DISCARD

In Pursuit
of Happiness

In Pursuit

of Happiness

BETTER LIVING
FROM PLATO TO PROZAC

Mark Kingwell

Ⓒ Crown Publishers • New York

Published by Crown Publishers, New York.
Member of the Crown Publishing Group.

Random House Inc. New York, Toronto, London, Sydney, Auckland
www.randomhouse.com

Originally published in Canada by Viking, a division of the Penguin Group,
under the title *Better Living: In Pursuit of Happiness from Plato to Prozac* in 1998.

CROWN is a trademark and the Crown colophon is a registered trademark of
Random House, Inc.

Printed in the United States of America

Library of Congress Cataloging-in-Publication Data
Kingwell, Mark, 1963–
    In pursuit of happiness: better living from Plato to Prozac /
by Mark Kingwell
    Originally published: Canada: Penguin Books, 1998
    Includes bibliographical references and index.
    1. Happiness.   I. Title.
[BJ1481.K53   2000]
1730—dc21   99-36083

ISBN 0-609-60535-6

10   9   8   7   6   5   4   3   2   1
First American Edition

for my parents

Contents

Preface to the U.S. Edition

We all know that some books work like ingenious traps. They begin innocuously, articulating a few genial sentiments or unobjectionable home truths designed to lure you down the false path of a deceptive familiarity. You stride ahead without fear. By subtle steps, each plotted with argument or example or statistic, you are moved closer to the place where artfully strewn leaves cover a hole in the ground. You know very well what is coming, or anyway suspect it, but at some point—if the author is any good—you fall, on cue, into conviction. Aha! You now think what the author thinks.

Maybe you're happy to find yourself there, and make yourself comfortable. Maybe you're feisty and seethe from your ignoble position in the trap, scanning memory and logic and the rest of the mental horizon for a means of escape. Either way, the trap affords complicated forms of pleasure. As trapping games go, there are not many better or more interesting than walking through a good book of argument.

Not all books, however—not even all books of argument, which this one surely is—seek to ensnare the reader in the author's own convictions. I knew when I set out to write a book about happiness that I faced a choice between setting a trap in the traditional philosophical manner, ascending to the high ground of objective detachment to observe the results, and doing something quite different: beginning an intimate conversation with one reader at a time. Books on deep and difficult topics can trumpet and they can whisper; they can declaim and they can hint. But for me, they work best when they just talk, in a manner as close as possible to the true voice of their author.

The difference is vividly illustrated by the enduring disputes, in manner and conclusion, between two claimants for the title of the first truly modern philosopher. On the one hand there is the generally acknowledged winner, René Descartes, whose brilliantly clear mathematical mind bent itself, with great success, to the task of achieving certainty by way of method. Descartes was a great doubter, as his celebrated contemplation of balls of wax, other people, and his own hand in the *Meditations on First Philosophy* amply show; but his doubt is only instrumental, used in the service of foundational truths. Descartes never really lacks certainty about where he is going. And, because he is both a great thinker and a great writer, we follow him there.

On the other hand is the unjustly neglected figure of Michel de Montaigne, the liberal essayist and skeptic whose personal motto, inscribed on a medal, was *"Que sais-je?"*—What do I know? Humane and literate, sometimes loose and rambling, but always charming and wise, Montaigne is never sure and he is never finished. Where Descartes finds positive proof and solid answers, Montaigne finds only variable experience and further questions. One favors treatises full of cold reasoning, the other personal essays full of warm intimation. Cartesian certainty, with its bedrock logic and stepwise proof, has built much of the modern world: its precise biaxial geometry is inscribed on every edifice and every trajectory of our experience. It is a remarkable, epoch-making achievement. But we would do well to attend, now and then, to the spirit of tolerance and open-minded inquiry to be found in Montaigne.

I try to write here in the other modern voice, then, the voice of the essayist—who is the one who tries, as the French *essai* reminds us. Though I certainly lack the rich gifts and hard-won experience of Montaigne, I have nevertheless striven for the conversational tone and playful, tangential style of argument he teaches us.

That is one reason you will find here what you might not expect in a book by a professional philosopher: details of my personal life, stories about challenges in career and marriage and friendship, jokes and anecdotes hopefully offered to enhance the pleasure of the text. I regard this book as my side of a conversation, a series of gambits and questions and, now and then, tentative answers about the tricky subject of happiness. If at times I break off and lecture for a while (as I have been known to do now and then at the dinner table), or tell you a little more than you thought you wanted to know about me—well, take that as your cue to step in and say something.

The choice of style for this book was born of something greater than mere personal preference, however. There is something about the subject of happiness, with its much-scored surface of confusion and vagueness, its crisscrossings of argument and counter-argument, that tends to produce writing either pompous or maudlin. I could not bear, in my regard both for myself and for the reader, to descend into either. Nor could I, in good conscience, pretend to a certainty I did not actually feel about the subject. It would have been deceptive, indeed irresponsible, to offer definitive answers about happiness when what I mostly felt was the power of the questions. Besides, reviewers of the book were sure to have all the definitive answers anyway, and who was I to steal their thunder?

If, like them, you already know everything there is to know about happiness, you have no need of this book. If you think there are simple formulas for happiness, in whatever form, then you need it but will have no wish for it. But if, instead, you want, as I did, simply to think about happiness, to probe it and ponder it in a spirit of humane and humorous inquiry—to investigate happiness philosophically, in the best sense of that much abused word—then welcome to *In Pursuit of Happiness*. And, I hope, better living.

Human life is about telling stories, about shaping a life's narrative out of the raw materials of experience and aspiration and contingency, and you will find a number of stories here. In that sense, this book functions at once as an argument about the importance of narrative and as an illustration of that importance. I could not have written about happiness without the tales that weave themselves through the pages that follow. No doubt the stories are as false as they are true, in the way that stories have of concealing even as they reveal—and therefore revealing, in turn, things I did not consciously intend.

My own story has advanced a little since this book was first published. In a turn of events too complicated to set out in detail (mostly involving that unfortunately common motive force, a job offer from another institution), the University of Toronto granted me tenure in the spring of 1998, just after *In Pursuit of Happiness* first appeared. That is relevant because I end this book with a discussion of my struggle with the challenge of imminent unemployment and exit from the academic world. This story was told not to elicit sympathy or to settle scores, as some have charged, but instead to address as honestly as possible the shape of a particular kind of unhappiness, one where a desire had stolen inside me without warning and had come to dominate my sense of my life and my self. Writing this book was my way of examining and transforming that desire, and I had no reason, while doing so, to expect things would change for the better; to my delight and surprise they did. The analysis of the desire itself remains, and I remain as troubled as ever about the way we are all subject to the power of self-imposed expectations to make us miserable.

This change in my professional status does not alter the views I express in these pages or what I have said elsewhere about the current state of academic scholarship. It does lift a huge weight from my shoulders, and makes me feel both very lucky and very happy. One of the ironies of happiness is that, just as your mother and mine used to say, sometimes you get what you want just as soon as you stop wishing for it. The rumors that my academic colleagues only gave me a permanent job so that I would finally shut up about them, or the theory that the surest way to tenure is to argue for its abolition on television, do not, so far as I know, have any basis in fact. Nor is it the case, as some people have suggested, that all tenured professors are like the tiny marine creature known as the sea squirt, whose unique evolutionary strategy involves finding a suitable home to attach itself to, at which point, finding the organ no longer necessary for survival, it consumes its own brain as food.

The particular challenge of finding the work I wanted has passed, at least for the moment. My task now is to make the most of the privilege of being paid to think and teach and write. Of course there will be other challenges to come, for my story is not yet done. True happiness, if it means anything, means having the strength of character to meet them when they arrive.

That is the one conviction of this book that I want you to come to share. So, let me tell you a story…

Preface

It can hardly be said that someone in pursuit of happiness should, above all other options, write a book about it. Happiness is a tricky subject, one whose pitfalls have swallowed up more than one writer more gifted than I. It is also a subject that has lately given birth to a boom in quasi-spiritual popular interest, the sort of thing that can be found in garish paperbacks listing "14,000 things to be happy about," including brake fluid and birdseed. And yet, happiness is too important a subject to be left to advertisers, self-help gurus, psychopharmacologists, and cut-rate therapists.

This book began life as an exercise in cultural criticism, an attempt to decipher the insistent ethos of happiness in our contemporary, media-saturated life. But I found it evolving, in the process, into a deeper kind of meditation—personal, historical, philosophical—on a profound subject that is close to all of us. It became an attempt to uncover the richer social and personal implications of happiness so that we can think more productively about them. Think about them, that is, in terms of a public morality of responsibility and obligation, and in terms of a culture that is rooted in character and action rather than in the current fetish of self-indulgence. When it is properly conceived, happiness, perhaps unexpectedly, makes deep ethical and political demands upon us. That, anyway, is what I discovered in my grappling with the subject. Call the result the virtue theory of happiness.

In pursuing these themes, I have drawn on my own perceptions and cultural experiences. I have employed my own enthusiasms, the things that make me happy, to make various points. I have also used the first-person plural on occasion, making reference now and then to "our" culture and "our" desires. I have not done this because I want to claim some kind of authority beyond my personal experience, or because I think there is a single all-encompassing culture to which we all belong, but rather because there is no better way for me to undertake the project of cultural criticism than to begin with my own perspective and trust that what I say resonates with you. I think it just might.

When I told some of my friends that I was writing about happiness, the most common response was: "What do *you* know about happiness?"—as if they could hardly imagine me being qualified to address the topic. I confess I found this somewhat deflating. Did they think I was so unhappy that I had no claim on the subject? Or, from the other side, so blithely happy that I could never appreciate how difficult it must be for other people to achieve contentment? I don't know. They never said. They just shook their heads.

After my last book, *Dreams of Millennium,* an exploration of cultural anxiety about the end of the world, was published in 1996, a friend of mine, whose book club had decided to read it, called me up. She said one of her book club colleagues had become very worried about me. "She thinks you must be awfully unhappy," my friend told me. "She thinks you might be considering something drastic. But I told her you're one of the happiest people I know—even if you are completely cynical."

Is it wrong to be cynical? Oscar Wilde famously defined the cynic as "the man who knows the price of everything but the value of nothing," and he was right—there is unarguably a significant loss in the move from smart to smart-ass, the decline from knowledge to knowingness. But cynicism has gotten a bad rap over the years. Personally, I align myself with the original notion of cynicism developed by the so-called "dog philosophers" of the ancient Greek and Roman world, who thought that happiness was to be found in "ascetic practice and mordant denunciation of established practice," as one commentator has put it.

A loose succession of thinkers rather than a coherent school, the Cynics were founded, more or less, in the fourth century B.C. by Diogenes of Sinope and flourished into the sixth century A.D. They argued that genuine happiness must involve critical self-knowledge, virtuous action, and a deep mistrust of external goods like wealth, reputation, and social convention. They were sharply critical of ignorance, however blissful, and favored the literary genres of diatribe and polemic to shock their listeners into an awareness of society's many somnambulant features. Radical, satirical, and iconoclastic, the Cynics believed that lasting satisfaction was to be found only in overcoming the cheap temptations of the cultural marketplace and in calling society to moral account. They were prickly, yes, but not dismissive. They advocated self-mastery and reform, not destruction or hopelessness. They were happy. So call me cynical; I consider it a compliment.

There is, of course, much unhappiness to confront when writing. Moments when you cannot see farther ahead than the next sentence, when the blank page seems to speak with a withering eloquence about your deluded aspirations and worthlessness of character. Or middle-of-the-night panic attacks in which the whole undertaking looks showy and absurd, the only option a degrading, apologetic call to your editor and a sheepishly returned advance check. Yet there are equally periods of elation, when phrases come to hand like palm-slapped surgical instruments, or ideas lock into place with the snap of injection-molded scale-model parts. One thing I have learned in working on this book is that the complicated satisfaction of writing, riding the up-and-down sine curve of word-toil, is a good illustration of a fundamental but easily misplaced distinction, one that turns out to be at the center of my conclusions. Happiness is too often understood as mere pleasure, a satisfaction of pre-existing, and usually banal, desires, when it should be seen as a deeper kind of reflective contentment, a project of examining desires as well as satisfying them. Writing books is a happy occupation only, I think, in the latter sense. While doing it clearly leads to a kind of rational satisfaction, it cannot be said with equal certainty to generate consistent pleasure.

If there is no necessary connection between dark themes and a dark soul, then there is also no strict entailment between the subject of happiness and its realization by the writer—or, indeed, the reader. For now I will just say that I hope this book brings you—even (or especially) when you disagree with it—the kind of multilayered satisfaction that I believe is the cornerstone of true happiness.

A word, finally, about my title. There are at least three resonances for me in the phrase "better living," which I use here with a measure of irony but also with the hope that we might reclaim the phrase from its bad commercial associations.

The best known of these is probably DuPont's slogan "Better Things for Better Living Through Chemistry"—an expression of uncomplicated faith in technological progress that is probably without equal in our culture. In more recent versions of the slogan, DuPont has at once shortened it and expanded its scope: their ads now read, simply, "Better things for better living." The physicist-theologian Frank Tipler once remarked that the original tag line was what gave him, as a boy, the belief that this was indeed the best of all possible worlds, one in which scientific acuity and the inevitable development of human intelligence would, one day, lead us to the Omega Point of human evolution, where we would be indistinguishable from the Judeo-Christian God.

At the more prosaic end of the spectrum, down where external goods reside, I recently noticed that the latest catalog from the Swedish furniture megastore Ikea offers "275 pages of better living at real life prices." And *Better Living* was also, of course, a popular house-and-garden magazine which, like so many others of its glossy type, flourished in the last few decades as people turned inward from the confusions and challenges of the outside world to "simpler" pursuits like decorating and cookery. The same impulse has made gardening the fastest-growing pastime of the 1990s. Indeed, gardening is not at all unrelated to happiness—there's the Garden of Eden, of course, site of archetypal (but unstable) bliss; Candide's overthrow of Dr. Pangloss's delusional optimism with the happy injunction that "we must cultivate our garden"; and even Bertrand Russell's oft-quoted remark that the only truly happy man he ever knew was his rabbit-murdering gardener.

The third echo is more local. When I was a boy and not yet old enough to work during school vacations, I used to spend the summers with my aunt and uncle and grandmother in a suburb of Toronto. For me, the highlight of the experience was the Canadian National Exhibition, a kind of big-city version of a county fair, with a midway and concerts and buildings devoted to the various wonders of modern life: Food, Automobiles, Sports, Flowers. Every year, I would take the train to the Ex as often as I could during the last two weeks of August and splurge my hoarded allowance on roller-coaster tickets and ice-cream waffles. And every year my grandmother, then in her late seventies, would insist on going with me at least once.

For an adolescent boy there are probably few hells more fiery than being in public with his wizened, slow-moving Austrian granny. But what could I do? Predictably, my grandmother had no interest in The Flyer or The Snake, nor did she care much about scoring free cheese samples in the Food building. She always headed straight to the massive concrete box distinguished by yard-high letters that spelled out "BETTER LIVING CENTRE." Filled with the year's latest consumer goods, plastic-covered power recliners, hideous dining-room suites, and space-age Hoovers, the Better Living Centre sang a hymn to cheesy materialism. As we worked through the crowd—me instantly submerged in terminal boredom, my grandmother suddenly avid—shills from Kenmore or Westinghouse would all but leap off the stands, extolling the virtues of their machines in tones of urgent near-panic. I found it somehow both dreary and overwhelming, a bit like watching too much television, but my grandmother, a woman who sincerely thought any entertainment other than *General Hospital* negligible, ingested the stream of hype like a channel-surfing teenager. I once left her in the building, against all the implicit rules of our engagement, and went to watch a water-skiing show—only to return an hour later to find her standing there still, enthralled by the vast array of fridges and stoves in fashionable chocolate and avocado.

Lately I have taken to imagining the Better Living Centre as it might be when I am in my seventies. Cosmetic-surgery vouchers, floating armchairs, automated kitchen sets, multimedia consoles, and custom pharmaceuticals have joined the banks of running shoes, stoves, and veneer furniture gathered under the big sign of happiness, but everything else is the same. Flacks still broadcast the virtues of the kitchen products on display; punters still push through the crowds, looking for answers to their deep longings to have more and better leisure time. They want what we all want, what we all think is our due. They want better living.

Eventually, unwillingly, they turn away.

Yes, I believe we may find ourselves forced to approach the whole question of happiness, which philosophers have gone round and about for so long. The idea of happiness is surely the sun at the centre of our conceptual planetary system—and has proved just as hard to look at directly.

—*Michael Frayn,* A Landing on the Sun

Part **1**

1

Happiness Is…?

But although a rational pursuit of personal happiness, if it were common, would suffice to regenerate the world, it is not probable that so reasonable a motive will alone prove sufficiently powerful.

—Bertrand Russell

MAXIMUM JOY

IT IS THE MOMENT THAT ANYONE WHO LECTURES ON UTILITARIANism, the influential school of happiness-driven philosophical and economic thought, learns to dread. I was in midflight, outlining the various versions of the principle of utility—the idea that an action or rule is justified if it results in more human happiness than its available rivals—when a hand shot up in the back of the room. It belonged to a middle-aged woman I hadn't noticed before. She looked triumphant, but then, people asking questions at such times always do. Reluctantly, I acknowledged the hand.

"Define happiness," she said, and sat back, crossing her arms.

I was, and am, in no doubt that the only appropriate response to this challenge would have been, "Not *now*. Can't you see I'm doing something really rather clever up here?" But you can't say that these days in a university classroom—not one outside of Oxford or Cambridge, anyway, where lecturers still get to enter by a separate door, speak from cramped, handwritten notes in an inaudible monotone, and then, without once looking up to see if the room is empty or stuffed to the rafters, exit by the same door. Besides, the lecture I was giving was a test of sorts, what we in the academic junior ranks know only too well as a "job talk." That is, I was a candidate for a permanent university appointment, and I was giving a guest lecture as part of the cruel inhumanity that passes for professional evaluation in today's oversubscribed academic job market.

Possibly that accounts for some of the woman's smugness. In my own classroom I might have passed off the challenge with a joke, turned it back on the student with an elaborate show of Socratic irony, or otherwise deflected the interruption with some diversionary tactic borrowed from the pages of P. G. Wodehouse—feigning a coughing fit, say, or suddenly noticing a nonexistent wasp. I couldn't do any of that, because for all I knew this middle-aged woman was not merely some irritating extension-class lurker but instead the dean of arts, maybe even the university president. More to the point, the search committee members were in the audience, and I could all too easily imagine their Precambrian thought processes slowly grinding to the conclusion that, yes, this was, after all, a pretty good question for a philosopher to have to answer without prior preparation.

A few definitions of happiness suggested themselves to me, some even possessing the sanction of philosophical authority, albeit of eccentric provenance. "What is happiness?" asked Nietzsche. "The feeling that power *increases*—that resistance is overcome." Good stuff. But the real definition of happiness, according to Rousseau (obviously in a rare playful mood), is "a good bank account, a good cook, and a good digestion." Once you start thinking that way, though, you're on the road to fatal wryness. "Happiness lies in good health and a bad memory," said Ingrid Bergman. George Burns once defined it as "having a large, loving, caring, close-knit family— in another city." Fun, yes, but you don't go that way if you want to impress search committees. I knew a few other answers, too, though I confess none of them came springing to mind at the time. Carlyle and Addison considered peace and quiet to be happiness. Cicero, Burke, Ibsen, and Bertrand Russell found it in tranquillity of mind. Corneille, Montesquieu, George Herbert, George Bernard Shaw, Sir

William Osler, Matthew Prior, and Victor Hugo all thought happiness had to be shared to be genuine. Epicurus, William Cowper, Thomas à Kempis, Benjamin Franklin, and La Rochefoucauld thought it consisted in the moderation of pleasures. Lord Shaftesbury and Mary Wollstonecraft claimed to find it in the exercise of the natural affections. Aristotle, Augustine, Philo Judaeus, and Coleridge all considered it a matter of being virtuous.

All impressive, and all somehow either absent or beside the point at that precise moment. I turned toward the blackboard, as if in thought but really to indulge myself in a *Lucky Jim*–style grimace of inarticulate rage, and briefly wished I was in fact Jim Dixon in the climactic scene of that novel, and therefore drunk beyond care or sense. Fighting to remain calm, I searched for a suitable answer, one that would serve the dual purpose of getting me off the hook and letting me get back to the business at hand, which was impressing the search committee. I might have felt like a hinterland animal trapped in a leghold device, fully prepared to gnaw off a limb in sheer desperation, but I like to think I projected a certain measure of aplomb. Or maybe I was just fooling myself...

The desire to understand happiness, to get hold of it, is one that is common in our culture, central to our many daily judgments about life, love, work, politics, and play. We do not always confront happiness head on, as it were, but it is nonetheless implicit in our decisions and undertakings, the ordering principle or end of our human projects. But if the desire to understand happiness is common, there is every kind of disagreement about what constitutes a good answer. Everyone thinks they know something about what happiness is; very few people manage to convince anyone else that they are right. Indeed, happiness seems to be one of those "essentially contestable concepts" that philosophers love to unleash upon an unsuspecting world. You know the sort of thing: justice, goodness, virtue, beauty, love. Thinkers since Plato have thought they could say what those things were, sometimes in great detail, but the fact that we are still asking questions about them demonstrates that no single answer is good enough.

Just so with happiness. Often we are inclined, like the woman in my lecture audience, to *demand a definition* of it. But, paradoxically, all offered definitions are waved aside like so many feeble tennis lobs, reducing the question itself to a mere ploy, a rhetorical device to confound the speaker (or make a visiting lecturer look bad). Nor is that sort of thing much improvement on the kinds of uselessly precise definitions you are likely to find in the dictionary. The *New English Dictionary,* for example, offers the famously unhelpful "state of pleasurable content of mind, which results from success of the attainment of what is considered good." Samuel Johnson neatly evaded the notorious problem in his own *Dictionary* by defining "happiness" as felicity and "felicity" as happiness.

The first thing to realize about happiness, I think, is that trying to provide a one-sentence definition of it is always a mug's game. (One critic of such vacuous definitions noted they mostly worked by "in effect defining happiness as wanting what you want and getting what you get and hoping that the two will coincide."[1]) There are many more questions than answers in this particular quarter of the philosophical field, and we must learn to accept that. No sentence beginning "Happiness is…" is likely to do us much good.

There is also a related and larger problem, as many a philosopher of happiness has discovered over the centuries. It is difficult to say anything intelligent about a subject that is at once so apparently clear and yet so resistant to explication. There is something about the implicit profundity of the issue of happiness, in other words, combined with the nearly inevitable banality of most sentiments given to it, that makes of happiness-talk a din of misfiring attempts at eloquence. Getting a grip on happiness is therefore far from easy. Indeed, for many, the concept is the paragon of ineffability, something about which nothing meaningful can be said or written. "Happiness writes white," said Henri de Montherlant of the banality of contentment when it came to literature.

John Stuart Mill fingered an even more troubling problem. "Ask yourself whether you are happy," he wrote in his 1873 *Autobiography,* "and you cease to be so." "The search for happiness is one of the chief sources of unhappiness," agreed twentieth-century essayist Eric Hoffer, while novelist Nathaniel Hawthorne famously compared happiness to a butterfly which, if pursued, always eludes your grasp, but which, if you sit quietly, may just land upon you.[2] The contemporary critic John Ralston Saul argues that notions of happiness have suffered such a decline from their ancient philosophical robustness that they now speak of mere material comfort or simply "pursuit of personal pleasure or an obscure sense of inner contentment"; accordingly, he suggests dropping the word from our lexicon altogether. "As economic and social conditions have gradually sunk, happiness, with its twisted meaning at the ethical and legal centre of our society, has seemed increasingly lugubrious and out of place," he writes. "In a more practical world, there would be a formal process for retiring a word from active use until it finds itself again."[3]

On this view, asking about happiness can only result in unhappiness or confusion, and therefore the project must succumb to its own self-contradiction. The question "What is happiness?" is judged by these thinkers to be a bad one, logically ill formed, misleading, or maybe just pointless. Pursuing it can only bring vexation and misery, the opposite of what we desire. (I don't know about Hoffer or Hawthorne, but Mill wasn't a very happy type: a celebrated child prodigy who learned Greek at three and had read all of Plato at seven, he suffered a nervous breakdown at nineteen.)

Those who would turn their backs on the pursuit of a definition for happiness would even seem to have scientific authority on their side. In 1996, several genetic and behavioral studies appeared in scientific journals that offered evidence to support the conclusion that one's achievable degree of happiness is genetically determined. You are either happy or you're not, and there is nothing that talking or writing about it is going to do to change that; indeed, nothing in your own life plans or aspirations and accomplishments will alter a built-in, hard-wired capacity for contentment. Try as you might, you cannot overcome the fact that, when it comes to happiness, biology is destiny.

Edward and Carol Diener, psychologists at the University of

Illinois, reported in *Psychological Science* magazine that their study of surveys from more than forty countries demonstrated that money, education, and family background were less important in determining one's level of happiness than was basic genetic predisposition. David Lykken, a behavior geneticist at the University of Minnesota, concurred in his report on a survey of more than 1,300 sets of twins. "People who have to go to work in overalls on the bus can feel as happy as people who wear suits and ties and drive a Mercedes," Lykken said (as if that should be surprising).[4]

The geneticists were far from confident in predicting a solution to the problem of happiness, but they nevertheless demonstrated a high degree of scientific confidence—a confidence shared by those who had reviewed the studies, including Dr. Jerome Kagan, a well-known developmental psychologist at Harvard University. "It's clear that T. S. Eliot was by nature dour, and Jay Leno is congenitally upbeat," Kagan told the *New York Times*. "But we're far from filling in the biological blanks. [Lykken's study] is a brilliant idea—it's well worth pursuing." The studies, and others that demonstrated a correlation between dopamine levels in the brain and expressions of subjective satisfaction, were widely reported in articles in publications as diverse as scientific journals and glossy in-flight magazines, often with jaunty titles like "How Your Genes Put a Smile on Your Face" or (rather illogically, considering the evidence) the old imperative "Get Happy!"[5]

Hawthorne's brand of common sense and these new genetic-predisposition theories, both of which seek to ground the happiness inquiry before it is launched, sound good—but only until you recognize their essential conservatism. If followed honestly and to their logical conclusion, such views would mark the end of rational human life, suspending us in intellectual nullity. So, while there is some measure of truth in the observation that questioning happiness will result in a certain kind of unhappiness, Mill, Hawthorne, Hoffer, and the rest of the nay-sayers are unnecessarily and preemptively pessimistic. So are the geneticists, who condemn us to a prison of biological limitation without ever raising the deeper question of what they, or we, mean by happiness—a failure that says more about the current popularity of this kind of reductive genetic "explanation" of human behavior than it does about the real limits of human life and experience. The happiness question is a good one, indeed a very good one. It is both answerable and important, and not just for instrumental reasons either. We can speak meaningfully about happiness, in short, and we can do so with intelligence and with reasonable prospect of results—not perhaps the kind of results that some happy-merchants promise you, but results nonetheless.

To say these things is to break ranks somewhat with my colleagues in professional philosophy. Expert in the techniques of bloodless analytic precision now so much in favor in the academic world, they have on the whole given up the attempt to discuss happiness in terms that speak to taste and desire. They don't often talk about happiness at all, in fact, and when they do it is often in language that is, to all appearances, designed to defy understanding, borrowing the finely spun distinctions and quasi-scientific precision of the "hard" sciences. The results inevitably have an air of parody. "For both the qualitative and the quantitative hedonist," writes one living philosopher, "happiness consists in a positive surplus of pleasure and ideally no pain at all over an extended period of time, and unhappiness consists in a surplus of pain over pleasure and at worst no pleasure at all over an extended period of time."[6] "The feeling tone of pleasure is one which we typically like," adds another contemporary philosopher, rather unhelpfully.[7]

Then there is this famous gnomic pronouncement from the godfather of analytic philosophy, Ludwig Wittgenstein, which manages to combine a spurious aura of profundity with a sentiment of such riveting banality as to be worthy of a Hallmark copywriter. "The world of the happy man," wrote Wittgenstein in the much-revered *Tractatus Logico-Philosophicus*, "is a quite different one from that of the unhappy man."[8] And the following, though it concerns love and not happiness, will suffice to illustrate the defects of contemporary philosophical thinking when it tries to tackle the big human subjects. "An idea of the concepts analytically presupposed in our use of 'love' can be gained by sketching a sequence of relations, the members of which we take as relevant in deciding whether or not some relationship between persons A and B is one of love," a philosopher writes. The relations include such things as knowing about, feeling affection for, respecting, and wanting the best for the other person in question. "These are relevant not in the sense of being evidence for some further relation 'love' but as being, in part at least, the material of which love consists," the writer continues, still not kidding. "The connection between these relations which we will call 'love-comprising relations' or 'LCRs' is not, except for 'knowing about' and possibly 'feels affection for,' as tight as strict entailment."[9]

We cannot allow ourselves to rest content with this sort of "comically solemn ineptitude," as one critic has accurately called it. And while it might be tempting simply to give up the hope that philosophy today might tell us interesting things about happiness, that would be a mistake. We must try to come to grips with happiness more richly and with, it seems, a greater degree of messiness: we have to get our hands dirty, rooting around in some odd places and perhaps talking to some strange people. While it is probably impossible to set out the necessary and sufficient conditions of happiness, and misguided to try, we *can* draw some important distinctions and possibly clarify our thinking about what it should mean for us. We must do so, because happiness remains a central—perhaps *the* central—motivating factor in human life, "our being's end and aim," as poet Alexander Pope had it. We all want to be happy, even if we do not know, even if we cannot easily say, what happiness is.

Back in the lecture hall, standing at the board with my back to the audience, I was on the brink of panicking. What would I say? Then I remembered the quick footwork of another lecturer caught in this very same situation, albeit in more elevated circumstances. A. J. Ayer, the dean of British analytic philosophy, the man who brought the logical precision of the Vienna Circle philosophers to

England when he published his first book, *Language, Truth and Logic*, at the tender age of twenty-six, once danced out of harm's way before my eyes while giving a lecture on utilitarianism at Edinburgh University. "Happiness," he said to his version of the middle-aged woman (actually a bespectacled young man), "is a satisfaction that continues to be satisfactory." There was a pause. "I challenge you to produce a better answer than that." The audience roared its approval. Of course "Freddie" (as his pals knew him) had the benefit of a superbly arrogant manner, years of experience in senior-combination-room sparring and a long nose down which he could, without effort, disdainfully look.

Lacking those things, I nevertheless took inspiration. I turned back to the audience. "In this context," I said, always a good opener, "happiness is whatever individual political actors take it to be." That seemed to silence, if not satisfy, her. She glared back at me in that you-can-run-but-you-can't-hide way and crossed her arms even more tightly in an elaborate projection of hostility. Crisis averted, if narrowly. But it was about then that things really started to break down.

First the giggling. Three young women, standard-issue undergraduates, suddenly launched an extensive campaign of smirks, sniggers, and helpless eye-rolling laughter from the back of the room. I could see them as they swayed helplessly around, racked by waves of silent merriment, the kind that passes over your body like an electric charge when you are somewhere, say a church or a lecture theater, that strives to enforce quiet. Anyone who tells you that people giving lectures don't notice this sort of thing, and get rattled by it, has never been on the stage side of a podium. You silently wish these people dead, but you have no choice but to carry on.

Obviously it had unsettled me more than I knew, though, because when, soon after this, one of the search committee members asked me a technical question I actually knew the answer to, I managed only a babbled series of unconnected sentences that may or may not have been in English. I dared to hope they sounded vaguely coherent, if not actually correct, but that was rank wishfulness. When the questioner took pity on me and answered his own question with the answer I knew but couldn't locate, I was shaken to the core. He smiled in a forgiving manner. You always know you're in big trouble when they start being nice to you. It was a rout.

Afterwards, the three young women came up to me and apologized. "We're sorry we were laughing," they said, "but there was someone in front of us being *terribly rude.*" I couldn't tell if they were kidding, because they were still smirking. There was also something smacking of mockery in the prudish phrase, which I found hard to connect with the ironic undergraduates of my own institutional experience. I nodded silently, wishing once more for the necromantic power to turn people to dust with a wave of the hand.

I left the lecture theater and went to the men's room to prepare for the next stage of the ordeal, lunch with the administrators. And I discovered—I swear this is true—that my fly was open. That in fact it had been open since, presumably, I left the house that morning after exhaustive but evidently incomplete attention to my appearance. Yes, there I was, competing for a plum job in a good university, out to impress and improve, and I was flying low like a snotty-nosed schoolboy. Humiliating hardly begins to describe it. The mind sometimes reels on these occasions, but I found instead that a preternatural calm descended upon me, as though I'd been suddenly bathed in a wash of chemical relaxants.

My first thought was: this must be why those students were giggling so much—the person being terribly rude was *me.* The little punks. How's that for undergraduate cheekiness, coming up to me afterwards, still laughing, to say so?

My second was: I'm not getting this job, because there is some kind of weird farcical karma at work here, which even I can appreciate as quite funny. (I'm not laughing yet, but maybe I will when some time has passed. Say, a few millennia.)

My third was: the spectacle of the otherwise well-dressed young academic posturing and declaiming, all the while undermined by his own fatal inattention to detail, at least made those undergraduates laugh—not to mention giving my objectors the perverse pleasure of making me squirm. Given the principle of utility, at least as narrowly applied—simple sum-ranking quantum welfarist maximizing, as one of my colleagues would no doubt put it—one could reasonably conclude that my state of relative undress was not only acceptable *but obligatory*. On the whole, I had brought more happiness into the room than I had sucked out of it. I considered rushing back to the middle-aged woman to communicate my insight in the form of a definition.

"Happiness," I would have said, "is an open fly on job talk day."

I felt ridiculous. I *was* ridiculous. But to speak seriously of happiness is, perhaps inevitably, to risk appearing somewhat ridiculous. We should not allow that to scare us. After all, appearing ridiculous has long been the philosopher's prerogative, far longer indeed than the self-conscious absent-mindedness that now passes for character in some quarters of the professoriate. Socrates says in *The Republic* that the lovers of wisdom, who have struggled out of the depths of the cave of his famous story, will be derided and mocked by the people still chained in place and forced to watch the shadow-play on the cave wall. The reason is that those who travel upward have their eyes dazzled by the true light of the sun, which makes the dim cave look black by comparison. And returning to the shadow realm, the philosophers are as if blind; they cannot convince the remaining prisoners that they are looking at mere shadows. "If the philosopher had to compete with perpetual prisoners in recognizing the shadows, wouldn't he invite ridicule?" Socrates asks. "Wouldn't it be said of him that he'd returned from his upward journey with his eyesight ruined?" Appearing ridiculous means asking questions that seem so silly as to be beyond doubt: Is that a chair that I see before me? How do I know anything at all? Can I *prove* that there is not an elephant in the room? When I sleep, where does my consciousness go?

Voltaire once said, "As for the obvious, leave it to the philosophers." His comment was meant to capture the common prejudice that philosophers only tell us what we already know or attack questions so clear as to be beyond sane inquiry. It was intended as an insult. It should be, instead, a rallying cry—a challenge to all of us to explore what we are, and perhaps succeed in becoming *who* we are. Even at the risk of appearing ridiculous.

IF IT MAKES YOU HAPPY...

Where should we begin to look for messages of happiness, then? Well, consider, as I recently did, some of the common ephemera of happiness in contemporary culture.

Perhaps the first place one notices claims about happiness today is in the transient realm of the pop song, whose lyrics, once stripped of the jangling guitars and thick backing tracks, often have all the depth of earnest adolescent poetry. "Happiness was when I was young and we didn't give a damn," sings Dolores O'Riordan of the Irish group The Cranberries. "If it makes you happy, it can't be that bad," according to American Sheryl Crow; "If it makes you happy, why the hell are you so sad?" Singer Jann Arden's new album for 1997 was called, simply, *Happy?*—introducing a welcome note of uncertainty. This brand of prosaic emotion is probably appropriate to the fleeting and market-driven confections of the pop-music world, which we consume as a form of daily sugar fix, as unsatisfying as the soon-gone glucose high. Yet we might well have expected more, since pop music provides some of our purest moments of self-conscious happiness (or sadness). A certain song, maybe against all odds, captures the essence of a moment inside its musically nugatory three-chord progressions or otherwise banal lyrics—and we welcome this, I think. But the strength of the lyrics cannot, absent the whole experience, sustain the weight of our expectation. This is the great disappointment of much popular music: it seduces us, but it cannot, any more than a meringue or a custard, support the burden of sustained critical attention. It is flattened, and ruined, beneath that kind of attention. Like Hawthorne's butterfly, these claims about happiness are frightened off, or maybe just crushed, by any attempt to close our fingers around them.

So we turn down different avenues. The evanescent sentiments of popular music give way to the would-be serious world of popular psychology. This is where you hear, today, more and more certain claims about happiness: programs of study and therapy, reassuring in their definiteness, that show you how to achieve the desired state. The ever-growing oeuvres of these authors—you know the ones I mean, the ones who wear their Ph.D.s prominently on their dust-jacket sleeves—confront us at every turn, from airport bookshelves and cable television to the far-flung reaches of the World Wide Web, demonstrating, if nothing else, that happiness is big business. Seminars, lecture courses, and mail-order products compete for your attention, and address your smallest misery, with their messages of alleviation, improvement, and solution. Pop psychology offers an easy target to the critic—it's like shooting fish in a barrel, really, which reflects badly on the shooter—but it is important to see the deeper issue, the issue that goes beyond the cheapness of the insight offered here or its self-aggrandizing tone, in which all profound conclusions are offered "quietly" and people who agree with the author are "courageous" and "born leaders" while all others are "rigid" and "fearful."[10] The important point is this: these quick-time programs of providing happiness make of it what the ancient philosophers could not, namely that very modern thing, a definite *problem*, with (it follows) a definite *solution*. "Let's Get Happy," *Psychology Today* magazine suggested in a recent cover story, complete with a beatifically smiling, poreless, and wrinkle-free model, "We'll Show You How!"[11]

So happiness programs and courses of study now arrive with the mail-order goods, as easy to order as a pair of wool socks or a chafing dish. Look at the "New Spirituality" and "Self Improvement" sections of your monthly book club and see works like *Simple Abundance: A Daybook of Comfort and Joy,* by Sarah Ban Breathnach, complete with lists of imperatives the author calls "Joyful Simplicities," touted as "concrete tips to brighten your life from within." "Revel in the last cookout of the summer," says the list for September; "go to an art store and buy exactly the kind of pen you like to use; create your own dried-flower bouquet." It's as if Martha Stewart and Deepak Chopra had united to have an illicit (but exquisitely tasteful) affair. Or notice some of the *14,000 Things to Be Happy About* that Barbara Ann Kipfer offers up in her similarly inspired work of happiness philosophy: blue skies, green grass, puppies. I'm all for buying exactly the kind of pen you like to use and reveling in cookouts. I even like puppies, though people tend to forget that they piddle on the carpet. But really, do we need people to tell us these things? And do they really imagine—or do *we?*—that this is the sort of stuff that true happiness consists in?

Even better are the books that promise to make us happy within specified periods of time, next to which *Simple Abundance* and its ilk seem to brim with intelligence. My personal favorite of the race-to-happiness books is one called *Become Happy in Eight Minutes,* by an Australian management consultant now living in America, Siimon Reynolds (don't ask me why he has two *i*'s in his name; some things are beyond human ken).[12] Eight minutes! You can't help thinking that books like this function as a kind of dare, a sort of name-that-tune version of authorial chicken, in which the writer implicitly challenges somebody else to come up with a book that will claim to make people happy even faster. You lose, Siimon, someone else can make people happy in six minutes. Or rather: *six minutes!* Sure, but yet another person can make people happy in thirty seconds! Fifteen! Five! No, no, listen to *me.* I have developed an entirely new technique. A program. A machine. A vision. A book. An audiotape. A drug. And I can make you happy…instantly.

But perhaps the most overwhelming evidence of a happiness obsession in the current culture is not all this talk but rather a simple image. I mean the proliferating and ever more insistent presence of the smiling yellow "Happy Face," whose associations with 1960s-revival pop culture and faux-psychedelic fashion seem less important now than its usefulness as a banner for the dominant emotional imperative of our day: Be Happy. Borg-like in its pervasiveness and disregard for opposition *(resistance is futile),* the Happy Face floats through the cultural landscape like an airborne virus, showing up here, there, and everywhere, in shops and on billboards, decorating T-shirts and baseball caps and even garbage bags, always with its lock-step message of enforced jollity. For those of us who think this banal form of contentment might just represent the end of culture, not its beginning—a sign of disease rather than health, smiling like idiots as we march into our own intellectual demise— even a trip to the corner store can be terrifying.

I recently got into a mild argument with a friend over a discovery I had made on a trip to the United States. In a top-of-the-line grocery store near Albany, New York, I came upon a new version of the Pepperidge Farm cocktail snack known as Goldfish. (If you don't know them, they are little baked crackers shaped, indeed, like tiny goldfish and, if I may say so, the perfect accompaniment to a large gin-and-tonic.) Instead of the pleasant blank faces of the original goldfish, with their suggestion of mute appreciation of your consumption, these new crackers sported minute smiles and dotlike eyes. The product developers at Pepperidge Farm must have thought we needed yet more smiles in our lives.[13] "Who wouldn't want the little smiley-face goldfish?" my friend wanted to know. "They're so sweet. I mean, who's going to buy the old *neutral* ones when they can have the smiles?" I tried to reason with her. "The smiley ones look like *idiots*. Look at them smiling away like there's nothing wrong. The other ones are smarter! Just look at them! They're the Mensa members of the baked goldfish universe!" She was unmoved.

Soon afterwards I came across a magazine ad for a new fragrance from Clinique called (what else?) "Happy." The ad shows the clear oval glass of the perfume bottle beside a black-and-white picture of model Kylie Bax throwing her head back in a grimacing spasm of deranged joy. She looks as though she has just been stabbed in the abdomen or had an electric cattle prod applied to her foot. An accompanying article on the new scent had this to say about our need for Happy:

Why Happy? Why now? Culturally we're primed for it like never before. For decades America has been under the spell of an enforced happiness (flash back to '50s housewives, to '60s peace and love, to '70s sunsets, even to the new-wealth exuberance of the '80s). But in the '90s, a gloomier attitude has prevailed. Happiness has been banished. Blown off the map. Which is why it is now ready to be reclaimed....That it's fresh, bold, even subversive to be happy.[14]

Within the usual breathlessness of magazine advertorial copy—"Why Happy? Why now?"—this article actually offers a small degree of truth concerning the "spell of enforced happiness." But then its potted, decade-driven sociology gives way to a standard paradox of consumer culture. Is it really "subversive" to be happy now, in the (allegedly) gloomy '90s? We seem as much in thrall to the idea of enforced happiness as people were in any of the earlier decades, perhaps more so. Moreover, subversive action surely requires more commitment than mere purchasing power, a consumer decision concerning eighty or a hundred dollars. Being happy (and wearing Happy) in dark times might be interesting, then, if it weren't for the fact that (a) the '90s are as insistent about happiness as ever, and (b) tossing your money into the coffers of Clinique in response to a hard marketing campaign (there were banners, spritzing flunkies, and even seminar presentations in my local department store) is hardly subversive, no matter how happy Happy—"floral with a hint of citrus"—might make you feel.

Distilling happiness into bottles of scent might seem a relatively benign feature of a culture much given to bland expressions of (or wishes for) contentment. Clinique even manages smoothly to unite consumer pleasure with the uplifting swing of pop music, adding Judy Garland's chirpy "C'mon, get happy!" to the campaign and referring, now and then, to other icons and images of self-confident contentment: Madonna's "Happiness lies in your own hand"; R.E.M.'s ringing "Happy...happy!" in a song ("Shining Happy People") that has always struck me as either ironic or deranged. But the bottling of happiness is a significant cultural marker, an indication of a fervent (if incoherent) collective wish. We want our happiness in buyable, obvious forms. How else, after all, to explain the explosion in sales of various antidepressants—Prozac is only the most well known, the brandname-goes-generic Kleenex of antidepressants—during the 1990s?

Clinically depressed people, and of course the drug company that manufactures it, Eli Lilly, often complain that Prozac is not a "happiness pill," that instead it simply allows one to cope with depression. But if that is so, why are so many people on it? More than 24 million prescriptions for various psychotherapeutic drugs were filled by Canadians during 1996; according to Intercontinental Medical Statistics of Canada, 20 percent of them were for Prozac and related drugs.[15] Something like 17 million Americans, including 400,000 who are under eighteen, were taking Prozac in 1996. (Indeed, the children's market for antidepressants is booming: Eli Lilly has recently attempted to introduce peppermint- and orange-flavored versions of the drug in liquid form, presumably to be enjoyed by kids with their morning cereal or toast.[16]) It is hard to believe that the incidence of clinical depression can be so very high, which raises the possibility that lots of merely routinely gloomy people are taking this drug, including hundreds of thousands of mildly miserable children and even many misbehaving pets. Why? It can only be because, for one reason or another, they think (or someone close to them does) that it will make them *in some sense* happier.

How did we get here? How did we arrive at a place where we think we can distil happiness into bottles, form it into little pills, and sell it?

MACHINES OF BETTER LIVING

There was of course a time when these versions of contentment, the cheap simulacra of satisfaction, would not have made any sense to people in pursuit of happiness.

Plato was taught by his master Socrates that the most basic philosophical question is "What is the life worth living?" and since then the question of happiness's true nature has been at the center of this larger project of examining a human life. The unexamined life is not worth living, Socrates famously said, and for the ancient philosophers there could be no happiness that was not rooted in the demanding task of systematic self-examination. Their idea of happiness embraced far more than the experience of simple pleasure or contentment; instead it included the idea of rational satisfaction, a sense (as Aristotle said) "that one is doing and faring well." For these thinkers that meant a life of ethical action, manifest in a well-formed virtuous character, and the associations typical of the good life: political community, friendship, family.

By the early modern era—roughly the first part of the seventeenth century and onward—this rich idea of happiness had largely been usurped. The great political theorists of the period claimed to understand happiness in stark psychophysical terms: the experience of bodily pleasure, the absence of bodily pain. To be sure, they, as much as Aristotle, thought a well-ordered life and a well-ordered society began with some basic notion of human happiness; they simply brought this difficult ethical and political issue *under control* by truncating the rich notion of happiness that had theretofore been operative in philosophical thinking. It was the Scottish "commonsense" philosopher Francis Hutcheson, drawing on Richard Cumberland's *De legibus naturae* (1672), who first made the connection explicit, and at the early date of 1725. "That action is best," Hutcheson wrote, "which procures the greatest happiness for the greatest numbers."[17] A century and more later, the English utilitarian philosophers were even more explicit about the centrality of pleasure-defined happiness in reaching ethical and political conclusions, and the possibility of performing that task by technological means. By the middle of the nineteenth century, the idea that one could socially engineer collective happiness was becoming dominant, an influence that continued well into the twentieth century.

Yet there was, and is, a deep confusion at the center of the project. The first utilitarians employed a reductive idea of happiness. In Jeremy Bentham's celebrated "felicific calculus," for example, all pleasures and pains are measurable on a single scale that evens out any differences in quality and duration, intensity, and suddenness, by translating them into a single unified language of numbers. Thus two disparate pleasures that look on the surface entirely incomparable—say, eating an ice-cream cone and listening to a Mozart concerto—can be converted to a single numerical scale and then compared. In this way, according to John Stuart Mill, Bentham's principle of utility made the crude children's game of pushpin "as good as poetry" because it no longer tried to distinguish between kinds of happiness, only degrees of it. Mill himself tried to improve utilitarianism by introducing the idea of qualitative difference in happiness. He concluded, in a celebrated phrase, that "it is better to be Socrates dissatisfied than a fool satisfied." Indeed, this was something Dr. Johnson had already raised to the level of aphorism. "That all who are happy, are equally happy, is not true," Johnson told the ever-attentive Boswell in February of 1766. "A peasant and a philosopher may be equally *satisfied*, but not equally *happy*. Happiness consists in the multiplicity of agreeable consciousness." True—yet this is an idea that thinkers trained in utilitarian principles still find difficult to grasp.

Not everyone, however, was as captivated by the technological prospects and social-engineering implications of utility as were the English. On the Continent, in particular, there flourished well into the eighteenth century a tradition of witty, worldly belles-lettres on *le bonheur* that drew its inspiration more from Renaissance sophistication and even medieval clarity of logic than from the newly fashionable scientism of the Anglo-Saxon world. In this tradition the great thing about happiness was its relation to taste and desire. The cultivation of these faculties of the human mind in beautiful and rewarding pursuits provided a kind of philosophical refinement, amateur in the best sense, that is altogether missing in the heavy treatises from across the English Channel. In her *Discours sur le bonheur,* for example, the aristocrat Madame du Châtelet writes movingly and convincingly of the important roles drinking and gambling play in the cultivation of happiness. This charming worldliness, which might appear to censorious eyes a little flighty, is then completed, and balanced, by her clear regard for the higher pleasures. "Finally, let us dream of cultivating a taste for study," she writes in the conclusion of the *Discours,* "this taste that makes our happiness depend only upon ourselves. Let us preserve ourselves from ambition and, above all, let us really know what we want to be; let us decide on the route that we wish to take to pass our life, and attempt to sow that route with flowers."[18]

Increasingly, this belletristic treatment of the subject of happiness begins to look more and more like an aberration. In our own day, the responsibility for trying to articulate happiness has largely, and on the whole unhelpfully, passed to professionals who comfortably assume that people are isolated atomistic individuals: contemporary neo-utilitarian economists like Harvard University's Amartya Sen, for example, celebrated for his attempts to enumerate the factors of human well-being,[19] from housing to leisure; or psychologists, whose variously conflicting systems have ranged from the modest (Freud's claim that psychoanalysis is intended to make the neurotic merely unhappy) to the grandiose (the wellness community's "peak experience" and "human potential" rhetoric). Meanwhile, one of the fiercest debates in the medical literature—fierce because in its implications it runs the gamut of hot-button issues, from eugenic manipulation to voluntary death—concerns the so-called "quality of life." Is all life worth preserving? Or is there a point beyond which a life cannot be judged worthwhile? What degree of happiness, in short, must there be in a life before we may consider it a life worth living?

That is an excellent question, but not one we are much inclined to pursue philosophically today—lately, we've preferred to do it medically. "Quality of life was not considered to be a component of health until 1947," a recent study notes, "when the World Health Organization began defining health as not only the absence of disease and infirmity but also a state of physical, mental, and social well-being."[20] A state, let it be said, that medical professionals have struggled to define, by holding large conferences on the topic and devising long questionnaires and indexes, beginning with the Sickness Impact Profile and moving on to indexes to measure self-esteem and social support.

These developments in medicine, important though they clearly are, leave the deeper question of what makes life worth living largely untouched. "There is but one truly serious philosophical problem," Albert Camus wrote in *The Myth of Sisyphus,* "and that is suicide." Hamlet's question, in other words, is, for him, at the base of all human wisdom: confronting the meaninglessness of existence squarely, without flinching, is to invite the only profound inquiry of life, whether or not it should continue. But if Camus begins his famous essay with an apparently grim sentiment, he finishes with a more paradoxical, and heartening, conclusion about happiness in human experience. "The struggle itself toward the heights is enough to fill a man's heart. One must imagine Sisyphus happy."[21]

Not everyone is inclined to agree with that brand of chastening wisdom. In the culture at large we now pursue the basic philosophical question of happiness—what is the life worth living?—with a decidedly *technological* bent. We believe we can settle the question of life's value with the precise tools of scientific reason, and alleviate any lack of happiness with the products of scientific genius. Happiness has declined from a vision of the good life into a prescription or an algorithm. The more one surveys the growing culture of happiness provision, in fact, the more dismaying it looks. How unhappy must people think themselves, to be striving and spending so desperately in search of relief for what ails them? All these tools and programs and objects! Can things really be so bad? For most of us in the so-called developed world, the material wants and needs of life are little more than consumer-choice issues. Why are we so apparently unfulfilled?

From this vantage point, we might be tempted to take our quest for happiness to a more spiritual realm. There is nothing in principle wrong with lifting our sights beyond material needs to spiritual ones—on the contrary, it provides many people with a richer and more satisfying kind of life than they could have in the more common round of desperate getting and spending. But the psychological idea that the spiritual quest is a natural ascent on the ladder of human development can obscure some dangerous implications. Framed this generally, the quest for happiness might be mistaken for a timeless psychological truth about human nature, an unavoidable natural fact of human life. It might even appear to be something that is hard-wired into the human brain rather than something conditioned by historical and cultural influences. We should not trust that kind of manipulation of our desires, which makes of them just another technological project to be managed. "Natural" explanations can begin to take on the hard impenetrability we see in the genetic view of happiness, the same attempt to cheat death that is characteristic of our technological drive to overcome limits. This kind of view then invites a quietism of natural inevitability: *You can't fight it, it's all natural, stop resisting.*

We may be constrained by our physical, genetic, and other natural limits, yes, but we are not altogether *defined* by them. We therefore cannot accept too easily the notion that whatever is, is right—even if vouchsafed by psychological or physiological theory. Within any natural box of limitations there is much freedom to choose, both individually and socially. That includes, significantly, the idea, so important to us, that the most interesting thing about natural limitations is that we can sometimes find the ability to pass beyond them. The desperate culture of happiness provision offers a retreat into animal pleasures and natural limits. It allows a simultaneous celebration of the basest desires we feel even as we denigrate ourselves for feeling them. It is a profitless reduction of ourselves to crude biological creatures. We *are* biological, we *are* animals—but that is not all that we are.

I therefore incline to a more historical view of how we have conceived the quest for happiness—a story of growing human self-interpretation in the modern world, the creation of a self-consciousness that goes beyond the limits of the earlier worlds ruled by ignorance, church authority, or other traditional forces.[22] The pursuit of spiritual self-fulfilment that marks so much of the happiness literature and that infects so many of our prereflective ideas about happiness—those confused ideas of what happiness is that stand up only until challenged—is not simply the result of material security (though that is surely an important enabling condition in individual cases). Of equal, if not greater, significance is the general movement of Western culture in the last two centuries toward ever-greater degrees of individualism.

The world that was born in Europe during the period of emergent liberalism and New World colonization—the early modern world of Descartes, the classical liberals, and *la scienza nuova* of determinate method—is a world in which the individual is granted an unprecedented moral, political, and epistemological influence. For these modern thinkers, the individual is now both the source and the purpose of political organization, arbiter of truth and falsity, and locus of moral direction. Think of Descartes's inward project of epistemological certainty (*"I* think, therefore *I* am") or the property-based individualism of the seventeenth-century state-of-nature thought experiments, in which property-hungry individuals imagined in some presocial condition agree to abide by a social contract in order to protect their rights to own things.[23] It is fair to say that, whatever we take our allegedly "postmodern" or "transhuman" condition now to be—whether we think, as some people do, that all standards of truth are relative because we can no longer believe in large stories of Progress or Salvation, or believe, with others, that death can be overcome with technology—we are still coming to grips with the implications, both positive and negative, of this modern, individual-centered world.[24] Old categories of understanding might be changing as we slide toward a new millennium, giving us markets and states and even people of a wholly new kind, but we have to accept the fact that, for centuries, the modern world has been populated by possessive, self-centered individuals.

This, then, is a world of predominantly *personal* projects: a world—especially in the Romantic version of individualism, with its

ideals of authenticity—of finding one's true self. With this conception of the authentic individual life comes a historically unique
focus on the idea of happiness as the point and privilege of every
individual life. Just as the early modern political philosophers would
argue that the bare life of the individual gave him or her (though,
in practice, only him) a fundamental right to life, liberty, and property—an insistence on egalitarian dignity that overturned at a stroke
the fusty justifications of hierarchy and privilege, the feudal and
immediately postfeudal strata of honor—so the same argument
would come to include a further right: to pursue happiness. Yet this
is a happiness that has very much been cut down, a one-size-fits-all
idea of good feeling or contentment that is clearly rooted in a dis-
trust of more pressing or particular notions.

The individualism of modernity is so basic to our self-conception
that we sometimes forget the relatively recent historical origins of
this "right" to pursue happiness. It is not that a medieval peasant
would not have understood the concept of happiness, or indeed
found it meaningless as a goal within life—just as he would not have
found the idea of an individual life entirely incoherent. It is rather
that the notion that human life, including political and ethical life,
could be organized around something so apparently selfish—and
indeed often godless—as personal happiness would for him have
fallen on deaf ears.[25] It would have *made no sense* to him to find that
people of exceptional material comfort—secure in their three meals
a day, warm, dry and sheltered, largely free of disease, with good
teeth, and likely to live for decades—were complaining, with all
apparent sincerity, that their lives were incomplete because lacking
in a sufficient degree of something called happiness, which they
could neither explain nor defend.

To be sure, the Christian goal of salvation would have promised
for many of these medieval ancestors of ours a form of eternal bliss,
thereby ordering their lives and providing otherworldly comfort for
their myriad real-world deprivations—even if, from a cynical contemporary point of view, such a goal might be no better or worse
than the ends of happiness, fitness, and sexual fulfillment subtextu-

ally offered in the latest advertising campaign from Nike or The Gap. But this idea of religious salvation is not what the authors of the Declaration of Independence had in mind when, in 1776, they combined a version of early-modern liberalism with some ideas of republican virtue borrowed from Cicero (who had in turn borrowed them from Aristotle). No, they thought citizens had the inalienable right to pursue happiness, *whatever* that meant to them—as I said, in my desperation, in that lecture hall. The resulting ethos of personal fulfillment, debased and manipulated though it too often is today, dominates North American culture, if not the Western world more generally.

Why debased and manipulated? Because once the standards of truth, rightness, and political justifiability are centered squarely on *the individual,* the elaborate machinery of persuasion and temptation, the honed and subtle techniques of persuasion we call advertising, begins to kick in. At its best, this machinery is at the service of our needs and desires, giving us new ways of reaching the personal fulfillment we believe is our birthright: that is, a kind of benign manufacture of happiness, the kind that supports our genuine experiences and contributes to a stronger sense of ourselves as engaged in a life worth living. A display of home furnishings or garden equipment might provide me with just the amount of inspiration I need to order my domestic world for comfort and safety, making it a haven from a hostile urban world.

At its worst, though, the same machinery declines into deceit, the creation of unnecessary desires—say, for fashionable tools and overpriced luxuries, platinum garden hoes or fur coats, that we neither need nor previously thought we wanted. This can lead, in turn, to a distortion of our sense of ourselves as we begin to crave what we ought to regard with wonder: thinking we deserve a hot gourmet meal on an airplane flight, say, when the fact that we are even there, flying in comfort at 400 miles an hour, is quietly miraculous. We begin to feel cheated if the salmon fillet is cold, angry if the chardonnay is not, or is served after we have already begun eating. Here our techniques of providing happiness in material goods and services turn back on us, twisting and perverting our perspective on life. At an extreme, in other words, this modern manufacture of contentment becomes harmful to our deeper selves. It does so by drawing together a powerful modern paradigm: the "tyranny of choice" we know as market freedom, where there are always more and more options but fewer and fewer genuine alternatives (you can buy any detergent, but they are all the same); the dangerous idea that self-fulfillment can be purchased and only purchased (your "true self" is to be found in what you buy); and a certain technological fetishism, in which we implicitly celebrate the ingenuity, the sleekness and novelty, of our material toys.

Let us say, then, that the central idea in the modern manufacture of contentment is what we might call the Machine of Better Living. The Machine of Better Living is a thing or program that embraces the powerful temptation, variously conceived today, of an algorithm, technique, process, code, or prescription that will *render us happy*. I am using the word *machine* to imply not only technological devices of various kinds, literal machines, but also the entire internal logic of power and control associated with the modern triumph of instrumental reason, the rationality of means to ends: metaphorical machines. The Machine of Better Living could be a drug, a program of therapy, or even just a material object that we invest with significance, which we think will cure what ails us. *(If only I had a BMW I would [finally] be happy…)*

The result of complex engineering and experimentation, the distillation of a vast system of psychotechnological relations and software design, possibly a result of intense pharmaceutical or marketing research, the Machine of Better Living makes happiness appear to us in a form not only purchasable but mechanical. No longer the life-plan and hard ethical commitment of the ancients, it is now something rule governed and linear, an ingestible pill or foolproof technique, an actual machine for isolating muscle groups or a metaphorical one for stimulating dendrites, the various and eerily Huxleyan means of artificial happiness, the real-world "soma" and "feelies" of our late-capitalist, postindustrial culture. Such Machines of Better Living, whatever else they may be, are the entire culture of modernity in microcosm. They mark the triumph of individualism, but also the dominance of technological and instrumental thinking in our age.[26]

When this kind of thinking dominates, happiness becomes, finally, no more than a program we run in the spongy, gray-cell wetware of our corporeal hard drives: a purchasable piece of software downloaded by capsule or program or airborne virus. That, indeed, is what the current imperatives of the culture would seem to demand. But is this program shareware or copyright protected? And what user-support hotline can we call when it crashes?

MYTHS AND MANIPULATIONS

The modern surrender of our conception of happiness to technological snake-oil and marketing manipulation is not inevitable. But it is strongly and multifariously reinforced by elements in our culture, from the technotopian cheerleading that says all upgrades are good, indeed inevitable, to advertising campaigns that promise to make you a better person; from economic preconceptions like the Consumer Price Index that purport to assess the quality of life, to political micromanagement that tries to buy votes by satisfying the short-term desires of citizens. The dominant technological version of happiness thus obscures many of the hard and rewarding questions that used to lie near the idea. *Technologizing* happiness makes it hard for us to think clearly about what it ought to mean for us, covering us instead in layers of images and information that tell us a great deal about what is for sale in the culture but little about what is of value. This distracts and confuses us. We must ask for more.

To do so we first have to arm ourselves with a clearer awareness of our culture's dominant myths concerning happiness. In their way, these myths are as pernicious as anything that contributes directly to unhappiness, because they create and foster false expectations in people who should be directing their attention, and their spiritual energy, elsewhere. In fact, it might be useful to orient ourselves, and the discussion to come, by enumerating eight dominant myths about happiness as they arise in our content-manufacturing culture. I do not pretend that this list is exhaustive, but I do think it captures, at least in outline, most of the bad ideas about happiness that seem to float through the cultural ether like intellectual fungus spores.

So, **Myth #1:** *Happiness is easy.* Everyone from best-selling authors to infomercial hosts to prescribing doctors would have you believe this is true. Indeed, we could easily break down the myth into several subversions based on specific kinds of market appeal. (1) Happiness is easy because it can be taken in drug form. (2) Happiness is easy because it can be generated with "simple, powerful steps to improve your mood—quickly" (to quote Siimon Reynolds's *Eight Minutes).* (3) Happiness is easy because you can be massaged, acupunctured, rolfed, or otherwise squeezed and prodded into feeling it.

I do not deny that any of these things might make you feel better; that they might alter the psychochemical balance in your brain such that more endorphins cascade through the dense tissue within the skull. I won't even deny that they might be worth doing. What I deny is that feeling better and being happy are the same thing. Unlike some forms of pleasure and the fleeting contentment we sometimes find and cherish, even as it vanishes, happiness is never immediate. Happiness requires thought, and, as anyone who has tried it knows, thinking is hard work.

Myth #2: *You can buy happiness.* "Annual income twenty pounds, annual expenditure nineteen nineteen six, result happiness," says Mr. Micawber in Dickens's *David Copperfield.* "Annual income twenty pounds, annual expenditure twenty pounds ought and six, result misery." Or as sensible Jane Austen wrote in *Mansfield Park:* "A large income is the best recipe for happiness I ever heard of. It certainly may secure all the myrtle and turkey part of it."

But even in her tartest moods Austen knew that the myrtle and turkey are, ultimately, the least part of it. There is no doubt in anyone's mind that material want can have the effect of decreasing one's chances of happiness, or that material satisfaction sometimes helps underwrite happiness. The mistake—and it is a fundamental one—is to think that there is a strong relationship of logical entailment between the two conditions. The extremes of poverty aside for the moment, there are clearly poor people who are happy and rich people who are miserable. Yet the hard connection between money and happiness is deeply maintained by the purveyors of Myth #2, for without it the sales pitch of easy happiness would fail. It is likewise a favorite of cheap cynics, who, as Wilde put it so penetratingly, habitually confuse price for value: they think that happiness is money, and that personal worth is equal to net worth.

Let them haggle amongst themselves.

Myth #3: *Happiness is simplicity itself.* Rejecting Myth #2 can, unfortunately, send us careering wildly into a countervailing piece of cheap pseudo-wisdom, namely, the idea that happiness must lie in wholesale rejection of the world's goods and temptations. The "New Simplicity" trend so evident in New Age bookstores is a prime example of this old lie in appealing new clothing (denim overalls, probably, and a flannel shirt). Renunciation is one of the great Christian holdovers in the free-floating spirituality of North American culture, but it is no less dangerous now than it was when Church authorities used it in the Middle Ages to protect their power, reconcile the unfortunate to their lot, and otherwise mollify the great majority of European citizenry.

There is, of course, a grain of truth in the theory of renunciation, because it is commonly our desires run rampant that lead to ever-greater levels of personal stress, conflict, thwarted ambition, and jadedness. Yet this affliction, if we can call it that, pertains mostly to those with ample power to do something about it. And if ever there is a hint that, for example, poverty is nothing more than "a lifestyle choice"—as the editors of the public policy magazine *The Next City* argued in an astonishing 1996 editorial[27]—we know we are back in the realm of right-wing, pull-yourself-together rhetoric. The goods of the world are genuine goods: eating out in fashionable restaurants is a great pleasure for those who can afford it, and driving a late-model Jaguar is surely (I wouldn't personally know) a superior experience to taking the bus. Only a fool or a saint would deny these facts of human life, and fools and saints, whatever their other merits, are on the whole bad company. You would not want one of them hitching a ride in your BMW or sitting across from you at Lutèce.

Material goods are merely material, to be sure, and one class of goods does not exhaust the Weld of things worth wanting.[28] But we don't call them material "goods" for nothing—they are, as we sometimes say in philosophy, *choiceworthy*, things worth wanting. It helps no one to wallpaper this truth over with self-abnegating hooey, least of all those people for whom such pleasures are denied by circumstance, not choice. It is not illuminating, only irritating, to find (as I recently did) a celebration of poverty as happiness in an upscale psychospiritual publication called *Why: A Magazine About Life,* which is printed in four colors on thick shiny paper and sells for $3.95 an issue.[29]

Myth #4: *Happiness is immoral.* Or at best amoral. "It is one thing to make a man happy," wrote that grim Prussian moralist Immanuel Kant. "It is quite another to make him good."[30] The wedge that has been driven between happiness and goodness is one of the most crippling myths of our culture, because it renders the search for happiness empty, even as it strips the ethical life of its real pleasures, leaving it hard-edged and forbidding. The real worth of what Kant disapprovingly called "negative pleasures"—the pleasures of occasional excess—gets drowned in a puritanical self-abnegation that has the effect of erecting a false opposition, characteristic of our culture, between hedonists and their enemies. The opposition is false because neither pleasure seeking itself, nor its diametric opposite, reflexive condemnation, helps us to see clearly what we lastingly desire.

The ancient Greek philosophers knew better, and so should we. Certainly, leading a life worth living is difficult—possibly the most demanding work there is. We must see that there is a morality in happiness, and a happiness in morality, that can only make the fleeting pleasures of mere contentment pale by comparison. If those fleeting pleasures are morally neutral or even, sometimes, positively immoral—as no doubt they can be—they are nevertheless pleasures. It helps nobody to deny it. But seeing the nature of these pleasures clearly can only underline again the difference between genuine happiness and any state of mere contentment, and further underline the old thought, too easily lost of late, that seeking happiness, properly understood, is the most worthy pursuit there is on this earth.

Myth #5: *Happiness is madness.* There are those who think that happiness, so far from being the human norm, is the exception. In June 1992, an article in a medical journal argued that "happiness meets all reasonable criteria for a psychiatric disorder," including abnormal levels of mental activity, disruption of work routine, formation of beliefs unrelated to evidence, and distortion of expectations. As a matter of psychological fact, happiness is not normal. This suggests, once again but in a new form, the conclusion that the aspiration to be happy is misplaced. Maybe, worse, the condition of being happy is in fact slightly insane, a form of mental illness.

But are the psychologists talking about happiness as I, or you, soberly understand it? It sounds more like joy, the sort of disruptively good mood, of necessity short-lived, that might come upon a person at the beginning of a new love affair, or from simple yet deep pleasure in the fact of being alive on a spring day. I have been known to walk down the sidewalk singing a Cole Porter tune to myself on such an occasion. No doubt I appear mad, swinging my arms in that exaggerated fashion, whistling inexpertly, even attempting, with potentially disastrous results, a nifty Fred Astaire dance move in my chunky rubber-soled shoes. Perhaps I *am* a little mad, by the world's reckoning. Yet this insane joy I feel is necessarily fleeting. It cannot be the sum, or the base, of true happiness, for that surely is a lifetime's work.

I suppose a second question is: was the author of this article just kidding around?

Myth #6: *Happiness is elsewhere.* It is consistent with Myth #4 that happiness should be deflected from this plane onto another one. That is, if we argue, as the Christian apologists traditionally did, that happiness here and now is not the point of human life, we often find ourselves holding out the promise of happiness in a life to come. According to this view, the point of doing one's duty is not to be happy but rather to be good, and therefore create "a worthiness to be happy." In other words, doing the right thing will not make you happy, but it will make you *deserve* happiness—should it come. Small comfort, but a bill of moral goods that has proved attractive enough over the centuries. Of course, this idea of duty creating a worthiness to be happy does rather tend to suck the strict value of obedience out of the theory, since rewards remain rewards even when they are deflected to another plane of existence. And if rewards are what motivate us to obey the moral law, the sense in which we can be said to do so purely out of a real motive of duty is attenuated.

All of which suggests, if one tends to be cynical about institutional religion, that this Christian view of happiness is more about obedience to external authority than anything else. Plato knew centuries ago that stories of reward in an afterlife might be necessary to convince the philosophically less inclined that living a just life was worthwhile, but he had the confidence that argument—albeit subtle, seductive argument—would suffice for those with a more philosophical inclination. Sometimes we need stories, fables, and paradoxes to draw us into the kind of critical awareness that will allow us to see the limits of what we believed before. Plato believed, as did Socrates before him, that this seduction was neither easy nor common, but it was possible. Let us share their conviction.

Myth #7: *Happiness is your birthright.* Not so. True, happiness happens, if it does, here and now—in this life. But that is not to say that happiness always happens, or that we have a right to be happy. It is one of the brightest lies of the modern age that everyone who manages to be born deserves to be happy. (Myth #6 at least had something right: deserving to be happy is surely more than a simple matter of luck in the genetic lottery.) The early liberal political philosophers talked, famously, of a right to the pursuit of happiness, and that indeed might be a part of the individual birthright now that we have left behind the hierarchical world of divine right and the medieval theory of the Great Chain of Being. But the etymology of "happy" (from *hap,* meaning chance or good luck) raises a warning hand: shit happens, as the vulgar T-shirts say. And it might, perhaps, happen to you, when you least expect it. The connection is even more obvious in German, where the same word, *Glück,* means both luck and happiness. Talk about contingency! We would like to believe that a happy life, like a good life, is entirely up to us. It is not.

Myth #8: *Happiness is fixed.* To say that happiness is to some extent ruled by luck is decidedly not to accept that the entire answer to our pursuit of it lies in the already rolled dice of the gene pool. And yet that conclusion has risen to dominance in our thinking about happiness. Partly, as mentioned, this rise is due to the fact that genetic science generally overawes us: we feel we cannot challenge any conclusion that purports to show hard-wired facts about us. Partly it reflects a deeper desire for definitive answers to hard, even eternally hard, questions. But the difficulty lurking here is that the more definitive the answer, the less compelling it seems.

"Want to know the formula for happiness?" a magazine article asked recently. "According to Paul Ekman, a psychologist at the University of California at San Francisco, the answer's simple: 12+6 AU." Ekman's formula, it turns out, is a matter of physiology, not feeling. His Facial Action Coding System (FACS) measures the movements of the forty or more facial muscles, and according to his research, "the closest we come to pure delight" is with a clench-combination of the zygomatic major (the grin muscles, or Action Unit 12) and the *orbicularis oculi* (the muscles around the eye, or Action Unit 6). In case you were wondering, your mother was right: it takes more muscles to frown than to smile. Sadness is defined in FACS as 1+4+6+11 AU, involving brow, cheek, and mouth action units as well as the good old *orbicularis oculi.* Ekman claims that FACS can help us interpret human behavior and decipher emotion (one of his books, *Telling Lies,* offers "clues to deceit in the marketplace, politics and marriage").[31]

It is true that how happy we are is never completely in our own hands. But to mistake that partial truth for the whole truth about human happiness is to shut down the possibility of living, and judging, one's life. We might be limited by our genetic makeup in all kinds of ways, but we are far more limited if we allow ourselves to be cowed by shallow scientific conclusions.

These comments are prickly ones, I know, and not the sort of easy, comforting solution currently peddled in the marketplace of ideas. For that reason, they may prove difficult to accept. I can only say that I think it will be worth the effort. On the whole, easy solutions to hard questions are only easy at first glance; worse, they are not really solutions. Grappling in a meaningful way with the idea of happiness may not increase your contentment. It may, indeed, make you in a certain way unhappy, as Mill and Hoffer warned. Yet I am convinced—or at least I dare to hope—that it will create the complicated forms of deep pleasure, crisscrossed with vexation and objection, that make for the true and lasting happiness of rational satisfaction. In a sense, Freddie Ayer had it right all along: the satisfaction that continues to be satisfactory is the clue to the elusive nature of happiness.

It is only fair to warn you, right here, that it's going to take longer than eight minutes.

2

I Want It Now

If you're happy, and you know it, clap your hands.

—*children's song*

HAPPINESS IS A CHOICE

I ARRIVE AT THE OPTION INSTITUTE IN SHEFFIELD, MASSACHU-setts, at about five in the afternoon on a Sunday, pulling in to the winding, steep driveway after a day of leisurely driving through Connecticut—coffee and bagel in New Haven, turkey sandwich in Litchfield. The Institute is ninety-five acres of rolling lawn and forest nestled in the southwest corner of the state, about fifteen minutes from the Berkshire hub town of Great Barrington. This is antique country, the sideroads dotted every few miles with one of those red-white-and-blue "Open" flags and a pile of colonial furniture in front of somebody's barn. Late-hippie craft stores and ancient roadhouses like Caesar's Shed Seafood are keeping the chains at bay. This isn't strip-mall hell yet. It could be 1970.

I have come here to get happy. The Option Institute and Fellowship (to give it its full name) is distinguished, if not unique, among the continent's many personal-development institutions in focusing explicitly on the elusive condition of happiness. The Institute is predicated on actually making its clients happy, and that is a prospect too intriguing, even intoxicating, for me to pass up. It's not only that I'm interested in happiness from the point of view of cultural criticism, either. If the Institute can do what it claims, and teach people how to choose happiness, I figure that is something worth knowing. I found it through a Lycos keyword search on the word *happiness,* and it boasts what might be the coolest e-mail address I have ever seen: happiness@option.org.

The Institute is the creation of Barry Neil Kaufman, universally known as "Bears," and his wife, Samahria Lyte Kaufman, formerly known as Suzi. A couple of decades ago, the Kaufmans had a son, Raun, who failed to respond to the world in the normal way. He would sit and rock for hours, or spin an object on the floor without apparent purpose, making eerie noises all the while. Instead of submitting to expert medical opinion that Raun be institutionalized, the Kaufmans devoted three painful years to trying to enter their son's autistic world, imitating his behavior and mimicking his array of noises. Apparently it worked. As Kaufman says in his 1991 book *Happiness Is a Choice,* "Raun went on to display a near-genius IQ and maintained an almost straight 'A' average in both grade school and high school, graduating with honors. Currently, he attends one of the finest universities in the country."

Kaufman wrote a book about the experience, *Son-Rise,* which was later made into an NBC television movie. In 1972 he also launched himself onto the lecture circuit, preaching a familiar message of positive thinking and unconditional love as the keys to happiness, but with an irrefutable personal experience to back it up. The so-called "Kaufman method" of connection through imitation was the vogue in treating autism through the late 1970s and early '80s, though many professional psychologists now dispute the original diagnosis of Raun, which was never official, and the merits of the method, which, they argue, only exacerbates genuine autism by reinforcing the child's disconnection from the world.

Undaunted, Kaufman founded the Option Institute in 1983 to spread the news to more paying customers. The Institute includes a Son-Rise House where dozens of couples take their "special children" each year to see if the Kaufman magic will work for them, in defiance of prognoses offered by "the medical mafia." The Institute is a registered not-for-profit charitable organization, and it runs on an annual budget of about $2.2 million. Twenty percent of revenues come from donations, according to annual financial statements made available as part of a recent fund-raising campaign, with the rest made up in fees and investments. In addition to the Son-Rise sessions, the Institute offers seven different programs designed to increase its clientele's happiness and productivity.

The programs are priced to exhibit a nice balance of expense and value. Most of the one-week programs are $1,275 a person, including room and board, while the four- and eight-week training sessions run to $4,500 and $8,500 each. Freud said people would not take therapy seriously unless it involved considerable financial sacrifice, and these programs are not out of reach for the kind of middle-range earners who could, say, substitute this for a week in the Bahamas. The program I'm here for is a one-weeker called "Inward Bound: An Activa Meditation Retreat." I had wanted to get into a basic program called "Happiness Is a Choice," but the timing didn't work out. Besides, Inward Bound was touted as the program "Bears" would be mostly running himself, a chance to see the master in action.

I learned all this from Zoë, one of Kaufman's enthusiastic assistants, when I called the Institute to sign up for happiness. (There is a small staff of paid assistants, but the bulk of the grunt work is done by volunteer college students beefing up their résumés, a group Kaufman has been known to refer to as "the munchkins.") Zoë was relentlessly upbeat.

"Mark," she said, "and I'm not just saying this—this is our most exquisite program. For a week, you're going to be asking yourself two questions, okay? Who am I? And what is my purpose in this life? This is a terrific opportunity to pursue growth in a supportive atmosphere. You're going to love it. The deposit is just $475." She paused. "Oh, but I see it's now less than a month before the program starts, which means we have to ask you to pay the full $1,275 in advance, okay?"

I said okay. Zoë went on to tell me just how much I was going to love it, and mentioned that I had to bring my own sheets and towels. Or I could have them supplied for a small extra fee. Then she suggested I order a couple of Kaufman's books to prepare for the program. "You should read *Happiness Is a Choice*, okay? And *To Love Is to Be Happy With.*" Eager to do my homework, I allowed her to add them to the bill. She also offered me other books, audiotapes, and videotapes, which I declined. Undaunted, Zoë asked me whether I might want to preregister for some personal counseling sessions, lasting an hour and ranging in price from $70 to $250. "This is one-on-one talk, Mark, okay? In a totally supportive and non-judgmental atmosphere." No thanks, I said. Once more she offered me videotapes, audiotapes, and more books. No thanks. Sensing defeat, she tried me on the counseling sessions again. "Mark, these slots fill up fast. There might not be any spaces left by the time you arrive." I told her it was a risk I was willing to take.

After more to-ing and fro-ing about these and other sundries, we finally settled on a total, which resembled a reasonable monthly household budget. I felt as though I had survived a bitterly con-tested salary arbitration or a trip through a Middle Eastern bazaar, but Zoë was jubilant.

"Fabulous," she said, when I finished reciting my credit card number. "Good for you, Mark! This is exciting! Are you excited?" I said I was. It felt like I was signing up for summer camp, only a lot more expensive. She laughed warily.

I called my wife Gail and told her I was going to spend a week at the Option Institute learning how to be happy. "Oh, god," she said. "Listen—I want a signed undertaking that if you come back brain-washed I get a divorce, no questions asked."

It was my turn to laugh warily. Was she kidding?

"I'm not kidding, Mark."

Why was everyone suddenly using my first name over and over, like my mother does when she's mad at me? We discussed what it would be like to be among the happiness-seekers for a week. "You'd better take a bottle of whisky in your luggage," Gail said. "You're going to need it." I suddenly had a vision of myself, blissed out and chock-full of personal growth and manufactured emotion, reeling back to my cabin to restore my normal personality with a few fingers of Laphroaig. I was starting to feel gloomy, but Gail was overcome with mounting hilarity, no doubt born of some mild form of matrimonial *Schadenfreude,* the joy in the suffering of the spouse that seems to come upon certain couples after long years of cohabitation.

"If you like," she said gamely, "I'll come down with you and you can put me up in a motel nearby, and then sneak out at night to have sex with me."

The next day, Gail placed on my desk a copy of an article that had appeared in *The APA Monitor,* a trade publication of the American Psychological Association. The article was by Philip Zimbardo, a Stanford psychologist famous for his work on the psychology of cults, in particular the idea that *anyone* can be vulnerable to initiation, given the right set of conditions. Zimbardo chided people who were, at the time, making great sport of pathologizing the thirty-nine disciples of the Heaven's Gate cult leader Marshall Herff Applewhite—the black-clad, Nike-wearing cultists who, in March 1997, uploaded their alien spirits into the flying saucer hidden in the tail of the Hale-Bopp comet, leaving their fleshly "containers" behind. She had highlighted a paragraph in the middle of the piece.

"What makes any of us especially vulnerable to cult appeals?" Zimbardo asked rhetorically.

> Someone is in a transitional phase in life: moved to a new city or country, lost a job, dropped out of school, parents divorced, romantic relationship broken, gave up traditional religion as personally irrelevant. Add to the recipe, all those who find their work tedious and trivial, education abstractly meaningless, social life absent or inconsistent, family remote or dysfunctional, friends too busy to find time for you and trust in government eroded.[1]

He made it sound as if anybody *not* in a cult was simply not paying enough attention.

A few days after that, I called my mother to wish her a happy

Mother's Day. I mentioned the upcoming trip. "Mark," she said, "you be careful down there. *They put things in your food.*" I told my upstairs neighbor, Jamie, that I was going to the Institute for a week. "You know, Mark," he said, "Gail should probably get some kind of signed declaration from you that if you come back insanely happy, she's not responsible for you." He paused. "A sort of pre-happiness agreement."

"A pre-hap," I said.

"That's right. A binding, airtight pre-hap."

A package of materials arrived from the Institute a couple of days later. It was full of enthusiastic prose about the transformative power of the programs, and pictures of smiling, multigenerational, multicultural groups in intense, meaningful, full-body clinches, sitting shoeless in circles on the ground or playing volleyball. There were testimonials, often from reformed skeptics from whose eyes the scales had fallen in the open air of the Institute's rolling campus. "I came here because my wife wanted me to," wrote Steve Sheller, a lawyer from Pennsylvania. "[The program] has enabled us both to be happier with each other and with our marriage." Others spoke of rejuvenated sex lives, promotions to vice-president, manager-of-the-year awards. Pictures of Kaufman showed him, bearded and smiling slightly, with his arms wide in that welcome-to-my-vision embrace, or else with fingertips pressed together, the very image of accepting and nurturing facilitation, listening intently as some whey-faced acolyte offered up his or her detailed revelations of pain and healing.

Along with various waivers and consent forms and order forms for books, guides, talismans, audiotapes, and videotapes, there was a good-conduct undertaking, in signing which I agreed not to bring any alcohol or illicit drugs onto the Institute grounds—also no pets or meat. I discovered, too, something I should probably have thought of before then: it seemed I was going to be sharing a room with one, maybe two, other people. "Comfortable, attractive guest houses with double occupancy rooms are available," the brochure said. "Single participants may be housed in triple rooms."

I experienced a form of anxiety that can only be described as Cub-Scout Apprehension. I hate sharing rooms: hated it at home, hated it at camp, hated it in college residence, hated it on road trips with my friends, hate it occasionally even now, approaching my ten-year wedding anniversary. I had visions of snoring, farting roomies, scratching their grubby jockey shorts on the way to a fungal communal shower. Or, worse and more likely, guitar-strumming beatific roomies who would want to "fellowship" late into the Massachusetts night, sharing and caring and leaning over for ursine hugs every few minutes.

The prospect of roomies also put paid to my original plan to skip out on the seminar early Friday morning so I could fly back to Toronto to attend an awards dinner. I had let slip to Zoë that my return flight was booked for Friday, and she was immediately suspicious, if not hostile: we were having our first fight. "I hope you booked a *late* flight," she said, almost threateningly. "The class doesn't finish until 4:30 and then most people stay for dinner. Most people stay over till Saturday." I knew I couldn't tell her that my plane was booked to leave at noon on Friday, could imagine all too easily the resulting encounter-group ideological detox session: Is happiness not worth *five whole days* of your life, Mark? Do you think you can experience this program without staying to the *end?* Do you think it's right to *skip out* on wisdom? I knew arguments about how unhappy I'd be to miss the dinner would be swept aside like so many spent matchsticks.

So I constructed elaborate Great Escape plans, with me sneaking out before breakfast, or in the middle of the night, or even the night before: casually tossing my bags in the car and taxiing slowly past the gates of the compound, then flooring it as I hit the asphalt, not stopping for anything, not even sirens and lights—who knows if the local police are in on it?—till I hit Hartford.

I couldn't see how I could carry off any of this if I had to share a room. Besides, I began to think it was irresponsible not to see the program through to the end. I bit the bullet, called the dinner organizers to give them my regrets and booked a later flight.

. . .

I park the car in the Institute's lot and walk up to the Mountain House for registration. I have to sign another waiver, this one saying I won't reveal enough detail of what's happening to me this week that the program could be copied for profit by the unscrupulous. (Fine: I don't want to cut into their revenue base; and besides, an exhaustive account of the week might be too much for some readers to bear.) I also have to undertake not to sue the Institute if I am injured while on the grounds. "[T]he programs, while didactic in nature, involve a degree of personal exploration," the form says. Therefore I must "agree to indemnify and hold harmless the Institute from any injury (whether physical or mental)." I sign away happily.

I go to find my room and confront the roomie, but there is no sign of him, only a nametag on the door and a mint on his pillow with a little card that says "Welcome Back Brilliant!" That's his name. Or rather, that's his Option name—participants are encouraged to take new names during their week at the Institute, and Brilliant has been here before. There is nothing on my pillow, which strikes me as a little particular for a place devoted to unconditional love.

I wander into the common room and find five of my fellow happiness-seekers already involved in a spirited extracurricular conversation about the Institute and its leader. I am surprised, not for the last time, by the skepticism and sharp critical humor of some of the people in the group. With a few exceptions, they are not the willing and enthusiastic disciples I expected. A guy called Steve, a salesman from Detroit[2] and more earnest than the others, describes a chance meeting with Kaufman in his home town, an experience he seems to consider somewhat magical. "I was in the mall, just shopping, and I turned around and—you're not going to believe this—there was the big guy!" He grins around the room.

"No kidding," says Beth, a medical student from Montreal. "Just like some regular person?"

There are one or two weird moments. Steve says his wife came to happy-camp and returned home feeling like someone who had been brainwashed or drugged, so displaced did she find herself back in the real world. And Thea, from Seattle, mentions how her husband started an affair shortly after attending a week-long course, waving away her objections. "Bears said your unhappiness is entirely within you," he told her, "nothing to do with me. Happiness is a choice." She was devastated. I ask her why, in that case, she has come here. "I know he couldn't have gotten what Bears was really teaching," she says. "That can't be the right way to see it."

It's getting close to midnight and still no sign of Brilliant. Seems I won't be sharing my room after all. I go to bed feeling oddly disappointed.

SCALING THE PEAKS

The first day of classes, and everybody has that new-semester, jockeying-for-position attitude. I gobble breakfast—waffles and fruit—make some desultory conversation and head over to the Option House, where all our classes will be held, passing along the way a lovely little pond, some of the rolling lawns of the camp, and the beautiful stone house where the Kaufmans live, perched on the side of the Housatonic River valley. Soothing Erik Satie music is being piped onto the grounds through loudspeakers.

We take our places in the upper room of the Option House, having left shoes and jackets at the door, and I get my first good look at the entire group. We are thirty-six adults ranging in age from maybe twenty to over eighty. There are eleven men, myself included, and I have some sense, from breakfast, of the range of occupations: lawyers, doctors, businesspeople, students and retirees, working moms, retailers. We are all white, middle-class, and apparently unmaimed: pretty high up in the *hierarchy of needs,* in other words, and ready for a little *self-actualization.*

.   .   .

Much of the intellectual cachet of the human potential move-ment—not to mention our culture's general approval of obsessing about happiness when you're already pretty comfortable—derives from the pioneering psychological research of the American Abraham Maslow (1908–1970), whose "holistic-dynamic" theory of human development provided one of the touchstones of well-heeled 1970s narcissism. Maslow's theory posits a "hierarchy of needs," leading from the most basic ones—physiological needs for food, water, oxygen, body heat, and so on—through needs for safety, love, and esteem, to a peak need for what he famously labelled "self-actualization." The theory holds that needs on the hierarchy are *pre-potent,* which means that one does not look to satisfy those at a higher level unless those at a lower level are more or less met. In many college textbooks, therefore, the hierarchy of needs is graphically depicted as a staircase, running from animal needs to the quasi-philosophical or religious fulfillment characteristic of the high planes of self-actualization.[3]

Maslow argued that all needs are "instinctoid," springing from a blend of innate human motivation and social reinforcement, but he thought that satisfying higher-level needs produced qualitatively different, and quantitatively larger, amounts of happiness. This insight is of course far from new—Aristotle had articulated that same point many centuries before. "When pressing needs are satisfied," the philosopher wrote in his *Metaphysics,* "the human being turns to what is higher and more general."[4] In Maslow's scheme, apparent conflicts of needs—when we seem to neglect food, say, when occupied with a conceptual task—are resolved when we examine them more carefully against the framework of the hierarchy. True, I may indeed become so absorbed in my work (higher level) that I forget to eat (lower level), but only for so long. Sooner or later I must return to the bottom of the staircase and meet the basic requirements for fuel and shelter that are indispensable to whatever higher pursuits make me happy. And of course when those physiological needs are not secured, there can be no thought of higher things. "It is quite true that man lives by bread alone," Maslow commented in his book *Motivation and Personality,* "when there is no bread."[5]

The staircase of needs is both simple and commonsensical, and that surely accounts for much of its popularity outside the confines of academic psychology. But there is also an undeniable whiff of self-congratulation in the idea of self-actualization. Maslow was led to the theory by three crucial life experiences. The first was an almost pathological degree of shyness while a child and young man, an affliction so dire that his sister had literally to force him into the arms of his cousin, whom he loved and later married. During his twenties he bounced from job to job, university to university, and came into his own only after 1935 when he returned to his native New York and, under the influence of European intellectuals then arriving from Nazi Germany, gradually shed a grad-school enthusiasm for behaviorism and adopted a more psychoanalytical approach to human psychology, a mixture that would later issue in his holistic-dynamic theory of personality. "I think it's fair to say that I have had the best teachers, both formal and informal, of any person who ever lived," he wrote in a letter to his friend Frank Goble, "just because of being in New York City when the cream of European intellect was migrating away from Hitler...I learned from all of them."[6]

The second crucial experience was exposure during this period to two teachers whom Maslow considered to have reached a peak of human development, Ruth Benedict and Max Wertheimer. In them he identified many of the fifteen traits characteristic of self-actualization: superior perception of reality, autonomy, continued freshness of appreciation, a penchant for the "peak experience," resistance to cultural conformity, and so on. "Self-actualizing people have the wonderful capacity to appreciate again and again, freshly and naively, the basic goods of life, with awe, pleasure, wonder and even ecstasy," he wrote in *Motivation and Personality*. They are "less enculturated, less flattened, less molded." In a celebrated series of papers, Maslow elaborated these characteristics by means of case studies drawn from his circle of academic acquaintance and from historical record. Thomas Jefferson, Abraham Lincoln (in his later years), Albert Einstein, Jane Addams, William James, Albert Schweitzer, Aldous Huxley, Benedict de Spinoza, and Eleanor Roosevelt are among those who get the nod as self-actualizing.

Not so the students that Maslow confronted at Brandeis University in Waltham, Massachusetts, where he taught beginning in 1951, an experience which marked the third signal event in his theory's development. Teaching at Brandeis tested his original assumption that self-actualization needs become potent whenever esteem needs—the "desire for strength, for achievement, for adequacy, for mastery and competence, for confidence in the face of the world, and for independence and freedom," in his words—have been met. In a study of 3,000 college students conducted in the early 1960s he found only one he considered definitely in the process of self-actualizing, despite the fact that these students, many from wealthy homes, had all basic and most nonbasic needs well met. They were safe, loved, and full of self-esteem. Nevertheless, they lacked the commitment to higher things that Maslow considered the sine qua non of the self-actualizing personality: the desire to seek out and treasure the so-called "B-values" (B for "Being"), such as truth, beauty, goodness, wholeness, justice, simplicity, and so on. Forced to lower his sights, Maslow then looked for those who were "relatively self-actualized" and decided that this group comprised about 1 percent of the Brandeis student population.

It's unclear how much of this finding is owing to the sort of middle-aged grumpiness that comes upon college professors when confronted with the typical undergraduate (the sort of thing that later led the conservative political theorist Allan Bloom to speculate about the closing of the American mind), but Maslow was certainly shaken. Self-actualization, he found, was the preserve of a small minority. In an attempt to quantify his findings, he estimated that a hypothetical average person—presumably one in a highly developed Western democracy, that is—has his or her needs satisfied to approximately the following levels: physiological, 85 percent; safety, 70 percent; love and belongingness, 50 percent; esteem, 40 percent; and self-actualization, 10 percent. Obviously, and by definition, peak experiences are not a feature of everybody's daily ken. In fact, the list of B-values and characteristics of self-actualization begin to make the peak-experiencer sound like a kind of philosopher-king in the

Platonic tradition. Self-actualization is "full use and exploitation of talents, capacities, potentialities, etc.," Maslow wrote. But failure to meet these needs is not simply a neutral condition. Instead, just as failure to meet lower-level needs results in various pathologies, from starvation to neurosis, absence of B-value commitment leads to a higher-level form of pathology: a "metapathology," in fact. The metapath, in Maslovian terms, lacks a meaningful philosophy of life. And without that, as Plato very well knew, we cannot be considered truly happy.

For Plato, the path to true wisdom was also an upward one: from the ignorance and self-preoccupation that he thought characteristic of most people's daily lives to the wisdom and enlightenment of contemplating the eternal and unchanging Good. In *The Republic*, Plato has Socrates compare everyday life to living in the bowels of a dark cave, chained in place and unable to look at anything but the cave wall, upon which are projected various shadows that the cave prisoners take for reality. The struggle upward is the struggle to escape the bonds of mistaking what we see and hear on this plane for true reality. What we see here is, like the shadows on the cave wall, just a wispy imitation of what actually lies above. By analogy, then, as the shadows on the wall are just imitations of real things, so the things of our experience are but an imitation of the truly real "forms" of those things: a beautiful person is but a pale imitation of beauty itself, a pious action just a fragment of the genuine reality of piety. The climb out of Plato's cave is therefore the ascension from ignorance to knowledge, from slavery to freedom. When one emerges into the light after long labor, one is bathed in the warm light of the sun, which represents for Plato the Good itself, or what he calls the Form of the Good: that which orders and gives meaning to everything else.

In fact, the Platonic resonance of Maslow's theory goes even deeper than this. In one college textbook on personality, the array of fourteen B-values is graphically presented as a series of spars radiating from a single source, as if on the face of a Tiffany-cut gem, with the caption "Maslow's B-Values: A Single Jewel with Many

Facets."[7] But to the eye trained in another, older tradition of self-actualization, the image is clearly reminiscent of Plato's sun, the metaphorical version of the Form of the Good, the light that draws together all the eternal verities of truth, justice, beauty, piety, and virtue into a single throbbing light source. The sun is the light that blinds those—the nascent philosophers—who struggle out of the ignorance and shadowy half-realities of Plato's cave. It is also the one source of true illumination. Philosophy, the love of wisdom which brings true happiness, is, in Plato's imagery, a heliotropic enterprise: a matter of turning oneself toward the sun of goodness and finding thereby the lasting happiness, the genuine fulfillment and justness of soul that must ever escape the grasp of those clouded by opinion, ambition, and the judgments of the world. It is not surprising that Maslow found his undergraduates lacking in self-actualization. On this view of things, it is an almost unattainable summit of human wisdom, almost a form of saintliness.

At the same time, Plato was much more clearly aware than Maslow of the dangers posed by base desire. He didn't believe that self-actualization was a matter of satisfying desires on an ascending scale; he thought lower-order desires had to be stifled, their loud, insistent voices shut out, if the soul was to be ruled by reason. To the modern mind, conditioned by advertising and the instrumental rationality of consumption—the mind in which, as Hume provocatively said, reason is the slave of the passions—that kind of hostility and suspicion about the appetites is, at the least, out of step, if not actually bizarre. We spend most of our waking hours stimulating and feasting on the appetites, walking through a world of images designed to heighten our desires, not stifle them. Maslow's version of peak attainment sits more easily with us than Plato's sharply self-abnegating version of genuine happiness.

As a result—and this, to be fair, was not Maslow's intention—his theory is at once appallingly elitist and charmingly seductive: it tells us that life is fundamentally ordered by a spiritual hierarchy, even while it appears to congratulate those who have passed on from "base" desires to higher things. It makes spiritual experience into a badge of human development, a sign of psychic and personal sophistication. Reading its tenets, one is sometimes tempted to offer oneself kudos for being in the upper echelon. Self-actualization? That's me. Of *course* I can take pleasure in the simple things in life, I say to myself. I can appreciate a cake, an orange, a good tuna-fish sandwich. And yet I also pursue the more spiritual and philosophical goals of meeting the needs of self-actualization; I don't live by bread alone. This is great—*I'm* great. I even approach the tuna-fish sandwich with a kind of spiritual attitude. And because the schema is so simple, I might even begin to think that the implicit Maslovian imperative—to self-actualize or suffer the disdain reserved for metapaths—is an easy one for someone like me to answer: just step on the rungs and start climbing the ladder, ascending from lower needs to higher ones, no problem.

The master himself thought otherwise. Despite his growing fame in the 1960s, Maslow became bitter and disillusioned as he got older and felt only scorn for those who thought that "metamotivation"—the attempt to meet self-actualization needs—could be consciously pursued. "They're doing it stupidly and inefficiently and incapably and they want it *now,*" he said in an interview recorded during the last year of his life. He also became increasingly dismissive of those who sold their psychotherapeutic wares by claiming that self-actualization was available to everyone (or at least everyone with the money to pony up). Maslow himself claimed he did not know what self-actualization could possibly mean for someone who was "feeble-minded."[8] But even as this sentiment appears to run the self-actualization merchants off the Weld, it simply reinforces the whiff of elitism in the basic theory. (Plato would, unfortunately, have agreed with him whole-heartedly: he thought that the philosophical life, the life of ascent to the sun of Goodness, was the privilege of a gifted few.)

Some of these problems Maslow glimpsed himself. What he could not have foreseen was the bastardization of his theory that would lead the Esalen Institute in California, for example, to create "Maslow Rooms," in which wealthy clients in search of self-actualization could convince themselves that satisfying material whims was part of a quasi-spiritual quest for happiness. Or the way boardroom explainers and jet-set consultants would tour the continent delivering potted versions of his ideas to executives eager for reassurance that plotting wage rollbacks or raising prices to fatten profit columns was worthy employment for a human, because there is no conflict between making a lot of money and pursuing a spiritual life of self-actualizing bliss.

Kaufman enters the room and is greeted, as he will be all week, by an enthusiastic round of applause. He is taller than he looks in his pictures, handsome in a rather self-conscious way—the carefully trimmed beard, the flowing mane of hair—and dressed in what will turn out to be a uniform of elbow-length baggy T-shirts and double-breasted sports jackets with the sleeves rolled up. Though the room is small, he has a cordless microphone that he will use to good purpose all week, making his voice low and resonant, taking us through our happiness exercises with a series of gently insistent orders, scraps of soulful New Age poetry, and much-repeated platitudes about "the comings and the goings" of human life. His amplified laugh, full of pleasure, barks at us like the sound of a marine-park seal asking for food.

Without preamble he begins to work the group, scrambling around the carpeted room to ask people questions in his patented Option Process® Dialogue style, which involves, according to the literature,

> a simple, respectful system of questions offered with a loving, accepting, and nonjudgmental attitude. The result is an extraordinarily effective and beautiful tool to help people be happy and comfortable, even in the face of difficulties. Beliefs and judgments which have created discomfort, distress, and self-defeating behaviors are gently uncovered, examined and discarded, leading to an increased sense of clarity, personal power and happiness.

Basically what this means is that Kaufman will seize on any sign of nervousness or confusion and push it to some piece of self-disclosure, usually painful—a process that can be, in practice, far from gentle: Why did you laugh just then? Can you guess? Why are you feeling uncomfortable? *Why* does somebody else crying make you uncomfortable? If you had to guess, what would you say?

And they *are* crying, even before 9:00 A.M., as people fall into gulping confessions and red-faced revelation. Much as I find myself despising these methods, which are about as nonjudgmental and nondirective as those practiced by the inquisitorial Jesuits at my high school, I am unable simply to dismiss the unhappiness on display here. The genuine emotion shown by these people momentarily overwhelms my well-trained critical faculties, which I am trying, with only limited success, to suspend. While it is true that nobody seems prepared to question, right now, the background assumption that self-exposure is always good, or to pause and examine the narcissism on continual display here—two issues I have a lot of trouble with—the people in this room are in obvious pain. These doctors, lawyers, students, and seniors are also recovering addicts, child-abuse victims, jilted lovers, near-suicidal depressives, possible schizophrenics, people whose partners have been murdered, people in career crisis, people who just can't keep track of the plot.

The morning's faux-Socratic encounters soon give way to some routinely unsettling intimacy exercises, the kind of thing familiar from any retreat weekend or encounter session: standing very close to a complete stranger, staring into his or her eyes for ten minutes, holding his or her face in your hands. As we do this today, changing partners with promiscuous rapidity, Kaufman's voice asks us what we're feeling, and I wonder if anyone else is silently answering: (1) slight intellectual disapproval, held mostly in check; (2) routine social nervousness (is my nose sweaty? do I have a zit today?); and (3) disconcerting wavelets of sexual desire(!). We do a little more touching and feeling, ending with a long, sweaty group hug, and then file out for a break.

In the second session of the day, after lunch, Kaufman gets down to business, setting out his philosophy of happiness. It is indeed a choice, he says, or what he sometimes calls "an attitudinal adjustment." Every event, no matter how potentially painful, is actually an exciting life adventure. His talk is studded with spiritualist hooey—"We are the ultimate imprint of what is!"—but it leans as much on quasi-scientific tidbits about brain power and neuropeptides. All the same, there is some unobjectionable wisdom in it. We could all use a more meditative attitude when riding the rush-hour subway, and who can honestly say that a few more everyday epiphanies would come amiss? I don't know if you can just *choose* to feel those things, but a week of bucolic idiocy in search of them is probably worth the price of admission. It certainly seems to be for my troubled classmates.

"Suspend your critical disbelief, and find the jewels in this experience," Kaufman says to the group, whispering into the microphone and smiling slightly. "Don't look for holes. You know, I spent part of my youth studying philosophy and I was trained to find holes in other people's work, to find fault with arguments. I read Aristotle to see where he went wrong; I read Sartre to find his weak spots. It was, in a sense, the *holiest* time of my life. Ha! Ha! Ha! But why not abandon your logic, your skepticism, your cynicism. Inward Bound pivots on make-believe. Give yourself this week. Let yourself go, and enjoy the emotional ride." This is the first time I have ever heard a teacher openly suggest his lessons be treated as no more reliable than a Hollywood movie, but I figure questioning this injunction, not to mention the identification of logic, skepticism, and cynicism, is a hole-finding thought, so I let it go and decide to get into the experience.

"I've been looking at you today and totally loving you," Kaufman says at the end of the afternoon. "I would love to give you all a big snuggly hug." As we line up, he has a little personal moment with each of us, the bountiful guru at ease, sharing his charismatic gift. "Hi, Mark," he says to me, "I felt a lot of strong energy coming from you today."

Dinner—pasta and vegetarian tomato sauce—is great, but there is no dessert. Beth and I go to Great Barrington for ice cream with a friendly, hard-nosed boutique-owner from New Jersey called Susan who says her friends kept kidding her about going to "The Clinic" for a week, like it was some form of psychic detox. Susan has a red Porsche 944 with a sunroof and a thumping CD player. Driving down the dark country roads, juiced on sugar, speed, conversation, and Sister Hazel tunes, I sink down in the low-slung passenger seat and think: happy.

CAMP CONTENT

We start the next day outdoors, going for a walk in the Institute's woods in silent single file. Kaufman, at the head of the line, is strolling at a contemplative two miles an hour, stopping every few yards to caress a frond or greet a tree. We climb up a small hill and array ourselves on little squares of plastic garbage bag. Our eyes closed, various objects—a fork, a playing card, a bullet, a tampon—are placed in our hands and we are asked, each time, to contemplate a question: "Who am I?" The idea is to open your eyes and see your-self reflected in the object in some way, to find the fork representing a fork in the road of your development, say, or to see that (in my case) the tampon is not something I need to use. Which might lead to thoughts of what it is to be a man, if I am one, and in what sense or senses I am or am not. Or, I don't know, it might lead to what it means *not* to be a woman in a world where the flow of menstrual blood is a subject unmentionable in polite company. Something like that. I play with these ideas and a few dozen more as we work our way through the inventory of objects. This is diverting enough, and the sun is warm, but by the end of it, the answer to the question "Who am I?" is, for me, a guy who needs to pee pretty badly—shouldn't have had that second cup of coffee—and apparently I am not alone. There is a rush for the bathrooms as soon as we troop back into the Option House.

There are just two loos in the building, and all week I will be spending time in slow-moving, awkward lines waiting to empty my bladder. A new social challenge: what do you say when someone who, seconds before, was weeping and spilling out their guts is now in front of you in the bathroom line, bouncing impatiently from foot to foot? New Agers like to say that every red light is a *bodhisattva*, a precious invitation to meditate. Is every experience of a nearly bursting bladder a revelation?

Upstairs again, we share our "learnings" about the forest exercise—the grinders in the class are already picking up the local jargon. I'm surprised at how inventive some of them are, making my own bored interpretations seem prosaic: the fork's tines as prison bars, or the prongs on a crown; the five of hearts prompting a moving story of family crisis and triumph from a mother whose third child was born autistic. But Kaufman cannot seem to resist interrupting these real moments with poetry and whispered questions, and I have a sudden guilty fantasy of snatching the microphone out of his hand and shoving it down his throat. *Eat this, happy man!*

At lunch Sharon, the woman with the autistic son, comes over to sit with me. The meals are cafeteria-style and, as in a college dining hall, each one is a mildly unnerving exercise in timing and savvy if you want to sit with someone interesting and/or attractive. Sharon is both, and now says she wants to know my story. I'm nonplussed. Compared to her, I haven't really got one: some career troubles, nagging worries about my marriage, simple curiosity about someone who claims to teach happiness. I tell her what is true, that I feel very lucky as a philosophy professor to be paid to contemplate my purpose in life, rather than having to pay someone else for the privilege.

"Bears studied philosophy too," she tells me, something I will hear many times over the week. "You must love what he does." What I would really love is to see some of these academic credentials—but that's my inner critic talking again. I tell Sharon that the raw emotion of her story impressed me, which it genuinely did.

After lunch I'm climbing up to the Option House with Paul, a playwright from San Francisco, and we pass the main building, now leaking Schumann-esque elevator music. "The *One Flew Over the*

Cuckoo's Nest music," Paul says. "I keep thinking, 'I have to go get my pillow from Nurse Ratched.'"

The afternoon session involves more of Kaufman's nondirected questioning, cracking people open like nuts, making them weep, and Paul is one of the targets. Despite some protests, he is verbally poked and prodded until he admits, his usual witty demeanor dissolved in embarrassed tears, that he hasn't been able to forgive his wife for an affair she had. For the only time during the week, and probably because I like Paul and identify with him, I have serious trouble watching this happen, an objection rising to my throat three or four times as Paul initially resists the pressure but then gives way. A bunch of us go and embrace him when it's over. He seems fine, relieved—happy.

In afternoon free time, the sun blazing, I go for a long run in the sweet Berkshire air. Afterwards Beth offers to teach me some Tai Chi moves on the fresh-mown grass in front of the main building. As we swim through the warm wind, I catch myself focusing on the sight of her small silver toe ring, a mole on her shoulder, a tiny heartbreaking hole in the back of her tank top. Since when am I noticing things about this woman?

I call Gail and tell her I love her.

That night's common-room discussion goes late, arguing the merits of Kaufman's methods, and by the next morning a couple of things are obvious.

First, the seven or eight of us in my cabin are now the unofficial but undisputed in-crowd of happy camp, a wisecracking clique of twenty- and thirty-something quasi-skeptics who find each other hilarious. Second, Kaufman's presence permeates the camp even when he is studiously absent, carefully maintaining his aura of slow-moving love god. (Samahria is even better at this: she doesn't make a single appearance all week, but nevertheless projects a powerful kind of gifted-madwoman-in-the-attic vibe throughout the grounds.) Steve will laugh at something Paul says and then cover his mouth, saying, "What would Bears think if he heard this?" We are regressing to grade school, and not just because we are eating peanut butter and jelly sandwiches after dinner every night. Kaufman is the all-seeing vice-principal, the unseen master of discipline.

This day begins early, six-thirty, as we assemble silently on the side of the valley and shout our names into the dewy morning air. It feels good. After some hugging—a kind of midweek physical-connection checkup—we stand around in the spring chill, meditating. As I stand there with my eyes closed, I keep hearing a song in my head, can't get it to go away. It is "(Everybody Was) Kung Fu Fighting."

Back in the classroom, we spend an inordinate amount of time eating small plates of fruit, living in the moment while Kaufman takes us through a predictable savor-the-details routine. "Send love to your small intestine," he says at one point, encouraging us to marvel at the ordinary miracle of mammalian digestion. And why not? As a friend of mine likes to say, "Never underestimate the role of the colon in human happiness." Before we can touch the fruit, however, we have to grant full notice to the cellophane covering, its wondrous transparency, its reflective qualities and clinginess. We are told to fashion it into some kind of shape or object. We play with a slice of melon, holding it in our mouths like a tusk. "This is called being a melophant," Kaufman mumbles into his mike. "Ha! Ha! Ha!"

Lunch is slightly chaotic, with some people trying to savor the brown rice and salad, others just shoveling. The afternoon session is devoted to a rambling discussion of why our group seems to be late for class so often. Kaufman seems to have something of an "issue" with tardiness, and, somewhat contrary to the acceptance-is-bliss rhetoric, he becomes scolding and disparaging as he offers us "observations" (not "judgments") about our abysmal punctuality record. Some of the others are rattled and sullen, but this little rant doesn't bother me: it is the first time that a vestige of criticism, not to mention a reference to normal social conventions, has crept into the feel-good rhetoric of the workshops. And anyway I'm a stickler for punctuality myself, back in the real world. Lack of it has always struck me as obvious passive-aggressive behavior, disrespectful if not offensive, and I'd lock the door on my late students if I could get away with it. So I'm happy. Judgments built the world.

The common-room group is in top form later, busting up the day's absurdity mercilessly, laughing crazily and horsing around with cans of sprayable plastic string that Thea purchased earlier in the evening in Great Barrington. Paul, who has perfected a viciously accurate imitation of Kaufman, does a riff on the cellophane business and how we all just sat there, dopey with fatigue and meditative stasis, doing everything we were ordered to, slowly ingesting the gospel of positivity with our nibbles of grape and apple. "Notice the beautiful cellophane," Paul says. "See how shiny it is. Now put it over your mouth and nose. Notice its texture, the way it shines in the light. Now breathe deeply. Do it again. And again. And again. Now feel how you struggle vainly for breath. Cherish that feeling. Own it. Make it yours. Now feel your life ebbing away. This is exciting! This is an adventure! Think to yourself, it's never the wrong time to die. You have to learn to live in the moment. Even if it's your last one!"

We're hysterical, falling about. The laughter goes on a long time, fading slowly to an exhausted pause. Then a big teddy bear of a man called Paolo, a veteran of one of the Institute's eight-week happiness boot-camp programs, says, "You wouldn't really do it, would you? I mean, even if Bears said something like that, you'd stop, wouldn't you?" I look at him. He's not joking. He really wants to know. Soon after, the group breaks up and heads off to bed.

Brilliant's mint is still on his pillow.

THE SPREADING VIRUS

I wake up at 5:30 and, unable to get back to sleep, read some of Anne Michaels's novel *Fugitive Pieces,* which I brought along as a tie to the familiar world I left behind in Toronto. "The night you and I met, Jakob, I heard you tell my wife that there's a moment when love makes us believe in death for the first time. You recognize the one whose loss, even contemplated, you'll carry forever, like a sleeping child. All grief, anyone's grief, you said, is the weight of a sleeping child." Can happiness be love if love is not love without the possibility of grief? Sometimes, I think, true happiness is a bitch.

I've had a headache all week, which I've variously joked away as detox jitters and TV withdrawal—there is no media exposure here, no papers or magazines or radio, so the week is a de facto media fast as well as everything else—but I am now coming to believe that the pain in my head is the result of intense mental frustration. I'm throwing myself into this as much as I can, and I am starting to feel emotionally hypersensitive. At the same time, the wheels of critical intelligence keep grinding away, noting the banality of the truths, the transparency of the ideological self-enclosure. Maybe all this inner conflict is making me sick.

It troubles me, for example, that every form of unhappiness is treated on the same level here, everyone's pain nonjudgmentally equalized, as if having your spouse die a screaming death from cancer is the same as having an asshole for a boss. That's a crucial assumption in the therapeutic culture—part, you might say, of modernity's unstable democratic legacy. We tend to think of emotional egalitarianism as something peculiar to self-indulgent America, land of ten thousand confessions. Or that it arose during the heady self-obsession of the late 1960s and early '70s, when the trend to take your merest mood incredibly seriously reached a kind of apotheosis of narcissism. But in fact some forms of indiscriminate self-regard are as old as Western individualism itself, and the creation, sometime around 1600, of an idea of personal identity so robust that everyone, no matter how lowly in social station or intrinsic interest, is granted inner depths to be plumbed, caverns of conflict to be excavated. The corollary idea, on naked display here and at dozens of personal-development institutions the continent over—not to mention elsewhere in the culture, from daytime television to the basic rhetoric of commerce—is that the creation of an individual narrative, an arc of self-fulfillment, is the most important piece of art any of us will ever create.

So these ideas of self-indulgent emotional validation are more deeply rooted, and older, than we sometimes suppose. Indeed, even the *forms* of pursuing the penchant for self-revelation are not so recent as we think. In America, where the idea of popular psychology now rises triumphant, the current crop of best-selling authors are simply drawing on a long tradition of by-the-book psychological health. By the turn of the twentieth century American popular psychology was already a booming industry, giving an eager public such works on "adjustment" and "mental hygiene" as Horace Fletcher's *Happiness as Found in Forethought Minus Fearthought* (1913), Orison Swett Marden's *The Joys of Living* (1913), Robert S. Carroll's *Our Nervous Friends* (1919), and Josephine Jackson and Helen Salisbury's *Outwitting Our Nerves* (1921), a trend that altered course only slightly to produce bestsellers on *Relaxation* (1943) and *How Never to Be Tired* (1944) a couple of decades later. Fletcher's treatise gives the flavor of the genre when he asks why, given that "the normal condition of man in civilized life is...happiness" and "the vital truths underlying the philosophy of life" can be "intelligently stated in a few hundred words," unhappiness still dominates our lives. The cause, he says, is "weak habit-of-thought" and the remedy is "good habit-of-thought," which in turn develops "appreciation." This leads to "habit-of-feeling," this to "habit-of-action," and this, finally, to happiness.[9] Aristotle could not have said it better.

In the 1930s, women's magazines such as the *Ladies' Home Journal* and *Woman's Home Companion* fostered an even more popular dissemination of the techniques of happiness. In one article that appeared in the latter, "Getting an Early Start on Happiness," someone called Lorine Pruette articulated the main elements of the position. Many people believe the legend that happiness is the gift of God, Pruette writes, "but psychology improves on the legend by showing us that happiness may be sought and found in any place, because it is in ourselves that it exists and only there. Happiness is... an individual product; it depends upon the chemistry of our hormones, the organization and health of the body's cells, the stability of the nervous system, the attitudes of the mind.... As such, it can be learned."[10] A few decades on, one Luther Conant offered in the same magazine "A 10-Day Plan for Happiness," which argued that unhappiness is "all in your head." "What you need is scientific guidance to help you regain true perspective and start living fully again," Conant said. "This ten-day plan does that. Its simple psychology should work for you. All that's demanded is that you give it the same fair test that you would give a ten-day reducing diet."[11]

We may indeed be inclined to view that degree of concern with self-actualization as a peculiarly American, or possibly North American, fetish. And it's true that this sort of thing has found particularly fertile ground in the United States, especially when combined with the spa-like environs of something like the Option Institute, which effectively fuses the Kelloggian wellness clinic with the encounter session, offering a regimen to reduce waistline and woe at once. But one of the most obvious effects of American cultural imperialism is the exportation of the language of self-help and self-actualization to previously sensible corners of the world. Pop psychology does not yet rank up there with *Baywatch* in terms of worldwide syndication potential, but it's on the rise.

Visiting Britain not long ago I was a little disturbed to find a happiness-provision industry as energetic and pervasive as anything detailed in the journalism of Wendy Kaminer or the fiction of Cyra McFadden. The BBC investigative journalism show *QED* was devoting two hours to a documentary about three unhappy people enrolling in an eight-week course in "How to Be Happy," run by a certain self-described "professor of fun" called Michael Argyle and a freelance psychologist called Dr. Robert Holden. The *Radio Times* offered no judgments on the show but instead a quiz designed to test your level of happiness. In the great magazine-quiz tradition, it had ten multiple-choice questions—number 9, for example, was "Do you feel your life has a sense of meaning and purpose? (a) Yes, definitely; (b) To some extent; (c) Not really; (d) Not at all"—followed by a key to rate your score. Each of the four categories, from "you should consider seeking professional help" to "there's very little you can be told about happiness," had a corresponding yellow "Happy Face" with an expression somewhere between deep frown and maniacal grin.[12] I preferred the judgment of *The Scotsman's* anonymous TV critic, who laced the newspaper's preview with the kind of bleak irony that only a resident of Edinburgh can deploy to full effect. "Tonight's fascinating documentary follows three misery-guts as they go on an eight-week course in how to be happy," the critic wrote, "and sees whether they end up feeling ripped-off as well as sad."[13] When I tune in to see Dr. Holden's prescriptions in action, I admit to feeling a whiff of that brisk northern common sense.

"I want to move people from wanting to be happy to getting happy," Holden says, looking improbably young in a sharp sports jacket and red turtleneck. "And I do it with ozone-friendly, non-chemical medicines like laughter and smiles!" One subject of the course, fortyish, bespectacled Caroline Ponting of Leeds, tells the interviewer that she is still, after the course, at home in a little flat looking after her aged mother. "There's been no change in my circumstances," she says, "only my attitude." The course, she adds, "was a good laugh—literally. A very good laugh." Dr. Holden, among other things, got her to lie flat on the floor, at which point she says she began laughing for no particular reason. "Your muscle tension relaxes, your nervous system relaxes, your immune system improves," Holden says of these quick-time happiness techniques. "If you want to make a great breakthrough around happiness, I would advise you to begin *allowing* yourself to be happy, without the idea that you have to *earn* it," he continues. "The good news is that everyone can learn to be a little bit happier. It's a change for the British public, of course. There's almost a fear of happiness here."

Which makes it all sound a little *too* easy, if you ask me. The columnist Charlotte Raven, writing in *The Guardian* a few months later, complained in a congenial way about the relentless new cheeriness-police of Britain's city streets and railway stations.[14] "So I am sitting on a station platform, lost in thought, when I notice this man looking at me," she writes.

Irritated more than intimidated, I recognize him, at once, as one of them…"Smile," he says. "It might never happen."

I picture him curled up in pain at my feet. Someone has punched him—not too hard, but hard enough to make him reconsider that line. "Actually," I would say, stepping over his body, "it nearly always does."

Or someone will say: "It can't be that bad, dear"—and then you'll have to kill them.

Raven has a point, and I like her John Woo style of making it: there are few things more annoying than being told that you ought to be happy—and that it's entirely up to you to make it happen. "We ne'er can be made happy by compulsion," Coleridge once wrote, rather more politely.[15]

The trouble with Dr. Holden and his Laughter Clinic is that being told to "play with the idea that you could be happy for no reason at all" is like being told you won't stop feeling ill until you are well. Indeed, as Raven goes on to say, "[t]autology lies at the heart of the new happy ethos," which, in its psychologism, often deflects attention from the difficult real-world issues of actually making people better off than they were before. In this way, its surface suggestion is that "[m]aterial reality has lost its role as the fount of all fulfillment," replaced by psychological well-being. But, she says, "[t]his conceptual shift is played out in politics as a retreat from economics to the pseudo-psycho language of self-help. The poor do not need money. You need only look at a pop star to know that they could be just as miserable with it as without. And so the poor will learn to be happy with their lot. They will laugh to themselves for five minutes hourly and teach each other massage techniques."

The ideological sleight of hand contained in the suggestion that money has nothing to do with happines is insidious, because even as it seems to repudiate old-fashioned material fulfillment as somehow tawdry or sordid and therefore beneath the true seeker, it blithely takes for granted that basic material needs are met. Thus those who are unhappy not because they lack self-fulfillment but because they lack food are wrong-footed, summarily judged to be spiritually impaired—or, more simply, unable to see the silver lining in life's inevitable clouds. It is no longer "Pull yourself together and get a job"; now it's "Pull yourself together and be happy." Here Maslow's plain common sense about the hierarchy of needs is turned on its head. Instead of seeing the hierarchy as based on pre-potence—fulfillment is not even an issue if I don't have enough to eat—it is shifted around to suggest that any failures in achieving happiness demonstrate an unfortunate attachment to the material things in life.

Notice, in another example of this inversion, the sort of twisted, quasi-Maslovian thinking that is buried in one of American culture's most endurable exports, Gene Roddenberry's *Star Trek* vision of the future. A gushing thirtieth-anniversary celebration for *Star Trek* and its various spinoffs happened to coincide with certain lively mani-festations of the happiness-therapy boom in Britain and North America during 1996, making the comparison illuminating and irre-sistible. (The same issue of the *Radio Times* with the happiness quiz features a *Star Trek* cover story and eighteen glossy pages of full-color raving; the show is as popular in Britain as in North America, even if the goofy, geeks-only conventions are happily less common.) *Star Trek* offers the most powerful utopian vision in cultural play right now in the various updatings and spinoffs of the original, rather cheesy television series; note in particular the techno-spiritual liber-alism and New Age corporate groupthink of Captain Picard's *Enter-prise D* on *Star Trek: The Next Generation*. Actually, there is little difference among the various mutations of the original concept once you get past the surface decoration and a few insignificant shifts in tone. Both vintages of *Star Trek* are actually apologies for American cultural imperialism, the gospel according to comfort, and market-based happiness. As one critic has put it, Picard, in con-trast to the overheated and boyish militarism of Captain James Kirk, "usually takes an anguished meeting with his senior officers before bagging the Prime Directive."[16]

Of course people love the future offered by Gene Roddenberry and his conceptual heirs. With no poverty, no hunger, lots of virtual-reality diversions, and little meaningful conflict—the wars and battles are often no more than special-effects window dressing, hardly challenging to the overall social structure—the subtext of the various series and movies is clearly one of self-actualization: a celebration of the human factor against encroaching technology, an insistence on psycho-spiritual development, the embracing of paradoxes as a means to hike humankind into the next evolutionary bracket. With synthetic pleasures and food on tap twenty-four hours a day, there is no reason to suppose anyone lacks the basic conditions of happiness. In other words, *Star Trek* doesn't just use soma-like devices in its basic fantastic infrastructure—recreational holodecks, frankly sex-for-sale holosuites, a popular vacation planet full of cheerful prostitutes—*it is itself a form of soma.* Ingested as a television drug, it dulls our sense of its own unreality by playing on immature teenage visions of a future where nobody is poor, sex is always free, and drinks make you witty and playful but never drunk.

Not that this vision goes entirely unchallenged. In one memorable episode of the *Star Trek* spinoff series *Deep Space Nine,* a group of renegades decrying the lack of moral fiber in the United Federation of Planets tries to sabotage the sex-driven resort planet called Raisa, offering a fine denunciation of the adolescent worldview that dominates the *Star Trek* empire. This is an astonishing piece of self-criticism—except that the moral revolutionaries, known as the New Essentialists, are eventually exposed in the episode as crazed right-wingers, Jesse Helms types with bright shining eyes and violent hearts. Thus the important kernel of truth in their message—that the Federation world is indeed one of greedy self-fulfillment that fails to confront the problems of economic inequality—falls to the ground, safely ignored. The tables are effectively turned so that our superficial political disapproval of the reactionary "solution" to dissipation is made to occlude the deeper, more insidious conservatism of the basic premise.[17]

These critical interventions drive us to the conclusion that the future imagined by *Star Trek*—one that resonates powerfully with many people around the world—is dangerously misleading. It asks us to conceive a world in which all the hard problems of political life are swept under the carpet, and suggests, along the way, that anybody who resists that piece of self-delusion is in fact a psychological and political neanderthal. *Star Trek* seduces us with a shortcut to self-actualization by cynically disposing of our baser needs with a too-simple solution. Happiness or nothing! *Star Trek,* like all cheap forms of self-fulfillment, is utopian in the worst possible sense.

For the record, it is worth noting that, despite what people like Dr. Holden would have us believe, Britons are not lacking in the ability to make themselves happy for no reason at all. They might look miserable, but really, to North American eyes anyway, British people are past masters at the game of finding happiness in the midst of abject material misery. It is an infectious attitude, as the transplanted American writer Bill Bryson discovered while living in Britain. Traveling around the country before heading back to the United States, Bryson came across a married couple sitting near a little seaside hut during what Bryson considered a blinding gale. "The man was trying to read a newspaper, but the wind kept wrapping it around his face," Bryson writes.

> They both looked very happy—or if not happy exactly, at least highly contented, as if this were the Seychelles and they were drinking gin fizzes under nodding palms rather than sitting half-perished in a stiff English gale. They were contented because they owned a little piece of prized beachfront property for which there was no doubt a long waiting-list and—here was the true secret of their happiness—any time they wanted they could retire to the hut and be fractionally less cold. They could make a cup of tea and, if they were feeling particularly rakish, have a chocolate digestive biscuit.

The English, Bryson argues, are *the happiest people on earth* because they have mastered this art of cheerfully diminished expectations: the sort of thing embodied in catch phrases like "Well, it makes a change," "Mustn't grumble," "You could do worse," "It's not much but it's cheap and cheerful," and "It was quite nice, *really.*" The sort of thing, in short, calculated to throw people like Charlotte Raven into a semimurderous rage.

"I used to be puzzled by the curious British attitude to pleasure," Bryson adds, "but gradually I came round to their way of thinking and my life has never been happier." The telltale sign of his conversion: the inordinate pleasure he took in being presented with a weak cup of tea and a slice of dry cake in a cold café on a dreary ocean promenade. "All this is completely alien to the American mind," he notes. "To an American the whole purpose of living is to cram as much sensual pleasure as possible into one's mouth more or less continuously. Gratification, instant and lavish, is a birthright. You might as well say 'Oh, I shouldn't really' if someone tells you to take a breath."[18]

Beneath the surface differences in cultural character concerning happiness, however, there is a shared assumption that there is something wrong with you if you are not happy. This in turn reinforces the idea that if you are unhappy it is your fault and not the world's, and, therefore, that nothing structural ever needs to change: what needs to change is you. Because of the presumed lack of connection between material goods and happiness expressed by Dr. Holden and Mr. Roddenberry—or, in what is really another version of the same idea, the relegation of material needs to an assumed background of shared enjoyment, where political questions are nonquestions—the just-do-it version of happiness therapy dominates. Moreover, it appears to be more necessary in highly materialistic cultures than elsewhere in the developed world, because here there is actual potential for conflict between those who have and those who have not. The result is an overwhelming emphasis on quick-fix happiness that ignores, or deflects, harder socioeconomic issues. For this reason, recent American happiness literature is breathtakingly instantaneous. Indeed, sometimes breath-taking is what it is all about.

Siimon Reynolds's *Become Happy in Eight Minutes,* for example, devotes minutes two and three to "changing your breathing." This follows minute one in which he suggests that you stimulate your thymus gland—an endocrine- and T-cell-producing lump in the middle of your chest—by smiling broadly (to stimulate the nerves, he says), tapping on your chest repeatedly and placing your tongue behind your front teeth so that "your two brain hemispheres become more balanced." T-cells are, the book reveals in deathless Reynoldsian prose, "the body's super police. They're always on the beat, looking out for abnormal cells—cells that can do the body harm. Once the T-cells spot a danger, they act like the Terminator and quickly destroy it. So you really owe a lot to those little Ts wandering around your body." I tried these three techniques, and while they didn't actually make me feel better, or not appreciably so, I did feel pretty silly. That's okay—Siimon says you will. I also found it easy to imagine wanting to laugh at how stupid you undoubtedly look smiling like an idiot, thumping yourself in the chest and "centering" your brain hemispheres by curling your tongue behind your teeth.

The point of breathing deeply is, apparently, that becoming happy is almost entirely a matter of moving around the lymph in your body, pumping it here and there, so that it can clean out the toxins that make you unhappy. For all I know, this is true. Breathing deeply, like regular exercise and a healthy diet, is undoubtedly a good thing (Siimon knows about diet, too: minute four involves drinking fruit juice for energy and vitamins). I have some grave doubts about the conceptual connections offered here, though. Most of Siimon's arguments are dubious tautologies cleverly disguised—well, let's be honest, not very cleverly at all, really—as medical claims: You smile when you're happy; therefore smiling will make you happy. You breathe deeply when you're contented; so deep breathing will foster contentment. "What works one way also works the other," he insists, building to slightly hysterical emphasis. *"If your moods change your breathing, then it makes sense that your breathing changes your moods.* It's a proven scientific fact. Any brain physiologist will tell you. So will any yogi."

When people say "it's a proven scientific fact," I'm always reminded of a shady butcher I once bought a roast from, who, in order to convince me to buy the cut he was holding, said, "It's really a nice piece of meat. Really. Believe me." I did believe him—until he said I had to. Still, Siimon is on to something: deep breathing does have a calming effect on the spirit. I try to remember to do it before addressing a large class for the first time or entering a room containing a search committee. And yet it doesn't really change anything, of course. Neither does smiling till your cheeks are going to spasm. It is hard to see how the forced smile could lead to a greater degree of happiness.

To test the thymus-stimulating properties of the wide smile, for example, we're supposed to "sit somewhere comfortable, away from noise and distractions." Well, if I could do that I'd be feeling better already, smile or no smile. Then Siimon says: "Smile as if you are the happiest person in the world. Smile as though you haven't got a care in the universe. The second you do this, your thymus gland will move into action and begin to stimulate the body in its very positive way." Meanwhile you're supposed to do the thymus tap twenty times and keep your tongue centered for at least a minute. Now, I don't know about you, but I'm fully capable of smiling "as if" I were Mr. Happy-Go-Lucky without actually feeling like him at all. My T-cells and lymph might be kicking butt all over my body, pausing to offer thickly accented tag lines before blowing the toxins away—I don't know. But from my point of view I'm just sitting here with a rictus of bizarre faux-merriment plastered on my face.

Still, I'm neglecting the even more powerful steps of minutes five through eight, in which I "reprogram my brain" by means of what sports psychologists call creative visualization (CV) and change my body movements to happy ones, consistent with the newly fashionable tenets of neuro-linguistic programming (NLP). NLP, like CV, is a technique of autosuggestion in which you convince yourself at some subconscious level—reprogram your brain, in other words—that something desirable is the case: you are a great free-throw shooter, a successful public speaker, a happy guy. You should create a movie inside your head, Siimon says ("Make the movie super-colorful, and nice and loud"), and use the movie to imagine the things you want to be true. "See yourself as happy as you've ever been," he says. "See yourself jumping for joy, smiling, laughing, playing, in total bliss. See that picture of yourself without a care in the world, free as a bird, delirious with happiness."

To Siimon, seeing is not just believing—it is actually being. If you follow NLP and start carrying yourself the way a happy person does, you will become happy. "It makes sense really," Siimon says in another believe-me moment. "If you move a certain way when you're happy, your brain logically concludes you must be happy when you move like that! This is known as a cybernetic loop." In circles where logic counts for something it is known by another name: the fallacy of affirming the consequent. Whatever Siimon might say, the proposition "If q then p" is *not* equivalent to, and does not follow from, the proposition "If p then q." [19]

Of course the skeptical are probably just failing to do the CV and NLP exercises properly. There has to be 100 percent commitment to the program—otherwise they won't work. The unspoken message here is this: unless you actually start feeling happier, you're not going to be any happier! But don't despair. It all comes down to acts of will and attitude anyway. In minute eight, you "change your focus" so that you see the good even in things that appear disastrously bad. Siimon's example is a household burglary. Bad, right? Not necessarily. Lots of good things can come from a burglary. You beef up your home security, alert your neighbors to risk, buy a guard dog ("You'll have a lot of fun frolicking with the dog that you wouldn't have had otherwise"), get a new wardrobe with the insurance money, appreciate the value of your family (you were burgled, not burgled *and murdered*). And if you think your problems are big ones, just consider for a minute the unimaginable vastness of the universe, the hundred billion planets in our galaxy alone. Don't you feel better already?

"We control our reality," Siimon eventually says, as he was destined to do from the beginning. "Our happiness or sadness is dependent on what we tell our minds. Never forget that."

TRUTH OR CONSEQUENCES

The next morning, Thursday, is a long Q & A session in which Kaufman alternately fends off mild challenges from the small minority of disgruntled seekers ("What kind of criminal justice system would you run?" "One based on unconditional love!") and tells long, rambling stories about how people, significantly his gruff, no-nonsense father, finally fell under his spell after long resistance. Dying of cancer, Kaufman Senior eventually peeled away his negativity and accepted the gospel according to happiness choice.

It is a typical example of the genre, comparable to M. Scott Peck's endless tales of former hard guys who *break down and cry* under the influence of unconditional love, but it also exhibits some fine points in the subtle aggression of ideology: the gentle mockery of outsiders who "insist" on being unhappy, the exclusive jargon of "intention" and "being present," the reliance on anecdote and crude either-or reasoning, and the all-encompassing nature of the belief, which is immune to challenge because proudly and cheerfully unfalsifiable. Kaufman, invariably right, invariably loving, basking now in the glow of adulation, starts to seem not just "irritating and pretentious," as Beth put it to me the night before, but also a bit sociopathic. I know that Beth's mother died not long ago of colon cancer. I look over at her and she is in tears—not happy ones, either, by the look of her, but tears of rage and grief.

In the afternoon the group dynamics begin to coalesce. We are run through an exercise on "seeing ourselves as God sees us," learning how to accept ourselves as we are—past the fickle gaze of Fortune and men's eyes. Nothing new here, just a version of the old take-the-long-view happiness maneuver. This argument, in which we put our woes in perspective by seeing ourselves from a long way off, as God or the universe looks at things, is hardly unheralded. It was, for example, much favored by the sixth-century Christian philosopher Anicius Boethius, and it still shows up as foundation in programs like *Become Happy in Eight Minutes*. Boethius's work *The Consolation of Philosophy*, maybe the first self-help text in the Western world, made the idea popular throughout medieval Europe and, along the way, laid some important groundwork for the later democratization and debasement of happiness concepts in the early modern era. "Why then do you mortals seek happiness outside yourselves, when it lies within you?" the figure of Philosophy asks Boethius in a key dialogue of the work. "You are led astray by error and ignorance. Do you really hold dear that kind of happiness that is destined to pass away? Do you really value the presence of Fortune when her departure will plunge you into sorrow?" God's favor, not Fortune's, is the source of all genuine happiness. Only in making the choice to turn to Him can we begin to see the trials—and triumphs—of this benighted plane for the illusions they are. This world is a vale of tears, and resigned acceptance is the only route to genuine happiness.

Sure, life is an illusion, and we all seek happiness in the wrong places sometimes. The Boethian attitude can look superficially compelling. But we should be careful not to mistake this form of resignation for the tough, here-and-now self-reliance of the Stoic, say. Boethius's thinking leads not to a thick skin but to a soft center: relax, God's will be done. Indeed, the argument is disreputable, not least in that it depends on prior belief in a benevolent Judeo-Christian God. Why do people fall for it? Well, it is intensely attractive when the world begins to overwhelm: many a nagging problem just seems to disappear in the bright light of eternity. Boethius, like Kaufman, also had impeccable personal experience to bolster him. A passionate scholar and writer who happened to get on the wrong side of a routinely bloody Mediterranean political intrigue, he wrote the *Consolation* in prison just before he was tortured and executed. Chaucer and Dante, not to mention C. S. Lewis and the Pulitzer Prize–winning novelist John Kennedy Toole, author of the thoroughly Boethian *Confederacy of Dunces,* thought Boethius was the real deal.

I can feel the waverers going over to the comforting embrace of Kaufman's view of the world—and the literal embrace of his body. "People say, 'But these ideas are not true,'" Kaufman now whispers into the mike, as if reading my mind. "And I always say, 'Who cares?' When I was a graduate student in philosophy, that's all I did, search for the truth. I was desperate to find it. Then I met someone who thought she had it, a brilliant woman, Harvard graduate, a psychiatrist and psychoanalyst. And you know what? *She was miserable.* She had the truth and all she got was pain and angst. So I stopped searching for the truth. If it makes you miserable, I don't want it. I'll take happiness. If searching for the truth brings pain, I'll take love."

The story has a familiar ring. It does so, I soon realize, because in *Happiness Is a Choice,* Kaufman describes, in virtually identical language, a similar moment, when he is confronted by a married couple, a psychologist and a philosopher, who object that he has nothing but banal maxims and anecdotal evidence to support his claim that happiness is a choice. What if it's just not that simple? What if he's just plain wrong? Kaufman pauses to consider this, and he "quietly" accepts the possibility. And yet, he *knows* that teaching what he admits may be an "incorrect belief" has nevertheless "altered lifelong attitudes and behavior patterns in profound and immediate ways." "Wow!" Kaufman writes in what has obviously become part of the set script. "So what we might have here is you holding the truth and being 'right' and us teaching something that's possibly false, no matter how helpful and healing....Well then, so much for the 'truth,' I'd rather be happy!" It was no more convincing in print than when whispered through the cordless mike.

Almost everyone nods at the sentiment, however. *Yes, Bears, you're so right. Screw the truth; ignorance is bliss.* I am nearly apoplectic, though fighting gamely not to show it. I want to shout at them: Wait a second, you crazy people. Is what he's saying *right now*—that truth doesn't matter—*true?* If it is, then truth matters, doesn't it? You can't ever say "The truth doesn't matter" without snaring yourself in a contradiction, because you have just claimed something, and claims are only claims if they are true. In fact, the whole issue collapses into one of the oldest paradoxes on record, the one usually attributed to Epimenides the Cretan, who said all Cretans were liars. (If that is true, then it is false; Epimenides is telling the truth. If it is false, then it is true; Epimenides is lying.) So if what Kaufman is teaching is *not* true, why should we be listening to it? And if he really doesn't care one way or the other, why is he charging us all a significant chunk of change to tell us about it? The Socratic *doctrina ignorantia*—the idea that true wisdom is knowing that you don't know, one of Kaufman's favorite philosophical touchstones—is a methodological assumption, not a conclusion. It's supposed to spur on the search for truth, not lay it to rest.

Kaufman likes to say that the world is all make-believe, a series of constructions that we could as easily shape into happiness as unhappiness. But logic, like gravity, is not just a good idea. It's the law.

In one sense, Kaufman and the other "get happy" gurus are part of a venerable philosophical tradition, one that in broad outline stretches back as far as Plato and the Stoics in the West and Lao Tzu and the Buddha in the East. This tradition offers only a small number of fundamental ideas about happiness, each more or less compatible with the others and sometimes, but not always, deployed together. Indeed, we may agree with these thinkers in deciding that these strategies exhaust the options of a theory of happiness, and yet there is much room for nuance, variation, and texture to these theories.

What are the basic theories of happiness, then? Well, we might distinguish three. We can make ourselves happy by (1) moderating, possibly even eliminating, our troublesome desires. Since desires can often go unfulfilled, they—not the world or the cosmic order— are the root of our unhappiness. We do not long for what we did not want; therefore, if we can only tamp down our particular wants, happiness will be ours. Call this first strategy the theory of the lowered gaze.[20]

In a related move of a similar kind, we may (2) insist upon the triviality of our concerns when viewed, as philosophers like to say, *sub specie aeternitatis*—from the perspective of eternity. "Our doings are not so important as we naturally suppose; our successes and failures do not after all matter very much," Bertrand Russell once wrote in this mood. "Even great sorrows can be survived; troubles which seem as if they must put an end to happiness for life, fade with the lapse of time until it becomes impossible to remember their poignancy." [21] Whatever we do, in short, and whether we do it well or ill, the universe will remain much the same in either case. As soon as we see this, many of the routine worries and miseries of daily life simply wither away as pointless preoccupations or mere narcissism now revealed as such. Call this second strategy the theory of the indifferent universe.

Alternatively, or in conjunction with (1) and (2), we may secure happiness by (3) concentrating on the positive aspects of what we actually have, even if it is invariably mixed with vexing and troubling features of this mortal life. In the words of the familiar pop song, "accentuate the positive and eliminate the negative." Happiness is thus largely, or perhaps entirely, a function of attitude with respect to one's particular situation. Even the worst outcome must, properly regarded, contain some shred of happiness. Gather those shreds together, and the result is the fabric of a happy life. Call this third strategy the theory of the silver lining. Russell himself gives us a nice statement of theories (2) and (3) working in conjunction: "Having looked at [a] possible misfortune in the face, give yourself sound reasons for thinking that after all it would be no such very terrible disaster," he advises. "Such reasons always exist, since at the worst nothing that happens to oneself has any cosmic importance."

The Irish playwright Oliver Goldsmith once professed himself very much of the silver-lining view, as well, though there is some reason to suspect a dark vein of irony in his defense of it. "I remember to have once seen a slave in a fortification in Flanders," he writes in his little essay "Happiness, in a Great Measure, Dependant on Constitution,"

> who appeared no way touched with his situation. He was maimed, deformed, and chained; obliged to toil from the appearance of day 'till night-fall, and condemned to this for life; yet, with all these circumstances of apparent wretchedness, he sung, would have danced, but that he wanted a leg, and appeared the merriest, happiest man of all the garrison. What a practical philosopher was here; an happy constitu-

tion supplied philosophy, and though seemingly destitute of wisdom, he was really wise.

"He would have danced but that he wanted a leg…" When we recall that in eighteenth-century usage the word "want" commonly meant "lack," the picture begins to cloud over a bit. When Goldsmith later adds, "I never pass by one of our prisons for debt, that I do not envy that felicity which is still going forward among those people who forget the cares of the world by being shut out from its ambition," you cannot help but think he's pulling your leg—one of them, anyway.

Goldsmith goes on to argue that good humor in the face of misfortune "is certainly a better way to oppose calamity by dissipation, than to take up the arms of reason or resolution to oppose it," and concludes that "struggling with misfortunes, we are sure to receive some wounds in the conflict; but a sure method to come off victorious, is by running away."[22] Don't fight it—and don't think too much out there.

Though the idea of willed happiness is old, then, older than most people currently engaged in its sale could know, it is not ageless and it is not something we should allow to be accepted without objection. There was a time when the idea that happiness could be as self-indulgent—and as ethically and intellectually undemanding—as simply choosing to have a positive attitude about your life would have struck sensitive minds as scandalous, if not insane. It is impossible for most of us to conceive now how alien such a thought would have seemed to Aristotle, Cicero, even Thomas Aquinas.

Something else has nagged at me all week, ever since Thea mentioned her husband's affair on the first night in the common room. When we were asked to write down our purpose in this life and share it with a rotating series of partners, not one person I talked to put anything but variations on "To be present," "To live in the moment," and "To love unconditionally." I was starting to get sick of all this unconditional love, anyway. "I should like to bring forward my two main objections to this view," Sigmund Freud once wrote. "A love that does not discriminate seems to forfeit part of its own value, by doing an injustice to its object; and secondly, not all people are worthy of love."[23] More than that, nobody mentioned ethical or political commitment, service to other people or a community, deferring or even submerging pleasure for the greater good. So, rather mischievously, I wrote "To live a good life," and was, predictably, regarded by my partners with some confusion. Was I talking about a martinis-and-Armani-suits kind of good life? Sure I was—bring them on, baby—but more than that I meant a more basic notion of the good life: the examined life; the life of reflection and ethical commitment, without which (Socrates said) life is not worth living. The life of happiness understood not as contentment or personal salvation or even unconditional love, but as ethical self-approval.

I tried to explain this to the other campers. I mentioned a superb episode of *The Simpsons,* one of my favorites, in which mother Marge drags the family to a psychotherapeutic barnstorm at the local rec center. A smarmy self-help guru in the John Bradshaw mode takes the stage.

"I don't have a lot of 'credentials' or 'qualifications,'" he says in fine Kaufmanesque style, twitching his fingers and putting a lot of sneer into the judgmental quality of those dirty words. "But I'll tell you one thing: I've got a Ph.D. in pain." Not surprisingly, irrepressible Bart immediately heckles him. So he calls the boy up on stage.

"What made you do that?"

"I dunno," Bart says. "I just do whatever I feel like."

"Isn't that marvelous, people? He just *does* whatever he *feels* like. This is the inner child I've been talking about. Be like the boy!" The ever-biddable Springfieldians take up the cry, and soon the town is a chaos of nonjudgmental, happiness-choosing layabouts and libertines. At the first annual "Do What You Feel Festival" (guest artist, James Brown), some people are hurt because somebody didn't feel like checking the safety measures on a Ferris wheel or double-bolting a grandstand. Fights breaks out; after that, it gets ugly and judgmental pretty fast. *Be like the boy! Be like the boy!* I found myself chanting this under my breath during slow moments in the afternoon session.

I had some trouble getting these points across to my partners, of course—people don't watch enough TV these days, never mind read enough Plato. Countless times over the course of the week I was told that it *didn't matter* what was making me unhappy, and also that it *didn't matter* what forms of belief or action, however mendacious, selfish, or fanciful, I adopted to stop feeling that way. My personal reclamation project took precedence over everything else in life, and anything, but anything, that "worked for me" carried its justification with it. The point, as Kaufman writes in *Happiness Is a Choice,* was to "stretch ourselves continually and passionately to live more fully with a clear and prioritized intention." Of course.

The same impasse happens now when I object to the idea of "seeing ourselves in God's eyes" to my dialogue partner. "Whatever you mean by God," she assures me, beaming away. But I think: Uh-uh, not good enough. Either we're talking about something in particular, or we're not even talking—we might as well be rubbing our tummies. Nietzsche's dismissive phrase for this kind of reassuring nonsense was "metaphysical comfort"; a simpler one is pleasant but dangerous delusion. People say Nietzsche was nihilistic—he said it himself—but there is no nihilism more degenerate than the one in which we make ourselves cheaply happy by refusing to face the challenges of reason, and life. With truth out the window, it's no wonder that whatever-God-is-to-you, that weak-minded bromide of the moment, has come in through the back door.

We line up for our hugs, and though I have been inconsistent with this part of the program—residual resistance, I guess, just like refusing to refer to Kaufman as "Bears," either to his face or when speaking with the other happy campers—this time I submit. "I'm aware that this is someone I don't hug very often," Kaufman says to the room at large as we go into the clinch. Yeah, well *my* love is conditional, bubba.

A bunch of people—the common-room in-groupers—are going off-campus for dinner tonight. There's been lots of schoolboyish talk of steaks and red wine, pepperoni pizza and beer. Initially I agreed to go, but I now find I just can't face any more of this, of these people, however much I like them.

I get in my rented Sentra and bounce down the driveway. When I hit the concrete I press the gas pedal to the floor, cranking the Offspring song on the radio till the ringing power chords begin to coagulate the air around my body. Tension rolls off my shoulders in waves. I head west for New York, driving into the sunset and the rising hills, shouting Green Day and R.E.M. lyrics into the onrushing air. I feel wire-brushed, rubbed raw with manufactured emotion and enforced intimacy. The sunset over the Adirondacks is so beautiful it makes me weep.

I turn around when I get to Hudson, New York, and drive back to an old aluminum-sided diner just off the Taconic Parkway, where I happily consume a Pepsi and cheeseburger with fries. Yes, I am on the lam from happy camp, eatin' meat and livin' large! But it's not enough to dispel the stress; my shoulders are still bunched with tension. Feeling the need to talk to some normal people, I go into the old wooden phone booth in the corner and start dialing up my friends in Toronto. Nobody's home. I get five voice-mail messages in a row, including Gail's. Good thing this isn't a real life-or-death crisis, just a philosophical one. Where are these people? Are they screening calls in my hour of need? Finally I catch my friend Janice, a book editor, who against all odds happens to be at home. She wants to know if I've discovered what happiness is.

"And don't give me any of that glass-is-half-full crap," she says.

Suddenly I miss her like mad. The week has clearly gotten to me. Janice listens patiently as, mental pressure easing all the while, I drone on for an hour about ideological indoctrination and love-bombing, unsettling crushes on grieving twenty-four-year-old women, sexual insecurity, fear of aging and death. Eventually the beehived waitress turns off the lights to make me leave.

CASHING THE CHECK

It is the final day of the seminar. For the hundredth time I think about eating Brilliant's mint but find I can't bring myself to disturb the little still-life arrangement on the other bed, which now gives off a certain bleak pathos.

There is a last-day-of-classes atmosphere at breakfast, people already failing to be totally present as they anticipate good-byes, return journeys, and piles of waiting bills. There is also a sense that time is running short for those of us yet to have some kind of public breakthrough.

Maybe a little churlishly, I refuse to credit Kaufman and his happy-camp gimmicks with my moment of existential insight from last night: I already know I have an "issue" "around" mortality. I know I'm afraid of dying. Who isn't? Talking to Janice about it, someone whom I will have to see regularly, is a lot more demanding than some tearful revelation to a group of strangers—attractive though that might be now and then, as an idea. And anyway, it is not that in my regular life I run short of little epiphanies about the fear of death and how sexual desire fits into that. (On the contrary, I spend so much time thinking about the prospect of my own death, and fixating on sexual attractions as some kind of palliative to that fear, that I sometimes feel like a Woody Allen character. Or maybe just Woody Allen.) The film director David Cronenberg once said that the Latin tag *Timor mortis conturbat me*—"The fear of death unsettles me"—could be considered an appropriate motto for all horror movies. As someone capable of scaring the living bejesus out of the most stable audience, he ought to know. So, a keynote of all horror films—but how about romances? Never underestimate the connection between death and love, I think, as we file out from breakfast and over to the Option House.

There is one more session, a "summary" of "points" by Kaufman, followed by a final stare-down contest and hugfest. Is it my imagina-tion or are some of these embraces getting a little, um, personal? All week there has been a lot of unacknowledged sexual tension in the air, and now the room is thick with it. This is not just me—there are some uneasy jokes as we leave the Option House later, a few rather clumsy gestures and feints of flirtation. This is not really a surprise to me, though possibly because I have sex on the brain this morn-ing. The therapeutic setting is ripe with erotic possibility. And yet sex was something we never discussed in the classroom. That's probably because unfocused Eros makes such an effective psychodramatic tool when it is present but unaccounted for. It's bound to open you up a bit—and probably mess you up a bit—when complete strangers are suddenly taking physical liberties unimaginable, for good reason, in the everyday social world. But some of the people here, I know at least three, are trying to deal with a painful legacy of sexual abuse: unwelcome attention from an uncle, a father who let his hands wander during goodnight embraces, that kind of thing. And for the rest of us, who will drop back into normal life in a matter of hours, this wash of fuzzy sexual feeling can only contribute to the feeling that the whole week is, in memory, a surreal dream—something, possibly, that we'll be desperate to recapture on a return visit.

And what about acknowledging, and maybe minimizing, the general dangers of transference and countertransference in this or any form of psychotherapy? Kaufman is entirely into his role as guru, the warmly beaming hug-meister. But any halfway decent teacher knows that creating a cult of personality in the classroom is one of the easiest things in the world, particularly when it comes to philosophy (or even pseudo-philosophy): a little wisdom goes a long way when people have not engaged in deep introspection before. All the more reason, I figure, to guard against becoming a focus for those intense feelings. Socrates knew well enough that the prospect of wisdom is intensely erotic, and the teacher-pupil relationship is therefore a charged one. His refusal to have sex with Alcibiades in Plato's *Symposium* is the first recorded professional-conduct decision in the history of Western teaching, long before Freud's injunction that psychoanalysts should not take advantage of their patients' transference of emotional attachments to them. (Even if, in the event, the refusal had a pretty seductive effect on the proud golden boy of Athens, more hooked on Socrates than ever.)

I am struck, not for the first time, by a suspicion that we have been duped by all this. We have been drawn here precisely because happiness is so important to us and we were, presumably, disappointed with the routine provision of happiness out in the world. What we have found is simply more technique.

This could have been predicted, of course. "The normal function of the human mind is the pursuit of happiness," the psychologist Hanns Sachs wrote in 1939. "That the soul is given to man as a means to lead him to happiness—if not here, then hereafter—is proof of the deeply ingrained universal conviction that happiness is the ultimate, if not the exclusive purpose of the psyche."[24] Hence, he adds, the common feeling that happiness is something for which a *demand* is justified: a kind of restitution, not of what we had and lost, but rather of something to which we have a preexisting natural right. Deep down we feel that happiness is the human birthright, something that fate or circumstance or perhaps human evil has denied us, yet which must naturally be restored—again, if not here then hereafter.

Listen to the complaint of the imprisoned Boethius in the first part of *The Consolation* and hear the slightly outraged voice of each one of us, confronted by fortunes that conspire to make us unhappy. We want to know: why has this happened to *me*? Nor is it merely a question of theodicy, a matter of squaring the alleged justness of God with the evident fact that bad things happen to good people. The psychological point runs deeper: our very self-consciousness, the basic ability to feel and discriminate among pleasures and pains both gross and subtle, seems to condemn us to a lifetime of grasping for what we feel we have lost. Benjamin Franklin once pointed out that only the *pursuit* of happiness, not its capture, was promised in the Declaration of Independence. But most of us would be inclined to regard that piece of Yankee common sense as marking the limits of government, not of human expectation.

Of course, there is no right to happiness inscribed in the foundations of the universe. Sensing that this is so, we must become aware of the difficulties faced by any psychotherapist—and indeed any individual—who must confront the collision of cold fact with the hot desires and demands of the human psyche. The point extends beyond the purely professional troubles of the psychotherapist, because the confrontation is a basic element in the pursuit of happiness itself. And the options Hanns Sachs considers are very much to the point in our present confusion regarding happiness. Some ways of coping with human unhappiness, he says, "are dangerously near to quackery or lead directly towards it." The first of these is what he calls "the pseudo-scientific method," in which we "withdraw into the rigid shell of mechanization and artificiality" and "find shelter behind the use of all sorts of new devices, gadgets, charts, statistics and what not." In short, the kind of thing now peddled with mounting shrillness on late-night television and in the vast self-help sections of the bookstore and the Internet.

The "technologies" on offer there, which range from dianetic theory to stepwise techniques on the order of Siimon Reynolds's eight-minute therapy, promise instant and decisive psychic alteration under cover of bad science, transparent jargon, and a flurry of alphabetical designations: CV, NLP, and so on. Such is the pervasive scientism of our culture that this sort of shameless creation of awe before the trappings of "the scientific" is not only successful with thousands of customers but rarely exposed for its sheer neuron-melting stupidity. Anything with the stamp of "scientific" authority overpowers our increasingly enfeebled critical responses, even when the science in question is bad or nonexistent. At the same time, genuine science is finding itself more and more rendered mystical by those who would have it serve their purposes of bolstering programs of spiritual progression. (Notice, for instance, the next time you find yourself in the bookshops, how many of the pop spiritualism and self-fulfillment books are now driven by obscurantist versions of neuroscientific and biochemical claims from mainstream science. It is odd, but far from uncommon, to see words like "neuropeptide" and "angel" on the same page.)

The other main temptation for the troubled psychotherapist, and for all us amateur psychologists, too, is what Sachs calls "the pseudo-magical method"—or rather methods, since these options proliferate like grapes on a vine. The essence of these methods, and "hence their immense popularity and their unreliable, but undeniable results," is that they "promise not only cure but happiness in their straightforward, undoubting manner." And in operating this way, they confess their technological bias as much as the pseudo-scientific methods: the pseudo-magical methods are also *machines* that promise consistent, and often instant, input-output connections. Follow this program and, as if by magic, you will be happier. (Don't ask me how it works; it's a secret.) Indeed, there is nothing startling in this, for if magic is simply the science of another form of belief—one in which not all connections need be causal, not all links logical—then what we see on offer in the marketplace of psychic technique is a peculiar mixture, sometimes in one and the same method, of pre-scientific and pseudo-scientific trappings decorating a blithe, and necessarily unfalsifiable, claim to generate happiness.

Unfalsifiable, that is, because the provision of happiness must be set up in these machines so that no critical rational response can be admitted: the technique must not include, as genuine science always does, the conditions of its own refutation.[25] After all, that might actually lead—as, again, it often does in genuine science—to an actual refutation. Hence the results of these machines must be both unreliable and undeniable. And yet popular, for they meet some part of the need to think ourselves deserving of happiness. "These people," Sachs writes of the happy customers, "walk on the air instead of on the hard and dusty earth, but they walk with crippled feet."

They also, most effectively, dance back and forth across a line separating the here and now from the hereafter, conceived either in the short term (when you finally break the cycle of co-dependency, say) or the long term (for instance, when God shall judge the quick and the dead). "This easy shifting from one side to the other is a great help when the expectations of happiness in this life become dimmer," Sachs says. "A rubber check is as good as a valid one when you don't present it in order to pay your rent or buy your victuals."

The trouble is, to many of us that springy check looks genuine. Worse, the people who made it out are good at suggesting that questioning its validity is, as they like to say, one of our *issues around happiness*. For some reason, the same charge does not seem to apply in reverse. Zoë made very sure my credit was good before I was allowed to go to happy camp.

"So maybe he is an asshole," Beth says to me as we drive to the Hartford airport later that afternoon, all but one of our awkward good-byes now behind us. She's still miffed about yesterday, and because, during the final snuggly-hug round of the week, Kaufman condescendingly suggested that a return visit could "really help someone like her."

"But you have to acknowledge that what he's teaching people is really beautiful," she says. "Maybe people have lost some deeper idea of happiness—happiness as civic commitment, the happy life the same as the ethical life. I don't know about that. All I see around me are a lot of negative people, a lot of people making themselves unhappy. If this kind of thing can make those people even a little bit happier, or if not them then maybe their children—my children, yours—isn't it okay? Isn't it?"

As we drive across northern Connecticut, though, I find the whole experience coming apart in my hands, collapsing down into an inescapable paradox. Apart from my long dark night of the soul about death and dying—which might well have happened anywhere, given a slight prompting—about the only wisdom I gleaned from the week's exercises, and this happened outside class, was a valuable reminder that happiness is not, as we tend to think, a prize to capture: not a condition to reach, a peak to scale. The attainment rhetoric that leads people back to the shopping mall every weekend, or into desperate flights after jobs, money, peak experiences, and multiple sexual partners, just *pathologizes* happiness.

The result is a culture that can no longer think straight about happiness. Happiness does come from within, but that doesn't mean it's a choice. Happiness comes from within in the sense that it is a matter of rational satisfaction with your character and actions, a mental and moral condition—hard-edged, lucky, demanding, and fragile. And there are no shortcuts—no twelve-step programs, no courses of therapy or drugs, no purchasing plans or career strategies—to that. It is not a place to get to, it is a state of mind and character to cultivate. The problem is that the Option Institute represents precisely the kind of technological, shortcut thinking that makes happiness hollow in our culture, the same cynical hard sell masked as benevolent healing that spills off the shelves of the self-help section. The staff may deny this, but the basic truth cannot be avoided. You pay your $1,275 and you get your payoff, such as it is. It's not as fast as Siimon Reynolds's eight-minute plan, but it has shaved seventy-two hours off Luther Conant's 1950s-vintage ten-day program. Who says there's no progress in human affairs? *Step right up!*

It is late by the time I get home. Gail is waiting for me in the living room. So are a pile of letters, a stack of phone messages, and a bunch of e-mail flags on my computer—the shards of a busy life, at once reassuring and annoying. I pour myself an inch of Glenlivet, mostly because I told myself I would. The week already feels like a dream, fading away fast as I struggle to close my fingers around the details.

"You look younger," Gail says, smiling. "Rejuvenated." She pauses. "Or maybe it's just the light in here." In the mail, along with

the bills and flyers and memos, are a couple of rejection letters—
jobs I applied for a while back in a fit of evidently misplaced optimism. The phrases are familiar. *Thank you for your interest. You have
impressive credentials. Many qualified candidates.*

I let them drop to the floor.

3

The Normal & the Pathological

Happiness is for idiots.

—*Charles de Gaulle*

PROZAC DAYS

IDECIDED RECENTLY TO PUT MYSELF ON PROZAC. IT WAS EARLY
summer, the university term over and the sun shining, and I
wasn't feeling particularly unhappy. My grades were all in and my
tan was under way and I had nothing weighing on me beyond the
usual long-term anxieties, as familiar now as well-worn shoes, concerning my future as a university teacher and whether I loved my
wife enough. Like a lot of people, I have bouts of mild depression,
in my case sometimes associated with insomnia, hangovers, or other
forms of physical depletion, in which color drains from the world,
joy fades from the achievements obsessively detailed in my C.V., and
friendships resolve themselves temporarily into desperate utilitarian
or drug-based pacts. But I have never suffered from the debilitating brain-chemical imbalance known as clinical depression, and
whether or not I agree with the assertions of those who do that their
affliction bears no resemblance to the blues I know, I can still appreciate that my lot is, by comparison, a lucky one. I am generally a
happy guy, with only occasional dark periods.

It is true that returning from the Option Institute to the routine
ups and downs of my normal life proved to be, as I expected, somewhat depressing. I spent forty-eight hours in a kind of daze and then

settled into several weeks of feeling a bit sad. I began to see why people like Paolo and Steve would return to what Kaufman called "our little corner of Heaven" every year for another dose. Unconditional love is a speed high—all that body contact and acceptance, the flood of endorphins, it can be like the first moments of sexual attraction, unsettling and exhilarating at once. But it wears off fast, and that's when you need a new stimulus. Back in the world, I tried hugging people more than before, but they were reacting warily. I saw my father on Father's Day, only the second time I'd seen him in a year, and ignored his outstretched hand to give him a hug instead of our usual handshake. When it was time to leave, he offered his hand again but I hugged him anyway. I hugged my friends, male and female, until their stiffening bodies and looks of mild alarm gradually sent me back to the kissy-kissy pecks on the cheek that are the standard in my part of the social world.

Around the same time there was a flurry of e-mail from some of the happy-campers, valiant attempts to follow through on those well-meant promises to stay in touch. I had almost readjusted to my regular life when Paolo suggested a reunion somewhere in New England for later in the summer, and I found the idea unwelcome. There is something foredoomed about attempts to recapture a serendipitous social moment, when a group of people has come together under unusual circumstances and suddenly bonded. Reunions offer the same mixture of pathos and idealization found in all forms of nostalgia, the peculiar pain of revisiting sites of former happiness. Trying to close your fingers around the past always has, to me, a bittersweet quality. I have some friends from college who are forever seeking to regain the feelings of shared purpose and emotional excitement that characterized our summers of softball and draft beer, our winters of existential philosophy and cheap red wine. But those days are gone, and keeping one eye forever on the past just makes me sad.

I tried to communicate some of this to Beth when we were talking on the phone one day. I said I had this fear that a reunion might expose the tenuousness of our connections, our lack of anything in common beyond a single experience, the very intensity of which was somehow false. "But don't you think," she said, "it would be great to just sit around with those guys in a motel room somewhere and smoke a lot of drugs?"

I didn't get the Prozac in order to ward off a documented case of clinical depression, or to treat an eating disorder or obsessive-compulsive condition. I didn't get it prescribed for me by a physician. I got it by making exactly two phone calls and explaining to friends that I wanted to see what taking Prozac made me feel like—and that I was certainly no less depressed than millions of people on the drug right now. The drug, Eli Lilly's cash cow, is the second-most-prescribed in the world—17 million Americans are on it, for starters, and the number of prescriptions or recommendations of the drug for children under twelve rose 212 percent between 1994 and 1997. Scoring some was the easiest drug deal I've ever made. Within a week I had a three-month supply of the pretty little torpedo-shaped lime-green and yellow pills sitting on my bathroom counter. When I started taking them at the beginning of June I had just heard some bad news, a small and I hoped temporary career setback. And while that wasn't the reason I started popping the Prozac at that point, it was a useful and, I thought, appropriate coincidence. I decided I would keep this self-administered drug trial to myself; only Gail and my supplier knew I was taking the pills.

One of my friends tells me that the practice of taking prescription medicine for kicks, something he dismissed as "very bourgeois," is known as *chipping*. This was news to me, but most of the lore concerning Prozac was not. It would be hard to exist in this culture and not know at least something about the most celebrated antidepressant of all time. First marketed in the United States in 1988, Prozac is the trade name of the drug fluoxetine, one of a class of newish pharmaceuticals known as selective serotonin re-uptake inhibitors, or SSRIs. They work by blocking the brain's tendency, under some conditions, to "absorb" the amounts of the neurotransmitter serotonin, a feel-good chemical produced by synaptic exchanges.[1] Typically, the serotonin generated by the brain's activity stays in the resulting electrochemical cocktail, in greater or lesser degrees, and we experience these variations as moods or changes in consciousness. Depressives have lower than normal amounts of serotonin in their brains because it has been reabsorbed by the neurons. When the brain's neurons take up the serotonin generated at the synapses, it has no chemical—and hence no phenomenological—effect on the person. Prozac works by inhibiting or blocking that re-uptake, leaving more serotonin active in the brain and thus alleviating depression.

Or so the story goes. "The antidepressant, antiobsessional, and antibulimic actions of fluoxetine are *presumed* to be linked to its ability to selectively inhibit the neuronal uptake of serotonin," one pharmaceutical desk reference says. "At clinically relevant doses fluoxetine blocks the uptake of serotonin into human platelets."[2] (Those are my italics.) Nobody actually knows how Prozac or other antidepressants work, and the presumption that its effects, which are observable, are linked to inhibition of serotonin re-uptake is simply pharmaceutical science's best guess so far. Even serotonin itself, which scientists—and increasingly lay people, too—speak about as if we all know exactly what it is, is something of a mystery. We know that brain-chemical levels and mixtures change over time, and we know that these changes correlate with our altered moods and states of mind, but we don't know exactly why or how that happens, and we don't really know which individual elements in the mixture are responsible for what.

Serotonin is, in some ways, as question-begging as the medieval humors. We know about as much as the Scholastic quack in Molière's play *La Malade Imaginaire,* who explained to a dubious patient that a sleeping potion worked because of its potent *dormative* properties. "Is serotonin the mystical spark of the postmodern mind?" one writer, a depressive himself, asked of his own increasingly desperate attempts to find a drug combination that would alleviate his depression. "I wonder if my depression is 'unbearable' without medication only because I know that this medication exists. Who am I without medication? Will I ever know?"[3]

Still, clinical evidence shows that Prozac and other SSRIs work in many patients, alleviating their debilitating depression. More important, SSRIs have fewer undesirable side effects than previous generations of antidepressants—though some evidence released around the time I decided to start my self-prescribed program suggested that impotence was still a risk, along with things like seizures, skin rash, anxiety, nervousness, nausea, weight loss, vomiting, yawning, and insomnia in something like 10 to 20 percent of users. These are what the medical literature calls, with a fine euphemistic flourish, "treatment-emergent adverse events." Coming off the drug can be even more unpleasant, entailing a long list of possible adverse events that includes high blood pressure, hemorrhage, nausea, asthma, taste perversion, tinnitus, amnesia, and suicide attempts. There was even a 1991 court case in Louisville, Kentucky, in which a forty-seven-year-old printing pressman and Prozac-taker named Joseph Wesbecker walked into his former workplace with an AK-47 assault rifle and four semi-automatic pistols and, proceeding to march around the building, shot twenty of his fellow workers, killing eight and injuring twelve. Wesbecker then took out one of the pistols, positioned it under his chin and, according to one wounded eyewitness, "shot his face off" next to the foreman's office door. Lawyers for the plaintiffs in a resulting civil suit charged that Eli Lilly was liable for the mood alteration that led to the violent incident, but the pharmaceutical manufacturer was eventually exonerated by a nine-to-three jury verdict.[4] The alleged murder of Rabbi Meir Kahane and the suicide of Del Shannon have also been linked, in polemic anyway, to the use of Prozac.

Despite the dangers of side effects, and the relative thinness of the research and clinical trials Prozac received before being allowed on the market, the drug continues to be prescribed in almost unimaginable numbers. In the town of Wenatchee, Washington, a clinical psychologist named Jim Goodwin diagnosed all seven hundred of his patients with a form of depression and put them on Prozac—an action that prompted appearances on *Oprah* and *Eye to Eye with Connie Chung,* not to mention a PBS *Frontline* documentary called "Welcome to Happy Valley." The millions of people who are on the drug or similar antidepressants like Zoloft, Paxil, Norpramin, and Buspar are contributing something like $6 billion to the world-wide market for happy pills. The pharmaceutical giants who market these drugs in increasingly aggressive and direct ways are among the most profitable companies in the world, racking up sales of $700 billion worldwide in 1995. The SmithKline Beecham company alone generated sales of $11 billion in 1995, mainly by acquiring direct access to patients by taking over physician management groups and pharmacy benefit managers, the organizations that administer the prescription drug section of health insurance plans to about half the American population.[5] Physicians are increasingly in the position where not prescribing the drugs supplied to them by sponsoring pharmaceutical companies is plain bad business. First do no harm? How about: first lose no profit.

None of this has much troubled the millions of Prozac users who rely on the standard 40-milligram daily dose to get them through the day, or the many thousands more who have taken the advice of Peter Kramer, in his best-selling 1993 book *Listening to Prozac,* that "cosmetic psychopharmacology" is a defensible way of exploring the mysteries of the human psyche. The opposite, and equally best-selling, view was soon advanced by psychiatrist Peter Breggin in his 1994 polemic *Talking Back to Prozac.* In it, Breggin countered Kramer's Huxleyan "doors of perception" view with another, equally Huxleyan reference: to the deadening "soma" of *Brave New World,* the feel-good drug that anesthetizes an entire population and, among other things, keeps them from questioning the rigid caste system of their self-imposed social engineering. The dueling Peters at once define the typical poles of happiness debate in our culture: "Just do it" versus "the devil's work." "Biologists do not know what depression is," Kramer flatly states. "The biological study of the self is so primitive as to be laughable." Breggin responded with denunciations of the quick-fix mentality and a long list of "Victims of Prozac": people, he suggests, who were killed, or killed themselves, because of the drug's adverse side effects.

I started taking my Prozac with no fixed views about its desirability simply as a drug, though I did have some misgivings about its current social construction. I suspected that it was overprescribed, partly because it was so easy to get some and partly because I heard many stories of physicians tossing out scrips like telephone numbers, making Prozac seem as innocuous as jelly beans. But what did it actually feel like to be on it? I wanted to know. Not, to be sure, as part of some kind of controlled scientific experiment. And not because I thought it would prove anything much about me. Prozac fails to work even for many people with severe depression, and it can often have no effect at all on the merely mildly depressed. But what about the side effects: anxiety, nervousness, and insomnia? It seemed to me ironic that an antidepressant, a feel-good drug, could increase anxiety levels. On the other hand, I had heard some people say that it did not make them so much less depressed as clearer in mind, more focused. "Prozac is great," a character says in Douglas Coupland's novel *Microserfs,* "and I think it goes beyond serotonin and up-take receptors and that kind of thing. I think these chemicals physically rewire your brain to think in parallel. It literally converts your brain from Macintosh or IBM into a Cray C3 or a Thinking Machine CM5. Prozac-type chemicals do not suppress feelings—they break them down into smaller 'feeling units,' which are more quickly computationally processed in the new, parallel brain."[6]

I wanted a new, parallel brain.

There were no effects in the first week or so I was on the Prozac, which is, I'm told, quite normal. After about ten days, I started noticing that I was sleeping more and having trouble waking up in the morning. I am not a Type-A morning person at the best of times, but I can usually jump out of bed and into the shower without too much trouble. Now I found myself staggering around with cobwebby brains for an hour every morning, trying to stop yawning and get to work. At the same time, my bouts of 4:00 A.M. insomnia were not alleviated—if anything, they intensified. I spent nights and some long early-morning hours in a strange state of combined anxiety and dopiness, lying in bed unable to move but with what seemed liked five billion neurons firing every second, my mind racing along in a manic survey of things to do, half-resolved issues, unreturned phone calls, future commitments, and past misdemeanors. Was this my new brain, with a cutting-edge operating system unaccountably stuffed into early Apple–era hardware? It was exhausting.

At the same time, and maybe for the same reason, I noticed a slight impairment of my gross motor skills. I fell off my bicycle twice in one week, something that I haven't done since I was a kid, and then tore up my knee and hands when I dove for a loose basketball on a concrete court. Certain emotional changes were soon noticeable too, although none of them was necessarily related to the drug. I found myself feeling increasingly antisocial, avoiding most engagements and not wanting to be at the ones I could not avoid. My editor, who is also a good friend, remarked on my "edginess" at one literary gathering, and it was true: I found myself beset by waves of flight-or-fight response to the agents, writers, and publishers schmoozing away around me. I felt as though I had to either bolt from the room that instant or take up one of the heavy, ornate ashtrays on the table in front of me and dash out the brains of the yammering foreign-rights manager standing a few feet away.

I found the same thing at another party, this time with a bunch of people I actually like. I felt hemmed in, trapped by crisscrossing lines of emotional stress, ready to throttle the attractive woman prattling away in front of me. My usually ample reservoir of bright small talk dried up completely. I had nothing to say—it was as though all the higher functions of my brain had been shut down, leaving me the mute, murderous caveman, or maybe the slithering reptile, of my distant phylogenetic past. I was regressing. I left this second party abruptly, suddenly unable to fathom why I was there. All these parties, what were they *for?* What could their purpose be? This action occasioned two concerned phone calls and an apologetic e-mail from friends asking if they had done something to offend me. (No, no, I wanted to say, it's nothing personal, it's just the *drugs.*)

All this was only slightly alarming, but it had some unforeseen consequences. Like some other people who take Prozac, I was apparently experiencing the (presumed) increase in serotonin levels as mild depression rather than as elation, or an increase in happiness—though, in truth, most depressives who find Prozac effective do not describe the experience as one of happiness anyway, but rather as an increase in clarity or "color" in their phenomenology. It was having the opposite effect on me. I went to a John Woo movie about three weeks into my course of self-imposed therapy and found, to my surprise, that his distinctive combination of operatic violence and over-the-top emotionality, which I usually find exhilarating, left me feeling deflated. Big explosions, so what? Guys shooting at each other while performing elaborate kung fu moves? Big deal. Lots of slo-mo and flapping doves—ho hum.

That was when I decided to double my dosage. I had been taking just 20 milligrams a day for close to a month, and I didn't think bumping it up to the standard dose of 40 was too risky—lots of people take that much. I started popping two torpedoes a day along with my daily multivitamin. The first thing I noticed was that my sleep patterns were even more disturbed than before, with long stretches of the humid night now spent in riveted contemplation of the ceiling, occasionally descending into heart-pounding anxiety attacks during which it felt as though I had a hooked rock bass flopping around inside my ribcage. I had a slight but constant tremor in my hands, imperceptible to most people but noticed immediately by my wife. Maybe unwisely, I continued to drink alcohol during this time, consuming what is, for me, a fairly normal amount: half a bottle of wine with dinner two or three times a week, a couple of beers after a basketball game now and then. I wasn't actually washing the Prozac down with alcohol, and I kept away from hard liquor for the most part, but I cannot say how it might have been reacting with the pills.

There was also, I soon realized, a certain kind of sexual dysfunction now evident. Not to be too indelicate about it, but I found that while I still showed visible evidence of sexual interest on occasion, I was finding it harder to—how can I say it?—*put the puck in the net.* By now I was spending hours each night prowling around the apartment, checking my e-mail or watching bad TV and wishing there were people I could phone and talk to. I have lots of insomniac friends, and we always joke about calling each other in the middle of the night, but we never do it. I also began noticing that people tell a lot of jokes about Prozac, usually about its presumed ability to make one instantly happy, and I had the weird awareness of ironic distance when a couple of my friends suggested I might go on Prozac to combat my evident listlessness. (Well, since you mention it...) At the same time, I experienced moments of voluble enthusiasm about subjects that did not seem to merit it, when I would reel off excited riffs about someone I knew, a book I was reading, whatever was on TV.

"Do you think I sound manic?" I asked Gail during one of these outbursts, brought on by watching an elegantly turned double play during the All-Star Game.

"Yeah, maybe," she said. "But you have your manic moments anyway."

I still wasn't feeling anything that could be described as happiness. Or was I? I noticed around this time that I appeared to be losing interest in my usual store of obsessions: social niceties, good food and drink, career prospects, deadlines, the limits of my talent. I just didn't care about any of it anymore. I left all my phone calls unreturned. I spent no time worrying about why that editor was not phoning me, or where the hell my check was. The texture of scab-fretting intensity that often marked my waking hours before was being rubbed to a downy smoothness. I felt bland, depleted, indifferent. My appetite was much reduced, and I couldn't seem to see the point in anything. I was talking to my friend Erin one day—she was worried because I seemed moody and altered—and I asked her, "Do you ever think there's just no purpose to any of this stuff we do, parties and work and writing and ambition?"

"Yes," she said, "but only when I'm really depressed."

We both laughed. Was this happiness—just not giving a damn

anymore? Could depression actually come full circle to encompass, to actually be, the only kind of happiness available to us?

CIVILIZATION AND OUR DISCONTENTS

Why does happiness prove so difficult to find? I have suggested that the problem might be that we are most of the time looking in the wrong places and, worse, seeking the wrong things. But the cultural debasement of ideas of happiness actually runs even deeper than that, and the costly seminars and quick-fix paperbacks are merely clues to this more profound malaise. The fundamental issue is the lack of clarity in our conceptions of happiness, combined with the fact that those notions of happiness we do have at our fingertips are created and molded by obscure social forces. To tackle the lack of clarity is going to involve drawing some distinctions that might prove controversial—and that might seem, at first glance, unhelpful. But they will repay our attention in the end.

The first important distinction is between what philosophers like to call the *hedonistic* and *eudaimonistic* senses of the term *happiness*.[7] Hedonistic happiness is happiness as a contented feeling, sometimes but not always identifiable with simple pleasure, usually of the bodily kind. Hence the hedonist is someone devoted to the pursuit of pleasurable physical sensations, whether in gastronomic, aesthetic, sexual, or other form. Eudaimonistic happiness, by contrast, is happiness understood the way Aristotle saw it, namely as a kind of rational satisfaction with one's character and actions: a form of reflective rationality that looks back on a life and—always in a provisional way of course, for things may change, luck may turn—pronounces it worth living. Put crudely, hedonistic happiness is simple and reducible to a kind of feeling, the jollies, more or less; while eudaimonistic happiness is complex and really a form of self-assessing cognition, a passing of positive judgment on oneself and one's projects. Indeed, so different are the two that they might seem to have nothing in common with one another. And yet, so long as we use the word *happiness* to describe both kinds of experience, we are leaving ourselves open to confusion. It is as if we had decided to use the word *pain* to describe both what happens when someone sticks a pin in our finger and what we feel when a lover of many years suddenly decides she is in love with somebody else.

Ah, but that is exactly what we do, and all the time, too. English, like most natural languages, is flexible and nuanced—or, if you prefer, confused and various. In fact, it is nuanced to such a degree that it gives philosophers and other advocates of conceptual clarity fits of despondency. Many, in a rage of logical desire, try to construct nonnatural symbolic languages in which things always make sense. In the world of ordinary language, where we speak and hear English without pausing to establish logical consistency, simple pleasures can soon shade into complex ones, so that it is far from easy to say whether hearing a Bach concerto or making love to one's partner or eating an exquisite meal is a physical, mental, or spiritual pleasure— or all of these, in some combination of measures yet to be (never to be?) precisely calculated. That potential for elision of meanings in the word *happiness* is one level of nuance that we must be aware of here. Matters get still more complicated when we, for example, become conscious of approving our own taste or accepting our pleasures as part of a well-ordered life, for here the line between happiness-as-pleasure and happiness-as-rational-satisfaction might actually begin to blur.

Suppose, for the sake of argument, that I am lucky enough to possess a Giorgio Armani suit.[8] Donning the suit, I am very likely aware of a number of things, ranging through any and all of: aesthetic pleasure at its superb cut and texture (those Italians are gods with a needle), awareness of myself looking good in the suit (its color and drape flatter me), a sense of confidence or power as I walk down the street (I'm The Man!). But there might also be a feeling of pleasure that comes to me because I am able to make these judgments about myself and the suit. I might, further, derive a good deal of pleasure from being not only the sort of person with enough money to buy an Armani suit but, more important, the sort of person actually willing to set aside that amount of money for such a suit—ability not being willingness, after all, nor thought deed. That might all sound pretty self-congratulatory, but what if I am saying these things to myself, or more likely just thinking them vaguely, letting them float just beneath the surface of my consciousness, as part of a larger inner discourse of self-regulation? I say to myself: I do not work simply for the money, and the work I do is valuable and rewarding in its own right—it has intrinsic value. But, at the same time, I do not despise the money that my work brings, and if that money is legally acquired, appropriately taxed and disposable, then there are many far worse ways to spend it than on fifteen hundred dollars' worth of fine Milanese tailoring.

Because the gap between hedonistic pleasure and rational satisfaction can be elided in this way, it might be tempting for us simply to refuse the distinction. It might be even more tempting for us to reduce all happiness to the concrete apparatus of pleasure, to mistake the suit for the object of our desire when it is, at best, something that prompts a potentially complex concatenation of feelings, thoughts, and judgments that we might be inclined to call happiness. It is just that temptation that we have to resist if we are to avoid mistaking cheap happiness for the real thing. The logical conclusion of that mistake—a conclusion that some forces within the culture have embraced all too enthusiastically—is a virtual economy of happiness, a kind of pleasure-generating machine-world as efficient, and as empty, as the orgasmatron of Woody Allen's sci-fi spoof *Sleeper;* or, maybe more terrifying, the various virtual-reality tropes of the numerous *Star Trek* series: the holodecks, holosuites, inverse worlds, and other confusions of appearance and reality that constitute a disturbing minor key in the dominant symphony of ambivalent faith in technology and triumphant individualism sounded in Gene Roddenberry's universe.[9]

That a distinction can sometimes be effaced, or that in the sophistication of human life the distance between two concepts can be bridged by something as intricate as a tailored suit (a pretty high-level cultural achievement, after all), does not mean that the distinction has no meaning. The conversion of all happiness into pleasure-happiness is indeed a reduction, and the idea that consumer goods—however lovely and desirable they may be—constitute the final end of human life is not just regrettable, it is pathological. An Armani suit is a wonderful thing to possess, or so I choose to think. It leads to pleasures of various kinds and can even play some kind of role in one's happiness. It is not, however, happiness itself.

The general declension of happiness to pleasure, a kind of positively evaluated feeling, which in many ways coincides with the rise of the modern era of individualism and technological optimism, has numerous negative effects that we still only dimly perceive. I will explore several of these in the succeeding chapters, but the first, and perhaps most obvious, is the implicit psychologization of happiness in our culture. That is to say, the largely unchallenged idea that happiness is primarily an emotional or psychological state, a particular kind of feeling or complex of feelings. We rightly lay much of the blame for this on Sigmund Freud, but the etiology is more complicated, and older: we must eventually go back as far as Thomas Hobbes's theory of physicalism, the revolutionary (and damaging) idea that humans are essentially pleasure/pain machines, and Jean-Jacques Rousseau's claims in *On the Social Contract* that society is the enemy of humanity's "natural" state of happiness and freedom. "Man is born free," Rousseau famously said in the first sentence of that essay, "and everywhere he is in chains"—that is, beset by the limitations of having to share social space with other people, thwarting ourselves and our desires.

A complicated story. Still, we can begin with Freud's flatly stated, and misleading, characterization of happiness in *Civilization and Its Discontents*—a dyspeptic book that was originally to be titled not *Das Unbehagen in der Kultur,* "Unbehagen" with its sophisticated sense of malaise or unease, but simply *Das Unglück in der Kultur:* unhappiness in civilization.

"What we call happiness," Freud says there,

in the strictest sense comes from the (preferably sudden) satisfaction of needs which have been dammed up to a high degree, and it is from its nature only possible as an episodic phenomenon. When any situation that is desired by the pleasure principle is prolonged, it only produces a feeling of mild contentment. We are so made that we can derive intense enjoyment only from contrast and very little from a state of things. Thus our possibilities of happiness are already restricted by our constitution.

Here we have, economically expressed, a number of our dominant ideas of happiness: its suddenness, its intensity, its quasi-orgasmic release, its evanescence, its need for contrast, its apparently natural and biological limits. More serious still, of course, are the limits placed on happiness by civilization itself: the way society is set up to create order, beauty, and utility, but also, to all appearances deliberately, to thwart our instinctual desires both loving and aggressive. This forces us, in turn, to sublimate desires in work or to turn them back on the individual as superego—or sometimes just to repress them, at which point they might squeeze out the side of the psyche as neurosis. "Civilized man," Freud says, "has exchanged a portion of his possibilities of happiness for a portion of security.... Civilization, therefore, obtains mastery over the individual's dangerous desire for aggression by weakening and disarming it and by setting up an agency within him to watch over it, like a garrison in a conquered city."

Freud says he reaches these conclusions simply by examining our "common sense" notions of happiness and unhappiness, but that is of course a piece of artful deception. Nothing is commonsensical until we accept it as such. Still, because these basic Freudian ideas about happiness are now so widespread, and because (as Auden once wrote) Freudian views have created a whole "climate of thought" that we all inhabit, like it or not—consider only how we now conceive dreams, slips of the tongue, and unequal power relationships—these ideas have begun to appear natural. So natural, indeed, that we rarely pause to challenge them. But that is precisely what I want to do now.

ARE WE HAVING FUN YET?

We all know people who might be described as "fun-loving," and activities—bowling, square dancing, water-skiing—whose primary, maybe sole, purpose is the provision of fun. (Disagreement about whether a given activity is fun is not to the point at this stage. Besides, we can be wrong about ourselves with respect to fun: lots of people who think they will hate bowling find themselves, after a frame or two, screaming and jumping like characters in an *I Love Lucy* episode.) The idea of fun is hardly ever examined, common though it is. We take for granted that, other things being equal, fun things are preferable to not-fun things. And why not? We even created the idea of leisure time for the sake of fun and erected one of the great cultural constructions of our times, the weekend, to make fun more culturally and institutionally available.[10]

Seeking and finding fun is one of the few lifelong projects most of us engage in with assiduity and a keen sense of purpose—alien observers might be forgiven for thinking that fun seeking is the main point of our lives, work reduced (as in Aristotle) to a mere prologue, an enabling condition of leisure. Numerous machines of the culture are expressly designed to facilitate fun, from the elaborate apparatus of quasi-aesthetic leisure (television, the movies), through the desperate creation of well-ordered domestic environments where every meal is a holiday feast, to the layered and demanding social order of bottle parties, dinner parties, cocktail parties, launch parties, and after-work parties. Martha Stewart might be considered the patron saint of this aspect of the culture, but only if flanked by the late Gene Siskel and Roger Ebert, with their must-see, thumbs-up imperatives—the unholy trinity of taking all the fun out of fun.

Yet still we seek it. The phenomenon of the party illustrates the paradoxical problem with fun. Jenny Standish, a character in Kingsley Amis's novel *Difficulties with Girls,* offers an eloquent if bleak assessment. "There was something in her that welcomed the idea [of parties], however faintly or briefly. It might be as she started to get ready, it might not be until they were going in the front door, but always she would have a moment of glad expectation that almost carried her away: perhaps *this* time…This time what? She could think of no answer."[11] Is there an answer? Does that floating sense of expectation ever leave us? Or are we its unwitting slaves forever, long past the time when a party might have meaningfully offered us the prospect of a new love interest, a stimulating conversation, a personal revelation? Freud called it infantilism, the cherishing of pleasurable fantasies in defiance of the lessons of life, rather than moderating the pleasure principle into what he called "the more modest reality principle." While at an extreme it leads to self-denial and the attempted elimination of the pleasure-instincts—a process that led to body-denying delusions, including religion—Freud thought that such moderation was actually a way to preserve happiness, since the option of pure pleasure-seeking was self-defeating, if not impossible. "An unrestricted satisfaction of every need presents itself as the most enticing method of conducting one's life," he remarks dryly, "but it means putting enjoyment before caution, and soon brings its own punishment."[12] No one can subsist on a pure diet of reality, however. So still we go on, racking up the party invitations as though they were personal honors, enlivening the daybooks of our lives with spots of fun that ease the pressures, and often enough the general monotony, of daily life. Where would we be without things to look forward to?

James Atlas, writing in *The New Yorker* not long ago, wondered if we had, as a culture, lost this sense of fun as something essential to hauling us through the banal diurnal rhythms of existence. Atlas describes a Jenny-like moment, only in this case it is the sense of thwarted expectation that envelops him when he has to leave a Manhattan cocktail party filled with agents, writers, publishers, and publicists. "A pang of regret comes over me; I want to stay for the party," Atlas writes. "Maybe it's the pleasurable stirring of sexual attraction without risk, that nerve-tingling aura of possibility accompanied by the knowledge that it's going nowhere. Or maybe I just thirst for a fourth drink. To relax and have—how can I put it?—fun."[13] There follows a celebration of the allegedly fun-loving literary culture of 1950s New York, with its long list of passionate, adulterous, drunken, and often suicidal denizens: John Berryman a suicide at fifty-eight, Delmore Schwartz found dead in a fleabag hotel at fifty-two, Randall Jarrell an apparent suicide at fifty-one, Robert Lowell dead of a heart attack at sixty. Harold Ross, Wolcott Gibbs, Robert Benchley, A. J. Liebling, Shirley Jackson—all of them dead before they reached sixty.

The contrast drawn here is to both domestic obligation (Atlas must leave the party because his wife and kids are expecting him) and the enforced safety of today's "anhedonic" culture. Anhedonia, significantly, is the name given to that symptom of clinical depression in which sufferers find they cannot take pleasure in anything. Sweet smells die in the air, tasty morsels turn to ash in the mouth, and the scene before me fades to drab brown and gray. "If I had to come up with a symbolic representation of the prevailing ethos," Atlas writes, "it would be a series of red circles, each with a line through it: No Smoking, No Drinking, No Sex. No Fun." It would be easy, as subsequent letters to the editor did, to dismiss Atlas's regret as the unseemly longings of an immature forty-seven-year-old who, like so many of his generation, has failed to come to terms with adult responsibilities—or, possibly worse, the delusional nostalgia of somebody who grew up uncritically ingesting the carefully created myths of the 1950s golden age of literary New York. But that would miss the genuine point that is being raised here. We do not have to go so far as to live like a Benchley or a Schwartz, but are we in danger of losing our sense of fun? Do those red circles and slashes symbolize a culture that is beginning to pathologize the pursuit of pleasure? If so, the fall of fun is more than just the preoccupation of an aging writer with domestic ambivalence. It says something potentially disturbing about our culture of happiness.

Now, I have been suggesting what looks to be the contrary conclusion, namely that the dominant culture is dedicated to satisfying pleasure, not denying it. But these apparently contradictory tendencies, denying and exhorting, are in fact two sides of the same coin. What we see here is actually a familiar cultural pattern of puritanical and hedonistic impulses in close, apparently endless conflict. Both the surrender to pleasure and the denial of pleasure proceed from the same source, rooted in the basic confusion of pleasure with happiness. We are, in other words, a culture suffering from a bipolar disorder, with manic and depressive episodes following each other by hysterical turns, bingeing and purging, sometimes existing in close proximity and annexing cultural forces in what looks like an attempt to destroy the opposite. But pleasure and its denial are, for us, locked in a Manichaean battle, inseparable one from the other. That is why it is always one-sided to complain, as Atlas does with an array of smart authorities to back him up, that the culture is against pleasure. True, but it's only half the story, for the culture is also decidedly, crazily, in favor of pleasure.

This can be hard to see, especially if the dominant forms of pleasure take on particular shapes. The late critic Christopher Lasch, writing in *The Culture of Narcissism,* noted the American tendency for "the invasion of play by the rhetoric of achievement"—a kind of cultural infection in which the virus of the Protestant work ethic steals into the otherwise un-self-conscious body of fun. Hence the aggressive, goal-oriented forms of play so much favored by weekend warriors of various kinds: mountain climbing, triathlon racing, extreme or high-risk sports, but also the slightly crazed Saturday-afternoon attempts to *get through* all the enjoyable leisure-time activities of gardening, decorating, cooking, eating, and socializing before sundown. Even the standard forms of urban dissolution—drinking and doing drugs, say, or staying up late—are annexed to the peculiar rhetoric of achievement, creating the odd spectacle of apparently nonconformist or antiestablishment hipsters bragging to each other about how drunk, how stoned, or how tired they are, just like plaid-sporting businessmen comparing golf handicaps.

This rhetoric of achievement, however, does not deny pleasure so much as it merely reinforces the machine imperatives of pleasure: the idea that happiness is, essentially, a problem to be solved, a psychological portfolio to be managed. Ersatz self-denial of the kind on offer in every Bally's gym in North America is nothing more than rampant pleasure-seeking in slightly deflected form. Thus the delicate dance of pleasure and pain. A recent ad for the sports drink Gatorade gives the gist of the pain-is-pleasure ethos: various slow-motion shots of athletes in pain—being tackled, being fouled, falling off a balance beam—are intercut with the song "Love Hurts." The tag line? "I never felt so good." Even what we might think of as genuine self-denial—selfless submergence in a larger project—can be, as Lasch well knows, merely one more form of self-obsession.

Atlas also enlists Peter Stearns, the man responsible for what remains the most probing reading of one of our culture's most important features, the idea of "cool." According to Stearns's book *American Cool: Constructing a Twentieth-Century Emotional Style,* the ethos of cool, which arose within the postwar economic prosperity, is an apparently antiauthoritarian stance that paradoxically collapses under the forces it seems to oppose. Cool was created by the emergent biker outlaws and pleasure seekers of the West Coast, the hepcat jazz buffs and coke-heads of *On the Road* and *Naked Lunch.* But its detachment and "anti-intensity emotionology," as Stearns chooses to put it, are soon set against the intensity of Kant's negative pleasures: the pleasure of boldness and daring, the transcendent high of rising up against, and maybe past, boundaries. Because cool is all about damping down and holding back, it ultimately conforms, Stearns says, to "the requirements of a corporate, service-oriented economy and management structure; small family size, with emphasis on leisure and sexual compatibility between spouses; consumerism; and anxiety about hidden forces within the body that might be disturbed by emotional excess."

Again, however, to say this is to tell only half the story. Cool is certainly now part of the overriding consumerism of North American life, but because of that it is no longer best understood as cutting against pleasure. Consumerism is all about satisfying desires—or rather, creating desires that must be satisfied—and hence is driven entirely by the hedonistic happiness so firmly rooted in our cultural consciousness. Cool is just a mode of that hedonism, a particular shape of the desire/satisfaction dynamic that happens to have a firm grip on our imaginations at the moment. The firmness of that grip probably has more to do with the perception of urban threat than with anything like the service-oriented economy or the desirability of small family size. Cool's shape has modulated from the West-Coast-jazz iconography of Chet Baker in his 1960s peak phase to the contemporary L.A. style of black kids, skate punks, and late-grunge neo-punks. Cool is now younger than ever, more urban than before, and almost entirely about *fronting:* projecting the aura of comfort in a hostile environment, sending a message of defiant self-assurance.

That is why sunglasses are the first and last iconic object of cool, from boxy Ray-Ban Wayfarers in the 1950s and '60s through ski-bum Vuarnets in the '70s and '80s to wrap-around Oakleys in the '90s: they hide the eyes, which might be shifty or afraid; they project a flat surface of confidence, like a mask or dangerous array of military equipment. Glasses "perfectly embody" the distinction between hot and cold media, Marshall McLuhan argues in *Understanding Media*. "[Clear] glasses intensify the outward-going vision, and fill in the feminine image exceedingly," McLuhan says, which is why Dorothy Parker was right that men seldom make passes at girls who wear glasses. "Dark glasses, on the other hand, create the inscrutable and inaccessible image that invites a great deal of participation and completion."[14] But like the self-denial of the athlete, this hanging-back ethos of cool is forever being outstripped by its own internal logic: whatever the surface might suggest, this is all about pleasure. Worse, it is about pleasure being bought and sold by marketing our own desires and uncertainties back to us as novelty and trendiness—as, ultimately, an illusory security, an empty identity.

This process is not restricted to cool but encompasses all the pleasures Atlas celebrates as *fun:* drinking, smoking, eating, having sex. Richard Klein, a professor of French literature at Cornell, is onside as a supporter of the cultural anhedonia thesis, with two recent books that champion, respectively, the forbidden pleasures of smoking and fatty food. "We are in the midst of one of those periodic moments of repression," Klein writes in *Cigarettes Are Sublime,*

> when the culture, descended from Puritans, imposes its hysterical visions and enforces its guilty constraints on society, legislating moral judgments under the guise of public health, all the while enlarging the power of surveillance and the reach of censorship to achieve a general restriction of freedom.

But it is actually much more complicated than that, as Klein acknowledges in his follow-up book, *Eat Fat.* "America," he writes, "under the sour influence of its persistent Puritanism, cruelly medicalizes the pleasures it most permanently indulges—turning every mild narcotic, even art, into a matter of public health and social morality." The culture's pathologizing of pleasure is obvious enough, issuing in the familiar, grim standard of judgment that insists if something feels good, it must be bad for you—and, contrarily, that pain is good. And Klein is probably right that it is nowhere more obvious than in the realm of food, especially fatty food, which has become almost the sole focus of a drastically impoverished language of iniquity and salvation: giving in to "sinful" chocolate binges, say, or "being good" and resisting the devilish temptations of cake.

Klein advises us to fight the power and *eat more fat,* but his urgings, paradoxically, are unnecessary. Pathologizing a pleasure does not make it less widely indulged; it merely folds the pleasure and its denial into a medicalized—and thus technologized—cultural shape. It can even, in a familiar twist, make the proscribed pleasure more intensely attractive than ever, which suggests that we might, as a culture, be subconsciously attempting to fortify and enhance routine pleasures through the added attraction of disapproval. "The feeling of happiness derived from the satisfaction of a wild instinctual impulse untamed by the ego is incomparably more intense than that derived from sating a desire that has been tamed," Freud wrote in the 1930s. "The irresistibility of perverse instincts, and perhaps the attraction in general of forbidden things, finds an economic explanation here." But whatever might be going on at a deeper level, at the conscious level North Americans are having no trouble deciding to eat fat. People who have never heard of Richard Klein are scarfing down the equivalent of eight sticks of butter a week. Not that we're happy about it. Americans dropped $33 billion on weight-loss goods and services in 1996, and yet 59 percent of American men, and 49 percent of American women, are still considered overweight by medical authorities. Our TV screens are dominated by washboard abs and manic aerobics instructors, yet the streets are a-bulk with the kind of fatties who, in another time and place, might have called forth emergency medical attention.

This particular cultural contradiction of late capitalism—call it the gap between the theory and the practice of fat—is brought to life by a unique television fixture, the funny fat man. From Jackie Gleason in the 1950s to Drew Carey, John Candy, and Homer Simpson in our own day, the addition of girth is one of the few surefire signs that we are in for wit. This is usually explained as a carefully maintained form of social oppression. As a former fatty myself (I tipped the scales at a zaftig 210 pounds when I was a five-foot-nine sixteen-year-old), I can tell you that being fat is no laughing matter, but becoming the jokester is often the only route to social acceptance when you exceed the brutal teenage norm. What your mother told you was true: nobody likes a grumpy fat kid. So start cracking those jokes, tubby.

Still, that does not explain the full extent of the fat guy's comedic persistence on television, which we can take, for the time being, as a personification of our strange unease and ambivalence about pleasure. In the current round of the battle between puritanical impulse and indulgent reality, the funny fat guy functions, too, as a form of cultural reassurance, a bulky sign that we can, in a sense, safely ignore the shrieking exercise wingnuts on the Home Shopping Channel and get down to the happy business of drinking beer, eating doughnuts, and cracking wise. He is a benign jolly presence, hailing almost exclusively from the trailer park or bungalow sub-division, a kind of ubiquitous Santa-analogue, dishing out the good cheer year-round. (Portly Uncle Phil on *The Fresh Prince of Bel Air* looks like the exception, being a big-time—and big—Bel Air lawyer, but think of him as just a former ghetto kid made good.)

Fat may be a feminist issue, but it is also a class one, and with these fat TV avatars before them, the disenfranchised lumpen-proles of North America can in effect shrug off the insistent cultural voice telling them that you can't be too rich or too thin. In fact, the inversion of the previous century's fat-to-money ratio is now com-plete. Yesterday's fat cats, who displayed wealth in the most basic attire of the well-fed body, are today's "social x-rays," to use Tom Wolfe's resonant phrase for the skeleton-thin Manhattan socialite set. The working class, by contrast, bulks large. At least since George Orwell wrote *Down and Out in Paris and London,* the working-class fondness for crude physical pleasures, especially the junk-food binge or beer-belly bender, has been revealed as a form of coping with mild social desperation. When you have no scope for more sophisti-cated pleasures and no sense that the future belongs to you, you might as well live life in TV's eternal fast-food present. Fat-guy sit-coms are just McDonald's fries in visual form.

Hence the deep appeal of both Carey and Simpson. Carey, a for-mer stand-up comic, is the hefty center of *The Drew Carey Show,* a witty prole sitcom set in Cleveland. Drew, a department-store func-tionary, is the kind of guy you used to see cheering the Browns every Sunday in the "Dawg Pound" section of Municipal Stadium. Brush-cut, bespectacled, and chubby, he is a charming Everyman, a down-to-earth paragon of normality who likes beer and pizza, shoots pool on a decrepit old table installed in the open air of his backyard with a brace of going-nowhere buddies, and hangs out at a quintessen-tially awful Alpine-themed midwestern beerhall. He also has had an incongruously beautiful and devoted girlfriend, which proves that, in the dream-space of TV anyway, being a funny fat guy has its con-crete social rewards.

The engine of the show's comedy is Drew's running battle with his coworker, Mimi, a hideous fashion criminal with a fondness for thick blue eyeshadow and mismatched floral prints. Mimi is a sharp-tongued chubster, a cruel and accomplished master of the ruthless practical joke, and that might suggest some kind of genetic predisposition here—the battle of wits for those in whom the battle of bodies is a nonstarter. But Mimi's exquisite horribleness is actually a clue to the limits of television's fat-person tolerance; she tends to upset the ambiguous pleasures of the funny fatty. As a fat *guy* it is easier to be, like Drew, both funny and likeable. But if you are a fat *gal*, the wit often slides into nastiness. Mimi is just Roseanne Barr with cheaper lines and uglier clothes.

The combination of Drew and Mimi is uncomfortable, then, because it draws attention to gender differences in the world of fat—a move likely to destroy the culture's ambivalence about fat-appeal. Even where the hefty woman is clearly in control—consider Roseanne's comedic dominance of husband Dan on *Roseanne,* played with some subtlety by handsome big man John Goodman— there is often a gradual demonization of her character. She is a rebel by social definition, a gender-expectation refusenik, and that makes her an unsettling presence. Viewers prefer the loose-cannon fat guy paired with a sensible and long-suffering thin woman. If Ralph and Alice Kramden started this TV pairing on *The Honeymooners,* Homer and Marge Simpson bring it to a kind of 1990s apotheosis. Homer is the funny fat guy we laugh at, not with, but he is all the more representative for that, the dark but hilarious underside of banal American culture. With every "Doh!" exclamation or slack-jawed "I dunno" reply, Homer entrenches his position as the satirical essence of 1990s cultural vapidity. He is the standard bearer for aggressively ignorant Ugly Americans everywhere. Nor is Homer's fat-guy status incidental to that role. From the notorious "All you can eat" seafood restaurant trial to the celebrated episode in which he succeeds in getting on worker's disability by becoming not just fat but obese— with a stop along the way for the deeply sick incident featuring a decomposing six-foot sandwich—Homer's capacity for ingesting anything and everything grounds the show's ongoing satire of

America's hysterical culture of consumption. The only time Homer, a devoted and inveterate slacker, displays the kind of initiative and concentration supposedly inscribed in America's can-do spirit is when the object is a fatty meal.

As always, Marge reacts to this aspect of her husband with earnest but loving disapproval. The two are the conflicted culture in microcosm: weedy Marge the wrinkled-nose pathologization of pleasure, eat-anything Homer the proud symbol of a relentlessly mythologized pursuit of pleasure. Shots of the family eating dinner invariably show them all gobbling their food with disgusting abandon, often in front of the television. "Why can't we get clear plates?" Homer wonders, licking the gravy off his. "I can't see the TV this way." Bart, his father's son on this issue anyway, suggests doing away with plates altogether and serving out the food in a long bowl in front of the TV. "You're talking about a *trough*," Marge says. "We're *not* eating from a trough."

What makes *The Simpsons* so watchable is this kind of wicked treatment of the culture's excesses. It is not afraid to sail close to the wind when it comes to bad taste. On live-action television, however, the whole thing becomes trickier. When the late Chris Farley, the largely unfunny fat guy who used to be on *Saturday Night Live,* did a sketch in which he and actor Patrick Swayze competed, shirtless, for the one remaining spot in a Chippendales dance troupe, he exploded not just the charming fat-guy stereotype (probably a good thing) but also the delicate chemistry of satire. Farley's hulking body and flapping man-breasts were set in stark contrast to Swayze's sculpted physique, and the idea that they were close competitors was, as a result, appalling. They both kept saying to each other that, really, *he* was going to get the job—a piece of irony so heavy it wasn't so much funny as *awful.* You wanted to put Farley in touch with Kramer from *Seinfeld,* so they could close a deal for a "bro," the invented breast-support garment for men.

The nature of Farley's subsequent movie career, which featured such instant video fodder as *Beverly Hills Ninja,* might have been a simple function of his meager talent, but it could illustrate, too, his inability to forge a fat-guy character that resonated with the oddly balanced public attitude about fat. It is probably too much to say that Farley should have kept his shirt on—though certain judgmental friends of mine would, if they had their way, legislate such things—but he did go further than most people were prepared to follow when it comes to challenging our ideas about fat. He accepted that fat could be ugly, and that is something we prefer not to confront.

Is there tragedy behind the humor, a thin man of sadness trapped within the funny fat-guy's culturally reassuring body? Probably. But that's not something most of us, watching television or sitting in the cinema, care to think about.

Jean Stafford, one of James Atlas's heroes and a woman of formidable literary gifts who died at age sixty-four from alcoholism and emphysema, once remarked that "happy people don't have to have fun." Suggesting, it would seem, that fun seeking of the booze-and-smokes kind is reserved for the unhappy, and that the merely happy are somehow fun-impaired. Atlas approves this sly identification and rounds off his paean to fun with an orotund sententiousness. "[Stafford] and her contemporaries messed up their lives and died—literally—for their sins," he admits. "But they risked pain in pursuit of a more ambiguous pleasure: the pleasure of living fully. They took seriously the admonition of Lambert Strether to Little Bilham in Henry James's *The Ambassadors:* 'Live all you can; it's a mistake not to.'"

There is something in that, to be sure, but there is a lot more melancholy in Stafford's bitter pronouncement, a feeling even of desperation in the false romanticism of the tortured artist, living life fully in rounds of drunkenness, infidelity, and personal conflict. Seen from another perspective—one not yet swinging into the conceptual trap of indulgence's twinned opposite, puritanism—we might be justified in simply calling that an unhappy life, a life devoid of lasting pleasure. But the question is even more complicated than that. Straightforward acceptance of Stafford's dichotomy between the happy and the fun—whichever side of that distinction we might choose to pursue—underestimates the ambiguity of the relationship between our culture's dominant notions of happiness and the fun-driven pleasures of ordinary life. Freud again:

> The program of becoming happy, which the pleasure principle imposes on us, cannot be fulfilled; yet we must not— indeed, we cannot—give up our efforts to bring it nearer to fulfillment by some means or other. Very different paths may be taken in that direction, and we may give priority either to the positive aspect of the aim, that of gaining pleasure, or to its negative one, that of avoiding unpleasure. By none of these paths can we attain all that we desire. Happiness, in the reduced sense in which we recognize it as possible, is a problem of the economics of the individual's libido.

How's that for a cold shower? Freud's suggestion here, and it is one that has crept deeply into the background of contemporary thinking, is that instinctual pleasures of the sort that are momentarily satisfied by intoxication, sex, or aggression are the sole root of the only meaningful notion of happiness available to us. And because social ties, not to mention our physical constitutions, impose numerous limits on the satisfaction of those pleasures, human life becomes a familiar tale of woe now recast in psychodynamic terms: repression, sublimation, neurosis. Freud, the prophet of the baser desires, is ultimately as depressing and chastising as any fire-and-brimstone preacher decrying a world of temptation. Once we accept the identification of pleasure and happiness, however, we begin to feel that our instinctual desires are continually thwarted in various ways, issuing in a familiar pattern of encouragement and repression. We arouse sexual responses with advertising or clothing, for example, only to insist that those desires not be fulfilled; we extol the social virtues of drink and drugs, only to give way to social censure and individual regret at any sign of drunkenness or mind alteration. The common pattern of switching between licentiousness and puritanism that marks our conflict is an essential element of how we seek happiness through pleasure. We are continually rolling happy drinking sessions into miserable hangovers.

Or at least I am. Alcohol is my recreational drug of choice, in large part because I like the way it has been incorporated into the fabric of better living by writers and artists and cooks and filmmakers—the way a well-chosen wine complements food, or the swanky feeling I get when I am drinking an ice-cold martini in an overdecorated hotel bar. But these pleasures have a way of gradually turning to dust in one's mouth. Kingsley Amis, who had reason to know all about it, has a character describe what he calls "alcoholic remorse": "Feelings of remorse for recent actions imperfectly recalled but suspected of having been unworthy in some way and certainly performed under the influence of drink."[15] Or, as a much superior comic novelist, Evelyn Waugh, once described it: "The effects of their drinks had now entered on that secondary stage, vividly described in temperance hand-books, when the momentary illusion of well-being and exhilaration gives place to melancholy, indigestion and moral decay."[16] This is not living life to its fullest; it is living life in a permanent state of alternating excitation and self-denial. Nor is this pattern of conflict merely a remnant of intoxication—though, to be sure, it receives its essential expression there and probably gets more literary and social approval than other forms of pleasure seeking. "The service rendered by intoxicating media in the struggle for happiness and in keeping misery at a distance is so highly prized a benefit," Freud said, "that individuals and peoples alike have given them an established place in the economics of their libido."

So long as we conceive happiness primarily as pleasure, then, so long as we accept the idea that the search for pleasure is at once desperate and doomed, we will never rise above the conflicted state in which, paradoxically, both happiness and unhappiness can be considered pathological. We pathologize unhappiness for obvious reasons, and in obvious ways. Because the pleasure principle dominates our thinking, we think that we somehow have a natural right to be happy or at least a natural capacity to be so. When we find we are not happy—even, as Freud morosely put it, in the reduced sense in which we recognize happiness as attainable—we begin to think that there is something wrong with us. Hence the extensive therapeutic apparatus of happiness. At the same time, happiness is so uncommon, given the many barriers to pleasure embraced in what Freud called the reality principle, that it begins to recede from view as the norm. So we pathologize happiness, too, as in essence opposed to the community and its collective goals of order, stability, and security. Anyone who was, in Freudian terms, completely happy would be, by the same token, a free-wheeling sociopath given to bouts of homicidal rage, ceaseless self-obsession, and nearly constant sexual arousal.

And that's taking things way beyond fun.

SO HAPPY IT'S NUTS

The simultaneous pathologizing of both happiness and unhappiness is intimately related to, indeed is merely another expression of, the alternating libertinism and repression of the dominant culture. What makes it a particularly significant version of that eternal conflict is the fact that it involves the invocation not merely of social and cultural forces of approval and disapproval but also the expert opinion, institutional authority, and (not least) insurance implications of medical diagnosis.

The classification of psychiatric disorders has become one of the most fiercely disputed pieces of intellectual territory in a fractious, psychologized culture, and small wonder. A great deal in the way of money, resources, and reaction hangs on the sanction, in both of that word's ambiguous senses, provided by having a condition or mood registered officially as a mental illness by the psychiatric profession. On the positive side, some dubious "illnesses" such as chronic fatigue syndrome or attention deficit disorder might not be eligible for state-funded medical support, or even simple acceptance by friends and employers, if they are not so classified. Nor, more deeply, will some kinds of disorder lend themselves to legal arguments under the vast gray mantle of the temporary insanity or diminished responsibility defense. One of the most important presuppositions in our moral and legal code is that an agent must be free in order to be held responsible for his or her actions. If freedom is impaired by coercion or (in some cases) lack of knowledge, then so is responsibility. And so, by extension, if a mental condition or nonstandard state of mind is judged by medical professionals to be severe enough to affect one's freedom of choice, one is off the hook.

This can of course go too far, in such perversities as the attempted "Twinkie defense" (junk-food sugar high leads to madness, crime, and exoneration) or the so-called "automaton defense" recently allowed in Canadian law (near-paralytic drunkenness leads to oblivion, crime, and exoneration). Here we are in grave danger of confusing the mad and the bad and allowing these dangerous-to-know people to walk away from violence without paying society's price. At an extreme, the idea becomes merely a black joke, a circular and bogus exercise in self-justification. "It's not my fault," a character in the late-1980s situation comedy *Designing Women* once said of her unpleasant moods, "I have obnoxious personality disorder."

On the other side of the coin, labeling someone mentally ill when they exhibit certain personality or mood traits can, instead of offering legal protection, have devastating personal and professional effects. People lose friends or jobs because of the social opprobrium, or suffer the humiliating interventions of well-meaning acquaintances: the sort of thing Kate Millet vividly describes in *The Loony-Bin Trip*, where her friends begin treating her with weary condescension, like a naughty child, when she chooses to stop taking the tranquilizer lithium because she doesn't like the way it flattens out her moods and her life. The power of psychiatric labels is that they make the odd, the eccentric, even the slightly threatening, into something reified and firm: mental illness, the pathological, a form of sickness.

Not surprisingly, the power to determine and affix the labels is hotly contested. Walk into a university bookstore sometime and have a look at one of the most influential books of our time. It is not where you might expect it: not among the topical bestsellers or maudlin advice books. It is over in the medical section, under psychiatry. The book is the *Diagnostic and Statistical Manual of Mental Disorders* (DSM), the bible of the mental health profession. Found on the shelf of every self-respecting psychiatrist or practicing psychologist, it is almost three pounds of detailed description of the various afflictions of the human mind. First published in 1952, the DSM is an encyclopedic compendium of mental illnesses, personality disorders, and aberrant behavior stitched together between hard covers and translated into a dozen languages. An indispensable diagnostic tool, it is also, by the same token, a powerful social weapon that determines who is and who is not crazy. The DSM is the American Psychiatric Association's vanguard publication—its manifesto, its Big Red Book.

It is also its cash cow; the DSM generates annual revenues of more than $1 million. Under American medical plans, insurance premiums can be issued only for diagnoses that are backed by clinical sanction: no name, no dough. The resulting temptation to make up more names is apparently irresistible. This also means that practitioners in the quickly growing mental health field—its numbers more than doubled in North America between 1972 and 1990—will feel obliged to buy any new versions of the DSM. The 1987 edition sold 1.1 million copies in less than six years; the 1994 edition (DSM-IV) has done even better. Knowledge doesn't come cheap, either. When it was published in 1994, the basic DSM itself ran to $78.25. A *Study Guide* (described as the "indispensable companion") added $42.75. There is also a separate *Guidebook* ("essential companion") that goes for $49.75. A *Quick Reference Guide* to keep on your desk is another $32.00, while the *Glossary of Terms,* important when the categories keep expanding, costs $34.50. If you are a real keener, there are additional workbooks, audiotapes, and videotapes. And if you're curious about the scientific basis of the manual, you might consider investing in the five volumes of the DSM *Sourcebook.* The first volume runs a measly $177.50. Most overburdened mental health workers will not look in the *Sourcebook,* since it concerns the details of the statistical compilation and long essays on how the DSM's various categories are assigned, but according to critics they probably should. The methodology sections reveal that the "scientific" foundation for many categories of mental illness is shockingly soft. Cited studies show methodological weaknesses of laughable obviousness (tiny subject samples, clear self-selection), and the reliability of the categories—which is to say, the extent to which they enable people to agree on a diagnosis—is ludicrously low. Apparently, when it comes to the vagaries of the human mind, greater precision is not always possible.

DSM-IV lists 374 separate forms of mental illness—up from 297 in the previous edition, published in 1987. Indeed, the rising number of disorders describes a steady upward movement during the last century and a half. In 1840, for instance, when the phrase "mental illness" had not yet entered the vocabulary, the U.S. census acknowledged just a single form of madness, idiocy/insanity, and failed to provide a definition, relying instead on presumed common sense and the sort of thinking captured by the common law's long-standing M'Naughten Rule (it dates from the time of Guy Fawkes and the Gunpowder Plot), which specifies legal insanity as the inability to know the difference between right and wrong. In the 1880 census, the number jumped to seven: mania, melancholia, monomania, paresis, dementia, dipsomania, and, incongruously to modern eyes, epilepsy.

Nothing new there: psychiatry also famously defined hysteria, the peculiar female disease of "womb-madness," and in the 1840s Southern alienists added to the store of dementia something called drapetomania: a slave's "uncontrollable urge to run away from slavery." The difference now is that the disputed categories are proliferating beyond all reason, giving us pathological behaviors like frotteurism (the irresistible desire to sexually touch and rub against fellow passengers on mass transit), fugue states (travel in foreign lands, often under assumed names), bad writing (and its close cousin, poor handwriting), coffee drinking (including coffee nerves), *bad* coffee nerves, and inability to sleep after drinking too much coffee. Not to mention snobbery, clumsiness, tobacco smoking, playing video games, and, sometimes, falling asleep at night.[17]

Still, "it cannot be said that the profession's urge to colonize the human mind proceeded at a blinding pace," according to one observer. "Many decades would pass, and much caution would be thrown to the wind, before things began to get really out of hand."[18] The turning point probably came in the years following the Second World War, when U.S. Army psychiatrists began to classify battle fatigue, shell shock, and the early versions of what is now called post-traumatic stress disorder. When the first DSM appeared in 1952, it listed twenty-six classifiable mental disorders, all understood to be reactions to observable causes. By 1968, though, when DSM-II was published, this strong causal link was broken, never to be reforged, and the list of mental illnesses began to mushroom. As ever, the issues of inclusion and exclusion were strongly influenced by social trends and the background of cultural assumptions. Though the revised version of the second edition (1974) famously banished homosexuality from the list of mental disturbances, for example, DSM-III (1980) introduced something call ego-dystonic homosexuality, which is the state of feeling bad because you are homosexual. Depending on your point of view, that is either politicized nonsense or a scientific recognition that such a condition is a reasonable response to social disapproval of a "deviant" sexual preference.

Do these jumps in the number of mental disorders mean we are getting crazier, though? Or just better at slicing up craziness into discrete categories? Do they perhaps mean something else entirely? Some insiders think so. Paula Caplan, a Toronto psychologist and academic, is one of the most outspoken critics of the DSM process, and her various recent books and articles, billed as "the inside story of the DSM," are an obsessively detailed diatribe against the institutional resistance, arrogance, and sheer lust for power exhibited by the people behind the DSM, the upper echelons of the APA.[19] Her exposé of DSM politics is based, in part, on a deep skepticism about the so-called "medical model" of diagnosis favored by the psychiatric establishment. Caplan's challenges mostly concern the DSM's most controversial sections, those dealing with personality disorders. The category is notoriously fluid, often more a message of social disapproval than a medical achievement.

Working from within by serving on APA advisory committees, Caplan attempted to get two dangerous categories removed from DSM-IV: "self-defeating personality disorder" (SDPD), a label often given to women who are thought to "enjoy" suffering; and "premenstrual dysphoric disorder" (PMDD), a pathologized version of PMS that has the effect of labeling half a million women mentally ill every month. Supporters argue that labeling PMDD will help acute PMS sufferers come to terms with their affliction. But is calling hormone-exacerbated stress a mental illness really a good way of coping? Won't that simply fuel claims that women are too emotional—mentally unfit, in fact—to hold positions of power or responsibility? SDPD, meanwhile, indexed in the revised third edition (DSM-III-R), is not so much a mental illness as it is an accurate description of how many people, and especially women, rationally respond when they are victims of abuse or violence: "a pervasive pattern of self-defeating behavior... [in which an individual may] be drawn to situations and relationships in which he or she will suffer, and prevent others from helping him or her."

In criticizing the PMS disorder, Caplan pointed out, among other things, that there was no corresponding mental illness associated with hormonal changes in men. So she created one, called it "delusional dominating personality disorder" (DDPD) and proposed it for inclusion in DSM-IV. In the proposal, published in *Canadian Psychology,* Caplan and an associate offered a table of behavior traits, any six of which indicate the presence of DDPD. These include "inability to establish and maintain meaningful interpersonal relationships," "an inability to derive pleasure from doing things for others," and "a tendency to feel inordinately threatened by women who fail to disguise their intelligence." The traits and diagnosis of DDPD are then discussed in the usual academic fashion, complete with extensive footnotes and replies from other scholars. One journal respondent said her first reaction to the thesis was amusement: an excellent satire. Another worried that it would once again provide rapists and batterers with an insanity defense. A third considered the proposal "consciousness-raising at its best." The proposal was, predictably, quashed—proving, if nothing else, that the APA is without a sense of humor.

The rejection also sent a serious message: it demonstrated that the categories set out in the DSM are rife with personal and political bias. "The process of revising and updating the…influential diagnostic manual is highly political," Caplan wrote in her journal article, "but most of the political issues involved…are unacknowledged. Naming DDPD and coming to understand the damage done by people characterized by its features is a step toward escaping the rigidity of the traditional view that a largely sexist mental health establishment has taken toward women." Fewer than two hundred people are involved in the process, culled from a membership that is disproportionately male (86 percent of the American Psychiatric Association members are men). In general, these professionals are resistant to change and jealous of their reputations. They discuss mental illnesses as discrete conditions even though there is strong reason to believe such precision is misleading, even dangerous. They insist, as always, that aberrant behavior is susceptible to treatment with medication, the patient considered in isolation from social and cultural forces. The standards of scientific proof acceptable for the identification of mental illnesses also seem to vary according to the desires of the small, inordinately powerful group of authors. A version of PMDD remains in DSM-IV, and SDPD was removed only following adverse publicity in the mainstream media.

Meanwhile, the deeper philosophical questions concerning normal and pathological continue to lie mostly unasked. That is why it is hard to decide whether Richard P. Bentall, a senior lecturer in clinical psychology at Liverpool University, was raising serious institutional and philosophical questions or merely kidding when he published a paper called "A Proposal to Classify Happiness as a Psychiatric Disorder" in the June 1992 issue of the *Journal of Medical*

Ethics.[20] Hard to decide, and probably pointless: the article's dry mockery of flat scientific prose and impersonal detachment from the world is both hilarious and cutting, a satire in the spirit of Swift or Waugh; it makes its serious point with a few deft flicks of a razor-sharp wit. "I will argue that there is a prima facie case for classifying happiness as a psychiatric disorder, suitable for inclusion in future revisions of diagnostic manuals," Bentall begins, adding parenthetically, "I am aware that this proposal is counterintuitive and likely to be resisted by the psychological and psychiatric community."

Conceding that formal diagnostic criteria are not yet available, the proposal nevertheless offers a psychiatrically precise definition of the condition. "[W]e can state that happiness is usually characterized by a positive mood, sometimes described as 'elation' or 'joy,' although this may be relatively absent in the milder states, sometimes termed 'contentment,'" it says. "The behavioral components of happiness are less easily characterized, but particular facial expressions such as 'smiling' have been noted" and "[u]ncontrolled observations, such as those found in plays and novels, suggest that happy people are often carefree, impulsive, and unpredictable in their actions." For some reason, happy people seem interested in forcing their condition on relatives and companions who are less happy, engaging in "a high frequency of recreational interpersonal contacts and prosocial actions toward others."

These outward signs are ultimately less telling than subjective reports of the condition. Happy people are in this way very much like depressives: if they say they are happy, then, psychologically speaking, we must consider them to *be* happy. But the incidence and epidemiology of happiness are less clear than this suggests. There seems to be an unevenness in distribution across social class and even across nationality (two studies, Bentall says, found Britons five times more likely to express themselves "very pleased with things yesterday" than Americans). The condition is statistically abnormal, sometimes reported in less than 6 percent of a study population. Bentall further suggests there is ample evidence that happy people are irrational:

It has been shown that happy people, in comparison to people who are miserable or depressed, are impaired when
retrieving negative events from long-term memory....There
is consistent evidence that happy people overestimate their
control over environmental events (often to the point of
perceiving completely random events as subject to their
will), give unrealistically positive evaluations of their own
achievements, believe that others share their unrealistic
opinions about themselves, and show a general lack of even-
handedness when comparing themselves with others.

The resulting "unrealism of the happy" clinches the case that the
happy should be regarded as psychiatrically disordered, and their
condition—rechristened *major affective disorder, pleasant type*—should
be added to Axis I of the DSM. Objections that major affective disorder, pleasant type, is not normally diagnosed as pathology by
practitioners, or that the condition is not negatively valued by sufferers, do not affect the case for its status as a disorder. "Indeed,"
the article concludes, "if psychopathologists persist in excluding
happiness from the list of psychiatric disorders, it will serve as an
admission that subjective values are the basis of their system of classification."

In fact, Bentall's point reaches well beyond the personal and
institutional biases in the DSM classification process. By reversing
the field of psychiatry's normal presuppositions of assessment, dis-
secting the unexamined baseline state of happiness with the same
tools of pathology used for everything else pulled under the banner
of mental illness, it cuts into the heart of the therapeutic culture to
expose its hidden assumptions. Psychological therapy, whether in its
various talking, surgical, or pharmaceutical forms, works from the
idea that unhappiness, especially when severe, is not normal. Or
rather, that it may well be widespread but should not, as a result of
that, be viewed as immune from therapeutic intervention. On the
contrary, the fundamental premise of psychotherapy is that people
can be dislodged from their misery, disconnection, and lack of per-

spective and returned, the triumphant hero arriving psychically home, to a "healthier" mental place. Therapists do not invariably promise happiness in their prescriptions, but enough of them do to make the point clear: if the benchmark of human existence is some (usually unspecified) form of happiness, then there is bound to be strong desire on the part of those who are themselves unhappy, *in whatever terms they find meaningful,* to seek out the cure on offer. But because unhappiness is so endemic to human existence, arguably a fundamental part of mortal experience itself, psychotherapy therefore runs the danger of conceptually molding and pathologizing unhappiness so that it becomes an iatrogenic illness: something whose suffering is caused by the cure offered to alleviate it. Were we really so *unhappy* about unhappiness before we had so many people claiming that they could—for the right price—cure us of it?

The labeling of various forms of unhappiness as mental illnesses is dubious for all kinds of reasons, not least of which is the basic etiological mystery of a lot of misery. Sometimes we can tell why we are unhappy, other times it just steals over us when that certain song comes on the radio. In fact, as the writer Nick Hornby has suggested, a devotion to pop, blues, and R&B music might have more to do with our unhappiness than we at first suspect. "What came first—the music or the misery?" a character wonders in Hornby's hilarious first novel, *High Fidelity:*

> Did I listen to music because I was miserable? Or was I miserable because I listened to music? Do all those records turn you into a melancholy person? People worry about kids playing with guns, and teenagers watching violent videos; we are scared that some sort of culture of violence will take them over. Nobody worries about kids listening to thousands— literally thousands—of songs about broken hearts and rejection and pain and misery. The unhappiest people I know, romantically speaking, are the ones who like pop music the most; and I don't know whether pop music has caused this unhappiness, but I do know that they've been listening to

the sad songs longer than they've been living the unhappy lives.[21]

Tipper Gore went after 2 Live Crew, sure, but did she ever consider banning Al Green's "Tired of Being Alone" or Dionne Warwick's version of "I Just Don't Know What to Do with Myself"?

Pathologizing happiness in response to the tendency of the culture to pathologize *un*happiness is a move that appeals on a straightforward level to cynics like me, because we have long suspected that people with that just-down-from-the-mountain look are, in fact, crazy. For example, I had a friend in graduate school who was otherwise a great guy but had two annoying traits. One was the fact that he would begin social gatherings by saying things like, "What do you think of the following argument?" and "Refute this if you can," conversational gambits on the order of "Would you like me now to bore you to death?" The second was that he walked around all day looking as though he had just seen the face of God, smiling away for all he was worth. This was in *graduate school,* where feeling mildly depressed is almost a code of honor ("Semper sigh"); more than that, it was graduate school *in New Haven,* which is nobody's idea of a great place to live (at the time, it had the highest per capita murder rate of any city in the United States). My friend wasn't seeing the world the right way, because, from the cynic's point of view, the rational response to the world's trials is not happiness, still less transcendental bliss, but rather some form of wisecracking *Weltschmerz.* I could only conclude that he was, considering the circumstances, unbalanced—just plain nuts.

The mock-pathologization of happiness has a deep message. It exposes the hidden underside of the culture of contentment, with its empty promises of returning us to an Edenic state of psychological health. The trouble with most people is not that they are unhappy. It is that they do not know how to think clearly about what happiness might be. Selling psychological contentment without raising that hardest of questions, indeed force-feeding it to people by convincing them that they are not normal if they are unhappy, is one of the most dangerous acts of collective manipulation currently operating. The trouble is, we all slide into the easy grip of this conviction, because we desperately want to believe that happiness is, if not quite as easily attainable as Siimon Reynolds would have us believe, at least attainable in the course of a year—or two years? three?—of psychotherapy.

JUST SAY NO

Coming off Prozac was a drag, as I'd expected it would be. I experience withdrawal when I don't have my usual second cup of coffee in a day, so I was ready for headaches, nausea, and the shakes. I had a few bad dreams about possible post-treatment suicidal moods, but I figured I couldn't feel any more depressed than I did toward the end of my pill-popping episode. What I wasn't prepared for was how much better I felt when the Prozac supply tapped out. There was no nausea, no plunging moods. Other than the fact that I gained back the four or five pounds I had happily lost while taking the drug, and experienced a weird increase in the number of involuntary twitches I felt while drifting off in bed—you know, those stepping-off-the-staircase spasms that jerk you out of half sleep—on the whole I felt great. It was as though a cloud had lifted from my personality, restoring good cheer and equanimity. I have no idea if surplus serotonin has the same effect on other non-depressed people, but for me it was almost the precise opposite of the desired result.

Around the time I came off Prozac, I noticed a chirpy three-page ad that Eli Lilly had begun placing in national magazines. There it was one day in my copy of *Sports Illustrated:* a black page with clouds and rain and the line "Depression hurts" followed by a blue page, sun shining brightly, with the claim that "Prozac can help." "Prozac isn't a 'happy pill,'" the ad said. "It's not a tranquilizer. It won't take away your personality. Depression can do that, but Prozac won't." On the sunny page, beneath the Prozac logo, which incorporated a little image of the sun in place of the "O" in "Prozac," appeared these words: "Welcome back."

Welcome back? To what, exactly? To the human race, understood now as a collection of beings possessing a "normal" serotonin level? To yourself, as someone free of depression? To clarity and contentment? *Welcome back?*

There is of course no way I can rule out placebo effects in my experience of Prozac because there was no control group. One recent report of fifteen separate studies, involving 1,082 patients, showed placebo cures in 58 percent of seasick patients, 35 percent of those with random pain and 35 percent of those with angina, tension, headaches, anxiety, and the common cold. Placebo cures are evident even in ailments that might strike us as less "in the head" than these, such as prostate enlargement. Side effects also surface under the influence of the deceitful little sugar pills: 50 percent of the patients in one placebo study became drowsy, 25 percent complained of headache, and 18 percent developed fatigue and a sensation of heaviness. Others complained of nausea, dry mouth, a warm glow, and reduced concentration.[22] In the case of Prozac, one 1996 survey of thirty-nine separate studies, encompassing 3,252 patients, showed that 27 percent of Prozac's effects were owing to placebo. "In pre-20th century medicine," said the survey's author, a University of Connecticut psychologist, Guy Sapirstein, "people were given lizard blood, crocodile dung, pigs' teeth, fly specks, all these things and people got better. Now we know that lizard's blood is not going to contribute to people's health, but if people believe it, they will do better."[23] Or, as Voltaire once said, "The art of medicine consists in amusing the patient while nature heals the disease."

Still, there are, it seems to me, several good reasons for challenging the stranglehold Prozac and other antidepressants like it currently have on the collective imagination. The first and most obvious is that Prozac, like all ingestible machines, reinforces the idea of the emotional quick fix. There is nothing as powerful to the desperate imagination, beset by the thousand daily stresses and tensions of contemporary life, as the brightly colored happy pill. But the happy pill, like all the machines of better living, is based on a confusion about the ends of human life. "Like ivy doth an oak, these miseries encompass our life, and 'tis most absurd and ridiculous for any mortal man to look for a perpetual tenor of happiness in this life." So wrote Robert Burton in his *Anatomy of Melancholy*, published in 1689, but three hundred years later that piece of dour wisdom is no longer much in fashion.

The most troubling thing about this is not the simple fact of the belief that pursuing happiness is important; after all, why shouldn't happiness be the goal of every life, the only human purpose really worth striving for? What is alarming is the way our imaginations can often seem so limited when it comes to thinking about what happiness means to us. A generalized feeling of emotional contentment? An oozy warm sensation? The play of sensual pleasures? Cheap thrills, all of them. To accept misery as part of the human condition is not to celebrate suffering, or to decline into quiescence. It is, instead, to embrace the range of human feeling and experience as inherently valuable because human. Forget for a moment any lingering technical or specific difficulties in the medical model's implied project of psychic perfection. Assume that it were possible to achieve, without discernible side effects, the end result of a perfectly, and perpetually, contented population. Would it be defensible? "Maybe if I were to wish for happiness, I wouldn't mind crawling," writes the humorist David Sedaris, describing a strange encounter with a woman who posed the question of what to wish for if having the wish granted left you on all fours. "But what kind of person would I be if I were naturally happy? I've seen people like that on inspirational television shows, and they scare me." [24]

A nation of anaesthetized citizens also raises a second specter: the implicit ideological commitments of this form of happiness. We already know the strong link between profit taking and the provision of drugs. What if the alterations in consciousness are themselves desirable from the point of view of a self-perpetuating system of production and consumption? A happy population is a noncomplaining population, and, provided they are not *so* happy as to think they want for nothing, it is also presumably a spend-happy population, one that continues to buy and enjoy goods and services without much thought about the more important ends of life. The politician Mustapha Mond, in Huxley's *Brave New World,* reflects on the social dangers of allowing people to wonder whether life has a point beyond feeling good. "[O]nce you begin admitting explanations in terms of purpose," he says to himself,

> —well, you didn't know what the results might be. It was the sort of idea that might easily decondition the more unsettled minds among the higher castes—make them lose their faith in happiness as the Sovereign Good and take to believing, instead, that the goal was somewhere beyond, somewhere outside the present human sphere; that the purpose of life was not the maintenance of well-being, but some intensification and refining of consciousness, some enlargement of knowledge. Which was, the Controller reflected, quite possibly true. But not, in the present circumstances, admissible.[25]

No, indeed. The self-indulgence of our culture, its pervasive and almost unassailable narcissism, is such that we believe—or anyway (and perhaps more significantly) behave as if—a perpetual tenor of happiness is not only possible but justified in this life.

Some critics of Prozac go even further. Peter Kramer argues in *Listening to Prozac* that it should be considered "a feminist drug" because it alleviates a condition that is disproportionately observable in women, the form of depression known as dysthymia, in which subjects exhibit passivity and lethargy. But so far from being a feminist solution to a preexisting problem, this analysis merely confirms a debilitating stereotype of women, while at the same time suggesting that they are ever in need of medical attention for their sickness. *"Dysthymic women,"* sniffs the critic Moira Farr, herself a depressive and Prozac veteran.

> The term itself is rather repulsive, calling to mind moist, slug-like creatures, dragging their logy, large-bottomed bod-

ies through their basement-bachelor-dwelling lives, in a perpetual state of feeling not so fresh, occasionally mustering the energy to raise their burdened heads and mewl self-pityingly. By all means, one would want to put such pathetic beings out of their misery, not only for their sakes, but to spare everyone else the unpleasant spectacle of their dreary dilemmas.

Farr has some fun imagining what would happen if the diagnosis, and drug prescription, were followed through to their logical conclusion. "[I]f every depressed woman in the world were to take Prozac and demand better living conditions," she says wryly, "then Eli Lilly had better stop manufacturing the drug."[26]

To be sure, it is never as simple as capitalism somehow "wanting" us all to be staggering along in a drug-induced bliss. Drugs might be related to productivity and that might give employers a motive, if not the legal means, for wanting them in their workers. But individuals themselves, having internalized the demands of pharmaceutical happiness, are much more likely to be the agents of their own better-living projects—and not because they want to be more productive or biddable, even if that is in fact one of the results. (There is some evidence that it is not, by the way. According to researchers at the Norwegian College of Business, miserable employees do better work than those who enjoy what they're doing. "Employees who like their work tend to overestimate their abilities," a report on the finding said, "whereas dissatisfied workers tend to delve deeper and come up with more creative solutions to problems." The study included surveys of workers but also anecdotal evidence, such as the fact that Albert Einstein was in a grumpy mood the day he began working on the theory of relativity.[27])

No, the real dangers of Prozac proliferation come from within, not without. They are rooted in a philosophical mystery that has puzzled humans since the beginning of history: Who am I? What is the nub of personal identity that lies at the heart of my experience? Substances that alter consciousness have always played a troubling role in the pursuit of this question, but the situation in our day is markedly different. Because biochemical explanations of human consciousness now dominate scientific and academic discourse, the mystery of personal identity has been, for the most part, pushed to one side. We still understand the human brain only imperfectly, but you will find few neuroscientists and, alarmingly, not many more psychiatrists willing to grapple with the complexities of the possible relationship between the brain and the mind, the individual consciousness, that is associated with it.

Cosmetic psychopharmacology looks as attractive to some people as cosmetic surgery. After all, if the tools are available, what possible reason could there be not to pursue the possibilities of improvement? But there is a difference between alleviating nearly unbearable suffering and merely playing around with brain chemistry in pursuit of a modified personality. I cannot pretend that there is a sharp line here, or that it is always easy to decide when to allow technical enhancements of body or mind as ethically unobjectionable. (I, for one, would not take away glasses from the near-sighted or prostheses from the maimed, for example. Who would? On the other hand, I do think breast and pectoral implants, nose jobs and liposuction are ethically indefensible—though I would not be inclined to legislate against them except under conditions of resource scarcity.)

What the anything-goes ethos of enhancement threatens is something important and worth preserving: the integrity of the individual experience, the variety of possibilities both good and bad that stitch together the tapestry of human life. What is reductive about reductionism, the shrinking of all accounts of human life and behavior into bare physicalist terms of neurotransmitters and brain electrochemistry, is not so much that we lose a part of ourselves. After all, consciousness does not simply disappear even when we decide to accept a strict physicalist account (Descartes's *cogito* still functions as part of our reflective experience, whatever the eliminativists and other scions of contemporary philosophy of mind would prefer). But what we do risk losing is part of the range of discourse about human life, the part moved by things that do not easily surrender to the available terms of scientific explanation.

No, what is truly reductive about reductionism is its truncation of our vocabulary, the all-too-human ability to sing both the highs and the lows of daily life.

Part **2**

4

Manufacturing Content

> He felt like the happy people in the advertisements for shaving
> soap who seem to have achieved very simply that peace of mind
> so distant and so desirable in the early morning.
> —*Evelyn Waugh*, Decline and Fall

WHO AM I?

W HEN I WAKE UP IN THE MORNING IT IS NOT UNUSUAL FOR ME,
like many people, to spend a few scant microseconds groping
for my self. The alarm clock goes off, and I experience a minute
period of disorientation in which I struggle, on the whole successfully, to reassemble the sleep-dissolved lineaments of personality
into their familiar relations.

Maybe struggle is the wrong word, for there is, with the notable
exception of the extreme version of this daily reconstruction (when
I am, for example, on the road and in the third unfamiliar hotel
room of the week), little of the consciousness of *effort* about the
process. It is more a springing back into shape, as if I were a squeez-
able toy with a kind of permanent involuntary desire to return to the
integrity of its original contours; or perhaps the morphing quicksil-
ver of that recently popular Hollywood special effect, in which the
pool of oozing moltenness repeatedly re-forms itself, following devastating blows or tricky spatial challenges, into a late-generation
Terminator or sojourning alien. Sleep may knit up the raveled sleeve
of care, but it also melts down the fragile alchemy of consciousness.

At the end of each day I calmly, even gratefully, lower myself into what should be, by rights, the frightening embrace of nothingness, blithely expecting that I will still be myself on the other side of that black pit.

How is it that I manage, out of the deep pools of oblivion, to find myself anew each morning? I remember, first of all. Suddenly it all comes back: the stock of filed-away experiences, recalled perceptions, and habitual judgments that form the bulk of the interior monologue I know as my self. It is not as though this recall is perfect, or anywhere near it, simply that the probing fingers of morning-emergent consciousness are able, like a swimming man straining after the edge of a dock, to close themselves around the just-firm-enough memories of who I am, allowing the relatively smooth transition from the nobody of Nod to the somebody of the ever-advancing present. *I come to myself,* as we say. It doesn't always happen quickly, or without its little bumps. When I was younger it was my self-punishing practice to spring upright from bed the moment the alarm clock began its circadian chirp, staggering into the bathroom and the shower before any thought of rolling over and going back to sleep could enter my sleep-addled mind. In those days, it felt as though that daily passage from bed to hot water was a dark Lethean journey of uncertainty and existential contingency, eight seconds of near nonbeing. I remembered myself, with some relief, only when the soothing flow of water enveloped me.

Suppose, for a moment, that this ordinary process of finding our memory-selves were, for some reason, to be impaired. What if I found, one morning, that the world of my memories did not coalesce in the normal manner? Would there be any sense in which I remained myself? What if I remembered, or anyway found that I knew, how to manipulate the ordinary machinery of life—showers, clothing, heating elements, ATM machines—but did not have any particular store of personal remembrance, none of what John Updike called (expressing a horror at what a biographer might take from him) "my life, my lode of ore and heap of memories." Would I remain myself? We have good reason to doubt it, for the very difficulty we experience in imagining such an eventuality seems to preclude the preservation of identity across the traumatic divide. Recognizing us, friends and lovers would treat us as always, yet this would not be sufficient to ground an identity so cruelly broken off.

But now suppose that instead of our store of memories, the morning alteration was, in the manner of Kafka's Gregor Samsa, a bodily one. Nothing as extreme as the beetle-mania of "The Metamorphosis," maybe, but instead something on the order of finding myself in the body of another, not wholly dissimilar human being. Let's say my upstairs neighbor, Jamie. The situation is not as completely debilitating as before, since this time I, at least, can continue to regard myself as personally intact. But now there is no confirmation of that sense of self forthcoming from the other people who populate my world. My wife is shocked—no, terrified—to find herself, as she sees it, waking up next to someone other than me. I am too stunned to realize what is happening. She points and screams; I stumble into the bathroom, look into the mirror and—the mind reels! I rush back to the bedroom to attempt an explanation: it's still *me* in here! I know I look like Jamie—the boyish good looks, the dark James Dean haircut—but I'm still Mark. It is no good, she is hysterical, and no amount of familiarity with the science-fiction narrative conventions of the body-snatch or the implanted memory will be sufficient to lay that hysteria to rest. She runs screaming from the apartment. I'm not sure what happens next, for I am now alone in a way that can be only barely imagined. Where can I go? What can I say? Who can I call?

Personal identity relies on (at a minimum) two criteria, then: memory continuity and bodily integrity. Though philosophers have attempted over the years to argue that one is more important than the other, or sufficient in itself, it seems that we need both threads of continuity in order to go about the simple business of recognizing our friends, greeting our acquaintances and regarding ourselves in the mirror.[1] There has to be a line of connection for us to follow. "I allow myself," writes Nicholson Baker, speaking of life-memory, "to move back from the burbling coffee maker of the present instant along those many linked extension cords of personal identity…that lead down to the basement of my simpleminded younger self."[2] Without these commonplace points of contact, we could make no sense of being someone in particular. And without that sense of our own uniqueness, and the presumption of the same in other creatures who look and sound like us, we could not do most of the things that we take for granted in this life, from praising and blaming people for their actions to forming lasting attachments and creating meaning together with others. Personal identity grounds our individual existence but equally it lays the foundation for social and cultural life.

That is why alterations of consciousness, when extreme, can be so unsettling to our categories of psychological and ethical integrity. If the individual personality is something that can be tailored through the use of prescription pharmaceuticals, presumably *made better* in the pursuit of some ideal of myself or of my life, then the very notion of the unique personality begins to slip through our fingers. Yet this can be hard to see, and not just because Prozac and other drugs come to us wrapped in the lustrous cellophane of medical approval. We have been altering consciousness, and life, to suit our purposes with the ingestion of chemicals for centuries.

The traditional herbal remedies, for example, that are abundantly available in health food stores and naturopathic clinics were first classified and popularized around the same time as Burton's *Anatomy of Melancholy* was published, by herbalists such as John Gerard, who in 1597 authored one of the first and most influential guides to herbal remedies. On a recent visit to Kew Gardens in London, I became fascinated by a beautiful herb garden behind Kew Palace, with its banks of *Beth officialis,* or balm, which, according to Gerard, "driveth away all melancholie and sadnesse"; or the patch of *Medicago sativa,* otherwise known as burgundy trefoil, which "driveth forth tough and slimie humours that cleave unto the guts." There were plants to cure everything that ails you, from *Silene maritima,* English sea campion, which "doth purge choler by the stoole," to *Anthriscus cerepolium,* common chervil, which "hath a certaine windinesse, by means whereof it procureth lust."

These pre-modern drugs, with their *humor*-ous specificity, effectively blur the distinction between mind and body (the descriptions predate, by several decades, Descartes's famous split of physical and mental substance in the *Meditations*) and suggest a richness of natural personality alteration that, at a distance, is entirely charming. There is a suggestion here of a holistic notion of self that blends into the natural world, its inner movements of phlegm, bile, and choler part of a larger, ordained complexity of the divinely created world. Surely, from a certain perspective, Eli Lilly is no more than our equivalent of John Gerard, the active ingredient in their little green-and-yellow Prozac pills functionally the same as certain herbs, and the new physicalism of the neurobiological consensus—that you *are* your brain—is merely the latest stage in allaying the mind-body problem with simple elimination of a separate mental substance, rather than accepting the richer holism of the high Renaissance. In that case, why *not* pursue the alteration of consciousness using natural sources to its logical conclusion?

The most popular product in the various health food stores in my neighborhood right now is something I decided I had to try. It is called St. John's Wort, and it is a natural remedy that purports to have the same effect as certain prescription drugs but without the pernicious hidden agenda of the medical establishment. St. John's Wort appears to act as a monoamineoxidase (MAO) inhibitor, which, like serotonin re-uptake inhibitors, works by altering the brain's chemistry so that more of the mood-enhancing neurotransmitters like dopamine and norepinephrine will stay in the wash. MAO is an enzyme that breaks down these neurotransmitters, and inhibiting its action theoretically increases the brain's levels of feel-good chemicals. My St. John's Wort is, in other words, an herbal version of such prescription drugs as Marplan, Nardil, and Parnate, arguably as effective but acting "less harshly," according to *Prescription for Nutritional Healing,* a self-help drug and food manual.

The editors of *Prescription for Nutritional Healing* listed many possible causes for depression, including contagion and low light levels, and suggested not unreasonably that "a poor diet, especially constant snacking on junk foods, is a common cause of depression."[3] I decided to cut out the taco chips and licorice while I was on the Wort. The caplets are little dark-purple speckled things that smell a bit like chocolate, and I popped three of them a day for a month. At first, there were the usual mild side effects that resembled depression itself—an increase in my insomnia and periods of grogginess when I did get to sleep—and some fairly alarming heart palpitations. I thought on one occasion that I was having an auditory hallucination when, in the limbo between waking and sleeping, I heard a hoarse, creepy, Linda Blair voice say what sounded like the words "Beg for me." I suppose it might just have been Gail yawning. (And no, I have no idea what such a message might mean.)

In addition to all that, I experienced another episode of what can only be termed violent antisocial sentiment: ducking commitments, avoiding invitations, just wanting to stay home alone. My friend Anne pried me out of this solitary confinement one evening by shamelessly playing on my guilt and telling me she had gone to extraordinary lengths to get me a ticket to a film festival schmoozer. "I don't know why you feel this way," she said. "Parties are fun." I confessed I wasn't sure why I felt that way either. Theoretically, like Jenny Standish in Kingsley Amis's novel, I like parties; parties *are* fun. So I went.

And you know what? It wasn't fun. I found I could not replicate the paradoxical social wisdom once expressed by a charming character in one of Nancy Mitford's novels. "It was just like any other party of that sort," she says of a New Year's Eve ball. "It had every element of discomfort and boredom and yet for no particular reason that anyone could see, it was divine fun."[4] "I know why I hate parties," I told Anne the next day. "You get dressed up, go somewhere far away, spend too much money, stand around complaining, fill your lungs and clothes with secondhand cigarette smoke, maybe drink a bit too much and then feel like hell the next day. Fun? This is not fun. Fun is exactly what it isn't." Even as I was saying this I realized that it all probably had little to do with the Wort. It was me. I got off the phone and then called a mail order company to order a novelty watch I had coveted for some time, decorated with the bilious green face of Dr. Seuss's Christmas-hating Grinch. Once more, there had been no increase in my sense of well-being or calmness as a result of chemical experimentation; if anything, I'd experienced the reverse. Was it possible that my neurotransmitters just weren't susceptible to chemical intervention, no matter whether it was taken under the natural or the medical model?

I kept waiting, while on Prozac and St. John's Wort, for some isolated experience or episode in which the elevated neurotransmitter levels would make me feel like someone else, make me sense that I was no longer myself. It never really arrived. In fact, the strangest feature of these periods of waiting, at least as I experienced them at the time, was realizing, with an awareness more physical than intellectual, that there was a fine-spun intricacy to my web of social relations, a complex equilibrium in the ordinary life of friends, coworkers, acquaintances, family and wife, in which my behavior was deeply embedded and, more than that, constantly adjudicated in countless tiny ways. It wasn't as though I actually felt myself to be different, it was more that other people experienced me as being so—and therefore forced me to bring those differences (edginess, melancholy, antisocial behavior) on board as part of myself. It was a lesson in the collective hallucination of personality.

At the same time, I felt that the bedrock of my selfhood was unbreached by these collective, consensual revisions. I was aware of the fragility of that individualistic substratum, as I often am—when we think of "the true self," in isolated acts of reflection, we tend to view it as unalterable and essential, when it might be neither—but I did not seriously question that, beneath the surface play of moods, I was still in possession of myself. Still, any kind of cosmetic psychopharmacology does prompt a disturbing question. How far down would any phenomenological alteration have to go before it changed something of my "genuine" self? How much chemical change would be necessary for me to become, in fact, someone else—another person entirely? I find myself thinking of a passage in Robert Penn Warren's *All the King's Men* in which a brain surgeon performs a prefrontal lobotomy on a catatonic schizophrenic to "give him a new personality"—something, he argues, more radical than a religious conversion. His friend Jack Burden, the novel's cynical narrator, watches the operation. "Then," Jack says,

> the little pieces of brain which had been cut out were put away to think their little thoughts quietly somewhere among the garbage, and what was left inside the split-open skull of the gaunt individual was sealed back up and left to think up an entirely new personality.[5]

That is extreme, and maybe inaccurate to the reality of psychosurgery, I don't know. But once we open the door to the similarly reductive physicalism of cosmetic psychopharmacology, there is no way in principle to argue that personality alteration *cannot* be done: we do it all the time, and ever more creatively. Worse, though, it sometimes seems there is no way to prove, even to ourselves, that it *should not* be done: that is, we appear to lack the arguments we need to back up our intuitions, assuming we have them, that such chemical and surgical alteration of the psyche is *wrong*, not just imprudent or tricky to perform.

Hence, perhaps, the desperation that now surrounds the quest for identity in our culture. We feel tempted, sometimes, to reel into metaphysical vertigo, unseated by the force of these dizzy ethico-physical reflections, and spend the greater part of our lives and incomes on what is probably a self-defeating quest to discover who we are. We undertake arduous voyages of self-discovery, pay for expensive retreats and seminars, go on challenging pilgrimages, both sacred and profane. Now, when we speak of finding ourselves in this deeper fashion, we do not usually confuse the Romantic ideal of authenticity, or what is left of it to us these days, with the apparently more basic issue of just being someone in particular. I don't spend those strange, disorienting early-morning seconds attempting to reconstruct a sense of myself in terms of long-term hopes and dreams, scanning actual achievements and unfulfilled potentials. No, it is enough that I gather together the few threads of memory sufficient to establish that I am, indeed, once more the person I was yesterday and that, thank god, the voluntary period of self-demolition we call sleep is successfully over for another day. Still, it would be misleading to suggest that the two senses of "self" are entirely unrelated, or that the project of finding myself could go forward without having a firm foundation in the poured concrete of identity. To seek my deeper self I need to know, with some measure of certainty, that I will be myself from day to day.

And our happiness is to a large extent tangled up in these cross-hatched notions of selfhood. Taking only the hedonistic understanding of happiness for the moment, we realize anew that memory in relative stability is essential for there to be any kind of pleasure associated with "my" experience, because pleasures necessarily exist in the three temporal modes: the anticipation of yet-untasted ones, the fleeting joy of their present moments, and the receding memory of their inevitable passing. The body, meanwhile, is the sensory vehicle for many, if not most, of the hedonistic pleasures we know and the physical site of the consciousness that enjoys all the others we call "finer," in particular those pleasures sometimes thought to be intellectual or aesthetic in tone. To be sure, we might imagine some forms of experience that transcend the limits of an individual body: implanted memories as a future substitute for actual experiences, say, as in the plot device of the epistemo-action thriller *Total Recall*. This film, Arnold Schwarzenegger's most Cartesian movie outing, involves a plot to eliminate a secret agent causing trouble in a Martian colony not by killing him but by reprogramming his brain with "memories" of another, and entirely ordinary, life. But even here we are limited by the other prong of personal identity, because we cannot conceive of the notion of pleasure in the complete absence of memory itself. Where there is no memory, there is no person, just the arid Martian mental landscape of *totaled* recall.[6]

When it comes to eudaimonistic happiness (the rational satisfaction with one's character and actions), the matter of happiness's strong link to the individual person is even more obvious. To conceive happiness eudaimonistically is to depend, implicitly, on the meaningfulness of the concept of a unified life and the actions and character that go into shaping it. We cannot be happy in this deeper sense unless we are whole in person, and we cannot be whole in person unless we have confidence that the project of seeking an identity beyond the necessary but insufficient continuity of memory and body is, in some large measure, within our control. I have to be confident that I am a person, in other words, before I can begin to think about whether I am a happy person.

The trouble is that one of the most powerful conglomerations of better-living machines we know is designed precisely to wrest that control from us.

COOL AND THE GANG

Like most people with functioning eyes and ears, I am bombarded daily with the colorful excreta of the advertising industry. From the moment in the morning when I reach for my shaving cream to the instant at night when I set my alarm clock, I am confronted by brand names and commercial packaging. In between I see, depending on how long I spend watching television, reading magazines and newspapers, and just generally hanging out in public spaces with their billboards, hoardings, and subway ads, something on the order of six or seven hundred separate ads for various consumer products. That is a very conservative estimate—some critics put the figure even higher, on the order of two or three thousand—and it takes into account, as it must, the maddening repetition of ads, especially in public-transit vehicles or on low-budget television stations, where the same irritating spot might run twice back-to-back during a single station break. (I actually tried to count the number of separate ads I saw on a given day, but gave up after the figure quickly passed a thousand and I became too depressed to continue.) Given the volume of marketing information that reaches my brain without my consent, any deliberate reading or thinking I might do is pushed rudely into a secondary position. It is part of the success of this advertising that we do not often pause to consider that we are, in a sense, imprisoned by it: enforced readers and listeners, we are the ultimate captive audience.

Why do we put up with it? It is not simply that we regard advertising as a necessary evil, something we would stamp out for good and all should we ever judge it worth the effort. Nor is it, for most of us anyway, a matter of some deeper political embrace of a free-speech provision (though a general regard for the principles of market freedom may be operating here, at some quasi-instinctive level). As a system of self-perpetuating norms, capitalism has few equals. It constantly acts to reproduce itself, sometimes in the face of stiff challenges, by convincing generations of its children that it is driven by nothing other than the commonsense tenets of that collective illusion we call "human nature." We are now so well schooled in the dominant ideas of getting and spending that we become foot soldiers in its defense, worker bees in witless protection of a gene-bearing queen—thus, in part at least, our cheerful acceptance of the commercialization of daily experience.

Some historians are fond of saying that advertising is as old as humanity itself, implying somehow that criticism of advertising is pointless. "It is customary to begin even the shortest account of the history of advertising by recalling the three thousand year old papyrus from Thebes, offering a reward for a runaway slave, and go on to such recollections as the crier in the streets of Athens, the paintings of the gladiators, with sentences urging attendance at their combats, in ruined Pompeii, and the fly-bills on the pillars of the Forum in Rome," says cultural critic Raymond Williams. "This pleasant little ritual can be quickly performed, and as quickly forgotten.... The real business of the historian of advertising is more difficult: to trace the development from processes of specific attention and information to an *institutionalized* system of *commercial* information and persuasion."[7] Indeed, the explosion of visible advertising and aggressive consumer marketing is a phenomenon less than two hundred years old, yet it is apparently riding a parabolic acceleration curve, such that things unimaginable only a few decades ago—say, that most middle-class North American children, and many adults, would prefer to wear clothing that bears some kind of commercial sign, slogan, or image—are now taken for granted.

The danger here is not simply that our daily experience has been rendered increasingly banal, but that the otherwise firm foundation of personal identity itself begins to be chipped away. In pursuit of happiness, we gather unto ourselves all the logo-bearing merchandise of modern life. We have been targeted, cajoled, niched, and typed. Our spending patterns have been made as predictable as the vectors of ricocheting billiard balls, leaving us with the illusion of free spending and unfettered consumer desire but contained within a larger scheme of demographic determinism. Can it be a surprise that we don't know who we are any more?

Consider a couple of examples. The writer Malcolm Gladwell has recently made a name for himself in *The New Yorker* by investigating what we might call the mechanics of merchandising: the principles of retail-store design, the success of male-directed advertising, and the peculiar species of cultural traitor known as the "coolhunter."[8] What Gladwell discovered—that marketers know what you're going to think before you're thinking it—will come as no surprise as a theoretical conclusion. But I for one was astonished at the precision of the findings. Store designers can tell exactly how many seconds someone like me, a white male in his mid-thirties with some pretensions to fashion and a moderate store of disposable income, will spend looking at socks if the rack is placed at the front, middle, or back of a retail space. They can tell me how much I am likely to spend on a sports jacket. They told Malcolm Gladwell how much he was likely to spend on a sports jacket and what razor he probably used, and I discovered, to my mild horror, that he and I use the same one—Gillette Trac II.

Meanwhile, the mission of coolhunters is to tell you exactly how far Dallas is behind New York in coolness—from six to eight months, on average—and to supply Nike and Reebok with tip-sheets and full quarterly reports on what is cool in Seattle, Chicago, San Francisco, and Boston, too, all for about $20,000 a year. Lots of lesser companies buy this information, too, or analogs of it, in order to stay ahead of the fragile business of what gets taken up by kids on the street. They then sell those things to the same kids *as* cool, and (with the exception of the genuinely cool people who offered the stamp of approval in the first place, and who have now moved on to something entirely different) people buy the products because they are, in fact, by extension, cool. But only until next season.

I can think of no experience in the modern world more unsettling, more vertiginous, than this one of realizing that my carefully constructed individuality is as transparent and manipulable to a savvy advertiser as if I sported a niche-market report on my forehead. It is far more threatening to my sense of personal identity to have someone know, with near certainty, which vodka or scotch I will buy than any mood-altering drug could ever be. For here, lost in the cash nexus of the modern commercial world, my very sense of myself as a unique, rational individual is thrown into doubt: I am suddenly nothing more than a blip on the radar screen of the marketing wars, a money-hoarding cipher who must be presented with enticements to part with my hard-earned cash and thus spin the turbines of the big engine of capital. I might *think* my choices are mine alone, considered and personal, but they reveal themselves as manipulated and predictable. So I am forced to wonder: am I a cultural dope after all, not free but determined? It's like the feeling I get when I look at a picture of myself from high school and feel the wrenching horror of realizing that what I thought was eminently cool then was, in fact, not only pretty goofy but, worse, only considered cool at all because everyone else deemed it so. Looking back, that experience has a comical quality: what nerds we really were! When it is constantly happening in the present, however, it is enough to make your head spin. In the midst of the coolhunting machinery of the commercial culture, which sells my desires back to me under cover of cool, *who the hell am I?*

The common use of the concept of cool, though it was originally rooted in the antiestablishment, grace-under-pressure ethos of the late 1940s and early 1950s, now casts a wider semantic net. After a period of relative cultural dormancy in the 1980s, when it was not (as I recall anyway) very cool to use the word *cool,* cool is now all-encompassing, widely understood as a simple seal of social approval, for the most part nonspecific and free floating. It retains some of its original aura, especially in urban settings where poised self-presentation and the appearance of courage are prized, but it has expanded to encompass any value judgment, particularly in the widely practiced Bart Simpson dichotomy: it's either cool or it sucks. Cool is therefore open to an unprecedented degree of cultural manipulation.

More troubling still, at least for those who like language to be precise, *cool* is now subject to the logical limits of interpretation, in the way that, for instance, the word *good* has been in more serious philosophical circles. You know the kind of thing I mean: Is a good martini good in the same way that a good person is good? If so, what is the connection? Is there, perhaps, a continuum of *good*s, from low to high? Or is the specifically ethical use of *good* somehow set off conceptually from other expressions of approval? Or is there, perhaps, nothing more in the ethical expression but an emotive exclamation on the order of "Yummy!" Those problems have exercised philosophers from Plato (who thought there was a connection) to David Hume (who thought there was not) to G. E. Moore (who thought the very idea of the good beyond analysis).[9] Cool now occupies much the same conceptual space and presents many of the same problems. What does it mean to call both a new silk jacket and a nifty basketball move, both a pop song and a new car, cool? These earlier philosophical thinkers would no doubt have bent their talents to the concept of cool, too, if they had known it was going to be so important to fashion-conscious consumers like those who dominate the North American cultural scene.[10]

Because he is clever, Malcolm Gladwell noticed the lingering paradoxes of cool, and he attempted to articulate three rules of cool for the presumably uncool readers of *The New Yorker*. "[T]he second rule says that cool cannot be manufactured, only observed," he writes in an essay called "The Coolhunt,"

and the third says that it can only be observed by those who are themselves cool. And, of course, the first rule says that it cannot accurately be observed at all, because the act of discovering cool causes cool to take flight, so if you add all three together they describe a closed loop, the hermeneutic circle of coolhunting, a phenomenon whereby not only can the uncool not see cool but cool cannot even be adequately described to them.

This passage came near the end of his lengthy article, at which point there was really little point in taking this claim seriously and doing the only logical thing, namely throwing the magazine away. Despite all his savvy in recognizing the various feedback loops and self-fulfilling prophecies of the coolhunt, and his cleverness in comparing cool waves to the dynamics of innovation, early adoption, and majority adoption articulated by so-called "diffusion researchers," Gladwell was unable to escape the inherent limitations of the idea that cool is a quality that some people simply possess, as if naturally, while others do not.

If you take for granted the kind of born-not-made instinct for cool that is so mythologized by the coolhunters—who then turn around and do the very *un*cool thing of selling that perception to shoe companies and clothing manufacturers—it is true that you can never escape, Gladwell says, this "hermeneutic" circle of cool. (I think he really means "hermetic."[11]) But that kind of attitude about cool, which makes it a form of second sight that some gifted individuals are blessed with, reduces it to the least interesting of social commodities, the thing that cannot be understood unless you already understand it—in other words, a self-enclosed ideology, what Gladwell himself calls "the triumphant circularity" of coolhunting. "It is not possible to be cool, in other words," he concludes, "unless you are—in some larger sense—already cool, and so the phenomenon that the uncool cannot see and cannot have described to them is also something that they cannot ever attain, because if they did it would no longer be cool." Right. So that means I might as well stop trying, yes?

No. Because like all ideologies, this kind of essentialism about cool is at once exclusionary and beckoning, teasing us, through advertising but also through this kind of smart celebration of the process of advertising, with the *possibility* of being cool. Gladwell's article becomes part of that temptation, because seeing through the paradoxes of cool is surely one of the first steps in being cool; or rather, only cool people are fully aware of the paradoxes of cool, and that awareness is part of the reason that they lead in being cool while the others follow. But the upshot of this metaview of things is that authenticity is reserved exclusively for the cool minority, since the rest of us are so hopelessly manipulated by marketing forces that we wouldn't know authenticity if it hit us in the face. This cool minority then becomes the chosen band of innovators whom the cool-hunters (themselves necessarily cool, except in being so coopted by commercial forces—a pretty overwhelming limitation) seek out and listen to. (This is all bad and elitist, if not unprecedented: listen to the self-aggrandizement of a Shelley or a Byron, say, and you realize that the idea that only a few people can be genuinely authentic in this sense is far from new. Those guys would have considered themselves very cool indeed, if they had known the word.)

But it's worse than that and worse even than Gladwell seems to think. When Nike and Reebok, in turn, listen to the coolhunters and market the things they think the kids will think are cool, the circle closes even tighter, because the original cool kids did not, in fact, get their cool from the gods as part of some native perceptual talent. Like everybody else, they learned cool from their social context—and cool only makes sense in a world of pretty narrow specificity: urban, media-wise, brand-conscious. The cool kids quoted by the coolhunters drop commercial names with more relish and precision than characters in a Jay McInerney novel: they never just wear a jacket, they always wear a Polo or a Nautica; jeans are always Levi's or Guess or retro-designer Jordache. This knowingness, the display of minute distinctions and arcana, is so much part of the current cool ethos that the basic contradiction lurking here never comes fully to light. *Not even the cool kids are genuinely cool!* They, no less than everybody else, have ingested ideas of cool already cycled through the cynical, profit-driven mechanisms of the fashion system, merchandising, and product placement. The essentialism of cool is itself an illusion, part of the pervasive ideology of consumerism; the idea of a cutting edge of hipness is nothing more than a piece of cultural self-congratulation that keeps some kids happy, some aging hipsters in work selling them out, and some smart journalists in the pages of a top magazine. The paradox is not, as Gladwell writes, "that the better the coolhunters become at bringing the mainstream close to the cutting edge, the more elusive the cutting edge becomes." The paradox is that there *is* no cutting edge.

And with that, the idea of cool itself finally comes apart. As does, at the same time, any attempt to forge an identity out of the manipulated materials of commercial cool. Where does this leave us? Post-cool, maybe; trans-cool. But how long can it be before the marketers begin to sell to us on that basis, how long before the current sandals-and-socks antifashion of the cultural resistance becomes the next moment in an eternal round of buying and selling ourselves? (The most recent attempt to transcend the influence of marketing, the alternative style of Seattle-based grunge, held out from the forces of marketing for no more than a year or two.) Is there anywhere to go, any identity to adopt, that is not already encapsulated by the forces of the market?

Before I deal with that question, consider a different kind of manipulation, this time directed not at personal identity but at another piece of the apparatus of authenticity: the idea of aesthetic experience. Philosophers from Aristotle to Moore have celebrated the perception of art as one of the fullest expressions of our humanity, an exploration of personality and psyche, and even a link to a collective soul or memory. Most thinkers who celebrate the aesthetic experience in this way appear to think that genuine aesthetic enjoyment is both straightforwardly accessible and untainted. But we must ask: can it be either for us today? I am far from sure.

Whenever I think, for example, of the variety of materials that pervert Edvard Munch's painting *The Scream* to commercial purposes—bastardized uses of the image in advertising, editorial cartoons, and urban design, not to mention the various "Scream" figures, sound-effect pillows, and other assorted knick-knacks available for purchase at gallery shops the continent over—my first reaction is a mixture of amusement and faint depression. Here we see on view the tiresome but all-too-familiar commercialization of our culture, which makes of everything, however serious and powerful, a possible image for coffee mugs and T-shirts. The more extensively replicated the image of anguish and dread becomes, especially as deflected from the serious context of contemplating a work of visual art, the more any significance in the image seems to leak away. So the first issue with Munch's *The Scream* is deadening commodification, which we can think of as represented by the fairly familiar figure—you have probably seen it if you've visited a gallery or novelty shop in the last year or two—of the inflatable doll in the shape of the original painting's main figure, the screamer him- (or her-?) self.

It is true that we may be able to offer little in the way of argument to explain our fetishizing of the authentic object. In his influential 1934 essay "The Work of Art in an Age of Mechanical Reproduction," the Marxist critic Walter Benjamin went so far as to denounce what he called the fascism of aesthetic "aura." For Benjamin, writing at a time when reproduction looked more liberating than delimiting, the glorification of the individual, "authentic" artwork reduced it to a mute object before which we must stand in equally mute rapture, an experience which, far from liberating, made us no more than unwitting communicants in a ritual of observance that preserved the elitist structure of the gallery as a kind of cathedral. (The muteness of this experience is particularly significant in the case of *The Scream,* since it is the very inarticulacy of the central figure, the frozen silence of its anguish, that opens up the painting's many associations in viewers—who nevertheless typically remain silent.) Thus in Benjamin's view mechanical reproduction of art could have liberating, democratizing effects, if it broke this unnatural—and politically reactionary—connection between art and power.

And yet even if we share this political goal, we find that the notion of the authentic work is resistant to challenge. Most of us, for example, would be unable to tell the difference between an original painting and even a fairly amateurish fake, but it nevertheless seems very important to us that *someone* be able to do so. Even attempts to deconstruct this cult of authenticity, like Andy Warhol's celebrated multiple silk-screens and commodified objects—including, notoriously, images of *The Scream* itself—eventually surrender to it. As Benjamin's contemporaries Theodor Adorno and Max Horkheimer noted in their grumpy mid-1940s essay on "The Culture Industry"— a negative assessment of mechanical reproduction from a similar political quarter as Benjamin's positive one, though made later and when the two co-authors viewed the process of reproduction with rather jaundiced, postwar eyes—the political impact of reproduction is most often nugatory, not liberating. Therefore the issue of the nongenuine copy in fact becomes more pressing, not less, as the means of reproduction become more sophisticated. The cult of authenticity seems almost antique as we surrender to a world of near-flawless reproduction, falling under the influence of the assembly lines of the culture which steal our authentic selves, flatten them out, and sell them back to us as slick (and banal) product. Thus does the supposed enlightenment of cultural experience become, in their words, no more than a "mass deception."[12]

The complementary problem is that, at the same time as the aesthetic image is divorced from its original and authentic setting and made into a cheap commodity, the experience of viewing the work of art itself becomes all the more closed into the regimented, bourgeois, culturally safe context of the gallery experience. The gallery and the gallery shop exist side by side, two features of the same process of commercialization. Thus the work, which we might by rights expect to be jarring or arresting, is instead enveloped in the deadening self-improvement aura of the modern art gallery, which people visit not so much to view art as to feel better about themselves. We begin to feel, in short, more or less like the stately, bourgeois, complacent figures in the background of Munch's painting, the figures of middle-class propriety that the screaming protagonist in the foreground is, to all appearances, trying to get away from. The irony here is not just obvious, it is structural: the emasculation of the artwork's presumed power to move and perhaps shock is something that apparently *must* happen as long as this two-pronged movement of commodification—selling the image in knick-knacks, even as we render the actual work little more than a piece of wallpaper in an institution—occurs. And that movement is deeply inscribed in the commercial imperatives of the culture. We sell dread, now in debased forms like fridge magnets and inflatables. We also sell safety, now in the odd form of viewing art that should, by rights, be shocking, with the same deadened gaze we nightly direct toward the television screen.

But that is only the first level of difficulty with the proliferation of *The Scream* and its attendant imagery. In these late-twentieth-century days, we don't simply commodify, we also kitschify. That is to say, we undercut our cultural and social experience with a relentless penchant for irony, for deflating the power of art by restlessly dancing away from its straightforwardness toward something we regard as sophistication or hipness. The image of *The Scream* is not merely replicated many times over; that trivializes the image, but at least leaves it more or less intact. The more advanced and refined forces in the culture are not content simply to leave the image as it is. They undercut it, invert its significance, make it a joke.

Examples of this abound. There is the famous "Scream" dress worn by drag-queen character Dame Edna Everage (invented and played, brilliantly, by Australian comedian Barry Humphries), which features the clichéd figure of anguish now picked out in sequins on a low-cut ballgown. ("I thought it was someone about to take a bite out of something that's just out of view," she said of the screaming figure, "until I realized it's a painting of a woman at sunset who has lost her earrings.") A recent ad for the Toronto art magazine *Fuse* reproduced a version of *The Scream* with the ironic tag line "Don't worry, be happy." The same message appears on a greeting card decorated with the screaming figure, inviting the sender to check off, inside, the reasons why someone might feel inclined to emulate the twisted-O mouth and writhing body language of the screamer. A now-celebrated Pontiac Sunfire car commercial uses the vivid colors and swirling brushwork of the painting to suggest the calming effects of driving the right car. As the screaming figure is confronted (and eventually seduced) by the beautiful, soundproofed car, driving away with a wink at the viewer, the wavy lines of *The Scream,* together with their suggestion of mental imbalance and an alien landscape, are straightened out and smoothed over; the formerly anguished figure chills out and dons a pair of sunglasses. *The Scream,* forever struggling to gain voice in Munch oils, is here decisively stifled, in other words, by the superior engineering of Detroit.

My favorite example of this second level of debasement of the artistic image, to be found in novelty shops and gallery stores, is another inflatable doll on whose head the features of voiceless anguish have been replaced with the smiling yellow happy face. (Like the other inflatable, the one that simply reproduces Munch's screamer, this one carries a printed warning that it is "not to be used as a flotation device.") It is clearly an allusion to *The Scream,* because it is an inflatable of identical type to the other one and the body language of the torso is identical. It includes the wavy lines of Munch's brushwork, now in bright yellows and oranges rather than the angst-ridden blacks and purples. The change of color, a repositioning of the arms—they are no longer clutching the face but are now flung open in a friendly greeting or a dancing excess of joy—and the replacement of the screaming face with the kitschy happy face of popular culture all indicate the kind of joke this is and the sort of object.[13] Here we are not simply commercializing Munch's image, we are mocking it. The archetypal vision of anguish is transformed into this thoroughly banal vision of happiness.

This inflatable figure is not a suggestion that happiness is possible, of course, or even that it is preferable to dread. Like any instance of the happy face, it is not really a claim about happiness at all. It is instead a joke on the very ideas of dread and happiness and, in this particular case, a further joke on the idea that such deep ideas could be communicated in art. We might be inclined to think that the happy-face inflatable screamer is some kind of ironic comment on the commercialization of the Munch image itself, nicely closing the circle of the joke. I confess, however, to finding that sort of argument about "reverent irony," as the novelist David Foster Wallace once put it, rather thin. What is abundantly clear is that we are now at least three conceptual steps away from Munch's original painting and, it follows, from the feelings that the painting was meant to evoke or illustrate. This is not just a reproduction, nor is it even simply a commonplace or silly reproduction; it is, in addition to those deflections from the authentic object, a debased quasi-reproduction and hence the final elimination of seriousness from the image on which it is based.

The happy-face inflatable is, in this way, a prime example of the growing virtuality of much of our cultural experience. A genuine image of anxiety, the one found in Munch's original paintings, is almost entirely drained of its power, first through reproduction and then through irony. The sad thing is that, in taking undeniable pleasure in the kind of joke this is—even, maybe, insisting that campy appropriation of the materials of the culture preserves as well as parodies them—we often fail to recognize that the joke might be on us. Our notions of dread and happiness are here in a sense betrayed, our anxiety packaged and manipulated to within an inch of its life.

Still, when I finally found myself before Munch's *The Scream*, I have to say I found it more powerful, even in its thoroughly mediated familiarity, even in the cobwebby confines of that thoroughly middle-class safety zone, the contemporary fine-art museum—even, let it be said, in the midst of the *ching! ching!* of the cash registers from the gallery shop on the other side of the wall—than I could have expected when thinking about my two inflatable friends. But however much I enjoyed it, savoring the complicated ice-cream swirls of sweet and tart that are the mouth-filling essence of all aesthetic experience, it was far from "pure" in its ability to move me. I was able, for a moment, to bracket much of the depressing commodification of my cultural experience, but not, in the end, to escape it entirely.

The inflatables carry the warning not to be used as flotation devices, yet they bob along behind me wherever I go, buoying up the commercial imperatives and ironic distance of our present confusion. I bought examples of the two inflatable toys, the anguished Munch screamer and his happy-faced cousin, to illustrate a lecture. They now stand side by side on a table in my office in a little cultural diorama, positioned so that the outstretched arms and big smile of the yellow one appear to lurch toward, trying to enfold the twisted and screaming original—who looks back in well-justified dread.

It is the very commonness of this sort of image reproduction, and of the irony that often comes in reproduction's wake, that holds the clue to how cultural industries subtly affect us. We have to expose the forces that lie behind such reproduction—the way commercialism and advertising work to colonize our very deepest desires, those centered on the wish to be happy, by playing on our various weaknesses and lack of critical training. These forces are, in their way, a form of ideological control: not the propagandizing of standard political indoctrination, to be sure, nor even some kind of well-orchestrated consumerist conspiracy, but rather a system of thought and representation that all of us, producers and consumers alike, implicitly accept (and reinforce) with every commercial transaction.

This system is so much taken for granted in our cultural milieu that it has become, indeed, *naturalized*—part of a set of background assumptions and ideas concerning life and work, even concerning what it means to be human, that we no longer pause to question. Yet we constantly communicate these assumptions in the materials of our daily cultural experience: the way, to take a simple example used by novelist and critic Gilbert Adair, that the apparently ordinary form of a meal like fish and chips which might act to communicate a surface message of democratization ("Everybody likes it!") even while falling within, and therefore drawing attention away from, a political structure (Britain) that is in fact extremely class-conscious and unequal.[14] We should pause to question naturalized ideas, though, to challenge anything that suggests it is "just the way things are," for nothing is natural until we make it so, and structures of commercialism are not metaphysical bedrock—they are not woven into the fabric of the universe. They are contingent, socially constructed and open to alteration or even elimination.

How to begin? In an early critical essay called *The German Ideology*, written before more programmatic revolutionary ideas and a one-sided economic determinism began to dominate his thinking, Karl Marx laid bare the mechanisms of ideological control under conditions of capitalist markets. Marx argued that the genius of capitalism was precisely its ability to make profit-taking, wages, and the marketing of commodities appear unquestionable. In the essay, Marx speaks of ideology as a kind of "false consciousness," a delusional process whereby the working class unwittingly adopts the interests that in fact serve the owner class. To take a contemporary example, false consciousness might involve thinking that a proposed tax on capital gains is a very bad idea, even though the elimination of such a tax would benefit only the richest few and arguably harm the rest in denying them new sources of public funding.

Yet this basic Marxist notion of ideology is actually misleadingly blunt. People are not simply cultural dopes who are moved by social and political forces beyond their control or comprehension. There are structures of economic domination that influence or distort our experience, true, but they are not entirely invisible to us; though we may be deluded or manipulated or confused at times, we are not staggering idiots ignoring our own true interests in the blind service of capitalism. On the other hand, neither are we the perfectly rational creatures, immune to deception and stupidity, on which contemporary economists model their increasingly abstract theories of market behavior. Neither side of this extreme either-or picture is the whole story: as one of my professors used to say, *"It's just not that simple."*

It is therefore necessary to refine the analysis of ideology to see the true influence of cultural forces on our daily lives. The first point in this subtler view is that ideology is troubling precisely because it can be difficult for even the most intelligent people to

see. "[I]deology by definition thrives *beneath* consciousness," according to the sociologist Dick Hebdige, a critic of Marx's crude version.
"It is here, at the level of 'normal common sense,' that ideological
frames of reference are most firmly sedimented and most effective,
because it is here that their ideological nature is most effectively
concealed."[15] Ideology, in other words, cannot be isolated as a mere
body of political opinion (the *descriptive* definition of the term) or
even as a set of views that we happen not to agree with (the *pejorative*
definition). It is, rather, the ideas and prejudices that are contained
in what appear to be the basic assumptions of normal life. (This is
what we might call the *critical* definition of ideology.) Understood
this way, then, ideology, to borrow a vivid description, "saturates
everyday discourse in the form of common sense."[16] It comprises all
the unquestioned preconceptions of the everyday, those structures
of cultural and social meaning that are so accepted that we cannot
even see them, most of the time, *as* structures. But the ideas we
blithely accept may often be, in fact, political ideas only masquerading as facts about the world. Ideology functions best when it manages to render itself invisible, immune to criticism because taken for
granted as impossible to change, like the weather. Like Poe's pur-
loined letter, ideology hides most effectively when it remains in
plain view. "Its very taken-for-grantedness," says the sociologist Stuart Hall, "is what establishes [the ideology of 'common sense'] as a
medium in which its own premises and presuppositions are being
rendered *invisible* by its apparent transparency."[17]

Any understanding of ideology as a form of consciousness,
therefore, whether false or otherwise, misses a key point about how
our thoughts are conditioned. It is not that we are being sold a bill
of goods by some "dominant" class that wants us to think as it does.
We have to look, rather, at the *un*conscious forces of a culture—the
environmental or mediated structures of social belief and action—
and there catch a glimpse of the systems of representation that
shape the existing scheme of things. Such ideological systems of representation "are usually images and occasionally concepts," according to the philosopher and critic Louis Althusser, "but it is above all

as *structures* that they impose on the vast majority of people, not via their 'consciousness.'...[T]hey act functionally on people via a process that escapes them."[18] Because they exist above all as structures that define whole arenas of social life, ideological biases and prejudices work to set the limits of what can be imagined or done; they envelop us in a circle of conceptual possibility, telling us that it is, for example, "unthinkable" not to work for money, or "unimaginable" that the world might be organized without social classes or markets. But such ideas are not, in the end, immune from challenge—if we have the right tools to put them into question.

What is an example of ideology understood this way, as a set of commonsense assumptions that is so taken for granted that it becomes invisible? Well, consider a structure that I am very familiar with, and which other critics have used to illustrate the point: the university classroom. Here seats and desks are arranged in rows, perhaps on a riser; a blackboard and lectern stand at the front; students, usually in multiple numbers, face a single person who, sometimes literally cloaked in authority (the academic gown), dispenses knowledge, perhaps even wisdom, from behind the lectern. The room not only naturalizes the lecturer's authority—he or she is given a special place at the front—but insists upon the auditory dissemination of knowledge. Furthermore, floors or buildings are assigned to different subjects or divisions of knowledge, working within the basic assumption of universities, contained in their very name, that total knowledge can be encompassed in one place, and doled out to paying or otherwise qualified apprentices. "Here the buildings literally *reproduce* in concrete terms prevailing (ideological) notions about what education *is*," says Dick Hebdige, "and it is through this process that the educational structure, which can, of course, be altered, is placed beyond question and appears to us as a 'given' (i.e., as immutable). In this case, the frames of our thinking have been translated into actual bricks and mortar."

If you doubt the naturalizing effect of basic structures like these, you have only to do what I do occasionally: invite students to imagine alternative forms of institutional framework. Their reactions to the invitation are illuminating. At first they protest: you cannot be serious, it is some kind of trick question or test. Then they are unwilling to participate, thinking that they are being asked to perform some kind of straight-man role in a routine they do not understand, a self-flattering piece of faux-hipness on the part of the aging professor. (Possibly this is based on hard experience.) Then a brave one or two will suggest the pleasant but hardly subversive notion of going outside. As most teachers know, the *al fresco* scene does somewhat alter what I suppose we must call the educational dynamic—there are more distractions, and perhaps a hint of eroticism that is missing in the sterile classroom—but it doesn't usually break through the most basic assumptions concerning teacher and taught. In my experience, very few, if any, students will suggest anything further, not even such traditional options as walking (Aristotle was a great walker, as the name of his school of followers, the Peripatetics, indicates) or even eating together, perhaps in the manner of Plato's *Symposium* (though that involved drinking, too, which nowadays no doubt rules it out immediately).

The paucity of the students' imaginations is not evidence of a lack of intelligence; rather, it is the sign of effective socialization. They have learned the assumptions and expectations of the classroom—indeed, they are past masters at them or they would not be in my university classroom in the first place—and they do not wish, on the whole, to consider alternatives. And to be fair, perhaps there is also some higher-level resistance, since I raise this question from within the classroom and therefore invite a certain kind of skepticism. But mostly their resistance is the resistance of common sense: *of course* university courses get taught in classrooms that lie within university buildings, according to disciplinary and scheduling demands contained in the institutional calendar. This, they want to say, is *just what it is* to acquire a university degree, with all the social validation and (one continues to hope) employment prospects that that implies.

The basic assumptions of advertising have now been naturalized to an extent equal to, or greater than, the degree of ideological taken-for-grantedness evident in something like the university lecture hall. Certainly far more people are exposed to advertising than to postsecondary education; it would be a rare person in an industrialized society who is not bombarded with it, in fact, even including those who voluntarily reject its currently dominant delivery system, the television. In order to understand advertising we have not only to deconstruct particular examples, laying bare the hidden assumptions of their slick imagery, but also to tease out an awareness of the more basic motives of advertising's system of representation, its way of ordering the world into conceptual parts that industry, and in turn we, accept as meaningful (product, campaign, target audience, spending patterns, and so on). The latter task is harder because we have to, in effect, denaturalize the natural, somehow isolate the medium from within the medium. It should be no surprise that this is difficult and as a result rare; it is also rare because it is the nature of ideology in this sense to want to remain transparent and therefore invisible. Good efforts toward this end are not common, but they do exist in the smarter magazines, journals, and websites.[19]

The material of advertising is often so fleeting, the ultimate cultural moving target at three minutes or less and a broadcast rotation of only a few months, that we can remain unaware of the ideas of class and success being peddled in a Crown Royal liquor ad, for example, or the aggressive technological optimism evident beneath the humorous pizzazz of an ad for a new electric car. But the thing to remember about advertising, as about all forms of ideology, is that these are contingent structures masquerading as necessary ones: in other words, things that could be otherwise pretending they could not. The more ideology succeeds at seeming unchangeable—the more it parades before us as part of "the way things are" or, even better, "just human nature"—the more difficult we find it to resist. And the mere important it is that we do.

FACILITATE ENVY

Everyone consumes advertising (as well as the products it advertises), but few of us know how ad campaigns are actually planned.

The business of advertising is a heady mixture of risk, manipulation, and renegade intelligence. Its practitioners will always deny this, however, and retreat into one of the deepest lies of the consumer culture: that advertisers are simply giving people what they want. It is as if they see themselves—or would have us see them—as generous dispensers of consumer bounty, the Father Christmases of the material culture. *Whatever you want, we got it. Just tell us what you want and we will make you happy.* Not long ago, the critic Howard Mumford Jones took upon himself the task of counting the smiling faces in the ads of a single issue of a national weekly magazine. He found that 178 out of the 257 depicted faces were smiling, grinning, or laughing, with 14 more singing and 3 tearfully smiling; of the remaining 60, 3 were asleep, 3 were blowing smoke rings, and about two dozen were enraptured children or infants; several others were "before" shots—the instrumental unhappiness of contrast—or comical frowns.

"In these advertisements an upset toboggan produces only gaiety," he notes in his book *The Pursuit of Happiness,* "a man up a tree with a saw is filled with joy, a mechanic carrying a can of engine sludge registers innocent merriment, a housewife pushing a vacuum cleaner bursts into song, and four salesmen of a storage battery join in a quartet." Nor are the happy-go-lucky denizens of the ads simply incidental mannequins of consumerism; they are, more than this, the grinning avatars of the culture's inner logic. "Advertisements reveal our folkways," Jones concludes. "They prove that the effect of purchasing American cigarettes, oil furnaces, laxatives, shirts, automobiles, house paint, television sets, coffee, nylon stockings, vacuum cleaners, chewing gum, coated papers, electric trains, and dog food is the instant creation of felicity."[20]

On the surface, yes, and yet the deeper truth is actually more troubling still. What makes a good advertiser good is precisely his or her ability to make us want something we did not previously feel any need for. The basic assumption of all advertising is this: *facilitate envy.*[21] And, as Bertrand Russell notes, envy is, together with boredom and fatigue, one of the three principal sources of human unhappiness. Still, like those other fonts of routine misery, envy is but imperfectly understood. We take it so much for granted, notes the philosopher Robert Nozick, that we rarely pause to investigate its *strangeness* as an emotion. "The envious person," says Nozick, "if he cannot (also) possess a thing (talent, and so on) that someone else has, prefers that the other person not have it either. The envious man prefers neither one having it, to the other's having it and his not having it." But why? "Why do some people *prefer* that others not have their better score along some [social] dimension, rather than being pleased at another's being well-off or having good fortune; why don't they at least just shrug it off?"[22] Good question. Nozick himself suggests that the answer is rooted in the comparative nature of all human achievement, the inevitability of measuring ourselves against proximate others (*proximate* because distance makes the heart grow less envious), and the resulting feelings of unhappiness that accrue to coming up short. He argues for a society in which achievements are celebrated along multiple dimensions, allowing individuals to think, however fleetingly, that they each have something uniquely valuable upon which to base their self-esteem.

Yet this is to ignore the powerful role of social isolation and celebration in making certain indices of success and worth dominant. On the surface, advertising proclaims the availability of the products it wishes to sell; indeed, modern-day television advertising is directly descended from the print-based advertising medium, which began simply enough as a means of letting the readers of periodicals know that certain services or goods could be had. But contemporary advertising actually works by playing on unavailability: the key is that the viewer *does not possess* the product or service in question. The ad is an attempt not so much to sing the praises of the consumable, though it may do that as one part of its strategy, as to create a sense of lack because one does not have whatever is being advertised. Here desire is created, not discovered. This may be done in many different ways—associating the product with another desirable thing or feeling, like sexual attractiveness; showing the product being enjoyed by sexually attractive or otherwise "successful" people; linking the product with an admired athlete or actor—but they all collapse down to the fundamental one: the viewer must feel that possession of the product in question will remove the troubling emptiness he did not know, until now, he suffered. Paradoxically, advertising is all about creating unhappiness.

Advertisers are therefore the contemporary world's leading experts at instilling desire and manufacturing longing—injecting us with images, humor, and state-of-the-art graphics, as a virus might be injected via a finely tuned hypodermic needle. This is no ordinary desire, either, unlike the desire simply for shoes or running shoes or even especially nice running shoes. The real genius of advertising is its almost incredible specificity, the ability to create in me a desire not only for Nike running shoes, say, but for a particular brand of them, Air Pegasus, which I will search out, high and low, because I find myself in a state in which *I do not regard myself as happy* unless I possess them. How's that for modern sorcery? If someone told us, up front, that he could get us to feel a desire so arbitrary and yet so overpowering, we would probably consider him crazy. And yet this is exactly what the successful practitioners of this black art can do on a daily basis.

Why "black"? Is there any harm in giving people what they want—even if you are the one who slyly whispered to them what they want in the first place? There is, indeed, and the harm extends in several directions, from the Indonesian assembly-line worker whose 16-cents-a-day wage created the shoe that I will pay $100 for, to the subtle twists and perversions of my personal desire under the onslaught of sexy imagery, spurious associations, and stirring rock music. "Envy," says Russell in *The Conquest of Happiness,* "is the basis of democracy," because it says that no one should have something that someone else does not. That democratic impulse can have both positive and negative effects, but with the array of expensive, harmful, or unavailable material goods that scans across our cathode-ray tubes night after night there can be no doubt that the sum effect is deleterious. One reason many people think themselves more miserable now, or consider themselves poorer than they should be, even though in real terms their standard of living is far higher than it was for similarly employed people a generation ago, is precisely that they now must confront not having (some of) the allegedly indispensable trappings of the good life. As Robert Samuelson argues in his convincing 1995 book *The Good Life and Its Discontents,* North Americans have allowed their expectations of comfort and leisure to rise so high that now almost any economic condition, or indeed social organization, that falls beneath utter luxury begins to seem inadequate.[23] (The perception of relative deprivation also leads, Samuelson says, to unrealistic and potentially harmful expectations about what government should provide in the way of "basic" goods and services: expectations that give rise to finger-pointing, conflicting rights claims, and dangerous social resentment.) Television advertising, and indeed programming (think of the unemployed yet beautifully clothed and luxuriously housed twenty-somethings of most mid-1990s situation comedies), has much to answer for in this regard.

The advertisers may say, for public consumption, that they are merely *persuading* us of their product's superiority over its rivals (a Toronto-based television show about TV advertising goes by the title *Media Television: The Modern Art and Science of Persuasion),* but this is linguistic sleight of hand. "Persuasion" implies rational conviction, a process by which we come to see a position's validity because of some combination of reasons advanced against a previous position. Advertising is not, by any reckoning, persuasion. I am not persuaded that Air Pegasus are the best shoes on the planet, though I may well comport myself as if I believed it: not the same thing. So why do we put up with it? Why don't we take a cue from Nike—it's their world, after all, as the tennis coach Tom Gullickson once said—and, when it comes to refusing the hawker's pitch, just do it?

In pursuit of an answer, I signed myself up for a day-long focus session for an advertising firm based in Montreal. I was hired as an expert to help the agency deconstruct the demographic characteristics of the eighteen-to-twenty-nine group it was targeting with its campaign. You might think it remarkable—I certainly did—that this firm was willing to employ my services in pursuit of a well-constructed ad campaign. But ad firms do this all the time, and I like to think it says something about their acumen that they believe expert opinion, even of the academic sort, is relevant to their enterprise. Now I won't lie to you: I took money for doing this.[24] I also signed a confidentiality agreement, which means, theoretically at least, that I'm not allowed to disclose any details of what went on during the eight or so hours of the session. So there are some ethical issues to deal with. When I called up my friend Janice, the book editor, to talk about the target group we were going to discuss in the session—Janice is part of that twenty-something generation—she had a typical reaction.

"I don't know why you're doing this," she said to me over the phone. "In fact, I don't know how you can sleep at night." Nevertheless she stayed on the line for more than an hour, long enough anyway to answer my questions about her population subsection, and in some detail. "Every single thing in our lives is being marketed, more for us than for any other generation," Janice said at one point. "I just feel like every time I turn around we're being told *what* to be and *how* to be. And every time we draw a line of rebellion, advertisers cross it. And then we get more and more depressed. It's very frustrating, because you can't find an identity or a comfort zone." Toward the end of our conversation, Janice pulled herself up short and realized what she had done. "I'm almost as bad as you, for answering these questions," she said, her voice rising. "Oh my god, I'm the Judas of my generation! I'm selling out my own friends to the advertising industry!"

I interviewed some other sub-thirty friends of mine, in all cases urbanites with some connection to writing or publishing, and opened a couple of computer files for the notes that I called, with heavy irony, "Faust 1" and "Faust 2." I began drafting the preliminary essay that I would have to send to the agency in advance of the session, searching in unfamiliar rhetorical territory for the kind of sweeping authoritative statements that make for best-selling books of demographic analysis. "This generation is not necessarily as aggressive or business oriented as those, say, ten to fifteen years older—successful 1980s urban professionals," I wrote,

> and they fear the uncertainty of the current job market. But planning for the future and a certain kind of financial hard-headedness seems to be as prevalent a response to this situation as the alienation and disaffection suggested by media caricature.... They have a political-cultural outlook characterized by social tolerance, often combined with personal conservatism or at least lack of interest in the politics of ideology.

Reading this bilge now is pretty cringe-making, and not simply because of its cheesy faux-anthropological tone. Who the hell was I to be making these judgments? It got even worse. "Some of them have a strong belief in their ability to adapt to changing social and economic circumstances," I said,

> and while they retain little belief in an overarching system of success to buoy them up—they don't have the blitheness of the Boomers that the world is their oyster—they nevertheless sense that their flexibility, intelligence, technological comfort-level, and initiative will see them through. Others are not so sanguine, finding that the world is not responding to their efforts and abilities quickly enough—partly because the world is overburdened with Boomers, whom this generation resents.

Nauseating. All I can say in my own defense is that I thought I was saying something reasonably valid at the time, even though the question at the heart of the project's premise—What is a given generation thinking, and how do we sell to them?—strikes me now as hopelessly pedestrian, if not downright dangerous.

But this is how such things can act on people with reasonably lively minds. The logic of the task is itself compelling: how do you sell something to someone whose defining characteristic is resistance to the very idea of being sold to? First you hit the initial meta-level of deciding to sell to them based on the idea that you're not selling anything, in fact you despise the very idea of selling—but that position is so transparently self-serving, and reached so quickly, that it can't possibly work for more than a few seconds, culturally speaking. A single wave of wannabe-cool, "do your own ironic thing" campaigns and the basic fallacy of being a rebel *just like everybody else* is ruthlessly exposed by the disdain of the very people you're trying to reach. So you search for a new level of self-consciousness, of marketable irony, to appeal to the rapid escalation of knowingness. But how far can you go up this ladder of growing awareness and rebounding attention before you get handcuffed by your own pattern of concentric feedback loops? When does the whole enterprise begin to collapse beneath its own weight?

It was that same fascination that took us over during the actual discussions of the focus session. I won't say that I would have done it for nothing, but I will say that it was no less interesting than many a philosophy seminar I've had to sit through. There were a couple of young cultural anthropologists and a magazine publisher, all under thirty; a television executive from a self-consciously hip local station and an art-school teacher both in their early fifties; and a business-woman, like me in her early thirties. Not surprisingly, there was a good deal of vocabulary clash, as often happens when you throw people together like that: cultural-studies-speak from the anthropologists, some warmed-over demographic nonsense from the TV guy, routine middle-aged grumpiness from the art teacher, and from me what they no doubt regarded as academic pedantry (I seem to remember quoting Leibniz at one point, for instance). Our leader—or facilitator, as he was naturally called—was a lean, athletic man named Mike who put us through our paces by splitting us into groups and demanding point-form characterizations of the twenty-something generation. Mike was one of those intense, weedy guys who probably runs marathons for fun and wears iron-rim glasses to make himself look more intellectual. He used the word *antidises-tablishmentarianism* several times, always incorrectly, to mean anti-establishment feeling. He scribbled things on a flip chart with a felt-tipped marker.

We spent the whole day doing this, adding up impressions from numerous different angles: what do they desire, what do they fear, what do they buy? I felt we had said all the interesting things there were to say by about eleven o'clock, but still we were driven on, through lunch and into the afternoon. By about two o'clock the absurdity of the enterprise, which had never been far from view, began to overwhelm me. It was becoming obvious, every time we groped toward a valid generalization about people eighteen to twenty-nine, that the very idea of a generation with a coherent and isolable identity is one of our flimsiest and most harmful social constructions. In every case, a sweeping statement ("This generation craves material success") had to be qualified and massaged beyond any sustaining interest, threatening at times to fold the project up like a cheap pup tent, leaving only the banal truth that *folks is sure different.* Other times we were confronted by bald contradictions, which is exactly what had happened when I polled my twenty-something friends in preparation for the session: confident but anxious, materialistic but spiritual, cynical but full of hope, libertine but conservative.

The demographic apparatus was proving enormously unhelpful, too, despite recent claims from some malpracticing surgeons of the population-slice game that birth year accounts for two-thirds of what will happen to you. There is no doubt that Boom-generation annexation of resources has meant certain kinds of limitation for people like me and those who are younger, and I still harbor dark fantasies about one day picking up a secondhand SS-20 from some cash-poor Armenians and dropping it on one of the eastern seaboard enclaves where the Boomers might be thought to be concentrated, but I doubt that being part of what Douglas Coupland called Generation X is really a decisive factor in my character or actions. The semantic extension of the term has been stretched out of all recognition: it no longer applies exclusively to the early-1960s cadre of post- or late-Boom kids who grew up on *Welcome Back, Kotter* and *Star Wars,* but has been extended to people as many as ten years younger. At the same time, this stretching has worked to distort Coupland's suggestions that late-twenties adults incline to world-weary confusion and thwarted romanticism, transforming that feeling, instead, into something altogether more passive, and boring, in the form of "slacker" or "mall-rat" stereotypes. It is probably true, for various reasons, that I have more in common culturally with someone who is twenty-four than I do with a home-owning, sedan-driving, forty-four-year-old father of three (I have no children and don't own a house), but I don't think seeing that fact in generational terms helps anybody or explains much.

In fact, I'm inclined to blame Coupland for a lot of this generational-sell nonsense. Not that he invented the idea of generational character, but, in trying to say something cool about the directionlessness of some twenty-somethings as they confronted the distant excesses of the mid-1980s, he unwittingly gave North American marketers a hook to hang their campaigns on. When the reaction to this naked grab at disposable income came, in the form of angry revisions of the media caricature by people who were, in fact, not Coupland's Gen-Xers at all but rather the younger siblings he had himself christened the denizens of Shampoo Planet, a reaction that mostly took the form of fervent denials of slackerhood, it just forced the marketers into increasingly desperate, and incoherent, follow-on labels: Generation Y, Generation Next, the Nexus Generation. In the resulting epistemological collapse, which was an identity crisis only in the sense that advertisers were momentarily confused about how to carve up the market's niches, the concept of generation was shown to be as manufactured and hallucinatory as zodiacal destiny or numerological determinism.

The problem is that we keep on buying in, or selling out, to it—and most often because the market-ruled world offers us no other choice. "The ultimate irony," one of the participants told me months afterward, when we had become friends, "is that I was sitting there

with this new master's degree in cultural studies and no money, trying to, you know, start some kind of career in consulting. And what
I was doing was helping people in their forties design campaigns so
they could sell my own ideas and identity back to me."

REACT AND RESIST

The paradox of all advertising is really the more basic paradox of
envy itself. The envious person takes no pleasure in what he already
possesses and feels only pain at the thought of what is possessed by
another. Envy is, moreover, activist in orientation: I fervently wish
that the other person did not possess the things I desire and would,
assuming no costs to myself in loss of status or infliction of punishment, take them away from him.[25] By creating envy, even if it is generalized and abstract rather than specific to a particular rival or
neighbor, advertising subverts its own stated intention of increasing
happiness in its consumers. Even in the paradigm case of advertising
that "works," which is to say a spot that forms in me a desire to buy
something which I then go out and actually buy, the sum total of created happiness can be neither large nor lasting. The relentlessness
of the ad barrage, the internal insistence on obsolescence and
replacement models, guarantees that any satisfaction achieved in
the realm of consumer goods is by nature fleeting. Sooner or later,
and usually sooner, I will be made to feel incomplete again because
I do not have something I see on television, something I begin to
believe in, however ironically, as part of the life I wish to be leading,
part of the life I suspect successful people elsewhere are leading,
part of what Pope called "my being's end and aim"—happiness.

Hence the incongruity. "[T]he only cure for envy in the case of
ordinary men and women is happiness," writes Russell, "and the difficulty is that envy is itself a terrible obstacle to happiness." Recent
economic evidence concerning the Consumer Price Index (CPI)
bears out the conclusion. It has become a commonplace that Americans were better off during the Golden Era affluence of the 1950s,

but a comparison of the facts is revealing. In 1950, when the median family income in 1994 dollars was a surprisingly low $18,000 (the same level is at about the 20th percentile today—that is, lower than 80 percent of the population), some 35 percent of homes lacked indoor plumbing, many people did not have telephones or cars, and of course most families did not possess a television set. Today it is unlikely that a family living even at the poverty line, which is set at about the 12th percentile, lacks a phone, running water, an indoor toilet and shower, or a color television set. They might even own a car. "Take into account improvements in the quality of many other products," the economist Paul Krugman writes, "and it does not seem at all absurd to say that the material standard of living of that poverty-level family in 1996 is as good as or better than that of the median family in 1950."[26] And yet the 1996 family is much more likely to be unhappy—to feel extremely poor and deprived, even bitter—in comparison to the national norms. "People don't just care about their absolute material level," Krugman says, "they care about their level *compared with others.*"

The implications of this finding (which has been obvious to everyone except a few economists for a long time) is that prosperity and happiness are not the same thing, which in turn lends support to a kind of radical egalitarianism that you are unlikely to see many people defending today: there would be more happiness if we evened out income levels, even if that meant lowering everyone's standard of living. "America in the 1950s was a middle-class society in a way that America in the 1990s is not," Krugman says. "That is, it had a much flatter income distribution, so that people had much more sense of sharing a common national lifestyle. And people in that relatively equal America felt good about their lives, even though by modern standards, they were poor—poorer...than we previously thought." Today, by contrast, while overall standards have risen in the traditional rising-tide-floats-all-boats manner of right-wing economic theory, the gap between "success" and "failure" is widening. "You could even argue that American society in the 1990s is an engine that maximizes consumption yet minimizes satisfaction,"

Krugman concludes. "Modern America is a hugely unequal society in which anyone can achieve success, but not many actually do. The result is that many—perhaps even most—people feel that they have failed to make the cut, no matter how comfortable their lives."

Maximum consumption, minimum satisfaction: the socioeconomic equivalent of junk food. The only way out of this bind without drastic economic overhaul—an unlikely prospect, for better or worse—is easy to state but not always so easy to achieve: forbearing from the uselessly comparative habit of mind that leads to disparaging judgments of one's own situation in the first place. This is a vice, says Russell, "partly moral, partly intellectual, which consists in seeing things never in themselves but only in their relations." My salary makes for a comfortable standard of living, yet it falls short of the level achieved by my less brilliant classmate. My wife is beautiful, but not as beautiful as the woman I see on the subway. This kind of comparison can, when linked to stronger reasons for fairness, lead to claims about justice: I do the same work as the other man, so why am I paid less? Hence the connection of envy to principles of democratic equality, and the political changes our century has witnessed in its attempts to render the social world one in which people should have less cause for envy. But that sort of genuine case for assessing one situation against another is a rarity when set next to the routine and endless comparisons of a less defensible kind, the kind that simply make me feel discontented with my lot for relative and not absolute reasons. Missing here is the calmness, the elimination of unnecessary and nagging restlessness, that contributes to well-being. "I should say," suggests a character in Michael Frayn's novel *A Landing on the Sun*, "that happiness is being where one is and not wanting to be anywhere else." [27]

Russell, a master of intellectual intensity and muscular good sense, thinks that the solution to all this is "mental discipline": thinking more clearly about what afflicts us. We may find his optimism in this regard of dubious value, but the neatness of his solution is worthy of admiration. "After all, what is more enviable than happiness?" he asks. "And if I can cure myself of envy I can acquire happiness and become enviable." But though Russell admits the pernicious influence of what he calls "propaganda" in realizing this goal, he could not have been aware of the all-encompassing power that the great envy-facilitators would have on our late-century consciousness. We might be inclined to say that envy is simply part of human nature, or more accurately of the basic forms of human life, but that does not deflect the question, which is this: Why do we subject ourselves to so much imagery and stimulation that has, as its unstated but obvious intention, the creation of envy, and thus unhappiness, in our minds? Why do we submit to the manufactured contentment of the consumer culture, which has the ultimate effect of manufacturing the contents of its own self-perpetuation: the cool-seeking, big-spending automatons of the shopping mall?

We are weak creatures.

5

On Earth as It Is in Heaven

Desire of Ease, and sensual delight, disposeth men to obey a common power.

—*Thomas Hobbes*, Leviathan

I T IS NOT ENOUGH, IN THE FACE OF THE ECONOMIC AND CULTURAL pressures of our times, simply to refuse the influence of envy in our strange psychologization—and pathologization—of both happiness and unhappiness. Even if we could, that refusal would leave a deeper problem unconsidered. For though we may feel some confidence in our ability to construct identities free of the influence of market and ideology (a confidence that may well prove misplaced or naive), we cannot forever avoid the issues raised by the extent to which our identities are embedded in social relations. Envy would not disappear even if we could, with a wave of the hand, destroy every ad agency and consumer durable in the world; nor would the problem of just how my happiness is related to yours. Can I be happy when you are not? More to the point, can I be happy when you are more so than I?

Putting individual happiness into our political visions has been an enduring preoccupation of the modern age, an attempt at accommodation that has become so distinctive, and defining, of the politics of the past half-millennium that we usually cannot fathom how things could be otherwise. At bottom, this project is born of the combination of a thoroughgoing physicalism, which conceives human beings primarily as pleasure/pain machines, and a desire to make sense of the happiness-seeking individual that this biological egalitarianism makes possible. The result is one of the most powerful machines of better living, the idea of the greatest happiness of the greatest number: the belief that the only possible justification for good actions, rules, or institutions—for social life itself—lies in a form of comparative calculation concerning people's degrees of happiness. At an extreme, this belief is not just a rule of thumb but a precisely calculable quantum which, in its apparently scientific way, represents an attempt to create a kind of earthly paradise of rationalized pleasure, social coordination, and algorithmic governance: a utopia of collective, complete, and constant happiness as vivid and enticing in prospect as any vision of heaven.

"No one can be perfectly happy," the forward-looking sociobiologist Herbert Spencer argued in the 1860s, "till all are happy." But some forms of happiness, like some kinds of victory, seem to depend precisely on invidious comparison, and the search for equality in happiness therefore contains within itself a nub of self-defeat. "It is better that some should be unhappy than that none should be happy," the more pragmatic Samuel Johnson had said a century earlier, "which would be the case in a general state of equality." Nietzsche was, typically, more pressing on the same point. How, he asks, do the weak and resentful exact their deepest revenge on the powerful? By means of envy raised to the level of a cultural force. "[T]hey succeed in *poisoning the consciences* of the fortunate with their own misery, with all misery," Nietzsche wrote in 1887, "so that one day the fortunate begin to feel ashamed of their good fortune and perhaps say to one another: 'it is disgraceful to be fortunate: *there is too much misery!*' But no greater or more calamitous misunderstanding is possible than for the happy, well-constituted, powerful in soul and body, to begin to doubt their *right to happiness* in this fashion. Away with this 'inverted world'! Away with this shameful emasculation of feeling!"[1]

THIS IS THE MATERIAL WORLD

Nietzsche's injunction is not liable to find favor with us today, at least not out loud. For, in writing the grand story of Western individuality, the triumphs of more than three centuries of taking each and every one of us seriously as individuals worthy of respect, we have in fact created a double-edged sword. At the same time as we rightly celebrate respect for the individual, we seem to make possible the pathologies of resentment and debased happiness. The ambition to build individual happiness into our political ideals, to make every person, morally and politically speaking, count for one—not more and not less—is a noble struggle constantly beset by the ineradicable differences among people and by some unpleasant facts about social psychology, not least that sometimes we want things *only because* other people have them. The struggle to manifest some version of the greatest-happiness principle as a political reality might be read as the history of modernity itself, the ever more technical attempts to realize the political ambitions of putting the individual first. But, even as our political ambition is rising in this way, our ideas of happiness seem to be reduced, cut down to size. Even as we expand the scope of political theory to include what look like general scientific principles, in an effort to make the messy realm of social life bend to rational will, we lose the richness and ethical stringency of eudaimonistic happiness.

Thomas Hobbes, considered one of the founding philosophers of modernity, is a key figure in this curiously twinned movement of elevation and truncation. Hobbes was born in England in 1588 when, as he later liked to say, news of the approaching Spanish Armada caused his mother to go into labor prematurely. He came to political theory late in his life, having spent the first forty years of it as a student and tutor to noblemen's sons. His first published work was a translation of Thucydides, completed in 1628, but travels on the Continent in the 1630s and an encounter with a copy of Euclid's *Elements* at a friend's home (Hobbes came across a theorem he could not understand, forcing him back to the definitions and postulates that showed it valid), sparked an interest in the possibilities of a science of society. Hobbes's relatively late entry into public discourse appears to have encouraged not modesty but, instead, a brand of intense middle-aged arrogance. The dedicatory letter to his *De Corpore Politico* (1644) captures the tone: "Galileus," he wrote, "was the first that opened to us the gate of natural philosophy universal, which is the knowledge of the nature of motion.... The science of man's body, the most profitable part of natural science, was first discovered with admirable sagacity by our countryman, Doctor Harvey. Natural philosophy is therefore but young; but civil philosophy is yet much younger, as being no older...than my own *de Cive*"—a work, it should be noted, that had been published just two years earlier.[2]

The first principle of Hobbes's science of society leans on Galileo's geometrical principles and posits that the universe is composed entirely of matter in motion. Even thoughts and memories— even imagination and dreams—are no more than conglomerations of material reality in particular local arrangements of "atoms." Hobbes was not the first to use this now-familiar word, but he was the first to offer a complete explanation of human life in exclusively atomic terms—that is, without reference to any reality beyond individual bits of matter, simple in themselves but sometimes arranged in complex ways. Even speech and emotion can be traced, Hobbes argued, to the material motions of smaller units of physical reality working in combination.

The second principle of this new science of motion was inspired by William Harvey and says that life itself is nothing more than "vital motion," just as, in Hobbes's own words, "the motion of the blood, perpetually circulating (as had been shown from many infallible signs and marks by Dr. Harvey, the first observer to it) in the veins and arteries." The brain, through the senses, detects the mechanical motion of objects in the external environment, and these acts of detection are themselves motions, which we call simple ideas. Simple ideas are, in turn, the building blocks of all more complex reasoning and of the apparently sophisticated processes of ratiocination. As the motions in the brain change over time, our thoughts recede as memories and, sometimes, disappear altogether.

Human beings themselves are also in motion, Hobbes argued, in that all human emotions, actions, and judgments are ruled by the two great passions of life: appetite, or the desire to increase pleasure; and aversion, or the desire to avoid pain. All states of mind, even the "highest" or "finest," have their ultimate source in increasingly fine-tuned combinations of simple appetite and aversion, covering everything from jealousy and love to moral evaluation. This point follows logically from the conclusion that thoughts themselves are material, for then mental states of all kinds can be reduced to constituent parts in the motion of an individual pleasure/pain machine. "[W]hatsoever is the object of any mans Appetite or Desire," Hobbes writes, "that is it, which he for his part calleth *Good:* And the object of his Hate, and Aversion, *Evill;* And of his Contempt, *Vile,* and *Inconsiderable.* For these words of Good, Evill, and Contemptible, are ever used with relation to the person that useth them."

Because humans are moved by their appetites and aversions, they are, Hobbes says, engaged in a constant search for power, which he defines as a person's "present means, to obtain some future apparent Good." Rational deliberation itself is no more than the calculation of the best means available for satisfaction of the desires, and the rational will is simply the ability to take the steps necessary for that satisfaction. Not only are appetites and aversions the single motive force in human affairs, they are also incessant and insistent. "Life it self is but Motion," Hobbes writes, "and can never be without Desire, nor without Feare, no more than without Sense." Which means, in other words, that humans are forever in pursuit of happiness, or what Hobbes chooses to call felicity, defining it this way: *"Continuall successe* in obtaining those things which a man from time to time desireth."

But of course such continual success is not likely, not simply because of the limitations of our individual constitutions but because of the existence of other appetitive humans, all of whom are necessarily in search of the same ability to satisfy desires—the same power—that we seek ourselves. Because my power might limit yours, and because we cannot assume that appetite is naturally limited in individuals (indeed, we can conclude from observation that it is without limit in some), conflict is the inevitable result of our pursuit of happiness. "I put for a generall inclination of all mankind," Hobbes sums up, "a perpetuall and restlesse desire of Power after power, that ceaseth only in Death."

The Hobbesian theory of human nature issues in the celebrated conjecture that humans once existed in a natural state where they were ruled entirely by these passions, a state without law or security. Unfettered by legal sanction, appetitive natural humans would attempt to increase their power, and hence their happiness, by control over the external world, including other humans. But because passions are unequal and incessant, this could only lead to a condition of what Hobbes called *bellum omnia omnes:* the war of all against all. In such a condition, with no authority higher than the insistent call of individual appetite, "every man has a Right to every thing; even to one anothers body." There is no morality in the state of nature, no justice, and no property; indeed there is no reality beyond the various operative appetites that issue in constant conflict, or fear of it.

"In such condition," Hobbes concludes, in one of the most famous passages in political theory,

> there is no place for Industry; because the fruit thereof is uncertain, and consequently no Culture of the Earth;...no Knowledge of the face of the Earth; no account of Time; no Arts; no Letters; no Society; and which is worst of all, continuall feare, and danger of violent death; And the life of man, solitary, poore, nasty, brutish, and short.

Natural humans are not unaware of the desperation of their condition, however, even though it would be impossible for them to imagine all that they are missing. The "continuall feare" they suffer forces them to the conclusion that the natural state is, for each of them, evil. "[S]o long a man is in the condition of meer Nature, (which is a condition of War,) as private Appetite is the measure of Good, and Evill," Hobbes writes, "and consequently all men agree on this, that Peace is good."

So they agree to surrender all their natural rights to the pursuit of happiness—with the sole exception of the right of self-defense—in order to create a common authority that can enforce the regulations necessary to constrain power. This common authority is, Hobbes argued, a Leviathan, a fear-born sovereign who, like the biblical creature of that name, is a man composed of many men. Individuals are not subsumed by the common authority; rather, they give life to it. While clearly motivated by the fear of violent death, the original contract of Hobbes's political theory represents a rational calculation of self-interest—an assessment of the prospects for happiness—by each of the individuals involved. They offer their consent to this contract, and retain their individuality in so doing. Indeed, the title page of the 1651 edition of Hobbes's *Leviathan* goes so far as to depict the philosophically crowned new king as a huge sword-and mace-wielding man presiding over a landscape of town and country, his body—that is, the body politic, the original civic corporation—composed of the individual bodies of a multitude, who have transferred their power to him for their own greater good.

It is tempting, sometimes, to think of ourselves exclusively in Hobbesian terms. My desires are purely my own, I say to myself, and need no justification beyond my having them. Happiness is nothing other than the satisfaction of those desires. So you, taking up two seats on the bus with your fat butt when I want to sit down, are blocking the satisfaction of my desire to sit down. My happiness is thwarted by you—unless I have the power, the present means, to move you over. That might involve fighting you, but it is more likely to involve my invoking the presumed authority of the rules of public space, themselves in turn backed up by larger structures of social authority like the police, the courts, and ultimately, Congress. So I ask you to move over because, after all, the seats are for everybody. (Actually, in my case—at least if I'm not on Prozac—it is more likely to involve standing there fuming ineffectually. On Prozac, I would be likely to get a little more violent; there might be shoving.) We all appeal, now and then, to the multipronged apparatus of social control when conflict between persons—between rival programs of happiness, we could say—is threatened. The shared background of civil authority is our version of Leviathan, our mutual contract to control the rampant desires that would, unchecked, toss us back into a state where life is solitary, poor, nasty, brutish, and short.

The advantage of this Hobbesian view of society is that it allows each of us to pursue the good life as we see it, free of overarching control: whatever makes you happy is perfectly okay, consistent of course with the same right granted to everybody else. The disadvantage is that social life is reduced to a state of suspended conflict, and happiness is reduced to nothing more than instrumental satisfaction of desire.

THE PURSUIT OF HAPPINESS

In many ways, Hobbes's hedonistic physicalism is at the root of modern confusion over the nature of happiness, our continuing inability to make sense of desire and its consequences. Hobbes's confidence that science held the key to solving all moral and political problems is also a significant advance in the idea that happiness is susceptible to technological intervention, a first important move in the drive toward creating machines of better living. For Hobbes and his followers, society itself is a kind of happiness machine: necessarily imperfect in satisfying all of our desires, perhaps, but nevertheless the best available choice, since the free-for-all alternative of the state of nature can result only in pain and death.

"The replacement of the power of the individual by the power of a community constitutes the decisive step of civilization," Sigmund Freud wrote in *Civilization and Its Discontents,* almost three hundred years after Hobbes first mentioned the idea. "The essence of it lies in the fact that the members of the community restrict themselves in their possibilities of satisfaction, whereas the individual knew no such restrictions." The various subsocial mechanisms of happiness we subsequently adopt—the goods and therapies, the drink and sex and food we so desperately crave, as well as the laws and norms, the diets and regimens, we use to curb excessive appetites—are really just fine-tuning of our desires within the larger constraint of being in society in the first place.

The links become more obvious as we note the powerful historical progression. John Locke, a philosopher who mimicked Hobbes in speculating about the presocial condition of humankind, argued for a similar social contract, but (among other differences) distinguished between the state of nature and the state of war, played down the role of fear in the move from nature to society, and wanted a government much more limited than the absolute monarchy of Hobbes's Leviathan. Locke, a Whig apologist writing against monarchical tyranny in the 1690s, believed in the natural freedom of men—and it *was* men, for him—and their natural right to hold property. "Whatsoever [a man] removes out of the state that nature hath provided, and left it in," he writes in the *Second Treatise of Government,* "he hath mixed his *labour* with, and joined it to something that is his own, and thereby makes it his *property.* " Men, while being naturally free, according to Locke, are also naturally rational about their self-interest—the two conditions are closely linked—and they soon see the threat of war as sufficient warrant to enter into a civil society, which acts more as umpire than monarch. "Those who are united into one body, and have a common established law and judicature to appeal to, with authority to decide controversies between them, and punish offenders, are in *civil society* with one another," Locke says, "and all this for the preservation of the property of all the members of that society, as far as is possible."[3]

The individualism secured by these philosophical efforts—the notion of the rational person as inextricable from his or her freedom to pursue a good life, however conceived—is one of the triumphs of the early modern age. It is the main achievement of classical liberalism and a dominating theory of human nature still. The high-flown philosophical speculation of the seventeenth century helped to produce the revolutionary fervor of the eighteenth, and then the inhabitants of the nineteenth century attempted to hammer out, in ever more elaborate detail, the bridge between the inner republic of Locke's individual to the outer republic of actual societies. Hobbes's physicalism about desire and Locke's notion of civil society as a defense of private property have therefore had a profound effect on our thinking about politics and happiness. Indeed, from this new, scientific point of view, the justification for government and law, even for morality itself, lies centrally in the notion of the greatest happiness of the greatest number. And while the notion of using calculations of happiness to justify ethical and political decisions is usually associated with the nineteenth-century utilitarian school, it actually has older intellectual and political roots—as old, according to some people, as Socrates's defense of a species of greatest-happiness principle in Plato's *Protagoras,* but certainly traceable to Hobbes in the mid-seventeenth century and to Locke's reduction of happiness to pleasure a few decades later.[4]

In 1774, some sixty years before the utilitarian theorist Jeremy Bentham attempted to defend his "felicific calculus," the rational quantification of individual desires and their satisfaction, Josiah Quincy Jr. stated as a general principle that the object of civil society "is the greatest happiness of the greatest number."[5] Thomas Jefferson agreed, arguing in a letter that the only aim of government is "to secure the greatest degree of happiness possible to the general mass of those associated under it."[6] And in 1776, John Adams summed up the vibrant American strain of proto-utilitarian thinking this way:

> Upon this point all speculative politicians will agree, that the happiness of society is the end of government, as all divines and moral philosophers will agree that the happiness of the individual is the end of man. From this principle it will follow that the form of government which communicates ease, comfort, security, or, in one word, happiness, to the greatest number of persons, and in the greatest degree, is the best.[7]

To which historian Howard Mumford Jones adds the important gloss that "[t]he only difficulty in this admirable sentiment is to determine whether the greatest happiness of the population is gained by insuring the private (and contradictory) happiness of individuals or by subordinating the individual's pursuit of happiness to some larger social aim." Freud was even more withering about the problems of reconciling the personal and the political when it comes to contentment: "It almost seems as if the creation of a great human community would be most successful if no attention had to be paid to the happiness of the individual."

That, indeed, is the rub. The greatest-happiness principle does not, finally, solve the problem of how the discrete individual will relate, in practice, to the community of which he or she is necessarily a part. And the ongoing potential for conflict can be obscured by the apparent nobility of statements like Adams's, which elevate social feeling even as they allow happiness to slip imperceptibly to a kind of lowest-common-denominator pleasure seeking. Yet the American Founding Fathers, who went furthest in putting the political theory of happiness into practice, did not much concern themselves with the problem. They were mainly followers of John Locke, and because of their Lockean ideas, the young American republic became a focal point for the task of creating the first genuinely individualist society, one based on the natural rights of all people (or at least landowners) to satisfy their desires. Here, after all, the right to pursue happiness was considered so important it had been written into one of the founding documents of the society.

Yet the distance between philosophical ideas and political reality, the gap between political rhetoric and constitutional practice, quickly became apparent. "In asserting the right to pursue happiness or to pursue and obtain happiness and safety, the eighteenth-century men asserted an absolute they failed to define," Jones writes of this noble American experiment. "For them the common sense of the matter was sufficient, and that which is sufficient requires neither casuistry nor metaphysics to defend it. But what seemed self-evident in the Age of Reason sometimes becomes ambiguous in the

Age of Anxiety." It is perhaps odd for us to hear that someone as clever as Jefferson should have failed to define a term that was so important to the structure of thought underpinning the American political experiment; and yet it is true. And it is instructive to identify the causes of this blind spot. There was indeed a self-evident character to the notions of happiness employed by Jefferson, Adams, and their contemporaries. That is not the real problem. The real problem is that these notions of happiness were elitist, propertarian, and exclusive.

Like Locke before them, the Founding Fathers were jealous of their private property and anxious to enshrine political structures that would safeguard it. They were convinced that Locke was right in asserting a natural right to property, whereby the land with which I mix my labor becomes mine, and government's first task was to preserve by law what I already possessed by natural right. So happiness in the first instance involved ownership, in particular the ownership of land. The natural right to property was itself part of a larger view of the universe as operating according to some kind of rational plan, the divine providence of the deistic worldview that certain influential European philosophers such as Leibniz and Spinoza had defended from the 1670s onward.

According to optimistic deism (a dubious philosophical and theological position that would later be viciously parodied), all things happened according to God's plan, even if He did not intervene directly in human affairs. There was a natural abundance of resources on this earth but not necessarily equal shares of these for everyone, since, though all are created equal, some work harder than others and greater labor does lead to greater prosperity. The righteous must, as the Scriptures suggest, benefit both spiritually and materially from their Christian virtue. Because natural law, including the right to property and the pursuit of happiness itself, is actually part of a larger divine law, humans will secure happiness when (and only when) they conform to universal reason—when they live in accordance with the clockwork mechanisms of the God-given universe, which can be rationally perceived. Commerce is not incompatible with God's will, in this way of looking at things; indeed, since God helps those who help themselves, the wider the profit margin the better when it comes to one's standing in God's eyes.

That is some of the intellectual and theological background in play in the pursuit-of-happiness language to be found in American political rhetoric—background that can, with variations, still be perceived in the work ethic, Christian self-righteousness, and hands-off property mania of contemporary American culture. But the Founders also projected another ideal with even older roots, drawing on a tradition of civic virtue that goes back at least to Cicero and Cato. This was the idea of the man of property as a man of public service who preferred quiet retirement on his updated version of the Sabine farm (the ancient ideal of a self-sufficient agricultural estate) but would rise to the challenge if called to help his community. There is something valuable in this idea, to be sure, but the bucolic vision of the Founders was dominated by an exclusivity and elitism they apparently could not, or would not, see.

This is Benjamin West, of Providence, writing in 1765 of "The Wish" he harbored for his own happiness:

> A small Estate, some hundred Pounds a Year,
> From Taxes, Tithes, and such Incumbrance, clear;
> A little Cottage, on a rising Ground,
> With nothing useless in it to be found:
> I'd chuse to have it front the Noon-Day's Sun,
> And not far distant from a neighb'ring Town,
> With some few Acres round it to supply
> What's just sufficient for the Family—[8]

Well, who wouldn't want a little cottage on rising ground and a few acres? Some friends of mine recently bought one in the Caledon Hills near Toronto—for close to half a million dollars. The deceptive simplicity of this vision is its most striking feature, the presumption of a superabundance of land and wealth its essential precondition. John Adams, Benjamin Franklin, Benjamin Church,

William Smith, and George Washington all expressed similar desires in the 1780s and '90s. The last wrote of his home at Mount Vernon in 1797 that "I am once more seated under my own Vine and fig tree, and hope to spend the remainder of my days, which in the ordinary course of things (being in my Sixty-sixth year) cannot be many, in peaceful retirement, making political pursuits yield to the more rational amusement of cultivating the Earth."[9] Here, the project of cultivating one's garden—an activity urged by the disillusioned Candide at the end of Voltaire's satire, a kind of keep-it-simple imperative to preempt useless speculation—is decidedly not an alternative to the dangerous optimism of Leibniz's best-of-all-possible-worlds deistic theory. It is, instead, a blithe accompaniment to it.

Perhaps worst was Thomas Jefferson himself, who in 1810 wrote to a friend about the quiet, happy life he enjoyed at his personal estate. "I am retired to Monticello," he said,

> where, in the bosom of my family, and surrounded by my books, I enjoy a repose to which I have long been a stranger. My mornings are devoted to correspondence. From breakfast to dinner, I am in my shops, my garden, or on horseback among my farms; from dinner to dark, I give to society and recreation with my neighbours and friends; and from candle light to early bed-time, I read. My health is perfect; and my strength considerably reinforced by the activity of the course I pursue....I talk of ploughs and harrows and seeding and harvesting, with my neighbours, and of politics too, if they choose, with as little reserve as the rest of my fellow citizens, and feel, at length, the blessing of being able to say and do what I please.[10]

No mention, here, of the slaves who served him meals in that house, or worked the land that produced the food in them. No mention that only a handful of Americans could afford, or even imagine owning, an estate as grand as Monticello, with its neoclassical details and expensive library. Do I simply begrudge Jefferson his wealth? Is this merely envy talking? Perhaps, but there is surely something a little offensive about the great advocate of political equality going on about his privileges as if they were within the grasp of everyone, if only they had the wisdom to pursue true happiness.[11]

These sylvan idylls, the visions of well-heeled rustic domesticity, are the unquestioned purpose and end of the idea of freedom and contentment championed by the Founders. The *limits* of the pursuit of happiness never really arise as political questions for them because they simply take it for granted that everybody wants what they want—and could have it if they so chose. And of course this romantic vision of countrified ease and plainness is still very much with us, in the form of a rarefied cult of gardening and verdant ease that is rooted, as it were, in the now long-standing tradition of patrician self-congratulation on one's enviable simplicity of mind. "True happiness is of a retired Nature," the essayist Joseph Addison wrote in *The Spectator* in the 1780s,

> and an Enemy to Pomp and Noise; it arises, in the first place, from the Enjoyment of ones self; and, in the next, from the Friendship and Conversation of a few select Companions. It loves Shades and Solitude, and naturally haunts Groves and Fountains, Fields and Meadows: In short, it feels every thing it wants within it self, and receives no Addition from Multitudes of Witnesses and Spectators.[12]

There is wisdom here—I would be the last to deny it. But retirement is a luxury the majority of us can scarcely afford, and it carries, moreover, a hint of passivity that is alien to the activist notion of happiness as a form of ethical and political engagement that leads to rational satisfaction.

The pastoral vision remains in American cultural life even when the obvious aristocratic features of its earliest versions are shorn away by the growing democratization of life in the New World. Remains, and indeed flourishes, producing a more egalitarian growth in the new green sprout of nineteenth-century American

Romanticism, the intense Emersonian and Thoreauvian daydreaming of "Self-Reliance" or *Walden.* "I look on that man as happy," said Emerson, "who, when there is a question of success, looks into his work for a reply, not into the market, not into opinion, not into patronage."[13] Thoreau, with his bean fields and wood-splitting in the sojourn at Walden Pond, would have agreed. "Every morning was a cheerful invitation to make my life of equal simplicity, and I may say innocence, with Nature herself," wrote the sage of Concord.

> I went to the woods because I wanted to live deliberately, to front only the essential facts of life, and see if I could not learn what it had to teach, and not, when I came to die, discover that I had not lived.... I wanted to live deep and suck out all the marrow of life, to live so sturdily and Spartan-like as to put to rout all that was not life, to cut a broad swath and shave close, to drive life into a corner, and reduce it to its lowest terms.[14]

Bracing stuff. And in the hands of the English Lake District poets, the same regard for simple earthly delights produced some of the most enduring, and beautiful, lyric verse in the language.

There is nevertheless something false even here, a new form of soulful, poetic elitism erected in place of the more straightforward economic superiority of Washington, Jefferson, and their peers. Thoreau's protests and little expense-accounts to the contrary (the charm of his text lies in these details, rendered with such joyous scrupulousness), the Walden experiment strikes me as somewhat self-indulgent. It smacks of the idealization of a Nature that is more man-made than we sometimes realize. The idea of the natural is itself, paradoxically, an artificial device, a social construction. Our notions of "getting back to nature" and "savoring the environment" are conditioned by a rich literature of social expectation, desire, and argument that are precisely not natural. Nature makes no sense, in this context, except as the encompassed opposite of Civilization, Thoreau's antlike society of men leading "lives of quiet desperation." Nature as we typically conceive it has much more in common with the garden—a small portion of wildness controlled, domesticated, brought inside the purview of the social—than it does with anything genuinely outside human society.

"Americans have a deeply ingrained habit of seeing nature and culture as irreconcilably opposed," writes the essayist Michael Pollan:

> we automatically assume that whenever one gains, the other must lose. Forced to choose, we usually opt for nature (at least in our books). This choice, which I believe is a false one, is what led Thoreau and his descendants out of the garden.... But my experience in the garden leads me to believe that there are many important things about our relation to nature that *cannot* be learned in the wild.[15]

And that is to assume what may sometimes be doubted, namely, that we might experience such a thing as "the wild" at all beyond what we are preconditioned to expect: the way nature films and photography, for example, falsely condition us to expect a wilderness of nearly constant animal movement, sometimes produced only with the aid of powerful telephoto lenses, prolonged exposure that is collapsed into a few minutes of film, or we are given staged images involving drugged leopards or common ferrets with feet painted to resembled a rarer species.[16] It can begin to seem that every celebration of Nature, every attempt to get natural, is already a socially conditioned experience.

This is not a popular view, or one that is easy to communicate. I remember having a fierce, protracted discussion with one of the other attendees at the Option Institute, a computer programmer from San Francisco named Jory, who asserted that her true happiness was always to be found in nature. When I suggested that her ideas of the natural were suffused by social expectation, by a long-standing Romanticism, she was not so much unimpressed as baffled: What was I talking about? Well, of course there *is* something lovely about smelling pine trees, hearing the lap of waves against the rocks of a Muskoka lake, hearing the soul-stirring plaintiveness of the loon. But we should never mistake it for anything other than a cultural experience, conditioned in dozens of ways by (among other things) my social expectations of the "uplifting" quality of the experience; my exposure to various literary geniuses, including Thoreau and Wordsworth and Cato; even other aesthetic moments that creep into my consciousness, like a sudden flash of Monet's sun-sparkled water or a memory of Turner's golden sunsets (for it is sometimes said that Turner invented the sunset). As Oscar Wilde famously argued, what is remarkable is not that art imitates life, but that life imitates art.

He also said, rather witheringly, that "anybody can be good in the country"—something Thoreau should perhaps have given more thought to.

These problems aside, how did the idea that one has a right to pursue happiness actually work its way into American culture? How did we get from the philosophical heights of eighteenth-century rhetoric to the dismal technological imperatives of the Prozac culture?

Well, that is a cultural story, but it is also a legal one. The problem faced by members of the American republic in its first century was that, though cherished as an "unalienable" right in the Declaration of Independence, along with life and liberty, the pursuit of happiness appears nowhere in the U.S. Constitution itself and therefore is not law. A number of cases during the nineteenth century grappled with the issue, using some inventive legal reasoning to bring the right to pursue happiness within the legal fold and, at the same time, give it substance. The most influential of these are, first, an 1855 Supreme Court of Indiana decision to strike down a prohibition law and, second, a trio of antimonopoly arguments known as the Louisiana Slaughterhouse Cases of 1869, 1872, and 1883.[17] The arguments deployed in these cases come up against, and then vault over, the apparently insuperable problem of providing legal protection to a right that does not, strictly speaking, actually have legal expression.

Personally, I rather like the fact that the right to pursue happiness was first defended in terms of the right to drink homemade liquor. The Indiana judges engaged in a fine denunciation of governmental paternalism and suggested, rather unconvincingly, that the life, liberty, and pursuit of happiness provisions of the Declaration are anterior to the Constitution but understood to be, as Jefferson himself said, self-evident. That is, they are matters of natural law so obvious as to be common sense. On this shaky basis these judges argued, you might say spiritedly,

> that the right of liberty and pursuing happiness secured by the constitution, embraces the right, for each *compos mentis* individual, of selecting what he will eat and drink, in short, his beverages, so far as he may be capable of producing them, or they may be within his reach, and that the legislature cannot take away that right by direct enactment. If the constitution does not secure this right to the people, it secures nothing of value.

The decision went on to describe the terrible slippery slope of state-directed fascism that prohibition threatened.

> If the people are subjected to be controlled by the legislature in the matter of their beverages, so they are as to their articles of dress, and in their hours of sleeping and waking. And if the people are incompetent to select their own beverages, they are also incompetent to determine anything in relation to their living, and should be placed at once in a state of pupilage to a set of government sumptuary officers; eulogies upon the dignity of human nature should cease; and the doctrine of the competency of the people for self-government should be declared a deluding rhetorical flourish.[18]

Now that's the kind of language you just don't hear in judicial decisions any more.

The response of the Louisiana judges a few decades later was more measured but no less legally resourceful. They used the anti-slavery provisions of the newly accepted Fourteenth Amendment, as well as passing references to Adam Smith's well-known injunction in *The Wealth of Nations* that the right to property is sacred and invio-lable, to argue that the right to happiness must include the right to follow a chosen profession. This natural right, they said, included the exclusive right of a corporate body such as the Butchers Union Live-Stock Landing and Slaughterhouse Company, an entity consid-ered to be in law not unlike a person, to make interstate contracts. (This decision, reached in 1883 in the third Slaughterhouse Case, overturned the 1872 judgment, which found for the individual's right to free employment as part of the right to happiness, and therefore declared the butchers' monopoly illegal.) Not only was this an odd, even outrageous, use of the Fourteenth Amendment, which does not mention inalienable rights or happiness and obvi-ously wasn't written to protect white business interests, but it was scarcely constitutional under any even mildly scrupulous interpreta-tion of the law. It also showcased the lurking fundamental problem of bringing happiness into law: mine and yours might not be in har-mony, especially if I am an independent butcher looking for work and you are a member of a consortium of butchers protecting a monopoly.

Still, as one later commentator has wryly noted, "[t]he butchers of New Orleans seem to have awakened American litigants to the rich possibility inherent in felicity." There was soon a boom of right-to-happiness cases, each more confusing than the last. In the latter nineteenth and early twentieth century, American courts were asked to hand down judgments on how the inalienable right to happiness might justify, among other things, smoking opium, carrying a pistol, selling liquor, using trading stamps, selling contraceptives, spraying citrus fruit with pesticides, sterilizing imbeciles, telling fortunes, divorcing an epileptic, and licensing both plumbers and prosti-tutes.[19] At different times and in different locales, these courts and the learned judges who sit in them found happiness something that only the state could secure, for instance in public education and welfare provisions; and something that individuals must vigorously safeguard from the intrusions of the state, as in the ability to make free contracts, eat and drink without interference, and fire employees at will.

On balance, and to nobody's surprise, the individual won out over the community when it came to happiness. "In some sense," Howard Mumford Jones says, "the norm of happiness being no longer determined by an elite (of whom Jefferson was characteristic), one can say that the concept of happiness has been democratized in proportion as the causes of unhappiness have been popularized, but that this concept has not yet acquired legal or constitutional force." Though never completely enshrined in law, in other words, the pursuit of happiness has become a cornerstone of American culture—and now, with the rise of global marketing, of most other world cultures. At the same time, Thoreau's idea that genuine happiness is antithetical to commerce and the hive-dwelling busyness of everyday life—is, indeed, a flight from that world— gained a strong hold on the imagination, creating a kind of cultural split personality: we support a growing industry of happiness, but we persist in understanding happiness as a refusal of the imperatives of industry. This is the same paradox, or a similar version of it, that afflicted me during my sojourn at happy camp, when I was suddenly so conscious of the controlling mechanisms meant to foster self-expression there, and the judgmental quality of the injunction not to judge. It is the same paradox that became evident in the combined puritanism and licentiousness of the culture's attitudes to food and drink, the confusion of a society in which people spend more and more on weight-loss products even as they get fatter by the year.

The problem lies in conceiving happiness as primarily individual, a view that cannot but encourage the idea that self-expression is self-fulfillment, and therefore that happiness means primarily an unfettered exploration of my own desires. These desires must then, sooner or later, come into conflict with the desires of others, and the resulting unhappiness will begin to seem intolerable, and maybe, as

I suggested earlier, pathological. Hence the many mechanisms operative in the current therapeutic culture. We all want to know why we are not happy, because we feel, American or not, that we have a *right* to be so: what has gone wrong? So we consult a psychotherapist or seek a prescription or drive to the shopping mall in search of... what? Our deeper selves? Our authentic identities? Or just the transient pleasures of servicing a desire, the quiet desperation of momentarily quieting a craving that can only grow stronger with every concession to its power. Indeed, entire consumer-goods and entertainment industries are predicated on their putative ability to satisfy the right to be happy, while other industries, like psychotherapy, no less commercial or opportunistic, try to make us understand why we continually feel that the right to happiness has not been satisfied in any complete or lasting way. Just to the extent that these offerings of goods and services *are* industries, however, and industries are always composed of mechanisms both literal and figurative, as solutions to our longings they can only be ensnared in a contradiction: here, the means of cure become the elements of infection. The presumed solution is now part of the problem. More than this, the artificiality and superficiality of the mechanisms of happiness-provision begin to create bastard notions of happiness: the cheap thrills and manufactured adrenaline of extreme recreation or the perpetual dissatisfaction of the perennial psychotherapeutic client.

Despite their limitations, these ideas of happiness dominate our cultural experience to such an extent that we cannot see, or perhaps choose not to see, that their very fleetingness is a sad comment on the distance we have fallen even from the elite Sabine ideals of Washington and Jefferson.

BIPOLAR UTILITY

Here is a story that I first heard from my academic adviser at Yale, a voluble law professor called Bruce Ackerman who, among other excellent qualities, bore a passing resemblance to Groucho Marx.[20]

There are two people, Manic and Depressive, in dispute over a certain amount of a malleable substance called manna, a form of good that everybody wants because it can be turned into anything. Manic will convert the manna into the joyful thrills of mountain climbing; Depressive will use it to engage in philosophical reflection. Now it happens that Manic is so constituted that he will generate ten times as much pleasure out of the same quantity of manna as Depressive will: one hundred units of utility, or "utiles," of subjective satisfaction from mountain climbing, compared to Depressive's ten from the painful work of philosophy. There are a couple of possible reasons why this may be so. The first involves no deep issue, just a physiological fact: it could be that Manic's hard-wiring is simply more efficient at turning resources into pleasure. He is a better engine of utility than Depressive, for reasons that have nothing to do with what he chooses to do—we all know people who seem to get more pleasure than others out of the same activities. On the other hand, there could be a more controversial implication in the difference between Manic and Depressive: the difference is not between them but between their choices. It may be, in other words, that, regardless of individual constitution, mountain climbing is, as an activity, just better at generating happiness *in anybody* than philosophizing is.

Who should get the disputed manna? If we are being utilitarian, the answer must be Manic. Why? Well, assume, as Ackerman does, that we have a computer that can calculate the precise utility—the amount of subjective satisfaction—a given person will enjoy from the use of a given chunk of resources. This computer, modeled on Jeremy Bentham's ideal of a perfect felicific calculus, can smooth out all differences of taste and inclination with an elaborate comparison of the duration, intensity, and proximity of pleasure in order to produce a single figure, on a single scale, that allows comparison of any discrete experience.[21]

Were we able to do this (most people, including even the most committed contemporary utilitarians, acknowledge that we probably are not), we could evaluate any and all disputes of the Manic-

Depressive kind by a simple nod to the numbers. And in such a case, Manic's one hundred utiles of pleasure must trump Depressive's ten, giving him not only a stronger personal claim on the manna but also an ethical one, for the ideal of the greatest happiness of the greatest number demands that we maximize the number of utiles generated from available resources.

The reason this result strikes us as abominable goes beyond the difficulties of interpersonal happiness comparison: the reason it would be wrong to give in to Manic's claim is not simply a matter of lacking the relevant technology of measurement. It is, rather, that there is something politically nugatory about a standard of distribution that relies on a common yardstick of subjective satisfaction. That is the most obvious and most serious problem with the happiness-driven theory of utilitarianism, the great product of nineteenth-century optimism about the scientific basis of ethical and political decision-making—an optimism that was born two centuries earlier in the physicalism of Hobbes. Even if it were true that mountain climbing always generates more happiness than philosophy, regardless of the physiology of the compared persons, it would be an error to think that this means mountain climbing is always preferable to philosophy. That is the sort of crude utilitarian thinking that leads to the infamous conclusion that the child's game of pushpin is as good as poetry. Indeed, we could go further and say, with some confidence, that following this logic pushpin is probably superior to poetry.

John Stuart Mill, the precocious son of Bentham's friend and associate James Mill, was aware of this problem of reductionism in the idea of utility. In his famous essay *Utilitarianism,* the younger Mill tried to remedy the problem by introducing the notion of *quality* into the assessment of satisfaction. Mill agreed without much argument that the only rational end of human life was happiness understood as pleasure. "The creed which accepts as the foundation of morals 'utility' or the 'greatest happiness principle,'" he wrote,

> holds that actions are right in proportion as they tend to promote happiness, wrong as they tend to produce the reverse

of happiness. By happiness is intended pleasure and the absence of pain; by unhappiness, pain and the privation of pleasure.[22]

This accords with Bentham's earlier definition of happiness as "enjoyment of pleasures, security from pains."[23] Yet Mill could not bring himself to conceive of pleasure as simply the satisfaction of base appetites. "Human beings have faculties more elevated than the animal appetites and, when once made conscious of them, do not regard anything as happiness which does not include their gratification," he said. "[T]here is no known Epicurean theory of life which does not assign to the pleasures of the intellect, of the feelings and imagination, and of the moral sentiments a much higher value as pleasures than to those of mere sensation."

And this is true. Even Epicurus himself, whose name has come to be associated with the dedicated, even reckless, pursuit of pleasure, especially sensual pleasure, had a harder ethical center than we tend to imagine. His notion of what is apparently a quantitative hedonism—gain as much pleasure as possible—seems to edge toward a qualitative idea of happiness, even a eudaimonistic theory of happiness as virtue. Indeed, in this his ideas resemble the sophisticated theory of the younger Mill, who said that when it comes to the virtues as a way to create happiness, "the means have become a part of the end, and a more important part of it than any of the things which they are means to. What was once desired as an instrument for the attainment of happiness has come to be desired for its own sake. In being desired for its own sake it is, however, desired as *part* of happiness."

Justice, for example, which is ultimately defended by Mill because it generates more happiness than injustice, may come to seem a quality that we desire without the intermediate calculation of its social utility: we just think it is good to be just. Despite some intemperate language that apparently argues the opposite view, then—"I spit on the fine and those who emptily admire it, when it doesn't make any pleasure"[24]—Epicurus actually has a considered view similar to Mill's: namely, that when it comes to pleasure and virtue, one entails the other. "It is not possible to live pleasantly without living intelligently and finely and justly," Epicurus says, "nor to live intelligently and finely and justly without living pleasantly. If a person lacks the conditions for living intelligently and finely and justly, it is impossible for him to live pleasantly."[25]

That sounds good—and true—but these considerations of quality and virtue in the theory of happiness can bring difficulties of their own. When happiness is said to entail virtue, for example, it is immediately open to familiar arguments: whose virtue, and according to what standard? The advantage of simple happiness, by contrast, as an ethical yardstick is precisely that it seems beyond such questions, universally applicable and unarguable as a motive force in human affairs. That, after all, was why Bentham and the other early utilitarians were so keen on happiness: it was impossible to deny its centrality. We all want happiness and we all want as much of it as possible, so making the greatest-happiness principle central to ethical and political decision-making seems an obvious move. Terrific—but then we find that we cannot compare my happiness to yours, or even one form of happiness with another. We are quickly reduced to the familiar position of a stalemate, which forces the conclusion that *de gustibus non est disputandum:* there is no accounting for, and no arguing with, taste. I always recall, for instance, the frustration I felt during a late-night pub conversation with my graduate-school roommate in Edinburgh, a Manchester native named Anjam, in which I tried without success (but with mounting irritation) to convince him that Bach's Brandenburg Concertos were aesthetically superior to "Hungry Like the Wolf" by Duran Duran.

Mill's answer to this problem of potential stalemate is that the person who knows only the lower pleasures has to bow to the judgment of the person who knows the higher ones as well. In *Utilitarianism* he writes:

> If one of the two [pleasures] is, by those who are competently acquainted with both, placed so far above the other

that they prefer it, even though knowing it to be attended with a greater amount of discontent, and would not resign it for any quantity of the other pleasure which their nature is capable of, we are justified in ascribing to the preferred enjoyment a superiority in quality so far outweighing quantity as to render it, in comparison, of small account.

In other words, "higher" happiness might involve a certain amount of discontent—as when we suffer to create art, say—but the depth of that happiness is such that no counterbalancing quantity of content could ever be enough to tip the scales the other way: quality eventually trumps quantity.

But by drawing this (otherwise valid) distinction between happiness and contentment, Mill has taken away with his left hand what he gave us with the right, collapsing the distinction that separated him from Bentham and, incidentally, reducing the intuitive appeal of the utilitarians' original resort to happiness as an ethical principle. Pretty soon the issue begins to resolve itself into two, equally unattractive choices. Either we accept Mill's view that he, and people like him, know which pleasures are more valuable, leading to the depressing (and hardly original) conclusion that "[i]t is better to be a human being dissatisfied than a pig satisfied; better to be Socrates dissatisfied than a fool satisfied." Or we rank all pleasures on a single scale, like Bentham tried to do, and find, in so doing, that we have reduced the utility principle to an empty tautology which says, more or less, that we all want what we all want, whatever it may be. In ethical theory, this latter view is known as *psychological hedonism:* the idea that whatever I do, even, for example, when I seem to be acting in a selfless manner, I do because at bottom it makes me happy. If I help old ladies across the street, it is simply because that is the peculiar way in which I get my jollies. But this claim, if true, is useless; it has no critical purchase on ethical decision-making because it applies indiscriminately to all actions, no matter what their cost or benefit.

Neither of these options, then, provides the scientific solution to the problem of moral disagreement that the utilitarians sought. The first interpretation is incisive but elitist; the second is acceptable but vacuous.

There is one further problem with the utility principle as the basis of a social order, and it is perhaps more serious than all the others. In Ursula Le Guin's short story "The Ones Who Walk Away from Omelas," she depicts what many people consider a logical outcome of utilitarian theory. Omelas is a society of perfect happiness, in which there is no poverty, no hunger, no suffering, no conflict, and no despair. Every citizen lives in perfect contentment, at ease with the world and with his or her fellows. There is only one problem. The price of this perfect social happiness is that some children, a very small number, must be forced to live in desolate conditions of want, neglect, and pain. They are housed in a filthy dungeon, chained and starving for the benefit of the majority. Groups of fortunate schoolchildren are taken to see the suffering few on improving field trips; they are made to appreciate the fact that they are not among the unfortunate ones whose misery purchases a great social happiness. Members of the Omelan society accept this bargain as not only justifiable but demanded by utilitarian principle. The alternative would be a greater amount of unhappiness, and so any misgivings about the one-sided contract are swept aside, indeed interpreted as antisocial. Some of the citizens, however, cannot accept this social bargain and they are the ones who walk away, leaving the comforts of a society whose moral underpinnings they view as insupportable for the dangers of social exile in the wilderness outside Omelas.

It is debatable whether utilitarianism actually provides warrant for this kind of social arrangement, of course. Mill certainly did not think so, since he believed utility led to the traditional virtues of justice and morality, and thus preserved the dignity of the individual; he also, in his book *On Liberty,* argued eloquently and powerfully about the dangers of a "tyranny of the majority" in a democratic society, a force of numbers that would crush eccentric or nonconformist minorities. But there have been many critics of utilitarianism who doubted whether it is possible, following the greatest-happiness theory, to *avoid* a conclusion that would sacrifice a few for the sake of many. For these critics, utilitarianism cannot completely eliminate the possibility of an Omelas situation without introducing moral considerations that are precisely not about happiness—or, at least, that go beyond happiness conceived as subjective satisfaction of desire. From this point of view, the trouble with utilitarianism is that it does not take seriously the differences between people, does not accord individuals the respect they are due as individuals, or properly regard their rights to self-determination.

The reason for this troubling conclusion is not that Bentham, Mill, and their followers were immoral, of course; it is, rather, that they could not, under the influence of modernity's unquestioned physicalism, see the limitations of their pleasure/pain view of happiness. So long as we conceive happiness to be primarily about the satisfaction of desires, the greatest-happiness principle will remain open to the possibility of a corruption that exacts its costs in the suffering of some. Adding sophistication in the form of a more nuanced account of happiness, as Mill did, cannot in itself solve the problem, for here we still face the age-old difficulty of deciding which forms of happiness count more than others. No, only other considerations—considerations of virtue, respect, and individual self-knowledge—can answer the difficulties the utilitarians faced in their attempt to subject human life, ethics, and politics to a greatest-happiness calculus. That particular machine of better living is broken beyond repair.

LIFE AT THE MARGINS

That conclusion is still hard for many of us to see. Utilitarianism, while currently unfashionable in ethical and political theory, leads directly to marginalism, which is the dominant school of thought in contemporary economics. Here the world is conceived of as an aggregation of individuals, lacking both class interests and political convictions, who function as utility-maximizing ciphers in a vast web of market relations. For them, "welfare" is defined hedonistically, as follows, to use the formula of one contemporary philosopher: "a person's life is going well for him just in case he is experiencing it, or its principal ingredients, as agreeable or satisfying; conversely, it is going badly for him when his experience of it is, on balance, disagreeable or distressing."[26] ("Just in case" is, in this usage, a logical formation equivalent to "if and only if"; it specifies that the relationship in question is both necessary and sufficient.) Under this conception of welfare, the individual person is reduced to the status of a consumer whose "rational" actions are a result of the presumed basic desire to be as happy as possible.

That presumption—that every choice made by a person is what he or she thought rational at the time—is in turn the basis of what is known as rational-choice theory. Here, all decisions and actions decline to a base level of perfect rationality where people are always free of manipulation, coercion, and necessity. That is, they always do exactly what they think will contribute to the realization of their goals, whatever they may be. The complexity of the world and my choices within it resolve themselves into a series of condition choices: If I want to eat dinner, then I must acquire the necessary food. If I want to get the food, I must have money to buy it with. If I want money, I must trade some good or service of mine for it. And so on. In each case, the "rational" action is the one that allows me to achieve the goal I have in view; I am rational when I act efficiently to realize my goals, irrational when I do otherwise. My happiness or unhappiness, by extension, is just a function of how well or badly I am able to perform this series of choices, moving by stages from means to end. Rational choices are ones that contribute to my personal happiness, allowing me to get what I want and so "maximize my utility functions," as the theorists say. Of course, not everyone agrees with this picture of humankind as a perfectly rational *Homo economicus* free of all outside influence. I was having lunch with an economist friend recently and I asked him why people live in depressed and dangerous urban areas like the one he was about to move to. "A sociologist would say they had no choice," John said. "An economist would say that was the choice they made."

This notion of rational choice is the basic assumption of most contemporary economic theory. Economics increasingly relies on mathematical models and the abstruse reasoning of game theory—an academic undertaking that begins in relatively intuitive situations like John Nash's famous "prisoner's dilemma" (in which two accomplices are interrogated separately and must decide whether to fink or stand firm), but quickly runs so far afield that it is divorced not only from the larger aspirations of individuals, but even from their actual spending patterns. The basic prisoner's dilemma posits a situation in which the two prisoners do better for themselves if they turn the other in, but better for both together if they do not. Under those circumstances it makes sense to defect, since neither prisoner can count on the other to cooperate. Subsequent iterations of the situation alter the case, however, to one in which cooperative strategies might be more effective over the long term—this is what game-theorists call "the shadow of the future."[27] Because it models self-interested contractual behavior under conditions of imperfect knowledge, game theory has increasingly become the basic theoretical tool in theorizing economic relations between people, rising to ever-greater heights of sophistication all the while. As a result, economics has lately acquired a reputation for technical rigor so arid as to approach the nullity of some contemporary analytic philosophy. Two economists, conversing before a blackboard in a famous cartoon: "You know," says one, "I've found this model works much better if you leave the people out altogether."

Robert Heilbroner, an economist himself, speaks with almost parodic understatement when he pronounces on the state of contemporary economics: "First rate analysts we possess by the dozen," he says; "worldly philosophers are hard to find."[28] But it was not always thus. The descent of economics from genuine worldly philosophy—a mixture of moral and political theory, aware of the realities of money and market—into self-perpetuating precision is of relatively recent vintage. Indeed, worldly philosophers are precisely what we used to find in economic thought, the field where individual happiness meets political reality. Take Adam Smith, the great hero of market-based liberalism. Smith was in fact a moral philosopher by training, and his book *The Theory of Moral Sentiments* was one of the most important ethical works to be published in the eighteenth century. It argued for the basic role of sympathy in human affairs and posited the existence of an "Impartial Spectator"—a conscience—that keeps us from falling into anarchy. This moral theory plays an unexpectedly large part in Smith's best-known work, *The Wealth of Nations*. Smith feared the "corrupting" influence of admiring wealth too much, knew that those who live by profit would naturally tend to oppress workers, and that government was necessary if economic liberty were to lead to a just society. He was, among other things, in favor of regulated banking, a public school system, public infrastructure, a central postal service, luxury taxes, and public hygiene measures.

Smith was distinguished, but far from unique, in bringing deeper philosophical, and even literary, concerns to bear on matters economic. Bernard Mandeville, for example, penned his thoughts on markets, cooperation, and selfishness in a 1705 poem called, variously, *The Grumbling Hive* or *The Fable of the Bees*, comparing commercial society to the apparently chaotic but in fact well-ordered activity of the beehive. The Physiocrats, a group of eighteenth-century French thinkers, believed that wealth was rooted in God's divine plan, arguing, with a strange combination of hard-headed analysis and pious theological conviction, that it was limited to what could be harvested from God's gift of land. But by the late nineteenth century, the market-based economic system was well established and these colorful philosophico-economic speculations largely disappeared into obscurity. They were replaced by a more and more technical attempt to put economic thought on a scientific footing.

The marginalist school, which now dominates the study of economics, "shift[ed] the emphasis away from land, labor, and capital, with their class implications, to the calculations of the classless and apolitical individual," Heilbroner writes. "Paralleling this was…the growing prestige and importance of science, with which economics wished more and more to be identified." The result is high-flown analysis trumping worldly philosophy, which is particularly evident in the current dominance of the discipline by the self-perpetuating nuances of game theory and rational choice theory.[29] The renegade Austrian economist Joseph Schumpeter identified the beginning of this decline with the English analyst David Ricardo, even going so far as to label it "the Ricardian Vice"—in Heilbroner's words, "the habit of theorizing at such a stratospheric level of refinement that 'nothing lacks save sense.'" But not even Schumpeter could have foreseen the extent to which game theory would come to mire the formerly worldly philosophy in abstract intricacy.

A vivid example is to be found in a recent issue of *The American Economic Review,* a leading academic journal in the field, which contains six articles driven by game theory, on topics from setting interest rates to selling nuclear weapons. There is even a now-notorious article attempting to apply game-theoretic approaches to *The Price Is Right,* the long-running daytime game show in which contestants try to price consumer goods accurately. "After detailed inspection of past episodes," the critic John Cassidy writes, "the authors reach the conclusion that most contestants follow simple rules of thumb, such as offering the amount that they think the prizes are actually worth, rather than solving mathematical optimization problems in deciding what to bid." (Both Cassidy and the authors of the journal article somehow missed the real rational-choice strategies that operate in *The Price Is Right*—for instance, the time-honored tactic of bidding just one dollar more than the person to your right. But perhaps that's not the sort of thing the existing models can make sense of.) The authors of the article were forced to a conclusion tinged with disappointment, if not outright disapproval: "Our results indicate that rational decision theory cannot explain contestant behavior on 'The Price Is Right.'"[30]

This being so (and no great revelation to anyone outside economics), there is good reason to cast doubt on the viability of analytic economics as a discipline worthy of the respect it enjoys in the halls of power. More deeply, this real-world nullity might make us begin to doubt the reduced model of rationality-as-happiness that dominates marginalism, and the crude utility principle that is the starting point of such analysis. Clearly, people often do not behave rationally, if rational behavior means the constant perfect maximization of their marginal utility. They have motives beyond the simple increase of personal happiness understood as choosing the clearest means to achieving a chosen end. In choosing to buy a gift for my wife's birthday, for example, I might be motivated by factors quite outside the calculation of self-interest in the terms available to me via economics. Certainly I take those things into account—I don't want to spend beyond my means, and I want to be efficient in realizing the goal at hand—but the accounting is more complex than any simple model of rationality can imagine, including (perhaps) twinges of resentment at "having" to buy something, a powerful cultural notion of romance, effective sociobiological conditioning in my wanting to be a good husband, and so on. This might suggest that people are irrational, but it might also lead to another, less bizarre conclusion: that happiness is to be found elsewhere than in the application of the utility principle to our daily experience.

For many, the answer to this "elsewhere" lies in projecting a happiness beyond the world we know. The conventional religious view, in the words of Sir Thomas Browne: "Were the happiness of the next world as closely apprehended as the felicities of this, it were a martyrdom to live." So bring on those divine felicities! Like justice, which arrives only sporadically, if at all, on this benighted plane, happiness can seem so desirable as to vindicate the existence of another place where it is perfectly realized—at least by the righteous. It can also provide the sort of long view necessary to get through the messy business of life. "I can easily overlook any present momentary sorrow when I reflect that it is in my power to be happy a thousand years hence," Bishop George Berkeley said in 1713. "If it were not for this thought I had rather be an oyster than a man." Or it can even provide a standard of judgment for the actions we undertake in this life. We know that the pursuit of happiness in this realm is founded on God's wish for our well-being, apologists say, and so we can create a kind of divinely ordained utilitarianism. "God Almighty wills and wishes the happiness of his creatures," wrote William Paley, an eighteenth-century clergyman and philosopher, in 1785, "and consequently...those actions which promote that will and wish, must be agreeable to him; and the contrary."[31]

But is this religious impulse itself dominated by the machine imperatives of happiness? Is the look to a world beyond just another advertising jingle lodged in the impressionable meat of our brains, yet one more mechanism of contentment working on false assumptions? We must confront the possibility.

I have always been fascinated by the expression "lapsed Catholic." It suggests an insurance policy allowed to expire or an estate permitted to revert; it hints, too, of the lapsarian moment of Adam's moral downfall; and, more distantly, it echoes the slip of the tongue (*lapsus linguae* in the more elegant Latin) or of the pen (*lapsus calami* in the same dead tongue). When it comes to religious belief, my life can be separated, it seems, into prelapsarian and postlapsarian periods, split by some defining moment in which I slipped, or fell, whether by tongue or pen or some other means, from grace and into something else. Personally, I am still afflicted from time to time by the vestigial Catholic superstition that good fortune must be the prelude to disaster: the feeling, as a friend of mine once said, that my life is going so well I must have cancer. Or as I prefer to think of it: "I just won that prize, I guess it's about time to be hit by a truck." I don't know a single Catholic, lapsed or not, who doesn't feel this way now and then, and it puts a crimp in your enjoyment of the moment, let me tell you. From here I cannot but view religious belief, of the traditional self-punishing kind, anyway, as an imperfect means to happiness.

Now don't get me wrong. Some of my best friends are religious and I have nothing against them. I respect their views—though I do find, as Emily Post suggested, that it is best not to talk about it over dinner. It is true that I am constantly astonished by the ease with which the otherwise fine-spun intellects of my friends surrender to the ideological self-envelopment of the language of faith: the injunction that you must believe something not despite its irrationality but precisely *because* it is irrational. A fine piece of propaganda, if nothing else, this position has the effect of closing down discussion and excluding the non-believer from some imagined state of perfect certainty. No political ideologue could have done so well. This sort of self-closure is more on the order of a blanketing paranoid delusion, the sort of mental state in which all attempts to challenge the belief are merely further proof of a concerted, and perfidious, effort at outside control. *It's all part of the plan!*

That's all just me being hyper-rational, of course. But there you are: my cards are on the table. The issue right now is not so much what I think of religious belief as how well religious belief succeeds in making us happy. Are religious people actually happier than non-believers? And if they are, is it simply a case of ignorance being bliss?

A colleague of mine likes to describe religious believers as "buoyant." Genuinely delusional people, he says, are walking on air; religious people are not quite that out of touch—their feet still touch the ground—but they bounce along as if supported by a flotation device. Is this really true? Certainly it is for some, but the ethical legacy of religious belief creates a more complicated picture, one in which feelings of guilt and shame, the terrible burden of living in sin, might begin to dominate. Bertrand Russell observes that there are three kinds of obsessive personalities who are pointlessly unhappy: the narcissist, the megalomaniac, and the sinner. "When I speak of 'the sinner,'" Russell writes in *The Conquest of Happiness*, "I do not mean the man who commits sins: sins are committed by every one or no one, according to your definition of the word. I mean the man who is absorbed in the consciousness of sin. This man is perpetually incurring his own disapproval, which, if he is religious, he interprets as the disapproval of God." In Russell's (essentially

Freudian) view, the judgment that one is sinful is composed of a murky combination of fear of punishment and good socialization, the sort of status-fear that children ingest in the nursery—the internalized superego, in other words.

Russell himself was proud to have overcome the childhood itch of his conscience, an accomplishment that led him to perform without remorse actions at which a more sensitive soul might have balked: seducing young women throughout his life, for example, and once, famously, simply turning to his then-wife during a country bicycle ride and dispassionately informing her that he was no longer in love with her. Russell and others who find the idea of "sin" infantile and worth discarding are also reacting against a characteristic Christian mistrust of those things that give pleasure, a self-denying asceticism whose roots in the Western tradition are actually deeper than Christianity, extending back at least as far as Plato's denigration of the body in the *Phaedo*—the famous comparison of the body to a kind of prison which holds the soul back from its upward journey, what a certain kind of religious believer would today call a *meat cage* or *container*. "This ascetic element in ordinary morality has become unconscious," Russell says, "but it operates in all kinds of ways that make our moral code irrational. In a rational ethic it will be held laudable to give pleasure to any one, even to oneself, provided there is no counterbalancing pain to oneself or to others." One has to wonder what his ex-wife would have said about counterbalancing pains.

For Freud, the creation of the religious superego was a clear outcome of the thwarted instinctual desires that arise when we find ourselves in society with other people. Where Hobbes and Locke had it wrong was in thinking that the transition from a natural state to a social one would be a painless, even rational affair of transferring some or all of our powers over to a common authority. On the contrary, the base desires for increased power—and increased pleasure—are not so much transferred as repressed. There are many cultural means of this repression, including the denial of desire and the creation of alternative realities, but religion has a particularly influential place because of its collective character. "A special importance attaches to the case in which this attempt to procure a certainty of happiness and a protection against suffering through a delusional remoulding of reality is made by a considerable number of people in common," Freud wrote in *Civilization and Its Discontents*. "The religions of mankind must be classed among the mass-delusions of this kind. No one, needless to say, who shares a delusion ever recognizes it as such." And yet not even religion can keep its promise of providing happiness, for its technique of doing so consists, Freud added, "in depressing the value of life and distorting the picture of the real world in a delusional manner—which presupposes an intimidation of the intelligence. At this price, by forcibly fixing them in a state of psychical infantilism and by drawing them into a mass-delusion, religion succeeds in sparing many people an individual neurosis. But hardly anything more."

In other words, all that religion provides is a complex way of feeling unhappy with my instinctual desires—a residue of guilt for having felt those desires, even when I denounce them—so that "the price we pay for our advance in civilization is a loss of happiness through the heightening of the sense of guilt." Indeed, in ending up by subjecting individuals to outside forces, in the shape of religious authority and church doctrine, religion succeeds only in returning us to the place we began: struggling to find happiness amid culturally imposed limitations. Religion claims to rescue us from the unhappiness, in the form of the sense of guilt, that it has itself caused. It is a detour to unhappiness that we might just as well spare ourselves. Yet we cannot, for our sense of ourselves is sometimes impaired by a painful longing for transcendence that religion claims to satisfy. "At this point," Freud concludes laconically, "the ethics based on religion introduces its promises of a better after-life. But so long as virtue is not rewarded here on earth, ethics will, I fancy, preach in vain."

Well, not necessarily. For someone so attuned to the pathologies of everyday life, Freud misses some of the appeal—and some of the perverse forms of happiness—that can accompany religion. For example: the sense of superiority and comparative pleasure that

comes from regarding the outsiders. This is *ressentiment,* a psychological motive that Nietzsche dissected carefully and at length in his
magnificently nasty anti-Christian tract *The Genealogy of Morals.*
Ressentiment is closely allied with *Schadenfreude,* taking joy in the misfortune of others, but it has a more complex economy: there is a
desire for the thing the other enjoys, combined with a denigration
of that enjoyment, which is in turn born of the realization that one
cannot have or enjoy that thing. In other words, insisting that the
grapes must be sour because I cannot reach them. (Hence the habitual self-righteousness of the believer.) Freud should have seen the
deep pleasures, and the real power, of this position. And he needn't
have read Nietzsche to know it. Here is Jonathan Edwards, the great
eighteenth-century American theologian, on the comparative pleasures of belief: "The sight of hell's torments will exalt the happiness
of the saints forever. It will not only make them more sensible of the
greatness and freeness of the grace of God in their happiness; but it
will really make them more sensible of their own happiness; it will
give them a more lively relish of it." [32]

The trouble with seeing oneself in terms of sin is that, ultimately,
this sort of moral judgment divides the personality against itself.
This not only reduces happiness, it destroys efficiency; and it can
lead to a form of self-absorption in which the pleasures of psychic
harmony are forsaken for the confused, momentary highs of guilty
pleasure. "The man divided against himself looks for excitement
and distraction," said Russell in *The Conquest of Happiness:*

> he loves strong passions, not for sound reasons, but because
> for the moment they take him outside himself and prevent
> the painful necessity of thought. Any passion is to him a form
> of intoxication, and since he cannot conceive of fundamen-
> tal happiness, all relief from pain appears to him solely pos-
> sible in the form of intoxication. This, however, is the
> symptom of a deep-seated malady.

It is, indeed, the original malady, the same form of disharmony
that Plato warned against in his typology of degenerate personalities

in *The Republic*. Injustice, Plato argued, was not so much a political condition as a psychological one, in which a soul is in conflict with itself. When the rational part of the psyche is overcome by the appetites, often aided by the fiery energy of the spirited part of the psyche, the result is a form of sickness that makes all actions and choices empty. A person in this condition either lurches from pleasure to pleasure, satisfying appetites but never achieving personal satisfaction, or he collapses into a psychic shambles of self-hatred. This, then, is the deepest form of unhappiness we can imagine, the one in which we are not at peace with ourselves.

How to avoid it? Russell, like most philosophers, is a great advocate of just *thinking* your way out of the toxic guilt of sinfulness. His goal is not unlike Freud's—"mental integration, by which I mean that the various layers of a man's nature, conscious, subconscious, and unconscious, work together harmoniously and are not engaged in perpetual battle"—though Freud had the good grace, as we know, to admit that his own ends were more modest: to take neurotic people and, via a long and painful course of therapy, help them to become merely unhappy. Russell is more ambitious and yet less helpful. "Whenever you begin to feel remorse for an act which your reason tells you is not wicked," he advises, "examine the causes of your feeling of remorse, and convince yourself in detail of their absurdity." Oh, sure; like it's as easy as that. Writing this way, Russell begins to sound like an atheistic version of Barry Neil (aka "Bears") Kaufman of the Option Institute or the "mental hygiene" advocates from the early part of this century. Refuse remorse! Happiness is a choice! Decide on mental harmony today!

Ah, yes. Just say no to regret. But can that be all there is to happiness?

6

The Consolation of Philosophy

"I always say you can have too much philosophy," Mrs. Kirkfield said. "It isn't good for you. It's disorganizing. Everybody's got to wake up sometime feeling that everything is terrible, because it is."

—James Thurber, "Midnight at Tim's Place"

MANUAL OVERRIDE

I FIRST HEARD OF THE NEW ACROPOLIS WHEN A POSTER PASTED UP on the lampposts around town caught my eye. "The Keys to Happiness," it said, advertising an upcoming public lecture. Looking more closely I discovered in the small print that the lecture was going to be about the early Roman Stoic philosopher Epictetus, famous for writing a little book of philosophical advice, *The Enchiridion.* "The richest countries of the world generate violence and the highest rates of suicide, especially among young people," the flyer said. "Our psychologists are so busy with depressed people.... We feel more and more tired and stressed, whereas technology was supposed to liberate us, and so on..." Despite the awkwardness of the phrasing, the message was encouraging. "Perhaps, that's why Epictetus's teachings sound so relevant and helpful, on the eve of the twenty-first century, telling us how to cope with the ups and downs of Life, how important it is to cultivate enduring serenity and move gently toward our higher selves."

Epictetus is indeed one of the most enduringly relevant of

ancient philosophers, though not as well known today as he should be. *The Enchiridion,* or "manual," has had a disproportionate impact on the history of Western thought. It was among Montaigne's favorite books, and Frederick the Great liked to say he never went on a military campaign without it. Pascal violently disliked Epictetus's slim book, but the Scottish Enlightenment philosophers Adam Smith, Francis Hutcheson, and Adam Ferguson all admired it, and Anthony, Earl of Shaftesbury, was comforted by its bracing moral courage during the long illness that eventually led to his death. Born between A.D. 50 and 60 in Hieropolis, in Phrygia, Epictetus was the son of a slave and was a slave himself until his late twenties, when he began teaching philosophy on the street corners of Rome, not altogether successfully. Together with other philosophers he was exiled from Rome during the reign of the emperor Domitian, probably between A.D. 89 and 92.

As well as being a nice test of Epictetus's own self-mastery, the enforced exile proved to be a blessing in disguise. It sharpened the former slave's philosophical commitment, and Epictetus soon founded a school of philosophy in the town of Nicopolis, which gradually began to acquire devoted students who were drawn to his conversational teaching method and to his practical teachings of philosophical happiness. His young pupils regarded Epictetus as a kind of Roman Socrates, a great teacher who had no interest in fame or honors and who lived the wisdom he taught. Among the students was Flavius Arrian, an intimate of the emperor Hadrian, who came to Nicopolis between A.D. 123 and 126 and copied down the lessons of Epictetus, which, later in life, he edited and published. *The Enchiridion* is one part of these writings, therefore not from the hand of Epictetus himself, but rather a form of lecture note or abstract, a kind of primer or companion piece to the four-volume work of Stoic philosophy that Arrian published around A.D. 140.

The Enchiridion, like much of Roman Stoic writing, is driven by the central conceit that life is akin to a military engagement, a field of battle on which only the well prepared and brave will flourish. It therefore teaches the value of forbearance and strength of will. Even more centrally, it enjoins the kind of willed detachment from worldly contingency that is characteristic of the Stoic outlook. "There are things which are within our power, and there are things which are beyond our power," it begins. "Within our power are opinion, aim, desire, aversion, and, in one word, whatever affairs are our own. Beyond our power are body, property, reputation, office, and, in one word, whatever are not properly our own affairs."[1] The correct attitude is therefore to control what is within one's power and to disregard what is not. To do otherwise would be as foolish as trying to attack a well-fortified position with only one's personal arms: bad strategy, necessarily leading to defeat and ignominy.

I didn't learn any of this from the lecture. Epictetus has long been one of my favorite philosophers, not just for the remarkable circumstances of his life but also for the clear-eyed strength of character evident in his thought. I discovered an English translation of *The Enchiridion,* a little yellow paperback in the old Library of Liberal Arts series, in one of my father's bookcases during a sleepy Sunday afternoon when I was sixteen. I was drawn initially, I have to say, by the book's endearing slimness: it is little more than a pamphlet and it stood out by its very fragility in the midst of the intimidating wall of books that dominated our Winnipeg living room. I have my father's copy of *The Enchiridion* still, indeed have it before me as I write this, and it is covered with the tiny capital-letter scribbles of his own notes on the text. "Only by willing it can you improve yourself," he has written on page twenty, summarizing Article IX of the book. "Do not fear the ridicule of others," he adds four pages later under Article XXII.

For some reason my father's marginalia stop abruptly on page twenty-seven with an obscure commentary on Article XXIX. It says only this: "Falk-like." Not surprisingly, I am baffled. I don't remember this note from my first reading of this copy of the book, and I certainly have no memory of asking my father what the judgment of Falk-likeness conveyed to him. Article XXIX concerns the need for planning and training before any undertaking. "You must conform to rules, submit to a diet, refrain from dainties," Epictetus says;

"exercise your body, whether you choose it or not, at a stated hour, in heat and cold; you must drink no cold water, and sometimes no wine—in a word, you must give yourself up to your trainer as to a physician." How is that plan Falk-like? Who, anyway, was Falk, and what was it to be like him? Was he a trainer, or someone dedicated to training? Was he someone who prepared well for tasks and hence performed them with skill and determination? Did my father perhaps resent him? Or maybe, on the other hand, admire him, wish to be more Falk-like himself? Could it have been the passage's very Falk-likeness, its discipline, that caused my father to decide to read no further, or anyway to put down his pen at this point in his reading? I don't know. I do know that I read this page in my first encounter with Epictetus because there is another note on page twenty-seven, in what I recognize as my own hand from almost two decades ago. Against Article XXVII, in which Epictetus offers a rather opaque comment about the nature of contingency ("As a mark is not set up for the sake of missing the aim, so neither does the nature of evil exist in the world"), I have written "classical notion of human nature...no original sin."

It makes me happy to pore over this book now, with its brisk and sane advice on shouldering the world's burdens, its smart confidence that reason can conquer circumstance not with sleight of hand but with tough-minded acceptance. "Begin by prescribing to yourself some character and demeanor, such as you may preserve both alone and in company. Be mostly silent, or speak merely what is needful, and in few words," Epictetus says in Article XXXIII. "Never proclaim yourself a philosopher, nor make much talk among the ignorant about your principles, but show them by actions." And, as he adds in Article XLIV, never give in to the envy and dislike that swirl around you in the heat of worldly battle:

These reasonings have no logical connection: "I am richer than you, therefore I am your superior." "I am more eloquent than you, therefore I am your superior." The true logical connection is rather this: "I am richer than you, therefore my possessions must exceed yours." "I am more eloquent than you, therefore my style must surpass yours." But you, after all, consist neither in property nor style.

It is invigorating to read such good advice, presented with the plainness and simplicity of experience. Epictetus knew how to live; we all have a lot to learn from him.

The New Acropolis lecture showed that we are not listening, however. It was held in a committee room at the City Hall downtown. I rushed in, ten minutes late and in a very un-Stoic mood—I had been cut off by a motorist while cycling there and had engaged in a small tussle with the man behind me in the line at the drugstore, who had put his bottles of Coke on the counter in front of me *before* I had received my change or gathered up my purchases, in what I regarded as a clear violation of check-out protocol. I'm not sure just what I was expecting at that point, but I was surprised to see that there were only three people in the audience, another man and two women, all in their early twenties. I paid my ten-dollar admission fee, was handed a paper cup of water, and sat down to listen.

The lecturer, Françoise, was an attractive Frenchwoman in her thirties with a mass of slightly graying Pre-Raphaelite hair, and she was speaking in an intermittently incomprehensible yet altogether charming Gallic voice. She paused every few seconds to beam meaningfully at us. Because there were just the four of us looking back, these soulful punctuations could not be ignored: she was always staring directly at one of us, who would invariably nod, as if to say, "Good, good. You're doing fine. I get it." Pretty soon the four of us were all nodding away like mad, tag-teaming our responses to Françoise so that the head-bobs were circling the room like a miniature, heads-only version of The Wave.

It was odd being there with just three other people, but it was depressing, too. The New Acropolis Cultural Association is, according to its literature, a worldwide organization founded in 1957 by an Argentine philosophy professor with the excellent name of Jorge Angel Livraga Rizzi; its aim is "to promote philosophical education, particularly for young people; a philosophical education that is adaptable to modern times, independent and unrestricted by any religious, political, or socioeconomic influences." I'm not sure the last part is entirely desirable, let alone possible, but you have to give the New Acropolis people credit for trying to take philosophy out of the classroom and into the world.

The recent growth of philosophical cafés and philosophical therapists suggests that there is a hunger out there for philosophical thinking, or anyway the sanction of it. The cafés started in Paris and Amsterdam in the early 1990s and quickly spread as part of an "applied philosophy" movement that captured the imaginations of ordinary people who wanted philosophical discussion (and even enlightenment) but weren't interested in the scholasticism and elitism of traditional universities. In some ways, this was a rather self-conscious attempt to re-create the kind of public forum that used to be more common: the coffeehouses and salons of the eighteenth century, the clubs and self-improvement groups of the nineteenth, and the sort of café society enjoyed by Proust, Wilde, de Maupassant, and Sartre. Like 1990s book circles, the "café-philo" idea speaks to a need to have intellectual discussion as a regular, and social, part of modern life. But while book clubs thrive in North America, the cafés have not—possibly because they are more argumentative and public than the book club, and more likely (I imagine) to be dominated by opinionated men.

Philosophical therapy has an older history. Indeed, philosophy has always offered itself, implicitly anyway, as a form of soul repair, and in this sense Socrates was the original therapist. But philosophical counseling in the psychotherapeutic vein familiar to most of us, the standard post-Freudian encounter between client and professional in an office, began in Germany in the early 1980s and has been growing slowly but steadily since then. In early 1997 there were only about twenty people worldwide who call themselves philosophical counselors, but more were in training, and conferences and journals are contemplated. The writer Laura Wexler recently described an encounter with one of these counselors, a Missouri philosophy professor named Kenneth Cust. Wexler was upset with her life as a graduate student, worried she was wasting time doing a Ph.D. in English and maybe being too intellectual about things in general. Cust asked her probing questions, forced her to confront a moral dilemma—a variation on what philosophers call The Trolley Problem, in which one must decide whether or not to divert an out-of-control trolley in order to sacrifice some human lives for others—and got her to see that perhaps her problem was not so much thinking too much as being afraid to accept that thinking was simply what she did. He charged her $50 for the session. "Am I any happier now than when I arrived?" Wexler asks herself on the way home, stopping at a fast-food restaurant for a snack. "I feel happier. But, as any philosopher will tell you, it's hard to know for sure why. Is it the philosophy or the french fries?"[2]

New Acropolis makes no explicit claims to heal the soul, and its chapters do not offer this kind of personal session with a counselor. But the organization's literature says it has ten thousand active members worldwide and "hundreds of thousands of supporters [who] speak in fifteen different languages and come from a wide range of religious denominations, ethnic origins, and cultural backgrounds." Professor Livraga has reached these people by diagnosing "a kind of apathy in the human soul," which he thinks is owing to several factors: "the ever-quickening pace of life in our cities, the lack of contact with nature, the artificiality of our relationships and communications, and the ephemeral and utilitarian goals we set for ourselves." We need to overcome these limiting pressures to discover our authentic selves, the selves that can distinguish between the essential and inessential to uncover true happiness. Only then can we become productive members of a tolerant and thriving multicultural society. Great stuff. And all the more reason to be surprised that only four people were there, one of whom was in the cultural-anthropological position of participant-observer. Maybe the New Acropolites need a better publicity person.

Or perhaps they need more lecturers. I liked Françoise and what she was saying, which was often reminiscent of the simple, wise tone of Epictetus himself. "We speak about idealism like it is a disease," she said at one point. "We tell you that you will grow out of it, as if you are being cured. Idealism is not a disease. On the contrary, it is a sign of good health." Yet there was a kind of aimlessness in the lecture, and a (to me) distressing tendency to squash every kind and manner of "philosophical" writing into one, acceptance-is-true-happiness message. Quotations from the *Bhagavad Gita* and the works of Plato were thrown together, with some rather dubious etymologies of the words *vocation* and *education*. It was all a little dissatisfying. And yet the overall message was unimprovable: people who are driven by external goods, by the false and harmful desires they internalize from peer pressure, socialization, and conventional expectations, have no direction because they are not doing the driving. "We need to dare to be ourselves," Françoise said. "This takes a lot of courage, a lot of assertiveness. But you must do it. You must live the life you want to live, not the life you are wanted to live. How can I know if I am living my vocation? I am happy. And not with a happiness that depends on the bank account. Marcus Aurelius said the true wisdom was to be able to sleep one night in a palace, the next on the floor of a hovel, with equal happiness."

After the lecture Françoise called for comments and questions, and the other man there, a young guy who introduced himself as Darryl, said, "I studied philosophy in university and I always found it rather impotent. This is different. This is principle driven. It's practical. You can do something with it." I am painfully familiar with this complaint about academic philosophy, indeed often share it now that I am some distance from the joy-killing professionalization machine called graduate school, but I was reminded, as he was speaking, that being definite, principle centered, and practical are not always good things. The Nazis were all of those things, more so than most people. And I thought of a joke handout I sometimes give to the students in my first-year philosophy class. It's called "Twenty Life Lessons from *Melrose Place*," and it codifies the operative ethical precepts of the group of beautiful twenty-something sociopaths who, on the Fox Network's hit television show, share a Los Angeles apartment complex, work space, and often lovers. It was first passed to me by a friend, who found it on the Internet.

The list of *Melrose Place* imperatives is worth quoting in full:

1. If your "significant other" leaves town for more than a week, sleep with whomever you want. After all, you can't be expected to wait around forever.
2. Never sleep with your boss or coworker. Just kidding. You should do both, often.
3. A good way to unwind after a hard day at the office is to build a fire, curl up with a good book, and rapidly drink seven large glasses of straight vodka.
4. Every once in a while, just go ahead and slap somebody in the face, really hard.
5. Pretend you're pregnant.
6. Feeling a little insecure? Buy a gun!
7. If marriage isn't working, consider a divorce. If divorce isn't convenient, fake your own death.
8. Don't walk too fast when feigning blindness.
9. Never base a relationship on lies and deceit. Just kidding! Dishonesty should be an integral part of any relationship.
10. When you leave someone to die of carbon monoxide poisoning, be sure to shut the door tightly on your way out.
11. Don't date drug dealers...unless they're really good-looking... or have a lot of money...or unless you can gain something from it in some way...or...oh hell, go ahead and date drug dealers.
12. Don't get too close to people in comas. Sometimes they wake up and try to choke you.
13. If you get fired, get drunk.
14. Call your ex-wife "Baby."
15. If you've got to fix your Harley, you might as well take off your shirt and do it by the pool.
16. Randomly insult the people around you.
17. Parents will be parents. Sometimes they'll nag. Sometimes they'll be judgmental. Sometimes they'll commit you to a mis-

erable insane asylum where you'll be bound in a straitjacket and heavily sedated.

18. If you lose your job, wait a few minutes and you'll get an even better job at twice the salary.

19. A good way to aggravate your sister is to tell her that Mom liked you best. Another good way is to sleep with her husband a bunch of times.

20. Just because you're in the midst of ruining someone's career doesn't mean that you can't carpool to work with them.

I love this list, and not just because I am an inveterate *Melrose* watcher. Douglas Coupland, in *Microserfs*, has the narrator say that the appeal of *Melrose* lies in watching people "start acting random and non-linear all of a sudden." But that's not it: they do not act in a random manner at all; on the contrary, their behavior is probably more consistently in line with the Melrosian "Life Lessons" than most people's lives are with their carefully chosen principles. The appeal of *Melrose Place* is precisely that, no matter how outrageous the acts of adultery and theft and professional betrayal, they are entirely in character. The acts are still outrageous, but the characters don't ever acknowledge that this is so, generating in the viewer a peculiar form of camp pleasure in which you know exactly what's going to happen but still can't quite believe it when it *does* happen. Call it the joy of confirmed outrage.

The larger point is that, appearances to the contrary, everybody has some kind of life plan, even someone who is calmly engaging in behavior we would consider unimaginable. Everybody is living life according to some sort of principle, however unreflective and even apparently instinctual. That's why the "Life Lessons" are important. They implicitly highlight, even as they parody, the idea that anyone could live a life according to insane moral precepts. People can, and people do (even if they are rarely as wealthy or beautiful as the people on television). The meaningful question is not: Do you have a principle guiding your life? The meaningful question is: Is it a good principle or a bad one?

The other good question, of course, is this: Now that I have decided a principle is a good one, how can I live up to it? The Stoic theory of happiness as virtue has always attracted me. It is firm, solid, and resolute. It shrugs off misfortune and routine unpleasantness as not worthy of attention, indeed faces all setbacks with equanimity. It lives in the present, preparing for the future but not caring too deeply about what is to come, and regretting nothing in the past because it is beyond changing. It faces the unpleasant truths of life without flinching, tempering them with familiarity. "Let death and exile, and all other things which appear terrible, be daily before your eyes, but death chiefly," Epictetus says in Article XXI, "and you will never entertain an abject thought, nor too eagerly covet anything." Above all, it teaches, as Article XXIII states, that there is no lasting or genuine form of happiness to be found in material goods. "If you ever happen to turn your attention to externals, for the pleasure of anyone, be assured that you have ruined your scheme of life. Be content, then, in everything, with being a philosopher; and if you wish to seem so likewise to anyone, appear so to yourself, and it will suffice you."

But will it?

JE NE REGRETTE RIEN

Eliminating regret and pointless striving from your mental life, as Epictetus and other Stoics advise, is really a version of the second happiness strategy I sketched earlier, a form of taking the long view. Philosophers have historically been big on this option, in particular because regret seems to them pointless and irrational, an emotion that merely adds superfluous negative feelings to what is, presumably, already a negative action, or at least one about which we already think badly. "Repentance is not a virtue, that is, it does not arise from reason," Spinoza wrote in a book published soon after his death in 1677. "Rather, he who repents what he did is twice miserable."[3] Twice, because he is already in moral debt for having done the wrong thing, and adding pointless remorse to what Spinoza considers the irrationality of failing to act morally is to redouble the foolishness. The point is that the *feeling* of regret adds nothing to the *judgment* of one's own wrongdoing; on the contrary, it might compound the offense by paralyzing one's character in self-loathing or else sloughing off genuine responsibility in the exquisite indulgence of one's own guilt. In an unusual, if not unique, point of intellectual contact, Nietzsche agreed with Spinoza on this point, expressing himself in characteristically sharper language: "Never give room to repentance, but tell yourself at once: this would mean to add a second piece of stupidity to the first."[4]

This advice can be hard to accept. We tend to believe that regret is an integral part of the "genuine" sense of wrongdoing, a prerequisite for a full recognition of our responsibility. We also might believe that feelings of regret make future wrongdoing less likely, or that some kind of suffering is necessary to atone for our bad actions, or that there is a threat to the integrity of our character if we do not regret the bad things we have done—a debilitating sense of moral detachment that allows us to look dispassionately on evil deeds. But however much these attitudes come naturally to us, the critics say, they do not stand up to rational scrutiny.

One of my favorite examples of recent philosophical arguments about regret and happiness was offered by Rüdiger Bittner, a philosophy professor who taught at Yale during the years I was in graduate school there. Bittner was a tall, thin German man with a graying pageboy haircut and the sort of fashion sense only someone of true intellectual prowess can get away with. In the muggy days of early September he used to lecture in high-cut khaki shorts and closed-toe sandals of the kind once sported by French schoolboys, and he was especially fond of a hand-knitted orange and purple sweater that his sister had mailed him from Germany. Contrary to cultural cliché, he was not grim, but his sense of humor was heavy and elaborate. I spent one semester working as his teaching assistant and was never entirely certain whether, or when, he was joking. This included the occasion on which I asked him for a reference letter and he refused, accusing me of doing it only for instrumental reasons and therefore being undeserving of his support. (It turned out he wasn't joking that time.) He baffled the undergraduates at Yale by teaching a course in ethics that did not tell them anything about the nature of right and wrong, good and bad, devoting himself, instead, to intricate criticisms of other people's equally intricate philosophical positions.

Bittner's argument about the irrationality of regret is deliberately counterintuitive, but it has a lengthy philosophical pedigree that begins with the original Stoics, extends through the worldly acceptance theories of the early modern era, and gets a hearing in Bertrand Russell's updating of Freud. Bittner's version appears in a smartly written article called, provocatively, "Is It Reasonable to Regret Things One Did?" "Regret does not in fact make doing better in the future more probable," Bittner writes in the article. Indeed, it can even make it less likely, for "there is the self-complacency of feeling terrible about what one did and leaving it at that."[5] As for atonement, it is, says Bittner, all about "scaring the children" and based on a natural but nevertheless indefensible bloodthirstiness. "However deeply it may have been inculcated in us that it ought to be the case that the good be happy and the evil suffer," he writes, "the truth is that, if anything, it ought to be the case that everybody, good and evil alike, be happy."

When it comes to the question of character and regret, matters are more complex. Do we not believe, with some justice, that feelings of regret tie us to our actions and their consequences in an important way? Do we not likewise believe that someone so detached from those actions and consequences as not to feel any remorse for them would be, in an important sense, a moral monster? But Bittner will not have it. Expressions of regret, he claims, sometimes allow us to forget actions all the more readily, as, for example, when the expiation purchased in the Catholic confessional is taken as wiping the slate clean. By the same token, a lack of regret does not imply a lack of awareness, or of willingness to repair the damage and avoid the deed in future. "On the contrary," Bittner says, "it is with mourning and regret left behind that we may come to see what we did in the sharpest light." Therefore it is not reasonable to regret things one did; more than this, it is reasonable *not* to regret them—and reasonable in a startlingly ordinary sense, too. "To look things straight in the face," Bittner says,

> unburdened by grief, is just a very good idea, and a good idea in the same sense in which it is a good idea, say, to have the snow tires mounted before the first snowfall. True, there is this difference: some people do mount their snow tires in time, but few people are likely to take in their failings without regret. Still, this shows only that some forms of unreason are more common and harder to eradicate than others.

In other words: get on with it.

This is good stuff, but I am forced to wonder—as, I suspect, are you—how helpful it really is. "All philosophy is only forcing the trade of happiness," said Goldsmith, "when nature seems to deny the means." Too true—you cannot make someone happier simply by telling them, in a dispassionate philosophical way, that it is irrational to be otherwise. This talk of mounting the snow tires makes it sound as though ridding ourselves of regret were merely another little chore to get through before the leaves fall from the trees. It begins to appear as just one more example of a philosopher taking the power of reason too seriously. Therapists are constantly confronted by the spectacle of patients who know, with every ounce of themselves, just what pathologies they are acting out in a given situation, but who are apparently powerless to keep themselves from doing so. This is not simply because they are mistaken in some way or lack the will to do the better thing; it is more complicated than that. Knowing what ails you is not enough to alter action, which is why the project of self-knowledge, championed for so long by philosophers from Socrates to Bacon to Bittner, and now the preserve of wholeness-peddling psycho-gurus from Bradshaw to Weil to Kaufman, is so often simply beside the point. What good is knowing myself, even in fine-grained detail, if it does not help me change the things about me that I consider bad? To grasp the other horn of this dilemma and simply accept myself as I am—the sort of thing you are liable to hear at happy camps the continent over—is to surrender the possibility of change. It is personal happiness achieved only through passivity and therefore no happiness at all.

All this assumes that we might, in a perfectly rational world, eliminate regret from our lives. Is that even possible? I decided to try it for a while to find out. As Bittner notes, eliminating regret is not as easy, or as obvious, as changing the snow tires, but as a piece of unreason, I thought, regret should be a susceptible target to somebody like me, with a fairly extensive philosophical background and reasonable stores of willpower. Could I actually be that rational? I wanted to find out.

The first obstacle I came up against was the residual traces of Catholicism in my psychological makeup, which are far from negligible. I remember deciding during my third year in university, when I was running for the position of editor-in-chief of the undergraduate newspaper, that I *must not* feel guilty about making people hate me. Guilt, I told myself in a graceless paraphrase of Spinoza (whom I had not yet read), is not a productive emotion; it creates nothing, it only destroys. This helped me feel a little happier about the tactics my faction employed to defeat our rivals, which were mildly Machiavellian, and I have no regrets about that incident, because, at the time, I sincerely believed that I was a much better editor than their man could have been. I would not consider that kind of ends-means justification convincing now, to be sure, but, all things considered, it was not entirely out of place there and then. I did nothing seriously immoral from any larger standpoint, and anyway it is all in the past. Yet I have found that feelings of guilt die hard in most cases, especially when you suspect that you have done something really indefensible.

I was reminded of this during my more recent period of self-imposed freedom from regret, when I failed to return a phone call from a professional associate and tried to eliminate any feelings of remorse for this minor social sin. It was easy. I never liked him much, and, anyway, he had failed to support me in one of those bitterly contested minor intrigues that take up so much of work life. Why should I care about maintaining social ties in that particular quarter? I found I felt the same way about some friendships that, through force of circumstance or difference of opinion, had lately grown distant. Though I certainly saw these events as, in some sense, unpleasant or even unfortunate from some imagined perspective of social harmony, they did not trouble me much. We all know the feeling of growing apart from people, or the momentary fits of antisocial behavior that make an unreturned phone call no sin at all. Things change, and so do we.

But then, one day, I did an unquestionably bad thing that could not be rationalized away. I stole the copy of the journal containing Bittner's article from the little library in my department, where up till then I had been reading it and scrupulously making notes on a piece of foolscap. I had planned to copy the article eventually on the mailroom photocopier, just to have a version in my files, but it happened that I didn't have my photocopy code number with me on this one occasion, and anyway, I thought, wouldn't it be so much easier just to put it in my knapsack and walk out? As I descended in the elevator I examined my feelings. Certainly I was prepared to admit the full weight of the wrongdoing involved. Though I had saved some paper and the power needed to make copies, I acknowledged to myself that stealing things from libraries is wrong. It costs money and it impairs scholarship. More to the point, it is selfish. How would I have felt had that number of the journal not been there because some other regret-eliminating philosopher had been there before me? I could not justify the theft on account of need, or scarcity, or overriding circumstances of any other kind. Any way I looked at it, whichever moral theory I chose to use, I had done something wrong. But I found I felt absolutely no regret for it—in fact, I feel none even now, as I write this passage, knowing full well that it means the revelation of my immoral act to you and everyone else who reads it. I was happy to have the journal, happy to feel nothing about its theft, and still ready to concede it was not right.

Or was I? You have to understand that I don't like some of my departmental colleagues very much, especially since they passed me over for some permanent jobs a while back and continue to treat me, and other people who work on limited contracts like mine, which cannot lead to tenure, with a barely concealed disdain. The same day I stole the journal, for example, I noticed that my name had for some reason been taken off the departmental directory. This had also happened the year before, with the additional indignity then that my mailbox had been removed from the mailroom, along with the mail that was in it. When I complained, the departmental secretary just looked at me and said, "You don't teach here any more," as if she knew better than I. It was almost as if I had been "disappeared." I cannot say that this year's directory removal played a part in my decision to steal the journal, because I only noticed it as I was leaving, the journal already in my bag, but it did strengthen my resolve to feel no remorse for the action as time passed—a sort of convenient post facto reason not to regret. And yet, this created a new problem, because now I had, in my own mind if nowhere else, introduced countervailing considerations that seemed to make the theft of the journal not only explicable but maybe even justified. Not rationally, you understand—not even I would go as far as to say that my feelings of frustration with my colleagues justifies stealing from them—but emotionally.

But this line of thought just meant that I was no longer confronting something immoral and failing to regret it. My action was no longer appearing to me *as* immoral, in other words, and hence the issue of regret was fading. If anything, my theft looked rather feeble as an act of revenge on my irritating colleagues: surely I could come up with something a little more drastic? So my lack of regret lost its piquancy, and this made me wonder whether there was any action that could meet the conditions of being both undeniably bad *and* sincerely unregretted. Surely one of the things that makes us regret actions is that we think they are, indeed, regrettable. If we cease to think of some action as something worth regretting, that is one thing—there is no point in regretting what one does not wish otherwise, and I might, like Edith Piaf, simply refuse the moral standards being applied to me by someone else and say, defiantly, *"Non, je ne regrette rien."* But just to the extent that I consider an action of mine wrong, must I not feel something like regret? Is it possible to separate the feeling that one has done wrong from the judgment of wrongdoing?

Well, I continued to try. Certainly, I thought, there is little to be gained, and much to be lost, from the toxic feelings of guilt that sometimes overwhelm us when we have done something bad. If you listen to people like Freud and Russell, a lot of guilt is imposed on us by other people or by institutions, usually with some manipulative or at least conformist intent, and that sort of thing might well be worth resisting—though I, personally, would not go as far as Bertrand Russell in completely denying the importance of a conscience. But regret sometimes has a more benign character than guilt, as I soon discovered.

When I began telling people I had decided not to regret my bad actions, it was a bit like that period after I came back from happy camp when I was hugging everybody for a week or two. Their reactions ranged from puzzlement to disapproval. How could I not regret bad things? Wouldn't that make it easier for me to do them? Well, yes, as a matter of fact it could, and did: once I had decided not to regret unreturned phone calls and invitations, for example, they just started piling up. I began lying, in a white or anyway off-white way, to all kinds of people, with motives both bland and self-serving. I didn't steal anything else, but I sure thought about it a lot, especially when I was standing in long check-out lines and it would have been so much easier simply to walk out with the stuff I was trying to pay for. Even though I regard slippery-slope arguments as mostly fallacious, I felt a bit as though I were on the crest of one now, and I realized that feelings of regret, because unpleasant, do in fact act as a routine moral curb, a kind of scaled-down version of the nausea that comes over the "reformed" thug Alex, in *A Clockwork Orange,* when he contemplates violence—or, unfortunately, hears his beloved Beethoven.

I was now fully prepared to look at my failings with clear eyes—

and to share that knowledge with other people. After all, if I didn't regret the things I had done, why should they? And yet they did, sometimes bitterly: What possible justification could I have for not returning phone calls or canceling social engagements? How could I lie with such ease? You can cause a lot of pain that way, as Russell should have realized but didn't. The reason is that morality is not simply a matter of your own judgments on yourself, however dispassionate. Morality makes sense only within a community of people to whom you owe obligations and about whom you care. The project of eliminating regret from your moral universe is therefore, from this point of view, itself inappropriate, even immoral. It would be, says Bernard Williams, "an insane concept of rationality" that insisted that a rational person should never experience sentiments of regret.[6] In attempting it, as I found, you take yourself out of the shared moral vocabulary and reciprocity of judgment that are the warp and woof of ethical life. You become, as Aristotle said of people who did not have communities, either a god or a beast. And in this condition, cries of "Grow up!" aimed at the irrational, still-regretting majority begin to sound either mad or bad or both.

Bittner is right that logically there is no necessary connection between not feeling regret and being a bad person, and no logical need to feel connected to my wrong actions in a relationship as close as regretting them. The "warning that by not regretting we fail to retain our identity and character as [moral] agents turns out to be another case of frightening the children," he says. "There is nothing detectably wrong with a failure to retain one's identity and character as an agent, in the sense of failing to identify with what one did. There is nothing detectably wrong with simply walking away from it." Perhaps I could, with enough practice, simply acknowledge my actions as wrong and then walk away from them. But in the complex web of social relations that gives point to ethical behavior, and in the creation of a moral character that is mine, surely there must be something missing in this. The nonregretting person becomes a moral cipher, a kind of blank spot in the social field. Worse, he risks becoming a moral monster or a sociopath.

Unsurprisingly, the project of nonregret was having negative effects on my sense of myself. It was, in a straightforward way, bad for my character—and I don't think that is because I am given to irrationality. It is not just, in other words, that I find it difficult to put the snow tires on. No, it went deeper than that. It did not succeed in making me happy, and it pretty clearly made other people unhappy. It was wrong. I gave it up.

CONSOLING THOUGHTS

I have spent some time dwelling on this project of eliminating regret because it is one of the most common answers philosophy has offered, through the centuries, as a reliable route to happiness. But as Bittner's position demonstrates, apart from its very real problems of implementation, the regret-nothing position has the effect of highlighting a troubling distinction between happiness and morality. One of the reasons we cling to regret as an inevitable outcome of wrongdoing is precisely because we want people to be unhappy about their bad actions. We might realize—indeed, it would be hard to avoid the awareness—that bad things continue to happen to good people on this earth, and good things to bad ones. We might even acknowledge that some of our feelings about a link between goodness and happiness are driven by resentment; we might find it necessary, for example, to believe that the devious bastard with the ill-gotten millions is really unhappy. (I'll bet he isn't; I'll bet he's ecstatic.) But these concessions do not alter our basic, apparently instinctive conviction that those who are good deserve to be happy and those who are bad do not.

How, then, to deal with the fact that this does not seem to be the case? Well, Bittner's position is one option: happiness is something everyone should have, regardless of ethical standing, so just forget about trying to bring character and fate into line. Are there others? I want to spend some time considering an influential one.

Before the world invented therapists, it fell to philosophers to deploy hopeful messages of happiness, and this they did with vary-ing degrees of commitment and success. It is part of philosophy's lament today that this role has slipped from its grasp, replaced by technical rigor and forbidding scholarship. "In our society," says one contemporary philosopher, "we have to turn to popular self-help manuals to find extensive discussion of questions of the best life, self-fulfillment, the proper role of the emotions, personal friend-ships and commitments, topics which in the ancient world were always treated in a more intellectual way as part of ethics."[7] Further evidence, if any were needed, that all is not progress.

Though there are many contenders, a quintessential expression of the robust theory of happiness is often thought to be Boethius's *The Consolation of Philosophy.* Boethius (A.D. c. 480–524), distin-guished civil servant and translator of Aristotle, brilliant scholar and statesman, had good reason, and ample leisure, to reflect on the question of personal happiness. In the second decade of the sixth century he became embroiled in a political conspiracy with roots in a papal schism. He was imprisoned in Pavia, interrogated and tor-tured there, and later bludgeoned to death at Ravenna. His book—a combination of mock-Platonic dialogue, devout Christian apologetic, and not entirely successful wisdom poetry—has proved to be one of the most popular pieces of happiness literature in the Western intellectual tradition.

It is also a prime example of a theory often found in the prison memoir, that strange form of cultural production that finds inspira-tion—not all of it admirable—in solitude. (In addition to Boethius, Sir Thomas More, Sir Walter Raleigh, John Bunyan, the Marquis de Sade, Fyodor Dostoevsky, and Adolf Hitler wrote what are arguably their greatest works while in prison.[8]) The theory I mean is amateur theodicy, or the attempt to "assert eternal Providence / And justify the ways of God to men"; in other words, to argue the case for God's justice on earth.[9] In his wrestling with faith and reason, providence and free will, Boethius prefigures, in his own version of philosophi-cal counseling, one of the central preoccupations of the early mod-ern philosophers who would follow him nearly a millennium later. Those inheritors of his mantle, in particular Leibniz and Spinoza, would begin to develop ever more elaborate theories of the human mind and its passions that would, eventually, spawn the now-distinct intellectual discipline we know as psychology. Boethius is not the first sophisticated psychologist in the Western philosophical tradition—that honor belongs to Plato—but he is the first to fuse classical and Christian versions of psychology in a form accessible enough to appeal to a wide nonspecialist audience. The religious writer and novelist C. S. Lewis, himself no slouch in that department, accurately regarded Boethius as "the divine popularizer."[10]

The Consolation itself is structured as internal dialogue, in which an intimate first-person narrator invites reflection on the turns of Fortune's wheel after he is confronted by Philosophy in the figure of a woman "of awe-inspiring appearance, her eyes burning and keen beyond the usual power of men." She chides Boethius for his evident grief and bitterness and, wiping away his tears, suggests he is suffering from amnesia: he has forgotten what he once knew, that wisdom conquers all worldly suffering. He replies with some spirit—and much bitter detail about the perfidy of his enemies—that he is falsely accused. Now he is about to die, all because he followed her lead, and Plato's, in thinking that philosophy and politics were natural partners. The situation causes him to wonder how such things can happen to good people:

> Grief has not so dulled my wits in all this as to make me complain that the wicked have piled up their crimes against virtue; but what does fill me with wonder is that they have brought their hopes to fruition. It may be part of human weakness to have evil wishes, but it is nothing short of monstrous that God should look on while every criminal is allowed to achieve his purpose against the innocent. If this is so, it was hardly without reason that one of your household [Epicurus] asked where evil comes from if there is a god, and where good comes from if there isn't.

The old question—and the right one.

Philosophy's reply to this complaint occupies the bulk of *The*

Consolation, and Boethius deploys many ingenious arguments in her voice. Some of them will undoubtedly strike the modern ear as mere sleight of hand: "God who can do all things cannot do evil," it is argued at the end of Book III. "What God cannot do is nothing"; therefore, "evil is nothing." But others have the deep ring of wisdom. "You are wrong if you think Fortune has changed toward you," Philosophy says in Book II. "She was exactly the same when she was flattering you and luring you on with enticements of a false kind of happiness.... Do you really hold dear that kind of happiness that is destined to pass away? Do you really value the presence of Fortune when her departure will plunge you into sorrow?" "If the enjoyment of any earthly blessing brings with it any measure of happiness, the memory of that splendid day can never be destroyed by the burden however great of growing evil."

More deeply still, Philosophy is inclined to wonder why humans are so preoccupied by Fortune in the first place. "Why then do you mortals seek happiness outside yourselves, when it lies within you?" she asks. "You are led astray by error and ignorance. If happiness is the highest good of rational nature and anything that can be taken away is not the highest good—since it is surpassed by what can't be taken away—Fortune by her very mutability can't hope to lead to happiness." If we realize this, we must live in constant fear of losing variable Fortune; if we do not realize it, we purchase happiness only at the high cost (to rational creatures like ourselves) of ignorance. Therefore none of the goods of Fortune—wealth, power, gratification, even life itself—can be judged the measure of true happiness. Revealing that is a project akin to dissolving the shadows of false belief described by Plato in *The Republic,* where ordinary life is a dark cave, we inside it chained and immobile and, as a result, taking the shadows projected on the wall for the full extent of reality.

All people are seeking happiness, Philosophy says, but most of the time they are misled in their pursuit. The following passage is expressive of the range of error in this regard:

Some believe that perfect good consists in having no wants, and so they toil in order to end up rolling in wealth. Some think that the true good is that which is most worthy of respect, and so struggle for position in order to be held in respect by their fellow citizens. Some decide that it lies in the highest power, and either want to be rulers themselves, or try to attach themselves to those in power. Others think that the best thing is fame and busy themselves to make a name in the arts of war or peace. Most people simply measure the possession of the good by the amount of enjoyment and delight it brings, convinced that being abandoned to pleasure is the highest form of happiness. Others again confuse ends and means with regard to these things, such as people who desire riches for the sake of power and pleasure, or those who want power for the sake of money or fame.... These, then, are the things that people long to attain.

But all of these are false paths and can lead only to illusory happiness. Though possession of these worldly goods might appear to increase one's self-sufficiency, in fact they lead only to greater fear, dependency, weakness, and imprisonment. True self-sufficiency—for such is the nature of true happiness—can only be glimpsed when the false paths and sidetracks have been recognized for what they are.

Of course, the Boethian version of true happiness can seem deeply unconvincing, since it is predicated on belief in the Christian God and on more logically dubious maneuvers to justify that belief. God, Philosophy says, is supremely good. Supreme goodness and true happiness would seem to be identical. Thus God is the source of true happiness, and individuals can find true happiness only in God. It is only a small step from that piece of legerdemain to the even more questionable conclusion quoted above, that God's goodness permits no evil, and therefore that all apparent evil is just that: apparent. And that is just dangerous nonsense.

Moreover, the arguments of Book IV of *The Consolation,* that God's justice is preserved because worldly evil is always punished after death, and virtue likewise rewarded there—begin to ring pretty hollow. There is the further suggestion, again prefiguring the theodical arguments of Leibniz, that everything that happens, happens for the best in this best of all possible worlds—which it must be since God, by definition a perfect being, created it. This notion is rightly scorned—vividly so by Voltaire, whose bathetic proto-novel *Candide* is a ruthless lampoon of the idea that a supernatural being has ordered this world for our benefit. Happiness, Voltaire suggests at the end of that comic masterpiece, consists not in metaphysical theories of preestablished harmony or God's will but in "cultivating our garden," surrendering the attempt to make sense of a senseless world in favor of a simple life of work and leisure. "Let's work without speculating," the skeptical Martin says to Candide in the book's famous final scene. "It's the only way of rendering life bearable." [11] The sentiment perhaps goes too far—speculation is not always pointless, nor is the world invariably evil—but while considerations of God's justice might have bucked up Boethius on his way to the torture chamber, Voltaire is surely right that they are not rationally respectable.

Of course, arguing this way begins to suggest an influence of philosophical training that Boethius evidently did not consider: namely, that a basic awareness of logical relations will effectively rule out some fallacious arguments that we might quite like to believe, because they are comforting, but in all rational conscience cannot. Logic is an austere master, heedlessly demolishing some of our most cherished illusions. (Call this the disconsolation of philosophy.) Yet all is not lost, for the Platonic influence on Boethius's position suggests a possible non-Christian version of the argument that might be more convincing. The distinction drawn between true and false happiness need not lead to belief in the Christian God, but it does lead to an awareness of the goods and goals that ascend higher than the immediate material and worldly things of this life. In *The Republic*, Plato argues that true happiness—the truly healthy soul, the one kind of justice that really matters—can only come about from orienting oneself to the Good. The reward of justice is the soul's health, the punishment of vice the pathological illness of the tyrant or libertine. True happiness is therefore enjoyed only by the virtuous, for happiness in a sense simply *is* virtue. And here the fatalism of the Boethian message is punched up to a higher ethical volume. The point of identifying true happiness is not merely to console oneself in times of trouble; it is also to provide the direction we need, here and now, to do the right and just thing.

LOOKING AT THE SUN

Despite my regard for *The Republic, The Consolation,* and *The Enchiridion,* my favorite piece of philosophical speculation about happiness is not an academic tract but a work of fiction, a novel by Michael Frayn called *A Landing on the Sun.* In it, an English civil servant called Summerchild has been found dead in mysterious circumstances near his Whitehall office—he has fallen, or jumped, or been pushed off a roof—and a cynical colleague, Jessel, is given the thankless task of closing the file on Summerchild's career and life. Jessel knew Summerchild only well enough to recognize him across the courtyard. All he has to go on now is a paper trail of old memos, requisition forms, incomplete reports, and notes from various meetings held and planned for. He must reconstruct the events leading up to Summerchild's death.

Summerchild was charged with a backwater bureaucratic task. He was to form a committee to investigate the notion of "quality of life" for the ruling government, which had promised to raise it for voters everywhere. But they can't begin to do that until they know in what quality of life consists. To Summerchild's way of thinking, communicated between the lines of his exquisitely crafted departmental memos, this is a wild-goose chase, a sloughed-off boondoggle designed to create the impression of progress when there is really nothing of substance going on. He decides to make the best of it without allowing the committee to get out of hand. To that end, he restricts the committee to himself and one other person, an Oxford philosopher called Serafin, with whom he begins a dry correspondence.

But Serafin is excited by the task, eager to make the most of it.

When the two finally meet, Summerchild is disarmed by Serafin's enthusiasm, and by her—he never considered that Dr. Serafin might be a woman. The two find an out-of-the-way office and begin a series of regular meetings, the absent-minded yet probing philosopher clashing with the process-oriented, memo-driven civil servant. Summerchild wants to write a report, while Serafin conducts their meetings in the style of a Wittgensteinian seminar, pushing concepts to their limit. "I have been attempting to identify and generalize the various things that we perceive as affecting or as constituting the quality of life," she tells Summerchild, producing a list of material goods including television sets, washing machines, central heating, and cars. "But what they have in common is something both blindingly simple to name and blindingly difficult to think about. The common factor is that *we do so perceive them!*"

Serafin keeps probing the limits of thinking about happiness, often to the point of gentle parody of the methods of analytic philosophy: Is happiness "a feeling tone," as one philosopher has argued, or a reaction to certain states of affairs? A purely subjective sensual state, or a perception of states of affairs? But there is something compelling about her attempt, at least for someone like Summerchild, who discovers that he has never actually asked himself the question "Am I happy?" When he does, he is forced to conclude that he can find only two hours and seventeen minutes of "unambiguous" happiness in his adult life—a period when the power went out one night, plunging his house into darkness, spent, in candlelight, with his wife, now dead, listening to his daughter play the violin. "I believe a good case could be made out for saying EITHER: (a) that, as a man who is happily married, with congenial work and fortunate domestic circumstances, *I am happy,*" Summerchild writes in a memo to Serafin. "OR: (b) that, as a man whose responses are so dulled by routine that he can recall only 2 hr 17 min of unambiguous happiness in the past few years, *I am not happy.* I think it is unlikely that there is any further evidence which would put the question beyond doubt. What seems to be required now is something more in the nature of a decision."

Serafin is struck by this, responding to the claim without recognizing the emotion that has forced Summerchild out of his habitual detachment. "[S]tatements about being happy have a strongly performative content," she says. "One so to speak *names* oneself as happy or unhappy, in the same way that one names a child." Performative utterances, for those unversed in the apparatus of philosophical analysis, are an unusual class of speech-acts that actually do what they say. For example, saying "I christen this ship the *Queen Mary*" or "I resign!" does not just provide information to listeners; such a sentence also, in its very utterance, performs the act in question. Another example would be the sentence favored by the guard at the University of Edinburgh philosophy library, who used to kick me and my friend Dave out every evening at five o'clock by saying, "The library is now closed."

Is the sentence "I am happy" a performative utterance in this sense? Well, it can be, in the way that articulating a state of affairs makes it, by that very action, more real. If I find myself uttering the sentence "I am happy," then surely I have been moved to do so by some awareness of happiness, but saying so also contributes to firming up that awareness. It is not, apparently, a strong performative, in the sense that simply saying it makes the statement true, as in the examples above. Yet it seems to retain elements of that peculiar kind of utterance, for saying it can have the effect of making us aware of a generalized, background contentment—which may be why some people tend to say "I am happy" so infrequently: they do not often find themselves in a position of wanting to assert their own happiness, not because they lack happiness altogether but, rather, because they somehow do not want to force the issue on themselves. On the other hand, we all know that merely saying "I am happy" does not, in itself, make the statement true, as with a genuine performative. There is a trickiness here that seems to resist analysis, a trickiness that always reminds me of a conversation I once had with my friend Peter. It seems to me now that it resembles one of Serafin's exchanges with Summerchild, in which the instincts of philosophical analysis, the relentless fallacy-alert, are gently mocked. Peter was trying to get me to sing the song "If you're happy and you know it, clap your hands—If you're happy and you know it, and you really want to show it, if you're happy and you know it, clap your hands." It's a bizarre song, I said, when you think about it, with the rising intensity of its imperative to *clap your hands,* and this strange distinction implied between being happy and knowing it. I wondered, further, whether somebody could be happy and *not* know it. You might not want to show it, true, but that is a separate question, really, conceptually distinct from the first one. Isn't it? Peter just looked at me with a raised eyebrow, like, I knew you were weird but now you're moving into wacko territory, my friend. Which is perhaps what happens when you spend too long studying philosophy.

So what is true when one says "I am happy"? Is happiness something superadded to my state of being, at that moment, a kind of cherry placed upon the cake of my contentment—a stamp of self-approval? Or is happiness, on the contrary, the very way of perceiving the world which, at that moment, allows me to utter these three words with a confidence that they are true? There seem to be elements of both, because an awareness of happiness is something more, an extra feeling, added to the state of affairs it refers to; but happiness is also, at center, a form of being-in-the-world, a complete sense of oneself as being in the right place at the right time, and wanting things to be as they are. It is a judgment, not simply a feeling—a judgment on the state of the world and one's place within it. That is why the hedonistic conception of happiness is so limited, because it does not account for this element of self-approval and external validation that resides in happiness: the sense that one is where one ought to be.

What causes this feeling, what warrants this judgment? Serafin and Summerchild begin, as they were charged to, with material goods. But they find that such goods account for very little, and that statistics about per capita income and the demographic distribution of consumer durables appear to glide over the deep question— though certainly the self-perception of happiness would often seem to be a function of socioeconomic circumstance, especially when that circumstance is regarded in comparison to those around us. Serafin suggests that happiness might consist in "complete absorption in some conceptual problem," the sort of thing psychologists call "flow-experiences": deep engagement in a mathematical analysis, for example, or reading a difficult book that takes up the entire store of our available attention and energy.[12] But this creates a paradox, for, as Summerchild puts it, "the pleasure there was precisely my *unawareness* of my feelings—indeed, the loss of all sense of self." Can happiness be happiness when it is not experienced as pleasure but as oblivion?

It is certainly a widely held idea of happiness. Not long ago, I was visiting some friends who have two young daughters, five and two years old, along with another couple who also have a daughter, five. We all went to a playground for part of the afternoon, and in the humid southern Ontario heat we sat watching the girls play, overcome by a mixture of glazed boredom and irritated attention. Watching them scramble on the swings and monkey bars, I wondered if it was true that only children are really capable of happiness—that sense of being lost in an activity so completely that time seems to disappear. The rest of us, the jaded adults with our worries and niggles and qualifications, no longer seem to fall through the present into that timeless cavern of joy. We are rarely lost to ourselves the way we so often were as children. On the other hand, there are moments—not many—when the complete absorption in an experience (usually, for me, one of writing or reading or maybe sex) annihilates time in that way most of us know, appearing to turn the clock faster and suddenly pitching me up on the other side of noon with a rumbling stomach and a mild cramp in my neck.

And yet, seeing the joy cast in bold relief on their dirty faces, their simple pleasure in simple pleasures, was somehow making me happy in turn. It was not a pure kind of happiness like theirs, of course, but murky and colonized by preconceptions, memories, and cultural expectations. And it was edged with, among other things, disproportionate sadness (Oh how fleeting is youth!), nostalgia (Whither the playgrounds of yesteryear?), pop-cultural mediation (I see Dustin Hoffman running with his injured son in *Kramer vs. Kramer;* also, bizarrely, the empty swing sets of a postapocalyptic scene from *Terminator 2),* an awareness of my own sentimentality (Milan Kundera's two tears of kitsch: the first of emotion; the second of self-conscious awareness of emotion), and simple adult impatience (When are we going to get the hell out of here?).[13] I was also aware of romanticizing the kids more than a little. ("Happy?" says a character in Minette Walters's novel *The Dark Room,* "I'm not 'happy.' Only children are happy.") But I don't really remember the experience of childhood as happy. I hardly remember it *as* anything: it was a series of events, some enjoyable and some not, embarrassments and minor triumphs, but almost entirely devoid of intentionality or awareness. The idea that childhood happiness is pure is itself, I thought, a rather dubious social construction, possibly indicative of a longing for more moments of oblivion in our adult lives—more times when we simply abandon the structures and expectations of grown-up existence and enter the manic, screaming selflessness of the merry-go-round.

The thing about the happiness of oblivion is that, despite its random and fleeting nature, it can still play an important part in grounding the ongoing sense of satisfaction that is essential to raising happiness beyond a simple, passing feeling. Regarded in retrospect, these losses of self are important markers of a life worth living, periods of occupation that are typically so involving that they lift us above time's tyranny and other mundane markers of anxiety. When writing or conversation or lecturing is going well, it has something of the transcendent quality of the perfect swish turnaround jump-shot or an occasion I still remember when, playing pick-up soccer, aged sixteen, I took an incoming midfield cross on my right foot near the penalty area, dribbled all the way up the pitch untouched, defenders tumbling in my wake, and then hammered the ball into the back of the net past the keeper's outstretched hands. Perfection! But there is a difference, even here. The reason clapped-out athletes so often seem sad figures is not just that their careers are of necessity over so soon; it is also because there are few things in life as simply and purely satisfying as the performance that rises above expectation, those exquisite moments when every shot drops, every pass is laser guided, every swing connects at the sweet spot. We say it's magic—and it is, until it is over.

Life offers few such moments, but they are essential life buoys on the roiling seas of uncertainty and disappointment. I think they are properly characterized as moments of joy, not happiness. We cherish them, but, at the same time, we often feel that genuine happiness must take the longer view. Genuine happiness must regard the bigger picture, and incorporate the uncertainty and disappointment of life within its ambit. The task of folding life's downsides into our conception of happiness is very difficult, of course—much more difficult than isolating a few transient moments of joy or pleasure or contentment and convincing ourselves that *these* are what happiness consists in. Such moments are not reliable; they come and go too sneakily, too unpredictably. Worse, they can often seem to exist only in prospect or retrospect, never in the crisscrossed present: yes, I knew joy at that moment; yes, I look forward now to a pleasure that is (might be) to come. But I think we rightly believe that happiness must also be something we can affirm in the present tense, however extraordinary and contingent such an affirmation might be.

"I came to the conclusion in an earlier report, I think," Serafin writes,

> that happiness was a state that existed only in recollection and anticipation—only in the past and in the future. I was wrong. It can also exist in the present. It exists now, as I say these words. I am at this moment happy. I know this with absolute certainty. I know this *incorrigibly*, whatever happens in future, whatever retrospective revisions the future imposes upon my understanding of the world. I know it in the same way that philosophers once hoped to show we knew the experience from which we supposedly inferred the world around us.

The qualifications she offers here are important: "whatever happens in the future"; "whatever retrospective revisions the future imposes." Such qualifications will affect her ongoing perception, and the affirmation of her own happiness—they must do so—but they cannot impinge on the truth of the statement that she *now* makes: I am happy. That is not a subjective feeling on which she is reporting—a report of her appetitive condition or even of her state of mind conceived more richly—but rather a *claim,* an objective judgment offered on herself and the world as it stands right now. It is not enough to conceive happiness, as some utilitarians and other philosophers often do, as a particular form of subjective consciousness. It must also be an objective condition, a state of affairs.

Is this true? Well, consider the implications of happiness being nothing more than a subjective mental state. In a well-known philosophical thought-experiment, we are asked to imagine that we have been given the option between life as we know it and existence in an "experience-machine" capable of synthesizing any desirable state of mind, including an obliteration of the awareness of its synthetic quality—a sort of super holodeck. (The philosophical counselor consulted by writer Laura Wexler offered her this choice as part of his therapy session: would you trade permanent happiness for your ability to think?) What choice would we make in such a situation? Constant pleasant illusion? Or the sometimes bitter realities—but more genuine happiness—of life? Despite the momentary attractions of the experience-machine, most of us, I think, would choose the risky self-determination, and the possible relative unhappiness, of life.[14]

Take an example. Imagine that something important to you, a close friendship or treasured accomplishment, were one day revealed as an elaborate deception, a long-term conspiracy of actors, drugs, and artfully revised newspapers. You would be devastated, the sweet love or pride you felt before suddenly reduced to so much emotional ash. Now, to be sure, the experience-machine has the ability to obliterate the subject's awareness of its own mechanical nature: unlike the situation in my example, the "deception" need never be revealed. So from within the experience of artificial happiness there is no awareness of its artificiality. Does that change the case? Not really, since the issue is still the *choice* that we must make, here and now, about trading life for happiness. The option of artificial happiness looks to us (or most of us) like a bad one. More than that, it begins to look like an incoherent one. In some important sense, the oblivious person inside the experience-machine would no longer be me; I can trace no concrete connection of personal identity from my choice to his experiences. In this sense, the option of the experience-machine is not so much unattractive as unimaginable. The reason for this is not simply that most of us have gotten inordinately attached to our individual lives through sheer familiarity. We also feel a clear attachment to life in general, the way it includes both the light and the dark, moments of joy and of despair, and, possibly, a larger background condition of rational satisfaction, the confidence that we are, by our own lights and others', living a life worth living. In other words, the reason for our attachment is clear: though we sometimes prefer to indulge in illusions for reasons of comfort or entertainment, on the whole what matters to us is reality. And it does so precisely because it is real. We don't just want to feel happy, solipsistically; we want to be happy, really.

The ancient philosopher Solon said it was not right to call any man happy until he was dead, since one could not know the unlucky things that might befall him later in life, the ethical failures he might unexpectedly allow himself. That is a dictum many people consider excessively demanding, or maybe just a little paranoid and depressing, but there is truth in it. The trick, I think, is to balance the awareness of the justness of Solon's observation with our ability, here and now, to look at life as it has unfolded and will likely unfold, and affirm our own happiness with it. In a sense, the claim about one's own happiness has to be made in the present, for only the present has the reality of lived experience—it is the crest of being that rolls along on the edge of potential and actual, future becoming past in a constant wave of time. That might seem to limit the scope of what we can possibly claim about happiness, or about anything else contingent on future eventualities, but in the present we can nevertheless assess not only how we *feel* right now but how we *judge* the totality of our lives, both lived and (we hope) still to come.

What prompted Serafin to this revelation about the incorrigibility of her present happiness? The formality of the bureaucratic committee has broken down in the close quarters of their room and in the intimacy of the question, and the eroticism of the philosophical quest has caught the normally unreflective Summerchild, and the normally professional Serafin, in a delirium of intense feeling: they have caught philosophy like a delicious virus. In pursuit of happiness, they have realized their own unhappiness—his with a dreary widowerhood and lost opportunities, hers with an unfulfilling marriage to a philandering poseur. But they have also realized the happiness of their shared pursuit, the devotion to a conceptual problem which is itself a form of happiness and, when experienced together, a form of communion. In short, they are in love. (Did you guess?) And now the question of their happiness becomes more complicated still, and ultimately—I won't sully the story with a clumsy paraphrase of the denouement—tragic. "We have to ask ourselves, I think," Serafin says, "and shall ask ourselves at a calmer moment—whether the intensity of our happiness is not in some way dependent on the intensity of our anguish—whether in fact happiness and unhappiness are not in some way logically interdependent."

Love is the form of happiness that invites this question most pressingly. At the crude, hedonistic level, we are all familiar with the experience of the pleasure that acquires sharpness and vigor by means of contrast—the hot shower after a long winter jog, the bracing cocktail after a hard day's work—and familiar, too, with the looming pathology of suffering pain simply in order to add relish to pleasure: say, lifting weights because it feels so good when you stop. More deeply, there is the complicated economy of expectation, in which artfully lowered ones can make an ordinary party seem excellent because I convinced myself it would actually be terrible; or, on the other side, the disappointment of a movie that fails to live up to its slyly edited trailer. But even beyond this, there lies something else:

I mean the terrible contingency of our deepest happiness, the frightening and vertiginous buoyancy of being in love with someone else.

For years now I have been afflicted by a form of morbid imagination concerning the physical safety of my wife, Gail, when she is out of my sight. I have nightmares about train wrecks and car crashes, muggings and violent sexual assaults. Each morning I spend the long subway ride to my office preoccupied with thoughts of phone calls from grim physicians or visits from a pair of businesslike police officers. I have viewed such scenes so many times in the movies and on television, the stock shot of the opened door and the face crumbling in shock, that they have a haunting vividness. There are a few variations: the police sometimes in plain clothes instead of uniform, a briskly sympathetic woman officer sometimes filling in for one of the crew-cut men. But the story is always the same. She is dead, or maimed, or lying unconscious in a hospital bed somewhere. I was watching television or reading while she was struck by a bus or beaten senseless or knifed or shot. Now there are tubes sticking into her arms and nose, a bank of dauntingly sophisticated machines beeping and pumping around the bed.

This ghoulish obsession began about seven years ago when we had to spend a year apart while I was finishing up my doctoral thesis in one city, and country, and Gail was beginning a degree in another. We were poor and overworked and saw each other maybe twice in the whole year, otherwise spending money we didn't have on agonized phone calls filled with expensive, frustrated silence. It was terrible and wreaked all kinds of psychic havoc on me. It was also the first time I realized that you could love somebody so much that it was painful. I do not mean the kind of all-consuming crush that, in the first throes of love, obliterates the everyday world in flinty, helpless jealousy or the exquisite anguish of separation. Much has been made of that kind of pain, and it is real enough, but I know from experience, as most of us do, that it passes after a certain amount of time, often replaced by a measure of indifference or even hostility. You can't trust it. Nobody seems to write songs about the pain I mean, the long-standing burden of love, the ever-present epoxy of gratitude for one's good fortune mixed with this terrible, unwholesome fear of having its source damaged or taken away.

It happens that, at the time I am writing this, Gail is preparing to move away again, this time to take up a teaching job in another city, and another country. She might be gone for two years, or four years, or maybe for good: it depends on how the job works out. We have more money now, more experience of ourselves and each other and more resources of maturity and tolerance to deploy in keeping our relationship going. But it is a daunting prospect all the same. When we tell people about Gail's new job the usual response is "How's that going to work?"—a question I confess to finding extremely irritating. I have no idea how it's going to work. What would you like me to say? That we're getting divorced right now, because it's not going to work? That I'm preparing to kill myself because I can't live without her? What? Either it's going to work or it isn't. *How* is not something anyone can decide before the fact. Shut up.

Of course I have lots of friends and more than enough work to keep me busy. And I am happy that Gail has landed a good job in a tough academic market, proud of her accomplishments in finishing the doctorate and moving to the next stage of career success. I would not wish it otherwise, in short, and, unlike the members of one search committee who interviewed her, I have never had the temerity to suggest she is doing a bad thing by leaving her husband to take up a job. I have never thought she has a duty to stay with me to the detriment of her career, just as I have always allowed myself the same freedom of opportunity, even if, so far, I have not been given an opportunity to exercise it.

Still, I can see the dark visions already, late-night visitations of scenes from bad thrillers: the 1:00 A.M. knock on the door, the somber faces illuminated by the weak porchlight. Awake at night, I place my left hand on the delicate fretwork of Gail's ribcage and feel the slow beating of her heart, wishing I could somehow cup it in my hands and keep it safe. How is it that happiness can include, apparently as a necessary condition, so much potential unhappiness? How is it that love, which brings so much strength, should also entail this enduring vulnerability, this dreadful potential for pain?

PLEASURES AND PAINS

In the face of this kind of vulnerability, some philosophers have argued that the only route to happiness is to strip yourself of the kinds of commitment that can make for unhappiness, an extreme version of what I called strategy one, the theory of the lowered gaze. In the grip of this form of pathology, we convince ourselves that nothing is worth caring about, partly for intrinsic reasons—consider the potentially defeatist wisdom of *Sic transit gloria mundi*, for example, which puts paid to worldly ambition—and partly as a psychic defense mechanism to avoid becoming, as lawyers say, "situationally exposed." The paradox of this attitude is that it appears to purchase happiness at the expense of taking no joy in anything. And yet it engenders a peculiar form of aggressive self-congratulation. "Men who are unhappy," says Russell in *The Conquest of Happiness*, "like men who sleep badly, are always proud of the fact." This is the conceited, cynical unhappiness of *As You Like It*'s Jacques or of Lord Byron in his darker moods.

"It is common in our day," Russell continues,

> as it has been in many other periods of the world's history, to suppose that those among us who are wise have seen through all the enthusiasms of earlier times and have become aware that there is nothing left to live for. The men who hold this view are genuinely unhappy, but they are proud of their unhappiness, which they attribute to the nature of the universe and consider to be the only rational attitude for an enlightened man.

What is curious about this attitude, apart from the sophomoric cheapness of its wisdom, is the fact that it is really, did its proponents but know it, a form of happiness theory: these people get their only form of happiness precisely by celebrating their own unhappiness. They are as concerned about their own happiness as anyone, only they pursue it in a perverse manner. If they could only see that, they might recognize the self-defeating character of the world-weary attitude once and for all, and give it up.

Still, even the most cheerful among us are now and then subject to the mood this position describes. There are moments, for me most common during the depressed early-morning hours following a night of one too many glasses of wine, in which I think that all is vanity: all the pleasures of social events reduced to so much posturing and preening, the achievements of working life no more than cheap acts of one-upmanship, personal attachments just shameful sexual attraction in disguise. Or those periods after a faculty meeting or editorial-board conference, when it seems to me that even knowledge and wisdom, not just human ambition and puffery, are rotten to the core: scholarship (I think then) is no more than jockeying for position, and literature just a mug's game in which grants and prizes and glossy author photos, not talent, carry the day. In these dark moments, the attractions of the world-weary position become clear. But, as Russell suggests, the mood is often brought on by excessive leisure and the too-easy satisfaction of material desires. The route out of this self-indulgent gloom and back to a more positive mental space is not through philosophy, Russell says, which might be itself powerless to alter a mood, but instead through some kind of work, or anyway exertion. He is probably right. I always feel better after sweating off my *Weltschmerz* along with a few calories—as long as I remember to forget that exercise is probably mostly vanity too.

What lasting consolation is there in philosophy, then? Its habitual answers—the theory of the lowered gaze (which says that excessive desire is the problem) and the theory of the silver lining (which says there is good in everything)—have the potential, in extreme forms, to lead to cynicism or passivity, or both. Too much philosophy, as Thurber's Mrs. Kirkfield reminds us, can tear our gaze away from the fact that everything is terrible. On the other hand, not enough means surrendering to that terror. We still seem to lack what philosophers have long claimed to provide for us, an argument for the kind of life that is worth living: an analysis of happiness that would not simply untangle its conceptual strands but offer us insight into how to live. Some thinkers think this is simply not possible. Freud was explicit in *Civilization and Its Discontents* about the limits of human reason when tackling the question of happiness: "I have not the courage to rise up before my fellow-men as a prophet, and I bow to their reproach that I can offer them no consolation; for at bottom that is what they are all demanding—the wildest revolutionaries no less passionately than the most virtuous believers." A more recent thinker took refuge not in disconsolation but in suggestive paradox. "The good life," he wrote, "is the life spent seeking the good life." [15]

There is a measure of truth in both observations, but they leave us grasping at straws when trying to decide, here and now, how to live. At the same time, the very question of the quality of life—the question that launched the sweet tragedy of Serafin and Summerchild, the question that we might say began the Western philosophical tradition, with its Socratic quest for the life worth living—has lately been taken over by medical and biological attempts to understand the nature of pain and its relationship to happiness. The physician Eric J. Cassell forces the basic issue of happiness in a suggestive way, for instance, when he draws a distinction between pain and suffering. Unlike the reductive hedonism of the classical utilitarians, in which all disagreeable sensations and perceptions are treated pretty much the same way, this view has the nuance to separate the physical sensation of pain from the cultural and phenomenological experience of suffering. Suffering, says Cassell, results from "injuries to the integrity of the person." Pain may not bring suffering if, for example, I find it a relief from a period of excessive indulgence, as in some kinds of violent exercise, or if I regard it as a badge of honor, as in taking a wound for the good of the battle. Moreover, suffering can accompany pain or be caused independently of it; blows to one's person are not always physical.

"With this in mind," Cassell writes, "we can also realize how much someone devoid of physical pain, even devoid of 'symptoms,' may suffer. People suffer from what they have lost of themselves in relation to the world of objects, events, and relationships."[16] That is why pain and its prevention are in many ways just the tip of the iceberg when it comes to well-being, which is much more about how one places oneself in the world. "In short," adds a philosopher, "how physical pain feels to us, how much it hurts, is one thing; how much it matters to us is another."[17] And the same is true of pleasure: sometimes too much pleasure is unpleasant, unsettling, or tawdry; sometimes we grow sick or wary of pleasure's warm embrace. But the issue of how much these things matter—the ethical questions of suffering and enjoyment, rather than the physical questions of pain and pleasure—is not something that readily surrenders either to simple measurement or to the reports of states of mind, despite what some sociologists and philosophers would have us believe. A recent study by social psychologist Ruut Veenhoven of the Netherlands, for example, defined a quality-of-life index that Veenhoven called "happy life expectancy," which gave social scientists the precise means of deciding which country on earth was the happiest. "If one multiplies the average life expectancy in a country by the percentage of people who declare themselves to be happy in opinion polls," the study concluded, "the happiest country is Iceland."[18]

At the margins of life, the problems of life's quality become more pressing still, and, increasingly, medical professionals and lay people alike are overwhelmed by the ethical indeterminacy of the issues. At what moment, precisely, does life become literally unbearable? Who will be sanctioned to decide that question, and according to what criteria? What quality must a life possess in order to be worth preserving? At what point, and according to what standards, does the quality of an individual life pass below an acceptable threshold? What amount of pain? What restriction of movement? What loss of hope? Fortunately, most of us never have to confront the quality-of-life issue in all of its stark, life-or-death possibility. Most of us never have to decide, for someone else, when a life is no longer worth living in this sense of no longer justifying medical intervention. Even for ourselves, it is not always the case that we will face a decision about whether, and when, life is no longer of sufficient quality to merit its continuance. (True, the difficult questions of continued care and pain management are often pressing ones for those who are ill and perhaps nearing death. But the hard cases of assisted suicide and the voluntary cessation of elaborate life-support are still, fortunately, the exception.)

In this sense, the medical issue of quality of life is not something many people concern themselves with. Indeed, most of us, when we think of it at all, tend to think of "the quality of life" in terms of the comforts and freedoms we enjoy within an existence that is presumed to be relatively stable, if not incredibly privileged. We do not, typically, ask ourselves the life-or-death question that confronts those who find themselves, as a result of disease or deformity or despair, at the edges of existence. Yet perhaps we should. Why? Well, not because Camus believed the life-or-death question the only really pressing philosophical issue, as he said in *The Myth of Sisyphus*. Nor because we want to be constantly on the edge of suicide, or wish other people to be. We should confront the quality-of-life question, rather, because it is, in its widest implications, really the basic question of the human condition. In other words, Hamlet's gloomy attempt to decide whether or not to live proves, when regarded properly, closer than we might think to Socrates' older, and apparently less pressing, attempt to decide what makes for a genuinely happy life.

The problem, as I have argued, is that more of us do not pursue the issue in disciplined ways. We seek happiness, all right, but with such a frenzy of confusion and aimless desire that the philosophical questions beneath that pursuit rarely come to the surface. What is a life of quality? What is a life worth living?

Part **3**

7

The Virtues of Happiness (I)

"Oh this *is* a happy day, this will have been another happy day! *(Pause.)* After all. *(Pause.)* So far."

—*Samuel Beckett,* Happy Days

LET'S GO TO THE EX!

GAIL AND I COULD NOT HAVE KNOWN, AS WE STOOD PRESSED together in the crush of people on the 511 streetcar, that the journey downtown to the Canadian National Exhibition and the Better Living Centre would actually be the high point of our afternoon. It was breezy and unseasonally cool outside, but inside the car a fug of expelled air, acrid sweat-smell, and disconsolate infant whining descended on us like a malevolent entity. It was nearly unbearable. In the long moments when the car was pointlessly halted or, worse, moving forward at geriatric walking speed, I thought I was going to have to scream, there was so much unresolved animal adrenaline shooting into my bloodstream.

We spilled off the car with enormous but short-lived relief. It was freezing. The sky was a bleak gunmetal gray and there was a stiff breeze coming off Lake Ontario. The crowds were no thinner than usual, though, and big phalanxes of baby-strollers and power wheelchairs moved across the grounds like malignant antipersonnel devices, pushed by and pushing through an assortment of pleasure-seeking people in ill-chosen shorts and T-shirts. Groups of them were huddled at picnic tables or on the grass, eating their massive

slices of pizza and messy hot dogs with the simple porcine contentment of Bill Bryson's British beach-goers, happy in their miserable
surroundings. Gail and I got cups of coffee and hot dogs and joined
them there, windblown and shivering, and I thought once more that
there really is nothing as simply gratifying and restorative as a cup of
good coffee and a sandwich on a cold day.

We strolled away from the bells and sirens of the midway, the
nearly deserted games of chance, and the standard array of thrill
rides which, in the freshening wind, were probably bordering on
genuine instead of apparent danger. We pushed our way through
the posturing teenagers, in their camouflage T-shirts and baggy
jeans, engaged as ever in the fearsome mating rituals of adoles-
cence, the attempted eye-locks and suggestive hip-swings that used
to terrify and fascinate me two decades ago when I was a pudgy four-
teen-year-old walking these same grounds.

The Exhibition complex had recently been subjected to a massive reclamation project, and there were new buildings and unfamiliar layouts. But the original structures, the lovely Victorian
architecture of exposition from Toronto's first commercial boom,
were intact—I love those soaring domes and cat's cradles of iron
and glass, the mechanistic nineteenth-century optimism of it all. But
the Better Living Centre comes from another period of technological aspiration, the 1960s, and it is a clean, functional cinder-block
shed that resembles a clock radio. We followed the thin stream of
people in through the main doors.

Inside, the space was divided into booths, or sections, spread out
before us in a patchwork pattern of dining-room sets, hot-tub gaze-
bos, and banks of televisions. The chairs in the furniture displays
had little signs on them that said "Not for rest purposes." Inside one
cedar hot-tub gazebo a family of three was sitting, actually in the
tub, going over a contract with the mustachioed salesman. Entire
extended families of nine or ten were walking down the narrow
passages between the booths—mom, dad, grandma, two strollers,
and several kids perambulating—and everyone had adopted, as
if instinctively, that glazed-eye, one-kilometre-per-hour shopper's

stroll. They wandered past the displays with every indication of indifference, if not somnambulance, only to halt without warning every now and then to gaze at this or that object and cause a severe human traffic jam behind them. It was the limbo-walk of the nearly dead, without purpose or destination.

The objects themselves were dispiriting in another fashion. I was surprised to find my memories of glossy appliances and scrubbed salespeople confronted by a tatty assortment of cut-rate kitchenware, low-end household aids, and big banners proclaiming "Everything $9.99 or less." An elderly woman walked past me and said, "It's like a dollar store in here." I thought sadly of my poor dead grandmother who, in days gone by, would have sacrificed a daily dose of *General Hospital,* in a time before videocassette recorders, in order to make her arduous way to this place, just so she could be close to the best the material world had to offer. I found the decline even more depressing than an aggressive increase in consumerism would have been. There was an overpowering air of hopelessness, the product demonstrators showing off their superpolishes and food slicers with a perfunctory and defeatist air, sometimes to nobody at all, as if they were not people at all but automatons on a mindless tape-loop. I couldn't even get excited when the biggest crowd of all, listening to a man called Graham Haley, of Haley's Household Hints, was told they could save money by shining their shoes with a banana peel or halve their ironing time by ingenious application of aluminum foil.

"One big infomercial," Gail said, and it was true. It was as if we had climbed into middle-of-the-night cable TV, or entered, by a magic portal, the terrifying parallel universe where the Home Shopping Network acquires all its products and hosts. Watching a young man go through the motions of demonstrating the Super Chef Deluxe, a revolutionary food-preparation system for some reason not available in stores, we ran into a couple of friends who had fallen into a similar mood. "Doesn't this have the stench of death about it?" one of them asked. We nodded dumbly. Their son, however, sitting cross-legged on the bare floor, seemed fascinated by the slicing-dicing action of the Super Chef Deluxe. It was technology you could see for yourself, not the opaque black-box necromancy of the computer or television set. He stopped short of asking for one—they were only $29.99, down from the regular price of $39.99—but I could tell he wanted it desperately. "He likes knives," his mother said tolerantly.

Farther away from the main doors it got even worse: Sweepa rubber brooms, large garish portraits of your pet, magic chamois cloths to wash your car. One man, showing off a brand of glass polish, was talking to the entirely empty air before him. "I don't do this for everybody," he said, to no one. "Watch carefully." I moved away in sudden embarrassment. We saw the smallest radio in the world, the Sushi Master sushi-rolling system, sale-price costume jewelry, and posters for all-but-forgotten pop-culture icons like Boy George and Bo Jackson. We saw clothes nobody would wear and gadgets nobody would use. It was as if we were in a garage sale in hell. The only time Gail got mildly excited was when she spotted a display of Miele vacuum cleaners, sleek little Italian numbers in Ferrari red and football-club azure that can probably make excellent cappuccino when they aren't engaged in tastefully sucking the dirt off your carpet. There were a few nice TVs, a couple of cool stereos, and about seven cars—all Chryslers. It was horrible.

We came out into the open air, where it was colder than ever. I felt unhappy and obscurely class-conscious. I realized that the good-life machines on offer in the Better Living Centre were for a *style* of life more trailer park than Victorian reno. Not that I lived in the latter, but my aspirations were all in that direction. I felt there was a shocking lack of taste in the things that better living apparently meant to the people at the Ex. I was slightly ashamed to have this thought, but what could I do? I wouldn't be caught dead putting an overstuffed massage-action recliner in my living room. On the other hand, I have nothing in principle against anyone who would, though I suspect we would never be close friends. Another thing I realized as we walked through the games of chance on our way to another building: there had not been a single computer in the Better Living Centre, nor even the trappings of one—no CD-ROMs, no games, no multimedia books or cutesy mouse pads. It was as if the entire booming industry of personal computer ownership simply did not exist for the shambling, overweight, baseball-capped denizens of the Centre. Their notions of the good life, of happiness, apparently did not include anything so newfangled. They wanted big TVs, loud stereos, fat chairs from which to watch and listen to these, and racks of overdecorated plates on which they could serve up meals prepared in miracle mixers and cooked in amazing waterless double boilers. Inside the Better Living Centre, it was still the 1960s, only the clothes were not nearly as nice and the ethnic mix not nearly as limited.

At the other end of the midway Gail and I walked into the cavernous new Heritage Centre, which was featuring a number of exhibits, including the NFL Experience, a celebration of Italian design ingenuity, and something called the Festival of the Future. Gail refused to heed my suggestion that she pose with her face visible above a headless dummy fully loaded with professional football gear, nine or ten of which had been placed around the display floor for this purpose. We didn't bother with punt, pass, and kick, either, hurrying instead into the Italian section. Here there was more of what I was looking for: smartly designed chairs, witty *objets,* and more slick appliances in deep, racing-car red, including a number of those pump-action Gaggia espresso machines that some friends of mine consider essential to human well-being. There was some weird Harlequin and Columbine play going on at one end, but it looked to me as though most of the people watching were simply taking advantage of the fact that the folding chairs ranked backwards from the stage were, in the absence of advice to the contrary, for rest.

The Festival of the Future sounded as though it might be all the Better Living Centre wasn't: space-age information technology, cool new inventions to ease and delight domestic life, hot new models of computer and multimedia hardware. But no. There was a little Internet café, where most people were ignoring the terminals and just sitting down to drink coffee, some piles of tatty discounted PC how-to books, and a small display of tamagotchis, those little Japanese electronic toys with identities, needs, and finite lifetimes that make little kids so unhappy when they "die." Across the way there were some listless kids standing in front of a connected series of displays called "The Home of the Future," which looked like any home of the present, except (according to the kids) everything was made of organic materials and designed to be recycled.

Another display suggested that the housing developments of the future would be like minicommunities, with general stores and dry cleaners all contained within a compound. Since this, too, has already come very much to pass (in fact, some places have gone to the preposterous length of creating fake little indoor "Main Street" malls, complete with Ye Olde Ice Cream Parlour and Ye Village Smithy), I felt the Ex version was veering toward dangerous understatement, even self-parody. A disembodied voice proclaimed, in tones of utter indifference, "We are entering a new era in which technology will transform the way we work, play, travel, and live." The voice didn't sound as though it imagined anyone could believe such a thing. I was just formulating a sort of satirical denunciation of this city-of-the-future project, in the form of an ersatz shopping mall modeled on an actual North American urban street, say Detroit or Bridgeport or East St. Louis, with boarded-up storefronts, dirty outposts of impersonal hamburger chains, swilling beggars, and lots of broken glass, when Gail called me over to another section of the exhibit.

"Look at this stuff," she said. "Now this—this is what you just don't see any more." It was a black-and-white photograph of an earlier incarnation of the Canadian National Exhibition. A large crowd of formally dressed people—the men all in suits and hats, the women wearing dresses and gloves—were lining up in front of a pavilion, patiently waiting in their hundreds to see an amazing new invention on display for the very first time in Toronto: television. The photo was in a little archival section of the exhibit called "Progress on Parade," which included photos and posters from more optimistic and, let's be honest, militaristic periods of Canadian history. In the poster illustrations, muscular men with the stern faces of Soviet labor posters stood in front of the CNE's main entrance, rolling up their sleeves in a visible expression of postwar determination. A few years later the same opening-day poster showed other men, or maybe the same ones, now dressed in sharply pressed suits and standing with pretty blond wives and chipper kids. Others were more straightforward, depicting the Ex as a showcase of Cold War military hardware and other industrial wonders from the first-city-of-the-colonies past some Torontonians cherish so much. It was pretty scary, in fact, seeing the notions of technological and social progress connected so un-self-consciously to the manufacture of instruments of death, machines expressly designed for the destruction of human tissue. But you had to admit there was a flash of energy still emanating from the faded colors and softened paper of the old posters that was entirely missing from the exhibits around us, and the very crispness of the trouser creases and A-lines in the old photos made the current crop of beer-belly boys and designer-jeaned women appear not so much tasteless as regressive. Progress on Parade, I don't think so. "Can you imagine how exciting it must have been to see television for the first time?" Gail said. "That's the problem. There's nothing *new* any more."

We were clearly descending into a peculiar form of nostalgic misanthropy, and it was about to get worse. We didn't know it, but while we had been shuffling around the anodyne vision of the future—where, I wondered, was all the genuine techno-optimism, where were the cool new machines?—it had started to rain outside. With the spirited winds, it was getting pretty hairy on the midway. As we watched from a sheltering doorway it started to pour, and now people were rushing into the nearest building in damp clumps, bottlenecking at the doorways as strollers clashed and wide butts blocked off possible exit routes. We were jostled in this manner for a few minutes as we tried to decide what to do; Gail suggested we make our way to the Food building in order to get a corn dog. That done, and rides out of the question, we could go home.

A big mistake. The Food building is frightening at any time, a shameless celebration of the deep-fried and high-sugar food groups, but now it was bordering on apocalyptic. Huge lines had formed at all the concessions except those for falafel and sushi, and there was nowhere left to sit, so people were just standing around, practically shoulder to shoulder, as they crammed in the hot dogs and big plates of chow mein. "You just have to pretend you're Calvin Trillin, in search of the perfect corn dog," Gail said. "Okay," I said. (I've always admired the single-minded pursuit of purity, even of the down-home kind; a long article on the relative virtues of Kansas City versus Louisiana barbecue is something I can really get into.[1]) So we threaded our way precariously through the rising volume and hot-fat stench of the building in search of the quintessential state-fair-style corn dog. But every time we thought we were about to complete our corn-dog quest, we'd notice that the stand was selling only Pogos, a brand of frozen corn dogs you buy at the grocery store and warm up in the microwave. Pogos are to corn dogs what Kraft Dinner is to macaroni and cheese: okay in certain what-the-hell moods but not to be confused with the real thing. We are corn-dog purists, and it is important to maintain standards of integrity even when it comes to junk food—maybe especially then. We wanted to see the wieners actually skewered on the sticks and dipped in actual vats of batter; we wanted to watch the bubbles foam as the dogs were lowered tantalizingly into the deep-fryer. Away with these frozen abominations with their brand-name uniformity, the Chicken McNuggets of the corn-dog universe!

After we had made our way around the entire building, hope of a pure corn-dog experience fading all the while, we were both murderous. While Gail waited in a line to get some fish and chips, I became fascinated with a little kid in a filthy red windbreaker and thick Coke-bottle glasses. He had smears of ketchup and mustard all over his face, a hot dog in either grubby hand, and he was kneeling on the dirty concrete in the middle of a passageway, dusty jeans and chunky off-white sneakers tucked under his little haunches, masticating away with his mouth open as the riotous crowd swirled around him. He seemed perfectly happy, the entirely contented consumer.

THE USES OF SOLITUDE

We have seen, in the past few years, a consensus building to the conclusion that there is now *too much culture to consume,* too many products to keep track of: a barrage of information and entertainment so immense that mere mortals are powerless in the face of it.[2] David Denby, writing in *The New Yorker,* recently compared the sensation of living in 1990s North America to being "buried alive" in cultural sludge.[3] As we approach the self-imposed calendrical deadline of the millennium, there is more and more a sense that cultural production is being stepped up in both volume and velocity. Images and information proliferate at rates unimaginable only a decade or two ago, coming at a speed that threatens to render us insensible. The depression that descended on me in the Better Living Centre was as much about the sheer number of products on display there as it was about their absurdly low quality.

Indeed, we could say without exaggeration that the characteristic feature of living in the current culture is that of being bombarded with product: advertising campaigns and model descriptions, logos and trademarks, films and television shows, books and magazines, e-mail messages and phone calls, speeches and sound bites, websites and newsgroups, fashion trends and revivals, pop songs and rock operas, new generations of software and new models of telephone. The sheer volume of this product is its most obvious feature. It makes the prospect of getting information or experiencing culture one filled with an unexpected element of risk. As Neil Postman says, Coleridge's "famous line about water everywhere without a drop to drink may serve as a metaphor of a decontextualized information environment."[4] To live today is, as a friend of mine likes to say, like trying to get a drink of water from a firehose.

Postman, following the pioneering analysis of Marshall McLuhan, speaks of the problem of the "information–action ratio" being altered by advances, or anyway changes, in the dominant form of communication. The concept works as follows. It is easy to act on relatively small pieces of information, say, when someone tells me that the building is on fire and it is clear to me that the appropriate action is to rise calmly from my desk and get the hell out of there. But the more information I must process, the less likely it is that I will be able to act on any part of it. Hence the well-known feeling of information overload. It is not so much that we cannot process the information, in the sense of simply ingesting it; the problem is that we cannot act on it in a meaningful way—cannot digest it— because we do not know where to begin. This, surely, is the root of our enervation when sitting before the television newscast: all this human misery, all these warnings and threats, and yet no concrete suggestion of how to act in response to it. "The news elicits from you," writes Postman, "a variety of opinions about which you can do nothing except to offer them as more news, about which you can do nothing."[5] To adopt more efficient techniques of ingesting information, such as the instinctive "multitasking" now common among younger people, does not alter the fundamental problem. There is always more information out there, more than you can ever digest properly; increasing the rate of inward flow is nothing more than a self-defeating surrender to the overwhelming imperative to consume.

This volume of information and imagery produces, too, a sense of deep restlessness or anxiety. In our age's version of the Rapture described in the Book of Revelation, many people have a pervasive feeling of being *left behind*—either by the simple weight of the information and imagery that is out there, crying for attention, or by the carefully crafted campaigns of planned obsolescence and continuous technological improvement that are the mainstays of any consumer-durables industry, from cars to computers. These "advances" take on an air of inevitability closely associated with the more general *fascism of speed* that appears to afflict every aspect of our cultural experience, from the delivery of information to the waging of war and conducting of business. As the critic Paul Virilio points out in his essay *Speed and Politics,* the widespread rule of speed is far from neutral: it orders our lives, dominates our expectations, even alters our deep sense of ourselves.[6] As a result, I suspect that all of us feel, to a greater or lesser degree, the energy-sapping anxiety that we might agree to call Upgrade Angst.

Its symptoms are common. Can I read all the articles that I want to, covering *The New Yorker, The Atlantic Monthly, Harper's Magazine, Slate, Salon, GQ,* and *Esquire;* or will I have to "catch up" with them by ploughing through a stack of glossies one weekend? Can I see all the latest movies before they are squeezed off the screens by newcomers; or will I have to "catch up" with *them* on video? Can I read all the bestsellers; or will I have to rely on just reading the reviews? Can I watch all the prime-time TV specials; or will I have to tape them for viewing later? When, later? Can I eat in the new restaurant everyone is talking about? Or will it be passé by the time I get there? Can I get the new version of Netscape? Of Microsoft Word? Can I download it from the Web? How do I get on the Web? Have I been to the coolest website of the week, of the day, of the hour? Am I running System 10.1? Do I have enough RAM to run System 10.1? What about System 10.2?

This feeling is not something we should mistake as unique to our own time, nor should we accept without ado the conclusion that such saturation is necessarily bad. There is good historical evidence that every era has at some point produced a feeling of being overwhelmed in this fashion, sensing that the world in general is going to hell in a handbasket and that the younger generation is exhibiting either lax morality or a shocking absence of idealism, or both. And it is possible that a culture suffused with product may, in its own way, create new opportunities for freedom: everything is available, so anything is possible.[7] Nevertheless, as people overwhelmed by cultural *content,* I think we feel a need for more *context,* for ways of making sense of the array. And yet that worthy project has an alarming tendency to decline immediately into mere trend spotting. And it can lead, in another familiar *reductio,* to stories like the one published not long ago in the *New York Times,* which argued that the newest trend was spotting trends—an effort that later led to a column by writer Rick Salutin in the *Globe and Mail* in which he noted that the newest trend was writing stories about how trend spotting was the newest trend. Yikes!

Indeed, in the face of that kind of self-defeating modishness, we might be inclined to try to extract ourselves from the culture in some way. It is enough to make you want to go, as they say, *off the grid*—to get a stone cottage somewhere, unplug everything, and live off homegrown beans in some Waldenesque fantasyland of simplicity and genuineness and purity. (In fact, I think I saw that the *Utne Reader* did a feature on off-grid living, but I haven't had time to read it yet.) We might think to find, in this media-fasting state, that we do not miss our former flow of information. "[O]ne of the first discoveries of his captivity," Evelyn Waugh writes of his character Paul Pennyfeather in the novel *Decline and Fall,* "was that interest in 'news' does not spring from genuine curiosity, but from the desire for completeness. During his long years of freedom he had scarcely allowed a day to pass without reading fairly fully from at least two newspapers, always pressing on with a series of events which never came to an end. Once the series was broken he had little desire to resume it."[8] But this fantasy of chosen simplicity is stacked up against a large and very powerful array of social and cultural forces that make satisfaction seem unlikely. "Our demands for security, identity and happiness," says the postmodern philosopher Jean-François Lyotard, "appear today irrelevant in the face of [the] obligation to complexify, mediate, memorize and synthesize every object, and to change its scale. We are in this techno-scientific world like Gulliver: sometimes too big, sometimes too small, never at the right scale. Consequently, the claim for simplicity, in general, appears today that of a barbarian."[9] That is, the claim of someone who is taking refuge in denial. The problem is clear: there is nowhere to run, nowhere to hide.

David Denby himself opted to return to his alma mater, Columbia University, and enroll in its famous first-year Western civilization, or Great Books, course. His resulting book about the experience describes, with some eloquence, the depth of response and challenge he felt from these midlife encounters with writers like Plato, Machiavelli, Hobbes, Kant, Nietzsche, Austen, and Woolf.[10] And certainly that kind of ascent to the pinnacles of human thought and writing is one worthy antidote to the banality and superficiality of much that passes for cultural production today. The scholarly solitude of the garden or the plainly furnished room is one of the most indispensable elements in genuine happiness, especially at a time when most of the messages of the culture insist that being alone and in thought is somehow suspect or even Luddite in orientation. Carl Malamud, founder and president of the Internet Multicasting Service, professor at the MIT Media Lab and at Keio University in Tokyo, recently made the following prediction about the wired future of what gurus call *seamless ubiquity:* the idea that message-carrying technology will soon be so extensive as to blanket our lives in connections, taking the logic of cellular phone and voice-mail to its implied conclusion. "Communications technology will soon disappear," Malamud said. "That's because it will be everywhere, the way electricity is now." In this omnipresent medium of communication, no one will ever be entirely alone again.

Solitude is hostile to some advances in technology—for example, the insistence of the clock, which cuts our otherwise flowing experience into the tyranny of hours and minutes so that we can, as we all say, be *on time* for assignments and appointments, ordering our days in terms of meetings with others.[11] It can also appear to discount the persistent idea that happiness is only to be found by being with other people, in particular some singular soulmate who is, per the myths, the completion of oneself: think of the roly-poly people described in Plato's *Symposium,* cut in half by the gods for their arrogance and then forever doomed to search for their other half. "It is widely believed that interpersonal relationships of an intimate kind are the chief, if not the only, source of human happiness," writes the psychoanalyst Anthony Storr. "Yet the lives of creative individuals often seem to run counter to this assumption."

The historical evidence for this proposition is overwhelming. "No man will ever unfold the capacities of his own intellect who does not at least checker his life with solitude," wrote Thomas de Quincey, and the examples of Descartes, Newton, Locke, Pascal,

Spinoza, Kant, Leibniz, Schopenhauer, Nietzsche, Kierkegaard, and Wittgenstein bear him out. None of these great thinkers ever married, and most lived alone for the bulk of their lives. (On the other hand, some of them went crazy.) Storr adds the great historian Edward Gibbon to the list to illustrate his larger point. "Modern insistence that true happiness can only be found in intimate attachments, more especially in sexual fulfillment," he notes, "does not allow a place for characters like Gibbon," who had many friends but no wife and whose main source of self-respect and satisfaction was work. But "[i]t is only since Freud advanced the notion that heterosexual fulfillment is the *sine qua non* of mental health that anyone would question Gibbon's status as a more than commonly happy and successful human being."[12]

There is, indeed, a great and unalloyed form of happiness, and freedom, to be had in the absence of any human contact, even (as Storr acknowledges) in the absence of traditional freedom. Some people, he argues, find their greatest contentment and creative fulfillment in the enforced solitude of prison—an insight that Waugh also had, albeit more satirically. Most of us would wish to stop short of the situation enjoyed by Paul Pennyfeather, sent to prison for unwittingly aiding his fiancée's prostitution ring in *Decline and Fall.* And yet: "The next four weeks of solitary confinement were among the happiest of Paul's life," the narrator says.

> The physical comforts were certainly meagre, but at the Ritz Paul had learned to appreciate the inadequacy of purely physical comfort. It was exhilarating, he found, never to have to make any decision on any subject, to be wholly relieved from the smallest consideration of time, meals, or clothes, to have no anxiety ever about what kind of impression he was making; to be, in fact, free.

There is, Waugh notes, something to be said for one's education and social background when it comes to this sort of peaceable acceptance. "[A]nyone who has been to an English public school will always feel comparatively at home in prison. It is the people brought up in the gay intimacy of the slums, Paul learned, who find prison so soul-destroying."

When Gail left to pursue her academic career in the United States I had ample opportunity to explore the condition of solitude. It was in many respects a painful adjustment. I realized once more the countless ways that her company shaped the contours of my daily life, the way small acts of affection tell the hours or exchanged stories create the shared materials of our marriage's joint narrative. I was struck again by a mundane insight from our last period of enforced separation six years earlier: that you don't appreciate how much routine instances of body contact—friendly hugs, holding hands—can matter to you until they are no longer instantly available.

At the same time, there was a new sense of space in my life, a feeling of greater control and serenity that comes from living in an environment unrestricted by another busy psyche. No interruptions when I was trying to work. No vexatious conversations about things I considered trivial. No packets of cookies finished and not replaced, no waits for the bathroom, no battles over the television remote or the sections of the Saturday paper. To be perfectly honest, I did not find living apart uniformly horrible. I found more opportunities for reflection, a stronger sense of being myself. There seemed, for the first time in years, enough hours in the day to do all the things I wanted to do. Like most people in long-standing relationships, I am well aware of the importance of getting away from my partner now and then to maintain my sanity. A person has to have some space, physical and mental, that is not shared by anybody else, however much you love them. It is by no means clear to me, in other words—and despite the clear and compelling statistical evidence that both men and women are happier and healthier in marriages than on their own—that all the arguments are in favor of a shared life.[13]

I know Gail feels the same way about some of this. One of our most overworked tag lines is that the ideal spouse is the one who is there when you want them and not there when you don't. And we both laughed helplessly at an episode of the situation comedy *Mad About You* that aired a few days before Gail's scheduled departure to the United States. The show features a married but (then) childless couple consisting of Paul, a witty but slightly gormless filmmaker, and Jamie, his know-it-all wife. In this episode Jamie leaves Paul alone one weekend when she goes to visit her father. He says good-bye to her at the door, turns, and suddenly begins skipping around the apartment. "I'm giddy with power," he crows, dancing into the kitchen, where he drinks milk from the carton with the fridge door open, recklessly replaces the nearly empty container, opens a cupboard to get a cookie, and then goes into the living room to watch *Baywatch, without closing the cupboard door.* Maybe Gail and I just need a bigger apartment. I have often envied the living arrangements of such famous couples as Jean-Paul Sartre and Simone de Beauvoir, who had separate but adjoining apartments, or the novelist Margaret Drabble and biographer Michael Holroyd, who, though happily married, maintain independent households in different parts of London.

Of course, this being 1990s North America, I was in many ways far from alone even though I was now living by myself. My experience was hardly one of solitary confinement. I talked daily to a host of friends, by phone or e-mail, and spent the usual number of hours servicing my long-standing television addiction. I read books and magazines, received and wrote letters, visited websites. I indulged in one of the great unsung urban pleasures, going to the cheap matinee showings of first-run films, sitting there alone with the company of just seven or eight other hookey-players, self-employed business-people, and losers. In short, I had all kinds of voices in my head every day of the week, and the sustaining conversation of human existence was livelier than ever. There was simply a greater sense of distance, a larger gap between me and my social interlocutors, which gave me a kind of perspective, and a kind of happiness, I could not have achieved otherwise. It was also easier, for clear reasons, for me to turn off the voices altogether, to find a deeper peace inside a Chet Baker vocal.

I felt the need for periods of silence, too, to be quiet as well as alone. I found them, as so many of us do, in the kitchen and in the garden. I have mentioned already the great pleasures of the restaurant experience, a sense of well-being I find it dishonest to denigrate. As the novelist John Lanchester puts it in *The Debt to Pleasure,* the happiness in eating out lies not entirely in the sheer quality of the food but also in the "blinding, consoling hugeness of the restaurant *idea*":

> Stiff napery; heavy, gravity-laden crockery; pristine wine-glasses, erect and presentable as Guardsmen on parade; an expectant commando of pronged, edged, and expectant cutlery; the human furniture of the other diners and the uniformed waiters; above all, the awareness that one has finally arrived at a setting designed primarily to minister to one's needs, a bright place of rendered attention.[14]

This combination of order and expectation makes of the restaurant at once a return to the womb and an imposition of confident order on a chaotic world. Still, there are equal if not greater pleasures to be had in ordering one's own world, in the kitchen, planning the menu, purchasing and preparing the ingredients with one's own fair hands, and presenting the fruits of these efforts—to others or simply to oneself.

Because Gail is such a prodigiously gifted cook, I rarely have the kitchen controls in my hands when she is around—I can't bear the little nose-wrinkling faces she involuntarily makes at my carbonara sauce, or the quietly conspicuous way she picks out the jarring ingredients in an otherwise acceptable stew—but with her out of the picture I could dabble away to my heart's content. I did not slide into a sleazy bachelor hell of unmade beds and dirty dishes; I cooked and cleaned like any normal human. I followed no recipes, because (as Le Corbusier almost said) a recipe is just a machine for cooking with; instead I reverted to the simple stand-bys of my mother's passed-on culinary repertoire: linguine with tomato-vegetable sauce, grilled steak and steamed asparagus, meatloaf, roast chicken. In addition to these culinary contentments I also felt the need, now and then, for a happiness of pure sylvan simplicity. To the garden go, I thought then, for there we may be refreshed and regenerated. I'm not crazy about working in the garden but I do like sitting there amid the foliage sometimes, a big cold drink in my hand. "God Almighty first planted a garden," wrote Francis Bacon in 1625.

> And indeed it is the purest of human pleasures. It is the greatest refreshment to the spirits of man; without which, buildings and palaces are but gross handiworks; and a man shall ever see, that when ages grow to civility and elegancy, men come to build stately sooner than to garden finely; as if gardening were the greater perfection.[15]

Who can doubt that genuine better living is to be found in the innocent Edenic confines of the cultivated earth, the profound pleasures of the well-tilled seedbed, and the first blossom of spring?

And yet, when I consider the cultural forms that seem to dominate the current search for solitude and simplicity, I find this form of happiness more in danger of debasement than ever. We can observe, for example, what marketers call "upscale simplicity," the detail-obsessive Martha Stewart version of the well-ordered life, where a garden hoe costing a hundred dollars and an inefficient push-mower are guaranteed to create a pastoral utopia in a Connecticut suburb. Stewart may exemplify the drive for domestic transcendence in a secular world, as people often argue, but it is a sad world indeed that finds its highest experiences not in what happens with solitude but rather in the neurotic creation of domestic perfection, which makes of simplicity the fastest-growing consumer trend of an already highly commercialized culture.

There is something both closed-minded and wretched about this current version of the simplicity response. It is a desperate and elitist retreat from the world of most people's daily experience, in which we allow ourselves to be dominated by purveyors of recipes and lifestyle advice, like the pair of cookbook authors a friend of mine always calls "those two Silver Palate bitches." Elite experience—for that is after all what we are talking about when we talk about kitchens and gardens and other perfect havens—has no justification if it is in the service of pleasing only a few lucky people granted the opportunity to indulge in it for a lifetime, spending money in search of the machines of better (now read "simpler") living. Simplicity becomes, indeed, something doomed to self-contradiction when the search for happiness is so dominated by inescapable technological-upgrade imperatives.

Such a result is not avoided even in the solitude of study, the form of happiness that Denby managed to recapture at Columbia. We commonly say that humanistic education is for its own sake, and I believe that: we cannot measure the value of Plato's dialogues, as some educators do today, by how effective they are in training students to do well on the LSAT. At the same time, the solitary experience of grappling with *The Republic* is not something that is supposed to end with that private conversation. It is meant to resonate outward. Yes, people need to know about Plato, and preferably in his own terms. But they need to know, too, that Plato's insights about political manipulation, ideology, and systematic deception apply to the advertising they are bombarded with, to the barrage of information and images that comes to them via the Internet, the terrible potential of television to distort and morph what we think of as reality. We cannot remain at the pinnacles of human experience forever; that, after all, is the route of retreat we rightly condemn as the withdrawal into self-indulgence. And even Plato knew, from hard and bitter personal experience with the Thirty Tyrants of Athens, that one cannot shirk the terrible duty of philosophy: to descend into the messy streets of what we sometimes call, misleadingly, "the real world." It is there, and only there, that the genuine battles over identity, happiness, and the good life can be fought and, possibly, won.

So let me suggest a different response to the apparently overwhelming supply of information and cultural content that marks our times. However essential solitude and reflection remain for our personal happiness, they should take their place as moderating activities or experiences in a fast world, not pure ends in themselves. You cannot engage in a perpetual media fast, for this is not a time for retreat to the ivory tower, whether that edifice is constructed of granite and ivy or merely of the plasterboard walls of your office or rec room—or even if it consists of the well-tended isolation of your garden, a place that should be used for refreshment, not occupation. What I have in mind instead is a strategy of what we might call *individual acts of cultural resistance,* the kind of thing known in some circles these days as culture jamming. This means the refusal to allow the messages of advertising, television, publishing, and conglomerated media to dominate our consciousness, the constant refutation and mockery of the hidden agendas and buried assumptions of the corporatist worldview.

In practice, this involves constant vigilance and the perpetual deconstruction of the taken-for-granted aspects of the culture. The way television truncates the news, or the way advertising facilitates envy, encouraging desires we did not previously have. The way Ted Turner can control what films we may see, or Wal-Mart what CDs we may buy. The way films promote soft drinks and shoe manufacturers colonize the desires of young people to construct identities. The way, more deeply, we all simply *accept* that consumption and marketing are part of the human condition, rather than the contingent products of observable historical and social forces that we can understand and, perhaps, change.[16]

The elevated rhetoric of the happiness-machine is now part of this web of belief, enforced as it is by the old ideology of technological inevitability. The promise of this rhetoric, that machines will set us free, can seem to handcuff us, to take away the very possibility of resistance with its message that those who do not adapt must die. Yet this too is a cultural idea, a dangerous piece of free-floating propaganda, and one that all of us, given the opportunities and the right kind of training in decoding the messages of the media, might be able to resist. But we have to make that decision, not in a foredoomed refusal to engage with the world of things, but in creating a critical consciousness about our own desires and the way they are tangled in the techniques and algorithms of better living. If we cannot avoid consumption, then we have to turn it into what it always potentially is: a form of production, a site of creativity, where we turn the messages of the dominant culture to our own purposes.[17]

I invite you to join me in the project of jamming this culture and, as a result, getting our individual experience of it back. I invite you to join me in being not buried alive but free.

PEOPLE AT WORK

But how? *How* do we dig beneath the layers of manipulation and distortion that blanket our ideas of happiness? Is there a residue of happiness, a substratum of genuine meaning uninfected by the viruses of technology, advertising, pathologization, narcissism, and popular culture?

I think there is, but to see it we need to alter in some fairly drastic ways our sense of what happiness means. The necessary precondition for that alteration is the kind of critical analysis I have tried to offer in the preceding pages. Such an undertaking begins in tranquillity, in the delicious enforced silence of reading, where the conversation is always internal and ordered and, one dares to hope, illuminating. Begins there, but cannot end there. There is indispensable happiness to be found in solitude, and there are forms of thought that only the written word can make possible; but we are, after all, associative animals and the hermitage option is really no option at all for us. It is, in the end, little more than an admission of defeat. Happiness happens, if it does, on the field of human community and in the performance of actions. It is not rest or peace so much as it is the disposition to act; not the invidious comparison that springs from envy so much as the self-applied criterion of rational satisfaction: am I living a life that I can judge worth living?

Nietzsche had this insight, even if his denunciation of the psychological perversity of Christian morality was more immoderate, and his celebration of individual strength more shameless, than we might prefer. "The 'well-born' *felt* themselves to be 'happy,'" he writes in *On the Genealogy of Morals,*

> they did not have to establish their happiness artificially by examining their enemies, or to persuade themselves, *deceive* themselves, that they were happy (as all men of *ressentiment* are in the habit of doing); and they likewise knew, as rounded men replete with energy and therefore *necessarily* active, that happiness should not be sundered from action— being active was with them necessarily a part of happi- ness...—all very much the opposite of "happiness" at the level of the impotent, the oppressed, and those in whom poi- sonous and inimical feelings are festering, with whom it appears as essentially narcotic, drug, rest, peace, "sabbath," slackening of tension and relaxing of limbs, in short *passively.*

The happiness derived from comparison, the false sense of well- being touted by the facilitators of envy, is ultimately weak: it lets us fall into a drugged slumber that leaves everything as it is.

Yet that point becomes harder to see just to the extent that the celebration of the individual begins to seem the point of all human life. "A good part of the struggles of humankind," warns Freud in *Civilization and Its Discontents,* "center round the single task of find- ing an expedient accommodation—one, that is, that will bring hap- piness—between the claim of the individual to liberty and the cultural claims of the group." We need to remind ourselves that this warning only makes sense in a context in which we presume a deep conflict between those claims—a presumption that Nietzsche, to his detriment, believed implicitly. It is true that such a context now obtains, but it is not true, as Freud appears to imply here, that this situation is eternal and unchangeable. Things have been otherwise and might be again. There might be a cultural space, in other words, where the notions of individual happiness and group health will be inextricably joined rather than in perpetual conflict.

To suggest that happiness is activist, that it is not the passive acceptance of what is, or the currently fashionable retreat into the characterless, self-indulgent pursuit of quietude, is implicitly to sing the value of work. The exercise of skill, the intense occupation in a task, is something that most of us know as a rewarding experience. In work we avoid both the routine unhappiness of boredom and the deeper malaise of cynicism. "[T]he most intelligent young people in Western countries tend to have that kind of unhappiness that comes of finding no adequate employment for their best talents," Bertrand Russell says in a comment that applies even more today than when he wrote it in 1936. "Cynicism such as one frequently finds among the most highly educated young men and women of the West results from the combination of comfort with powerlessness."

In full occupation, furthermore, we find scope for our ambition, and we extend the range of our interests beyond the strictly personal: work projects go past our particular points of view and broaden our concerns so that one task may occupy us when another fails or loses its piquancy. In work we taste the joys of competition, a form of human happiness that is far from negligible. We tack along on the winds that flow between effort and resignation, testing the edges of our power—and our desire. Clint Eastwood's Dirty Harry Callahan infamously said that "A man's got to know his limitations," and you will hear baseball players say almost every day that the key to good performance is "keeping within yourself," but sometimes those lines can only be drawn by risking failure in the pursuit of transcendence. You have to push the envelope. A man's reach should exceed his grasp, not because there is no point to heaven otherwise, as Browning had it, but because we cannot know how far we may rise above ourselves unless we believe, at least now and then, that anything is possible. Dr. Johnson dismissed the desire to be remarried as the triumph of hope over experience; we cannot allow that worldly-wise tartness to obscure the fact that such refusal to curb expectation *is* a form of triumph.

At first blush we might not be inclined to call the experience of work one of happiness, but part of the move from the hedonistic to the eudaimonistic is to recognize the depth of personal fulfilment as not necessarily limited to experiences that furnish us with good feelings of the transient kind. Happiness is not about feeling good all the time. It is, rather, about the ability to reflect on one's life and find it worthwhile—to see it as satisfactory. Work is an important ingredient in that satisfaction, because it gives purpose to our existence, places us in a structure of goals and tasks and furnishes the incomparable personal rewards of achievement: the sense, so deeply pleasurable, that one has done something impressive and maybe even lasting. There is a sense, when one has completed a degree or built a cabinet or finished a lawsuit, that the achievement is incorrigible; that, as lyricist Dorothy Fields had it, *they can't take that away from me.* Yet in a culture of instant gratification and vicious repression—a pathological culture of desperate fun and guilty punishment, of marketing and identity manipulation—this insight can slip from view.

Not all work is equal. It is not enough to be, for example, a self-fulfilled professional killer who derives a great deal of satisfaction from a job well done. (John Cusack, in the 1996 film *Grosse Point Blank,* hints at this possibility, which of course arises as bleakly comic; but even here, Cusack's character is trying to get out of the business and is getting therapy for the resulting psychic conflict from a terrified psychologist played by Alan Arkin.) It is not sufficient for genuine happiness, in other words, that one simply be happy in one's work. It also has to be work worth doing. And this is one point at which the subjective awareness of happiness (which in hedonistic conceptions occupies the entire conceptual space, rendering all forms of external challenge null in a deft solipsistic closure) is importantly connected to the objective value of the things I do. Happiness is not simply a feeling or emotion; it is a connection to the world, a realization of one's place within it.

What makes work worth doing? I realize that to speak of the objective value of work is to risk alarming those of postmodern mind, for whom all claims of objectivity have a dubious odor of repression and Enlightenment hubris. But I don't mean anything scary or inflated by using the idea of objective truth. Our thinking on this question has been distorted by false expectations, the sort of thing embodied in the idea of perfect detachment, or the so-called God's-eye-view of objectivity: as if the only available alternatives were the fiction of perfect impartiality or a gooey mire of individual affection, subjective bias, and incommunicable self-interest. As if, in other words, the inability to attain the Enlightenment goal of a "view from nowhere" meant that we have no alternative but to fall into a chaos of free-floating, and indisputably subjective, claims and counterclaims. The subjective side of this false dichotomy is a position just as incoherent as the idea of complete and certain objective knowledge, namely, the self-defeating relativism that says everything is relative—including, presumably, that statement.

As usual, the truth is less spectacular than the extremes that dominate the debate. It is true that the very idea of cultural authority no longer has the hold on us that it once did, when the modern age reached its full flowering in encyclopedic projects and universities, which, as their name implies, attempted to encompass the universe within their ivy-covered walls. Instead we are now confronting a multiplicity of cultural authority nodes, some of them local and limited, others occasionally wider and apparently solid, but none of them *absolute* in the manner that our earlier aspirations promised us. Confronting culture must in future mean responding to that multiplicity, surrendering the encyclopedic impulse, honoring the particular, the unusual, the strange. Legitimacy of the rigid kind will give way to smaller and more private cultural undertakings, or ones dedicated to particular, even subcultural, purposes. But in saying this, I am certainly not trying to make some kind of cheap relativist point about exploding all myths of legitimacy and progress. The norm of truth may be local, or contingent, or open to constant correction, but it exists, and it must exist if we are to do anything as commonplace, and as remarkable, as sitting in a room somewhere reading these words printed in black ink upon a white page. Nor am I trying to suggest that an increasingly diverse culture means a disintegrated culture. There can be a kind of unity in the multiplicity, a form of order in the chaos.

So we *can* make judgments of value, in work as in other things, that are not merely subjective. They are, instead, as objective as we need them to be: they are intelligible to other people with whom we are engaged in the common project of living and conversing together. Some philosophers, especially recently, have argued that objectivity is once more available in morals and epistemology. To the extent that relativism can be shown to be incoherent, it follows that a meaningful notion of objective truth can once more be vindicated.[18] Meaningful, but not perfect or absolute. We surrender, as it appears we must, the *detachment* model of objectivity which required us to stand outside ourselves and judge the truth of propositions or the reliability of concepts. Inside a given context or horizon of concern, however, it still makes sense to speak of "true" and "objective" because of what one philosopher has called "the disappearing 'we.' "[19] When we say something "is true" it follows—if the detachment view is incoherent—that this really means "true for us." The view *sub specie aeternitatis* is no more accessible to us than immortality or godhood. Yet the "for us" condition drops out of the equation once we see that detachment is indeed impossible, no longer an option to be entertained. *For us,* sure—but who else could we be talking about anyway? True, we are left speaking only to those who can understand us; but then, no other situation is, after all, intelligible. Objectivity is vindicated by, paradoxically, taking the limits of context seriously.

From this point of view, what makes work valuable? In one sense, that is a matter for the ongoing conversation in which any genuine human community partakes—in which, we could say, the community consists. But we can offer some general statements before the fact. Work, we might say, has value when it contributes to the welfare of the community. But we cannot conceive "welfare" in the narrow terms of crude utility. Work also has value when it cultivates the intrinsically interesting qualities of human life, the things we find fascinating about each other. That is why sports, art, and philosophy, for example—none of which, as occupations, bakes any bread—are nevertheless inherently worthy human activities. What we consider valuable may of course change over time, for that is part of what it means to surrender the notion of absolute value: we do not regard hunters the same way now as we did six hundred years ago, for example. As well, there are likely to be many disputes about the details and at the margins, for a healthy human community is also one in which challenges to value are constant. Some of us think serving the rule of law is a high and noble calling, others that "The first thing we do, let's kill all the lawyers" is the finest line Shakespeare ever wrote. On the whole, the things we find valuable are those that help us live more comfortably, more equitably, more joyfully, and more beautifully. They are the things that make life worth living.

They are also, arguably, the most secure form of happiness we can know, the form based on creation or attainment. "One gains the most if one can sufficiently heighten the yield of pleasure from the sources of psychical and intellectual work," Freud says.

> When that is so, fate can do little against one. A satisfaction of this kind, such as an artist's joy in creating, in giving his phantasies body, or a scientist's in solving problems or discovering truths, has a special quality which we shall certainly one day be able to characterize in metapsychological terms. At present we can only say figuratively that such satisfactions seem "finer and higher."

The problem for Freud is that even these finer and higher things are, like all forms of human activity, merely desperate masks for the psychosexual conflict that he believes is characteristic of our existence. When I find satisfaction and what I imagine to be lasting happiness in the performance of a certain creative task, the joy of the job well done, I am really just channeling my libidinal energy into a socially acceptable form. What I *really* want to do is not to finish that journal article or complete that lecture preparation, but rape and pillage with abandon. The intensity of "finer" pleasures, Freud says, "is mild as compared with that derived from the sating of crude and primary instinctual impulses; it does not convulse our physical being."

The elevation of happiness into the higher faculties creates other problems too. Since it can apparently be undertaken only by a few, it is dangerously elitist; and while that might not bother someone like Nietzsche (who thought we should never impair our own capacity for happiness just because other people were too limited to make the most of life), for most of us it is troubling, if not absurd, to think that happiness should be confined to a small class of artists, scientists, and philosophers. Let's assume, then, that this is not the case: that finer and higher things, at least in the sense of finding fulfillment in valuable work, are accessible to nearly everyone. After all, the most robust form of creative human activity there is, parenthood, is a project most of us can undertake if we so choose—though how well we perform it is another question altogether.

Yet even thus qualified, this work-driven version of happiness must still face the possibility of its own self-defeat. It was meant, Freud points out, to protect us against the pitfalls of fate by taking us to a more secure place where happiness was less subject to variation: a combination, in other words, of long-view and lowered-gaze theories that is not unlike Boethius's form of consolation, though without the dubious theology. But does it work? Disconsolate Freud thinks not: the finer-and-higher strategy "creates no impenetrable armor against the arrows of fortune," he says, "and it habitually fails when the source of suffering is a person's own body."

That is true. Sometimes the best-keeled ships of happiness founder on the shoals of fate. "Call no man happy until he is dead," as Solon said. We must confront the fact that luck plays a greater part in the good life than we might like, and not simply because happiness is a matter of happenstance. Even the deeper forms of happiness, the rational satisfactions of a well-lived life, can surrender to the whims of fortune. Yet, confronting that fact does not mean surrendering to it. On the contrary: to agree with Solon is to accept not the absurd proposition that only the dead are happy, but rather to see that we cannot judge happiness except on the scale of an entire life. As Aristotle and Machiavelli both knew very well, in their different ways, the proper response to an awareness of fortune's turns is not dismay but good preparation. To habituate character in the virtues (as the former recommended) or to anticipate reversals with back-up plans and long-term strategy (as the latter did) is no more than to accept the variability of human life. Seeing that, we minimize, even if we cannot finally eliminate, the sharp unhappy rocks of possibility lurking in the seas of fate.

Branch Rickey, the legendary commissioner who helped bring Jackie Robinson into the major leagues, had the same insight about the highly contingent universe of baseball.

"Luck," he used to say, "is just the residue of good design."

8

The Virtues of Happiness (II)

There is nothing which has yet been contrived by man, by which so much happiness is produced as by a good tavern or inn.

—*Samuel Johnson*

THE TELLING OF LIES

TAKING LUCK AND CONTINGENCY SERIOUSLY AS FORCES IN OUR destiny must lead to alterations in our view of human life and happiness. We might view personal identity and character differently, seeing these essential features of existence not so much as static qualities but rather as *projects:* in effect, tales full of planning and reversal, foresight and fate. This is what we may call the "narrative hypothesis"—that is, the claim that I make sense of my life largely, if not wholly, in terms of a story I tell about myself. To be human, in this way of looking at things, is to be primarily a spinner of yarns, a renderer of accounts.[1]

We all engage in this ongoing work of revisionist history when we speak about ourselves and the people we know. We frame actions in terms of previous experience and explain character by reference to childhood influences or educational transformation. That is uncontroversial. The deeper idea is that the *best way* to make sense of human personality is in terms of this story, the ongoing narrative construction in which the present is simply the front end of the story that is my life. In therapeutic language, the narrative hypothesis carries healing potential: I come to terms with a traumatic event or drastic personal failing by successfully constructing a story of my life that makes it mesh with the other acts or chapters in the drama. (To the extent I cannot do this, I might suffer from neurosis or a sense of personal fracture: I will remain unhealed because my story is untold.) In ethical terms, the narrative hypothesis forces us to confront the issue of moral judgment in a wider context in which no act stands alone, and no simplistic judgment of a person can hold sway. In political terms, finally, the narrative hypothesis gives us a way of explaining the conflicts of identity and membership that are so characteristic of modernity: the limitations inherent in a notion of citizenship divorced from concrete historical experience, and the tension between our individual desire to be free and our apparent need for ethical substance to give us direction, to provide a life-guiding role.

The narrative hypothesis does not solve these problems—it merely provides a useful way of thinking about them. One feature of this way of thinking is its exposure of the apparent contradiction between objective roles (those ordained by religious or cultural tradition, say) and subjective ones that we consider to be entirely our own creation. Thus the classic story of modern identity, in which the individual shrugs off the layers of expectation imposed on him by tradition and finds a nub of pure individuality, freely created and pursued, somewhere beneath. In this version of individuality, I gain the personal freedom to tell my own story after long and painful struggle.

But we cannot fail to notice that this tale of overcoming traditional expectations is now itself a classic narrative, with its own expectations and traditions, and is in no way free of the complex interplay of actor and role. Neither of the dramatic extremes—neither, that is, the idea of rigidly determined roles that leave no room for personal freedom nor the incoherent idea of a subjective story *entirely* free of expectations and conventions—is accurate to the reality of our actual narratives. In practice, we construct our personal stories in a dynamic fashion, moving back and forth between the stability (but limitations) of preordained roles and the freedom (but indeterminacy) of creating new ones. It would not be an exaggeration to say that the modern self is an exercise in sophisticated narrative, with each one of us cast in the role of a director who might decide to produce, say, a Western version of *The Seagull* or a staging of *Hamlet* in Nazi Germany.

A continuum is therefore exposed, different in detail for each one of us, between rigid or "conservative" scripts, largely determined by stage props and prescribed moves—we might think of Peking opera, say, or commedia dell'arte, or pantomime—and "liberal" scripts of personal freedom and individual innovation: improvisation, perhaps, or street drama. These visible extremes post the limits of human happiness: it must be neither so rigid as to bulldoze individual desire nor so innovative as to threaten meaningfulness. Nor are we committed to a single production, even if we are, obviously, engaged in a single performance. We may change roles, and shift direction as well. But one consequence of this is that we are constantly involved in a process of *bringing the story into line:* attempting, with greater or lesser degrees of success, to make the entire tale coherent by reconciling past with present, part with whole. And here we face many new difficulties, for we are constrained not only by our desires but by the desires and expectations of others—let's call them the audience and the other actors.

Consider a simple example of this process of revision.[2] Brenda is married to Susan's brother, whom she met in college. Susan is a few years younger than Brenda, and when they first met—the Thanksgiving weekend when Tom brought her home to Brookline from New Haven—they found that they didn't have much in common. Brenda was studying French poetry, was something of a poet herself (she had published five poems in various undergraduate journals and had a sonnet accepted by *The Southern Review),* and favored the sort of draping, multilayered dark clothes that Susan considered pretentious. She had silver rings of intricate design on eight of her ten fingers and wore a big piece of amber twisted in silver on a chain around her neck. Susan herself preferred the neat look of little plaid skirts, ironed cotton blouses, and penny-loafers. She had no jewelry except a small gold signet ring and a gold Cartier watch, a present from her father on her eighteenth birthday. She disliked makeup and wore her hair in a clean blond bob, while Brenda's hung down in messy swirls or poked suggestively out of her various slouchy hats, which shaded eyes thick with mascara and eyeliner. Susan saw herself going on from Smith to Wharton or maybe Georgetown law; Brenda wanted to find a loft near St. Mark's Place and write thoughtful, witty essays for *The New Yorker* while she waited for an editor at Random House to realize she was the next Sylvia Plath, only without the damaging neuroses. The two young women regarded each other warily during the weekend. Susan went so far as to roll her eyes when Brenda politely declined a helping of turkey over Thanksgiving dinner, explaining that the slaughter of imbecilic birds in celebration of imperial violence and genocide was not her idea of a good time.

Tom loved them both. His sister because she was such a smart-talking straight-shooter, the kind of girl who could tie a bowline and bake a pie with equal assurance, a pretty deb with a high IQ and a wicked forehand. Brenda because she was one of those brainy midwestern misfits with artistic aspirations that get quietly nourished through dark high school days in bleakest Kansas City, only to flower in the sudden approval of the Ivy League. He desperately wanted them to like each other, and he knew they would if they gave themselves the chance. For his sake, they tried. There were no girlish heart-to-hearts, but each recognized the intelligence in the other's eyes, and over the course of time they grew closer. Brenda and Tom were married three years after graduation from Yale, the summer he completed his law degree at Columbia and she finished an internship at *Harper's Magazine* and placed a short "Talk of the Town" piece that was rumored to have coaxed a smile from David Remnick. Susan flew in from London, where she was working on a short-term contract with Saatchi & Saatchi before deciding on postgrad options. Brenda asked her to be maid of honor and the two smiled and cried, the first time they had done so together. They were now fast friends.

But Tom's legal career, so promising in prospect, did not fly as high as he had anticipated. Even though he passed the New York bar exam on the first try, a clerkship he coveted fell through, and then he found that even extensive wining and dining from Manhattan law firms did not guarantee a permanent job. He wasn't hired back by the Wall Street office when it came time to cull the associates, and so he faced the prospect of private practice or moving to another city, with a less overburdened bar. He and Brenda started having fights about money, nasty spats during which he ridiculed the meager earning power of her literary efforts and raged about the mounting credit card bills from Bergdorf's and Dean & Delucca. Things got worse. He started drinking too much, and she had a stupid little fling with a semifamous novelist whose last book had been short-listed for the Pulitzer. Within a year they were divorced. They had been married for a total of thirty-six months, and both found themselves confused and desolate.

During the breakup, Brenda tried to talk to Susan about her problems, careful not to cast too much bad light on Tom because she knew it would strain Susan's familial commitments. Susan was back in the States now, in the second year of her own law degree, at Duke, where her boyfriend was studying political science. Brenda really needed Susan in her life, to stay in touch with Tom and with the life she, Brenda, had tried to find with him. But Susan's loyalties were torn, and she found she couldn't avoid blaming Brenda for the breakdown of the marriage: Brenda was too artsy, too otherworldly, to appreciate the problems Tom was having. She wasn't supportive as he struggled with his thwarted ambitions and a mounting sense of failure—really just some bad luck and a stiff job market. Susan thought that, secretly, Brenda despised the law as a career and quietly hated Tom's squash-playing, red-suspender-wearing, cigar-smoking legal buddies. The two women had several long phone conversations that started civilly but quickly degenerated into recriminations and hurt silences. They stopped talking.

At this point, Brenda engaged in a typical piece of moral story-telling. She began to ask herself whether Susan had ever liked her for herself. She had thought so, but now she wasn't so certain. She knew Susan liked her, or had anyway, but now she thought that the liking had been entirely for the sake of Tom. Motivated by hurt and resentment, Brenda was moved to, as we say, rewrite the past. She decided that Susan did not like her for herself and never had; that any regard from Susan was, instead, a function of Brenda's having fallen into the category of Susan's brother's wife. With the end of the marriage, and the change in her in-law status, there came an end to the closeness between them. Brenda found she could not interpret this change in any other way than to decide that Susan had never liked her intrinsically, for her own sake. She felt obscurely betrayed.

Now is this really a *rewriting* of the past? We might be inclined to doubt it, because Brenda's motives are so understandable, but it is, because the story Brenda now settles on is, while seemingly accurate to the facts on the surface, one that involves a deliberate suppression of certain important elements. We cannot say that, from an entirely objective point of view, we know that Susan's regard for Brenda went beyond mere sisterly loyalty. At the same time, we can be reasonably certain, as outside observers not influenced by Brenda's feelings, that there was probably more to Susan's friendship than consideration of her brother. It might have started there, but it did not end there. This is not something Brenda can admit into her story right now, however, for it is very important for her to tell a different story, one in which she was deceived into mistaking Susan's well-bred politeness for friendship. This revisionism is not in error so much as it is *a limited interpretation,* one that preserves Brenda's dignity at the cost of judging Susan too harshly. Though the revision satisfies an important moral and narrative impulse in Brenda, it is not, as we might say, the best literature that can be made of the situation.

Why not? Well, Brenda has gone back over her history to bring it into line with her current emotions, and in the process she has changed its value. In truth, the question "Did Susan like Brenda for herself?" is not something Brenda can know for certain. (It is not clear that anyone can know this for certain, or absolutely: Susan's motives are probably as various and vague to herself as to anyone else.) This indeterminacy of both knowledge and fact about whether Susan liked Brenda "for herself" shows that the story Brenda is now telling herself is flawed because it is one-sided. However satisfying to her own interests, it does not satisfy the demands of the narrative hypothesis for a substantial fit between the parts of a tale and the available facts of the matter: there is a gap between Susan's actions and Brenda's version of them. Brenda finds fault where there might be no fault to find. This is not a question of whether Brenda's revision is aesthetically pleasing or a riveting story, but whether her self-told story makes narrative sense given the stock of available knowledge. This, then, is what the narrative hypothesis enjoins: not only that we make sense of our lives in terms of stories but that, as storytellers, we attempt to be *responsible* narrators, who do not change the facts to fit the mood or alter interpretations too drastically for the sake of self-protection.

Of course, Brenda's particular form of faulty (and fault-finding) narrative is extremely common; in the same circumstances, many of us would perhaps be inclined to tell some very similar version. That is partly because, when we each construct our narrative tales, we are inevitably the stars of the show. And if we have unpleasant emotions to explain, it is natural to construct the tale in such a way that the fault lies elsewhere. More precisely, psychological evidence suggests that we each tend to view our own lives as very much in flux—stories still under construction—even as we regard others' characters as more fixed and determinate. Whereas I see in you something I regard as a character flaw, a permanent (if perhaps forgivable) aspect of who you are, you may see in yourself merely an aberrant act or unseemly adventure, something that demonstrates not a pattern of behavior or, still less, a feature of your personality, but only a rather unfortunate and atypical lapse. Or you might admit a pattern of behavior but think of it as "something you are working on"—not a permanent or established character trait, as an outsider might see it, but part of an internal struggle that could go either way. It is not that we view others as entirely non-narrative beings, simply props and furniture in our own solipsistic dramas; it's just that we tend to be more determinate with them than with ourselves, holding them in place more rigidly even as we grant ourselves all kinds of poetic license.

More positively, though, the ability to construct our stories gives us a strong clue to one element in the nature of happiness: how much of it is about fitting the past into a narrative structure that confirms rather than unsettles our sense of ourselves as living and faring well. I suppose to put it that way sounds both abstract and high minded, but take a common example of this capacity. I have a friend, Elaine, who is among the most relentlessly upbeat people I have ever met. During a low period not long ago, when I was feeling hard done by and unjustly criticized, she and I were talking on the phone. "Don't worry, honey," she said. "Everything will work out for the best." I found this intensely irritating at the time, maybe because it is the sort of thing my mother always says when I am trying to communicate some righteous anger about the small-mindedness of the world. "What does that mean?" I wanted to know.

"Just that you might come to see this as something that was meant to be," Elaine said. "I know you don't believe in God, but He has a plan for you anyway."

I was about to launch into a rant about this idea when I suddenly saw the kernel of sense that is buried in theodicy. It's not that bad things won't happen to good people—they will—it's just that humans have an apparently infinite capacity for reinterpreting bad things in positive ways. We tell stories about the past to make sense of where we stand in the present. We are constrained by what happened, and by the facts of human psychology and the laws of physics, but we are free to increase our chances for happiness by, in effect, telling ourselves the best possible story. I tried to say this to Elaine.

"You're making it sound like some kind of delusion," she complained.

"Not a delusion," I said, "just the ability to be happy." But of course there is indeed a certain element of willful self-deception in this, the kind of thing enjoined by the well-worn imperative to accentuate the positive and eliminate the negative. I thought of Jonathan Swift's wise, if rather cynical, definition of happiness as "the perpetual possession of being well deceived."

This can go too far. I consider the strong theodical position—that God has ordained all suffering in this best of all possible worlds—to be not only excessively delusional but, in addition, bad narrative. The idea that one can exercise mental discipline to become more satisfied with one's life is, by contrast, in my view a good example of the capacity to be happy. Those judgments are of course debatable. The larger point is that human actions, and human life more generally, make sense only within the framework of a narrative. And when we judge people's actions and lives, we are always implicitly, and sometimes explicitly, attending to the stories they tell about themselves and the corresponding stories we are telling about them. (One major source of moral conflict is that these stories often fail to mesh.) "In what does the unity of an individual life consist?" asks the philosopher Alasdair MacIntyre. "The answer is that its unity is the unity of a narrative embodied in a single life. To ask 'What is the good for me?' is to ask how best I might live out that unity and bring it to completion."[3]

Philosophers and critics have no special purchase on the moral issues and problems that go into the creation of these personal narratives. But they do have something to say about the way narratives in general get constructed. In particular, philosophers have the skills of argumentative precision to identify indeterminacies in the narrative materials, to see how gaps open up between what we wish to be true of ourselves and what is often the case. This, then, suggests a role for the moral philosopher as someone who clarifies the moral point of view, and hence the possibility of genuine happiness, by giving what might be considered a form of story advice. A faulty story might answer well to internal needs of the agent to explain hurt, resentment, and the like, but it is nonetheless faulty—and can be shown to be so. The philosopher is thus a kind of script consultant or, if you like, a dramaturge. He or she cannot construct someone else's story but can identify the many common ways a story can go astray. Ultimately, the moral philosopher, just like the literary critic, must make it clear how difficult a task it is to construct a *good* story, a story that entails fulfillment, whether the subject is myself or someone else who plays a role in my story—for to remember that others are busy writing their own personal stories is part of what it means to be a good storyteller yourself.

This can be difficult to accept. It happens that I am moderately addicted to gossip, or what the novelist Laurie Colwin preferred to call "emotional speculation." I have an abiding curiosity about the details of other people's lives, and I like nothing better than to spend an evening with one of my friends as we sort through the sexual peccadilloes, political entanglements, and minor humiliations of the members of our social circle. In my own defense, I think this is an ethical exercise as well as a voyeuristic one: in exchanging gossip we assess character, try to divine motives and conflicts, evaluate courses of action and situation-responses. Like most in my social circle, especially the journalists and TV people, for some reason, I can be harsh about my friends on occasion, especially after a martini or two, and I have been known now and then to offer rather withering assessments of a recently published short story or ill-advised haircut. Fine. But, again like other people, I find it mildly distressing to realize that my friends are somewhere, sometimes, doing the same thing to me. I know this is true, but I know it mostly as a distant theoretical proposition rather than as a meaningful reality. "One of the most universal forms of irrationality is the attitude taken by practically everybody towards malicious gossip," Bertrand Russell says.

> Very few people can resist saying malicious things about their acquaintances, and even on occasion about their friends; yet when people hear that anything has been said against themselves, they are filled with indignant amazement. It has apparently never occurred to them that, just as they gossip about every one else, so every one else gossips about them.... We know that our friends have their faults, and yet are on the whole agreeable people whom we like. We

find it, however, intolerable that they should have the same attitude towards us.[4]

It has occurred to me that people must gossip about me as I do about them, yes, but not *really* and not about my supposed faults, in definite terms—like when my friend Janice unwisely told me one day over lunch that some people we knew considered me untrustworthy and condescending. I was shocked and unsettled: it ruined my afternoon. Was I really? Were those features of my character? I was forced to look back over previous actions and situations to reassess them. Were my interpretations faulty; was I telling myself a bad story? Was I, for example, really being arrogant when I thought I was being charming? Did people interpret my admittedly idiosyncratic whimsy as a kind of moral flightiness? I had to examine the script again, look over the story and see if I had missed something, as if I had just read one of those intricate academic articles that purport to prove that *David Copperfield* is really an anarchist manifesto or *Four Quartets* an elaborate celebration of good sportsmanship.

This kind of experience can be trying. Most of us manage to come to terms with people saying critical things about faults we acknowledge in ourselves. The much harder thing is hearing, perhaps for the first time, that someone considers you guilty of a fault you did not think part of your character. We have to be aware that our self-told stories often include negative self-assessment as a kind of moral prophylactic: like the funny man who rushes to tell the tale of his own humiliation, we are really trying to gain control of the director's chair before someone else can grab it. (No doubt the same motive plays into my decision to include the detailed self-revelations scattered throughout this book, though I flatter myself I had nobler purposes, too.) The trouble is that, sometimes, as soon as we leave the room the others turn around and tell the identical story without any of the hilarious self-deprecation. It's one thing for me to call myself an idiot; it's quite another for one of my friends to do the same. Seeing ourselves as others see us is always instructive, as the poet Burns suggested, but it is rarely entirely pleasant.

Still, most people don't give us a second thought; it is easy to overestimate the degree to which they care about us and what we do. Indeed, much unhappiness can result from too great a preoccupation with the swirls and trends of public opinion, and a good deal of solace can be gained from an awareness that everyone is as self-obsessed and insecure as you, if not more so. It matters what our friends think of us, just as, at another level, it matters what the community thinks of us at the margins of acceptability. But on the whole, Russell is right when he says that "[o]ne should respect public opinion in so far as it is necessary to avoid starvation and to keep out of prison, but anything that goes beyond this is voluntary submission to an unnecessary tyranny, and is likely to interfere with happiness in all kinds of ways."

All my talk of stories and tales might be thought to open the door to too much indeterminacy in human life, of course, and that is a clear danger of the narrative hypothesis. But I think it is a danger worth accepting, for the narrative hypothesis captures something important about our moral lives. Morally speaking, we are neither entirely acts nor entirely character; nor are we even merely some combination of these. We are agents who live and act *in time*, and only a narrative conception of human agency can attend to that *Zeitlichkeit*. Indeterminacies of various kinds crop up in these narratives all the time, certainly, as we face the limits of our knowledge, our will, our luck, and our courage. But that entails no surrender of judgment, either about people and their acts or about the resulting narratives we and they construct in seeking to understand ourselves.

Nor do we need to say that every story is as good as any other, because we have surrendered the non-narrative idea of a final moral truth, the detached objectivity of the impartial observer. There is no necessary sacrifice in moral judgment when we adopt the narrative hypothesis, because all the hard work of deciding which stories to tell, which elements to retain and which to jettison, remains. By contrast, to ignore the narrative dimension of human life in favor of some absent principle of entirely extrahuman moral truth constitutes an enormous sacrifice in nuance, detail, and moral truth. Yes, and happiness. It is very bad literature indeed.

BY VIRTUE OF

We can now draw out a conclusion about human happiness based on the discussion of external goods, solitude, friendship, work, luck, and narrative that has made up the bulk of these last two chapters. What I want to suggest is this: the only possible way the notion of happiness can be reclaimed from the machinery of manipulation and self-indulgence is to recast it as *the possession of virtuous character and the performance of virtuous action.* I want to agree, in short, with Russell's insight—one familiar to Spinoza and Aristotle, too, in their different versions—that "[t]he happy life is to an extraordinary extent the same as the good life."

To say this is to invite immediate objection. For fairly precise historical reasons, especially the dominance of Kantian ideas of morality in the modern era, we tend to think of "the good life" (when we do not think of it in terms of material goods) in terms of a strict program of self-denying imperatives: do this, don't do that. The traditional ethical virtues of the ancient Greek world shrink into the stern moral Virtue of the Enlightenment: we move from an organic form of good life to an impersonal, punitive, external standard of judgment. Doing the right thing is now associated with the inflexible demands of duty, uninfected by thoughts of happiness or benevolence. This Kantian idea that happiness and morality are in conflict, the one variable and untrustworthy, the other unchanging and enduringly beautiful, is so deeply inscribed on the modern (especially Christian) consciousness, in fact, that it sometimes issues in the extreme, almost pathological conclusion that if something makes us happy, that is prima facie evidence that it is morally suspect.

At the same time, the rebellious response to this grim moralism is equally pathological, as I argued earlier. It says: if it feels good, do it. The result? An endless, helpless cycle of extreme indulgence and punishing denial. It is this strange idea of virtue that leads Freud to a devastating judgment about the paradoxical nature of morality. "[T]he more virtuous a man is," he writes,

> the more severe and distrustful is [the conscience's] behavior, so that ultimately it is precisely those people who have carried saintliness furthest who reproach themselves with the worst sinfulness. This means that virtue forfeits some part of its promised reward; the docile and continent ego does not enjoy the trust of its mentor, and strives in vain, it would seem, to acquire it.[...] Moreover...temptations are merely increased by constant frustration, whereas an occasional satisfaction of them causes them to diminish, at least for the time being.

In other words, morality is *designed* to make you unhappy: the more dutiful and moral you become, in these terms, the more self-hating and frustrated you are.

If happiness-denying duty is one face of modern thinking about morality, the empty happiness of the utilitarians is the other. We seem confronted with a choice between a notion of the good life that rules happiness out of bounds and a utilitarian theory that works only at the cost of reducing happiness to quantified units of pleasure.

It was not always thus. Aristotle firmly believed that happiness and goodness were allied, and therefore that no conflict existed between pursuit of the virtuous life and a greater share of personal satisfaction. On the contrary, virtuous character and action were the only secure routes to lasting happiness. To pursue happiness was, he thought, no more than fulfilling human nature: it was a matter of becoming who we are, manifesting our "metaphysical biology," as the philosopher Alasdair MacIntyre called it. But that required careful thought about what human life was for. It could not be, as it was for lesser animals, simple procreation or species survival. And there was much ignorance and disagreement about what else the point of human life might be: pleasure, honor, study, money, external goods. But all of these, though apparently pursued for their own sakes, are also pursued because we think they will make us happy. "Honor, pleasure, understanding and every virtue we certainly choose because of themselves," Aristotle says near the beginning of the *Nicomachean Ethics*,

> since we would choose each one of them even if it had no further result, but we also choose them for the sake of happiness, supposing that through them we shall be happy. Happiness, by contrast, no one ever chooses for their sake, or for the sake of anything else at all.[5]

Given the ability to reflect on the conditions of our own existence, a double-edged gift we apparently enjoy uniquely, humans are both social and contemplative by nature. We form associations and have intentions, not just instincts. We make judgments about the world and ourselves. We possess character, which surrenders its secrets to rational insight. In short, we pursue happiness actively, for it is the end of human actions, that for the sake of which all things are done.

For these reasons, human life is, for Aristotle, ordered by ideas of excellence: what serves our interests, what makes for success rather than failure in the pursuit of ends. This is what we mean by the good: not a universal, supernatural presence, as Plato argued, but the contextual judgment that a thing, person, act, or idea is helping us achieve a desired result.[6] Indeed, excellence is just another word for virtue, in Plato's and Aristotle's lexicon (the Greek is *areté*). The judgment of virtue describes the qualities or actions that contribute to human flourishing. In the context of human social life, or politics, an excellent person is a virtuous one, one who participates in the flourishing of his or (we may now add) her community. To be conscious of possessing excellent character, to have an awareness of one's place in a well-ordered form of human life, is to be satisfied with the course of one's life: to realize that one is living and faring well. This is not as austere as saying that virtue is its own reward; Aristotle believed that virtue included the feelings of contentment, well-being, and comfort that later moralists would dissociate from ethical life. Virtuous action and dedicated contemplation brought pleasure, honor, and abundance—all the things that are generally considered to be happiness itself. When a person participated in the life of a social group, forming and maintaining ties, doing work that supported rather than destroyed what was shared, the result was the only genuine form of happiness.

Thus a powerful, and attractive, connection is forged between the good life and the happy life. It was a connection that lasted for centuries after Aristotle, even if it has been misplaced in our own time. Cicero, in the fifth book of the *Tusculan Disputations,* found that virtue was sufficient for a happy life, and Seneca, writing "De Vita Beata," of the blessed life, in his *Minor Dialogues,* says:

> A happy life, therefore, is one which is in accordance with its own nature, and cannot be brought about unless in the first place the mind be sound and remain so without interruption, and, next, be bold and vigorous, enduring all things with most admirable courage, suited to the times in which it lives, careful of the body and its appurtenances, yet not troublesomely careful. It must also set due value upon all the things which adorn our lives, without overestimating any one of them, and must be able to enjoy the bounty of Fortune without becoming her slave.[7]

That is why Aristotle devotes his study of human life and happiness to an analysis of the virtues. "Since happiness is an activity of the soul expressing complete virtue," he says, "we must examine virtue; for that will perhaps also be a way to study happiness better." The virtues of character, together with the theory of the golden mean—that is, the powerful idea that virtue is always a matter of moderating between deficiency in a quality and excess of it, hitting the target of courage, say, somewhere in the productive middle between cowardice and rashness—and a necessary modicum of good luck and reward, sketch the nature of the happy person: complete, self-sufficient, blessed.

The details of this theory are naturally controversial, and Aristotle's very specific list of virtues of character has come under attack in the twenty-five centuries since it was first mooted. Temperance and mildness, friendliness and wit—these virtues of character have lost much, if not all, of the specifically ethical and political seriousness they had for the Greeks. At the same time, the virtues of character that govern the disposition of wealth and honors—proper self-regard that borders on arrogance, a certain degree of ostentatious spending—are precisely those items on Aristotle's list we may now incline to view with some misgiving. As translator Terence Irwin says in the Introduction to his translation of the *Ethics,* "we will not be immediately inclined to find the magnanimous person as admirable as Aristotle finds him." For, although we still speak of a virtue of magnanimity, it no longer means what it did to Aristotle, for whom the magnanimous person is "one who thinks himself worthy of great things and is really worthy of them." By extension, the vice of deficiency concerning this virtue is weak-heartedness, a tendency to think oneself less worthy than one really is—something we might rather describe as the virtue of modesty. (Notice, though, that the current preoccupation, in schools and therapy sessions, with the idea of *self-esteem* does not touch on Aristotle's aristocratic idea of virtue. He didn't mean feeling good about yourself no matter who you are or what you do; he meant being capable of noble and impressive actions and willing to take credit for them.)

Even friendship, arguably the central theme of the *Ethics* and the virtue allied so closely to justice and the pursuit of civic flourishing that they are sometimes spoken of as identical, is something we tend to detach from the political. If we did not, there would be no sense in E. M. Forster's celebrated challenge: "If I had to choose between betraying my country and betraying my friend, I hope I should have the guts to betray my country." There is for Aristotle no choice to be made (and therefore no issue of courage) between my friends and the civic body to which I belong. Particular friendships may be, as he says, "subordinate" to the larger community, but without community there is no friendship. And friendship demands, in Aristotle's discussion, a host of obligations and duties that are unfamiliar to our notions and practices of friendship. The true friend, he says, is my equal in virtue; he or she is "another myself." With the exception of familial or conjugal friendships, and perhaps a rare close colleague, many of us would, I suspect, find that the bulk of our routine friendships are defective in Aristotle's view, "incomplete" associations based on pleasure or utility. Indeed, the reason Aristotle can argue (as he does in Book V of the *Ethics)* that justice and friendship have the same scope and extension is precisely that the series of relationships that make up the good life—together with their rewards and responsibilities, and the character traits associated therewith—are exactly what he defines as justice: the complete exercise of virtue with respect to another.

By contrast, a contemporary map of the same terrain would be likely to say that friendship and justice are notions divorced at or near the root, since (merely) doing justice to our friends is not treating them properly, that is, not treating them with the exclusive love and loyalty that friendship demands. Likewise, in contemporary terms, the complete exercise of virtue is something properly limited to a sphere of close association that is, by definition, separated from the public or political sphere. Justice might remain the ruling principle of this public/political sphere, but only insofar as it is divorced from friendship: we must be just to our fellow citizens, certainly, but asking us to be friends with them is asking all too much. Overall, we are left with only a debased version of the public thesis of the ethical and political virtue of happiness: an imperative not to complain too much in times of trial. "In this democracy," Dorothy Thompson wrote chirpily in the *Ladies' Home Journal* in 1941, "it has become a public duty to be as happy as one can be."[8]

When we consider these divergences, the question arises as to whether this ancient way of thinking about the link between virtue and happiness is available to us, whether we can navigate a virtuous middle course between the duty-based theory of Kant and the happiness-based theory of the utilitarians. "[T]his is to take a modern journey with a mediaeval map—an artificially neat map combining detail in places with large unsatisfactory areas, unexplored and assigned only to monsters," says philosopher Julia Annas.[9] But if we could undertake that journey we might be able to resist "the notion that morality is a life harassed and persecuted everywhere by 'imperatives' and disagreeable duties, and that without these you have not got morality," as F. H. Bradley put it.[10] We might be able to replace the "imperative" notions of duty, obligation, and rule following with "attractive" ones of character, happiness, and the worth of a whole life.[11] And if we could do that, we might be able to bridge the deep divide, so common now as to appear instinctive or natural, between doing the right thing and doing what we want to do. As Ogden Nash had it, "O Duty, Duty! How noble a man should I be hadst thou the visage of a sweetie or a cutie!"[12]

Such a move to happy virtue would counter an overly negative kind of morality, which is excessively technical or algorithmic, in favor of more contextual and natural ethical standards; but it would also, from the other side, counter the dominant view of happiness, which relies on truncated psychological notions of contentment and passivity. Before we pop the corks, however, we must accept that there are problems with the notion of virtue itself. Not long ago the philosopher Bernard Williams could opine, with good reason, that in our culture "[t]he word 'virtue' has for the most part acquired comic or otherwise undesirable associations, and few of us now use it except philosophers."[13] Williams meant by this the way "virtue" might seem to strike us as an outdated or pious concept, the sort of thing seriously appealed to only by people named Laetitia or Murgatroyd, and hence usable by everybody else only in ironic or scholarly contexts. He could not have foreseen a new set of undesirable associations with the word because of its appropriation by puritanical neo-conservative ideologues like William Bennett, David Frum, and William Kristol, with their books and tables and tales and fables of nonthreatening traits like chastity and obedience. Nor could he, or anyone else, have foreseen the resulting publishing boom, with countervailing left-wing virtue books now shouldering in next to

Bennett's bestsellers. The result is a familiar point-counterpoint game of moral one-upmanship, in which each interested party claims privileged access to *the* virtues.

What this illustrates is an enduring disagreement about what the virtues really are. If there is insufficient agreement in our culture about what constitutes a good life, talk of the virtues is rendered impossible. Without a deep background of shared ethical assumptions, the kind of thing Aristotle could hope to articulate when he wrote the *Nicomachean Ethics,* can we even speak of the character traits and dispositions to action that make for the good life? It would seem not. Liberalism, the dominant political theory of the modern age, was adopted to deal with precisely this problem of the fracturing of ethical experience. If people disagreed about the life worth living (or in the beginning, more specifically, the proper route to Christian salvation), then a political philosophy of tolerance and respect of the individual seemed like the only possible alternative to the endless conflict that would otherwise dominate life. Liberalism, in its various forms, has this shared center: it tries to rise above moral disagreement, which it regards as insoluble, in order to deal with the more pressing, but more tractable, political question of simple coexistence. It purchases social survival at the price of putting to one side the question of what is really good. Thus liberalism, individualism, and modernity are intimately linked: they are, we might say, three faces of the same project.

The problem with this Holy Trinity, as we have seen, is that individualism brings with its many achievements a drastic reduction of our ideas of well-being, and hence of the self. The paradox of the idea is that, in granting status to every individual, we invite a kind of narcissism or even solipsism that issues, eventually, in the pathological institution of confessional talk shows, ad-dominated cultural experience, and a sense of the good life that is wrapped up in the acquisition of material goods. Hence the ongoing dissatisfaction with the liberal individual on the part of conservative moralists and radical reformers alike. If you have a deeper sense of ethical conviction, especially an idea that ethics and politics cannot be easily separated in the manner suggested by classical liberals, the modern individual appears in so many ways to be *beyond repair:* self-involved, acquisitive, complaining, and nonparticipatory. Here we see the reduction of the citizen to the taxpayer or shareholder, someone who might or might not vote every few years and otherwise tends to regard the state as a nagging intrusion on the multifarious project of getting and spending.

It should be clear that I have no fondness for this peculiarly modern creature, despite my belief that individualism is, on the whole, a very good thing. At the same time, I am troubled by the very real difficulty of taking a modern (or perhaps it should be post-modern) journey with a medieval map. Can talk of the virtues of happiness make sense to us any more?

I think it can, for several modest but important reasons. First, even Aristotle faced the problem of addressing a culture that included profound ethical disagreement. We tend to assume that his ethical theory was a close reflection of fifth-century-B.C. Athens, an articulation of what oft was thought but ne'er so well expressed. Yet the matter is not that simple. By engaging in a *theoretical* investigation of ethical life, Aristotle took tacit assumptions and unquestioned practices and raised them to unprecedented clarity—they were solidified, molded, even changed radically in the very act of being spoken. In other words, Aristotle did not simply mirror his times, he helped create them.

More than this, his ethical theory is such that the virtuous person must be prepared continually to go beyond the conventional or accepted ways of acting, for sometimes a rational assessment of the matter will suggest a different decision than the rule-governed, all-inclusive notion of morality might suggest. We cannot wait for a coherent ethical context to appear before we try to speak of virtue; it will never come. Contexts change and demand sometimes drastic shifts in emphasis: the virtues of physical courage and daring, for example, will be highly valued in wartime but of lesser importance, even undesirable, at other moments. (Think of the inability of the great general Coriolanus, in Shakespeare's play, to shift his undoubted military excellence into the more discursive, and compromising, sphere of civic politics.) There is therefore no algorithm for *ethics,* as there is for dutiful *morality.* Through imitation and habituation, we try to aim at the moderate and virtuous middle. Despite these indeterminacies, then, we may speak meaningfully of virtue, and trust that the act of so speaking lays one brick in the foundation of a flourishing future.

There are other reasons to be hopeful. Even in the midst of much ethical disagreement it is possible to speak of *political* virtues, since politics is, by common agreement, the one realm of life that all citizens share. This gives us a beachhead for further talk of the things we might or might not share, and the ideas of well-being and rational satisfaction that might make sense under these conditions.[14] It is unlikely we will ever come to agree on all the details of what makes a life worth living, of course: I like watching college football games on Saturday afternoons, a cold beer and bowl of taco chips at the ready; you think that time must be devoted to eating a single peach and then practicing arpeggios. But there are larger truths that we can converge on, concerning the need for rational satisfaction and the idea of a life worth living. It is wrong to live life without a sense of its possibilities, to simply wander through it. It is virtuous to pursue goals that are both productive and satisfying. That may all sound hopelessly abstract, but it is a place to start, and soon we may well find ourselves talking, or arguing, about courage, temperance, generosity, civility, and the other traditional virtues of the Greek, Christian, and other systems of thought that lie in the rich background of our culture.

I do not know—or anyway I am not prepared at the moment to claim—that these truths are universal, part of some unchanging human nature. I rather doubt it, in fact. What I *am* prepared to argue is that if they make it easier for us to continue a conversation, really the only meaningful conversation, about what it is to be human, then that is enough for me.

ARE WE HAPPY YET?

Aristotle's theory of virtuous happiness leaves one large problem unexamined, and I want to confront it now, in conclusion. However admirable the defense of virtue might seem, it sometimes appears to have literally no connection to happiness as we *typically* conceive it. Certainly it appears to have little to do with the mundane searches for the right household object that drive the sluggish steps of the crowds in the Better Living Centre. We are forced to wonder how much help it is for a philosopher to tell us, as I am attempting to do now, that the truly happy life lies in living and faring well. Fine, you might say, but *what's that got to do with happiness?*

This is not a problem that arises only with the distance we have come since Aristotle, though our materialism and physicalism certainly make the problem worse. As Julia Annas points out in *The Morality of Happiness,* these ancient theories of the ethical nature of happiness were counterintuitive to nonphilosophers even at the moment they were deployed. "They give an account of happiness," she writes, "which, if baldly presented to a nonphilosopher without any of the supporting arguments, would sound wrong, even absurd." They make some mention of external goods and their role in creating happiness, but seem to play down the very real pleasures of possession and enjoyment. They nod to pleasure, honor, and so on only perfunctorily, sliding the terms of reference around even as they do so, such that happiness is the only end worth pursuing for its own sake. And then, in the vacuum of confusion that naturally arises at this point—of course happiness is the end of life, but now *define* it— they slip virtue into the picture while the rest of us are trying to decide between a new dining-room table and that CD player we saw, because we can't afford both.

So we are forced to wonder: Is virtue sufficient to happiness, as Aristotle and the Stoics said, and Boethius seemed later to agree? Or does it require external goods—and if so, how many? "Resolve not to be poor," Dr. Johnson said in December 1782. "Whatever you have, spend less. Poverty is a great enemy to human happiness; it certainly destroys liberty, and it makes some virtues impracticable and others extremely difficult." Is there, then, a sense in which virtue is possible only when one has the material wherewithal? Do you need to have money to be good? We tend to think not, at least in our pious public moments, but actually the question is far from easy to answer. Aristotle says explicitly that the happy person is blessed with both luck and a decent share of external goods: virtue requires a degree of wealth and leisure even as it demands moderation.[15] (It never demands vicious self-denial of the ascetic kind, such as the Christian world fixated on.) External goods and virtue are not opposed, though it is clearly true that the man blessed with plenty of external goods is not necessarily the virtuous man. By the same token, while it is usually true that the virtuous man and the happy man are the same, it is possible, under negative circumstances, to possess all the prerequisites of virtue except external luck, and hence to be not happy but unhappy.

But whence these external goods, anyway, and how important are they? It is arguable that Aristotle never fully solved this problem.[16] Nevertheless, his view is more nuanced in practice than any simple refusal of external goods, as later Stoic philosophy made clear. What it asks is not for us to forswear external goods but rather to aim at external goods in a way that expresses the prior commitment to virtue. External goods are not despicable; they are just not the end of human life.

The result of this attitude is an extensive revision of our notions of happiness, one that involves two important paradoxes. The first is that this instability in the notion of happiness is brought to our attention only by the kind of deep reflection on the nature of happiness that Plato, Aristotle, and the other ancient philosophers enjoin—and which I have tried, here, to continue. We could not confront the problems of happiness without beginning the philosophical investigation of what it is to be human. And thus a second paradox: that very act of investigation inaugurates a kind of life, a life of critical contemplation, in which we might just come to see that happiness is more than pleasure, honor, peace, or material goods. Like Socrates and Plato before him, Aristotle's philosophizing succeeds best not in laying a deep question finally to rest but as a form of seduction. By posing a question both vexing and profound—What is the life worth living?—he draws us into just the kind of life that *is* worth living, namely, one in which we reflect on the very conditions of our own possibility.

Now, as someone who teaches philosophy, I am perhaps a little overfond of paradoxes. Think of Epimenides the Cretan saying, in his confounding way, that all Cretans are liars. True or false? Well, if he is telling the truth then he is lying; and if he is lying then he is telling the truth—at least about himself. But this last paradox is so basic to philosophical reflection that it might be its defining problem, and one that in a way applies to all projects of self-discovery. It first comes up, as so much does, in Plato's *Republic*. Socrates is trying to convince his ambitious young friends Glaucon, Cleitophon, Polemarchus, and Adeimantus that the life of philosophical study is the best life, vastly superior to any life of worldly gain and honor. Indeed, he says, the unexamined life is not only inferior to the examined, it is not even worth living. He does not claim to be able to define justice—the set topic of these opening scenes of Plato's dialogue—but he does claim to know that the kind of moral skepticism offered by Thrasymachus the Sophist will not do.

In a celebrated exchange in the middle of Book I of *The Republic,* Socrates defeats the blustering Thrasymachus, who tries to defend the idea that justice is "the advantage of the stronger." But is it possible for the stronger to make mistakes? Socrates wonders. Of course it is, Thrasymachus replies; they do it all the time. Then they are not acting to their advantage but to their disadvantage, Socrates says. According to Thrasymachus it is just for the weaker to obey the stronger, for that is part of what "the advantage of the stronger" must mean, but if the stronger make mistakes, then sometimes the weaker will, in obeying them, actually act *against* the interests of the stronger. Whatever they say about justice is what goes, Thrasymachus says; granted, says Socrates, but this might be either good or bad for them.

Now, what this implies is not simply that the strong may be mistaken about their own best interests. That would hardly be either surprising or interesting. It also implies that there is, that there must be, *an independent standard of advantage* that stands outside what a given person might think or say is to their advantage. This is so because the possibility of error logically implies the possibility of correctness, and both necessarily imply the fact of a standard of judgment. (Where there are no standards we can be neither right nor wrong.)

At this point Thrasymachus shifts ground and tries to argue that the unjust man is always better off—always profits more, is what he says—than the just man. But he is similarly caught here. If the unjust man can be wrong about his own advantage, then he is not the sole arbiter of it—contrary to what relativists wish to say. This lays the nature of profit on the table, a move that Plato has, to all appearances, cleverly engineered through the ironic posturing of Socrates and the imperious bluster of Thrasymachus. The unjust man, Socrates says, appears to live in a disharmony of ambition and deceit. His soul is disordered, regardless of the amount of worldly profit he may amass in the form of wealth and power. Yet we know that the soul is that part of the person that lives, the vital part. Its excellence or virtue is living well. Living well must mean harmony in the soul. Harmony in the soul is just another way of speaking of justice—and, indeed, of happiness. "The just soul and the just man will live well, and the unjust man will live badly," Socrates says near the end of Book I. "Surely the one who lives well is blessed and happy, and the one who does not is unhappy. So the just man is happy, and the unjust man is wretched. It profits no one to be wretched, but to be happy. And so, my good Thrasymachus, injustice is never more profitable than justice."[17]

The reason the unjust person lives poorly is not because he lacks for wealth or power—he might enjoy a surfeit of these—but because he has a soul in grave disorder, in which the various parts outlined in Plato's somewhat proto-Freudian psychology are in constant conflict with one another; while the just person has an excellent, well-ordered soul. Compared to this latter *kind* of profit and advantage, in other words, all the glory in the world is as nothing. Thrasymachus, after setting out to defend a sharp and worldly-wise notion of justice, has been caught in a series of humiliating and rather obvious self-contradictions. The reason is simple enough. In denying the *choiceworthiness* of justice he has not actually overturned the definition of justice as psychic harmony, or happiness. On the contrary, he has accepted it. His resulting argument, the only one he can make—that the unjust man is better off than the just—simply reinforces the virtue of justice by inviting a discussion of advantage and profit that he cannot win because his notions of advantage and profit are faulty. In the dialogue, the character of Socrates says: "Thrasymachus agreed to all this, not easily as I am telling it, but grudgingly and after being pushed; and, since it was a warm summer day, with a copious amount of sweating. And then I saw something I had never seen before, Thrasymachus blushing." After that, though Socrates continues to badger him, it is all over but the shouting: Thrasymachus retreats into sullenness, and he is soon dropped from the action altogether.[18]

That is all very satisfying, if a little stacked against poor arrogant Thrasymachus. Yet Socrates still faces a problem. The goods that philosophy delivers—wisdom, virtue, and happiness—are seen to be goods only by those *already* initiated into the philosophical life. They are not the things typically valued by the world, as his young friends do not hesitate to point out to him. Glaucon, who takes up the main burden of the discussion in Book II, sincerely wants to know why he should be a just (that is, good) man when the world seems to reward injustice as highly—or even more so. Indeed, the cynical view would seem to suggest that an unjust disposition succeeds best, especially when combined with an outward reputation for justice. The problem for Socrates, therefore, is that he apparently cannot convince those who are still operating outside the philosophical notion of the good life that it is good for them, because they come to see that only from *within* that form of life. Hence the enduring Catch-22 of "useless" goods: you value philosophizing and the goods of wisdom only when you already value them. So unless you are already engaged in the happy life of self-examination, you cannot see why it might be worth living in such a way in the first place.

Now, Socrates manages to lure his young friends into philosophy despite themselves, using subtle techniques of irony, parable, and professed ignorance—the sort of thing you might still find, if you're lucky, in a gifted teacher. Socrates was a master. The rest of us must continue to struggle, and one of the central features of this struggle now is the tendency we have to sell activities not on their own terms of value but rather according to the consumer-driven marketplace. This is a potentially disastrous mistake. The genuine reasons for ethical reflection on happiness lie not in the market possibilities or prospects of pleasure but in the personal and community possibilities during a lifetime of regard for the great conversation concerning what it is to be human.

But you won't know that for sure until you plunge in, heedless of the world's crude utilitarian advice to the contrary. The question of the life worth living is not, as we often assume, an issue so large and abstract that it is appropriate to raise only in a philosophy class or therapy session. It is not an overwhelming matter of considering the whole of my life all at once; it is, rather, a matter of broaching the much more tractable and pressing question of what I am going to do *now*, in the next thirty, sixty, or ninety minutes of my life, over the rest of today, then tomorrow, and the next day. What, right now, is the action that would make my life one about which I can be rationally satisfied? How I ought to live is not a matter to be put off for another time—for life has this insistent feature, that it will not be put off.

At the same time, asking the question of how I ought to live is to confront, and accept, that basic mystery of my life, namely, that it comes to an end sometime. In contrast to the technological versions of happiness, which, like technology itself, seem to be motivated by a desire to overcome death, to cheat the contingency of the world— which scares and disturbs us—this richer version of happiness takes seriously the finitude of individual existence. *Timor mortis conturbat me.* Of course it does: we are, so far as we know, the only species capable of reflecting on our own mortality, the only creatures on this planet able to envision our own ceasing to be. This fear might be considered irrational, as fear often is. "To be afraid of death,"

Socrates says in Plato's dialogue *The Apology*, "is nothing other than to think oneself wise when one is not; for it is to think one knows what one does not know. No man knows whether death may not even turn out to be the greatest of blessings for a human being; and yet people fear it as if they knew for certain that it is the greatest of evils."

Well, fine; but that kind of clear thinking is in short supply most of the time, and little solace anyway. "So far as I know," the humanist scholar Robert Ingersoll said in 1879, "the only evidence about another life is, first, that we have no evidence; and secondly, that we are rather sorry that we have not, and wish we had." Nor is the simple fact of passing on cultural meaning likely to assuage our existential fear of death. "I don't want to gain immortality through my work," Woody Allen once said. "I want to gain immortality through not dying." But the desire for immortality is full of danger, the kind of desperate striving and questing so apparent in the culture of happiness provision. The real question is: can we accept our finitude rather than fleeing it? That is an existential challenge of unparalleled magnitude, but it should be an occasion for wonder and happiness rather than fear and trembling. Do we have the courage?

Only in asking these questions will we find precisely what is missing in any and all of the better-living versions of happiness, in all the complex and sophisticated machinery of our contentment: not the simple satisfaction of our desires but the revision of them. Only here can we put our inherited priorities and conventional expectations into question. Only here can we find a happiness that goes beyond the untrustworthy waves of fortune and pleasure, the fast-fading glories of objects and excitations.

Only here, finally, can we become who we are.

9

Postscript: Happy to Be Here

We think that change occurs suddenly, but even I have learned better. Happiness is wild and arbitrary, but it's not sudden.
—*Anne Michaels,* Fugitive Pieces

O H, BUT IT *CAN* BE SUDDEN, IN THE INITIAL SHOCK OF RECOGNItion if not the actual achievement: the suddenness of an intellectual revelation, akin to the first hot glimpse of a mathematical problem's solution, say, or the clear route from premise to conclusion in a proof of formal logic. The awareness of happiness can come upon us without warning, all unbidden. And when it does, when it is properly seen, we realize, if we are wise, that it is neither wild nor arbitrary—though I grant it can often feel that way. I started this book with a story of flying low and I want to end it, appropriately, with one about flying high.

My discussion has been in part about the dangers of technological thinking, the power of machines (both literal and metaphorical), and their persistent distortion of our ideas concerning happiness. But only a fool or a Luddite would deny that technology aids and facilitates our pursuit of happiness in countless ways, and I am neither. Sure, there are moments when, like most people, I am overcome with inarticulate rage against my machines: grabbing my computer monitor in both hands with every intention of hurling it through the plate-glass window in my living room, barely restrained by my alarmed wife, like a vignette from some kind of cheap 1950s psychodrama ("Don't *do* it, Biff!"). People say computers can't have personalities, but mine clearly does, ranging in expression from the strange wistfulness evident in its auto dial-ups to the Internet late at night, when I will hear the number tones beeping from another room, to the sort of jokey malice that only an older brother or college roommate would indulge, when it deliberately messes things up in my part of the world just to see how mad I can get. Yet there are other moments, on reflection not less numerous, when the sophisticated tools of modern life seem to be clicking together with every appearance of perfection, producing on cue the variously desired products of (as it might be) laser-printed text, beautifully cooked food, or video-recorded television drama. There are moments, in short, in which we feel justified in loving our machines. We ought to savor these little epiphanies of technological success, not least because they are fairly uncommon.

My favorite of recent memory took place on a transatlantic British Airways flight, London to Toronto, when I found myself suddenly aware of blissful comfort. Sitting there in my little slippers, big gin and tonic in hand, looking out over the rosy cloud landscape at 30,000 feet with a rousing aria from *Aïda* blasting in my ears, I was conscious, in that moment, not only of my state of simple happiness with these creature pleasures but of the amazing convergence of human effort and ingenuity that made it possible. The genius of distillation, the sweet alchemy of juniper and quinine and ice. Verdi's native brilliance and the celestial mathematics of music, conveyed in recording and reproduction. The apparently magical warmth and ventilation of our little capsule, suspended over the earth in the icy near-space of the stratosphere. Most of all, the powerful mystery of the airfoil, perhaps the twentieth century's most beautiful technological achievement, those big metal wings holding us all up there, speeding over the ocean, emancipated, like gods.

Then the movie came on and I started to cry.

SHALL WE DANCE?

We all have our lists of cinematic tear-jerkers, and mine is probably no quirkier than most. It has some obvious candidates: that scene in *Casablanca* when they sing "La Marseillaise" in Rick's Café Americain, drowning out the nasty German officers and their Prussian drinking song—and some embarrassments: the schmaltzy final sequence of *It's a Wonderful Life,* a movie I hate, and the deathbed scene in the Winona Ryder version of *Little Women,* when young Beth (Claire Danes) finally surrenders to lingering illness in a blaze of courage and noble sentiment. I blame this last weepy episode, and another even more embarrassing, involving a juvenile comedy starring Kelsey Grammer, on the rarefied air in transatlantic planes. I'm convinced there is something about the low pressure and confined spaces of the economy cabin that make me more susceptible to cheap cinematic emotion—I once teared up during a phone company commercial set to Elton John's execrable "Rocket Man." I usually end up watching the movie with a hand blocking the view of tears rolling down my face. I don't do this because I'm ashamed of crying at movies; I'm ashamed of crying at such *bad* movies. "What I love most is that it's almost the only time I cry," the novelist David Shields writes about the movies, obviously a kindred spirit. "The worse the movie, the more I cry."[1]

My two favorite weepy scenes, however, are in exquisite movies, and I want to mention them here to record, if possible, the nature of this complicated kind of human joy. More important, perhaps, is that these scenes speak deeply about the fragility of happiness, about the sweet pangs of loss and memory, the terrible fortuity of love.

They are pivotal moments in films of almost identical structure, starring the same actors, Fred Astaire and Ginger Rogers, and released within a year of each other: *Swing Time* (1936) and *Shall We Dance* (1937). Both films have elements of screwball comedy, the genre of sophisticated, talky romance perfected a few years later by Cary Grant and a stable of leading women—prominently, Irene

Dunne, Rosalind Russell, and Katharine Hepburn—who created such cinematic masterpieces as *The Awful Truth* (1937), *His Girl Friday* (1940), and *The Philadelphia Story* (1940). In his book *Pursuits of Happiness,* the Harvard philosopher and critic Stanley Cavell labels these films "Hollywood comedies of remarriage," adding *It Happened One Night* (1934), *Bringing Up Baby* (1938), *The Lady Eve* (1941), and *Adam's Rib* (1949) to his personal A list.

In some cases the remarriage label is strictly apt, for the arc of the one hundred minutes of cinematic narrative describes a revelation on the part of divorced partners that they still, indeed always did, love each other. In other cases, the same line of development—a smart, grown-up version of boy meets girl, boy loses girl, boy gets girl back—is played out over conflict, mistaken identity, some drunkenness, and a brace or more of doomed rival lovers. Inevitably, against a background of wealth, bright talk, and social mobility—"contexts," says Cavell, "in which there is satisfaction enough, in which something like luxury and leisure, something beyond the bare necessities, is an issue"—the pursuit of personal happiness is revealed as a *transformative* quest, a reorientation, a return to something that was glimpsed or possessed before. In these films, we learn that "the achievement of human happiness requires not the perennial and fuller satisfaction of our needs as they stand but the examination and transformation of those needs."[2] Just the sort of inward change, in short, that Plato taught us to pursue so many centuries ago.

The sublime moments at the center of *Swing Time* and *Shall We Dance* are sexually less explicit versions of that same revelation. In the first film, Fred plays dancer Lucky Garnett, leader of a vaudeville troupe and soon-to-be husband of a wealthy local beauty. But Lucky's fellow dancers don't want the act to break up and they sabotage the wedding by a subterfuge involving the state of Lucky's trousers: to cuff or not to cuff? (Is he, we wonder, the soul of elegance or merely a vain clotheshorse?) The marriage is off, but the penniless Lucky, despondent, leaves the vaudeville act anyway and travels to New York to seek a new fortune. He bumps into Penny Carrol (Ginger) on the streets of Manhattan, and when she rebuffs his boyish advances, he follows her to the dance studio where she works. Asking for a lesson, he begins what we know will be the eventual seduction with a bravura performance of Jerome Kern's "Pick Yourself Up." The dance, here as so often a displacement of sexual activity, is a revelation of their suitability: they move together as if made for each other, as if by magic. Penny is suspicious but overwhelmed; Lucky dances her off her feet.

The pair decide to audition for a nightclub spot, but the attempt is foiled, again by a question of sartorial propriety: Lucky lacks the proper formal wear. Penny is of course livid, at once downcast and self-chastising. A betrayal so soon after the initial rush of communion! She should have seen it coming. She retreats into sullenness while Lucky and his sidekick picket outside her door with placards asserting Lucky's innocence. (What *can* a man do when it's a matter of proper attire? It's as if love were clashing with honor.) Finally he enters the suite and tiptoes over to the piano. In the next room Penny is sitting disconsolately before her vanity mirror, clad in bathrobe and with shampoo in her hair. Lucky seats himself at the piano and, as Penny listens and eventually enters, sings "The Way You Look Tonight."

With its suggestion of a bleak future and an uncaring world ("Some day, when I'm awfully old, and the world is cold"), the song is on the surface a straightforward invocation of the reality principle—nothing good ever lasts—but the romance lies in the cherished image of the loved one's face, a barrier against the world's frigidity and the harsh inevitability of age. The way she looks tonight, shampoo and all, will be sufficient to keep him warm when all else fails: "I will feel a glow," he says, "just thinking of you." The slow swing of the Kern melody tugs at us, gently insistent, just as the Dorothy Fields lyrics tug at Penny: she is already lodged deep in his heart. Seduction again, only this time charged, and chastened, by the prospect of a real future of loss. Lucky and Penny will dance, and dance around it, for the remainder of the film, but this is their romance's key bittersweet moment, its still center.

Shall We Dance follows an almost identical storyline and includes a scene of identical semantic weight, though in somewhat more involved circumstances. Pete Peters (Fred) is a Paris-based ballet star who falls in love with revue dancer Linda Greene (Ginger), from a distance. He decides to follow her on a transatlantic voyage and proposes to her on the ocean liner's kennel deck. Linda is not interested, but as the result of a misunderstanding Linda and Pete arrive in New York to rumors that they are already married, and Linda's manager, fearing she will retire if they *really* get married, tries to maintain the mistaken impression. Pete and Linda realize that to quell the rumors they must actually get married—and then divorced. So they take a ferry across the Hudson to New Jersey for a quickie wedding, and on the return trip, during what amounts to an abbreviated (and of course fake) honeymoon, Pete sings George Gershwin's lovely "They Can't Take That Away from Me."

The song's melody rolls with the river swells, its gentle syncopation again radiating persuasion, as Pete tells Linda of the series of moments, impressions, and gestures that not even enforced separation can remove from his store of cherished memories. They are married only to be divorced, but the undeniable fact is that they *are* married—and he loves her. It is an invocation of the doomed lover's habitual metaphysical claim, that not even God can alter historical fact. Astaire's elegant tenor picks out the plaintive obstinacy of the song's "No, no" bridge and the devoted, even obsessive attention of his impressions, the lovesick swain's sharp eye for detail: "the way you wear your hat, the way you sip your tea." It is the fineness of his memories, as much as the raw emotion of his love, already imagining a future in which they are all he has, that convinces us—and Linda. We are made to see that love is first and foremost a cognitive state: a way of looking, a form of knowledge, that finds heartbreaking poetry in the details. The insight completes the circle opened by the old Platonic link between *Eros* and *epistémé*, the idea of carnal knowledge. To love is indeed to know.

Once again, although there are twists left in the plot, a corner has been decisively turned—and, not coincidentally, it happens while the main characters are in limbo between two states: New York and New Jersey, obviously, but also marriage and divorce, resentment and love. The film pivots on the scene, and the song, just as in *Swing Time* the invocation of a dark future appears to illuminate an uncertain present, and cement the connection with a mixture of melancholy and relief. That commingling of happiness and resignation, the dark essence of romantic love—even in these apparently lightweight comedies—brings on a rush of feeling. "What is more natural than that we should persist in looking for happiness along the path on which we first encountered it?" Freud asks of the happiness of love. Yet "[t]he weak side of this technique of living is easy to see. It is that we are never so defenseless against suffering as when we love, never so helplessly unhappy as when we have lost our loved object or its love." True, but Freud misses the point with his better-living talk of *technique*. When it comes to love, we don't have any choice. There is surely a wide spectrum of emotions that mix happiness and sadness, sometimes in near-equal measure: the tears of joy when we are reunited with a long-absent friend; the exquisite and indulgent gloom of the jilted lover; the cheerful *Weltschmerz* of the committed cynic, happy in his unhappiness. None of them is as powerful as the sad awareness of love's lucky gift, its insistent and frail reality, in a world where time, of necessity, passes—where things change.

When I see these movies, I weep for sheer happiness.

THE BITTER AND THE SWEET

We all have our chosen paths to what we imagine happiness will be. I hope I have provided in these pages some ways to think constructively about that human journey, to be critical of what we think we know, and to remember some of the hard but true things about ourselves. I want to conclude with one further personal reflection, not so much because I think it representative but rather because it illuminates some of my conclusions about the pursuit of happiness and, incidentally, goes some way to explain how I came to write this book.

For the past eight years I have, in common with many scholars of my generation, sent out applications for university teaching jobs: sometimes just nine or ten; sometimes, as in the first year after actually completing my Ph.D., as many as sixty-five or seventy. Over the years—twice as many as it took me to get the doctorate in the first place—I have probably mailed more than five hundred applications to university philosophy departments. I have applied in Canada, in Britain, in the United States. I have applied to famous research universities and backwoods liberal arts colleges that I had never heard of until the day I sent off a package asking to spend the rest of my life there.

Despite this annual ordeal, I have found it hard to shake a certain kind of optimism, namely, that there were good and explicable reasons for my failing to get a raft of offers: I had not finished my degree, I had not published, I had not published *enough*. So I did all those things. The applications went out every November—cover letter, C.V., teaching evaluations, writing sample, promise of reference letters to come, a little paperwork assembly line—and I waited for the phone to ring in early December, the call asking me to come to the annual philosophy conference where job interviews are conducted.

For those who have never attended these gatherings, there is nothing to prepare you for the atmosphere of aggressive dread that seeps from the walls of the various convention hotels in which they are staged. Fingering tight collars and wincing in new shoes, the overdressed job candidates haunt the hallways with blank eyes like the academic undead, offering surplus copies of their C.V.s to anyone with a heartbeat. They form lines to enter a little room in which, posted on bulletin boards, are the dregs of the job offerings, the ones too insignificant to make it into the advance issues of the professional-listings newspaper called, without irony, *Jobs for Philosophers*. They prowl through massive hotel ballrooms during soul-destroying cocktail parties, armed with maps to who is sitting where and ready to buttonhole the embattled members of the various search committees. The lucky ones take their earnest dissertation summaries and rehearsed pedagogical ideas into overheated hotel rooms, where they confront the same search-committee members, now perched on beds or window sills, sometimes eight or nine to a room. If they manage to impress, they make the jump from the long short-list to the short short-list and are invited back to the campus for a visit, several socially nugatory meals, and the happy ordeal of the job talk.

Now, I fully realize that failing to land a cushy job matters little, if at all, in a world where people are routinely dying for want of enough to eat or murdered because their skin color or ethnic origin proves unpleasant to someone holding a gun. I am aware that there is something even a little obscene in considering oneself unhappy because a particular kind of employment doesn't come one's way. Even compared to a casting director's cattle call, say, or the stream of unsolicited manuscripts, screen-test videotapes and eight-by-ten glossies that arrive daily at film studios, talent agencies, and literary quarterlies the world over, this event probably ranks only in the middle of some universal scale of human futility. It is, however, the part of that scale I am most familiar with, and it is, moreover, depressing enough in its own right to exemplify something essential about the risks of human ambition. Also, it helps very little in making you happier to know that other people are worse off than you, even drastically worse off. Because, after all, *they are not you.* Unhappiness takes no prisoners, and one of the first casualties of its irreducible first-personal character is the felt awareness, as opposed to the rational conclusion, that we ought to be thankful for the many things we have.

I might derive some perverse happiness from the misfortunes of others if I resent or hate them, of course. "Mine is a most peaceable disposition," Heinrich Heine once confessed.

> My wishes are: a humble cottage with a thatched roof, but a good bed, good food, the freshest milk and butter, flowers before my window, and a few fine trees before my door; and if God wants to make my happiness complete, he will grant me the joy of seeing some six or seven of my enemies hanging from those trees. Before their death I shall, moved in my

heart, forgive them all the wrong they did me in their life-time. One must, it is true, forgive one's enemies—but not before they have been hanged.[3]

So true. Occasionally, too, simple awareness of comparative misfortune will bring me to my senses and help me count my blessings. But on the whole I am unlikely to dispel my own deep unhappiness by having my attention drawn to the fact that there are many unhappy strangers throughout the world.

When a friend of mine with an English literature Ph.D. from Princeton was first on the job market, he actually went so far as to call up departments where he had failed to get a job and request some kind of feedback. This action is a common response to failure in a job competition in the corporate world, mainly because you can't learn from failure unless the causes of it are made clear, but in this case it was greeted with incredulity, even hostility. For reasons that are not entirely clear to me, the academic hiring process is often covered with a veil of silence, its decisions defended by reference to opaque notions of academic excellence. Over the years you learn about job-search realities and how the decisions are actually made: dire reports of personality conflict, back-stabbing, institutional pathology, even envy of a candidate's success. Fame, however modest, is particularly frowned upon. The Cambridge classicist F. M. Cornford, who penned a still unsurpassed satirical manual on academic politics, *Microcosmographia Academica,* captured the idea in what he called the Principle of Sound Learning.

"[T]he noise of vulgar fame should never trouble the cloistered calm of academic existence," Cornford wrote in 1908.

> Hence, learning is called sound when no one has ever heard of it; and "sound scholar" is a term of praise applied to one another by learned men who have no reputation outside the University, and a rather queer one inside it. If you should write a book (you had better not), be sure that it is unreadable; otherwise you will be called "brilliant" and forfeit all respect.[4]

Hence academia's favorite backhanded compliment: Ah yes, Dr. X
…I hear he *writes* well.

AT LONG LAST, LIFE

Though I've long been a small-time Scrooge on anticonsumerist
grounds, I soon became an unredeemed Grinch every December as
I waited for the phone to ring. I manufactured elaborate revenge
fantasies, usually involving a high-powered rifle, a lofty vantage
point, and a list of departmental search committees tacked to the
chimney next to my telescopic sight. Some of my more sensitive
friends grew mildly alarmed when I talked about this with every
show of seriousness. ("Don't worry," I'd tell them. "It's too hard to
get the weapons in Canada.") Less violently, I indulged feelings of
mild contempt for my colleagues. Various passages from Amis's
Lucky Jim, the basic primer of the academic *Untermensch*, would pop
into my head during colloquia or departmental meetings: the eva-
sive journal editor who has actually stolen a submitted article; the
senior professor reacting to a question about the future of a young
academic on contract "as if he were being asked to make some concession which, though theoretically due, no decent man would
claim"; the same professor being "known to be taking the whole day
off, as distinct from days like yesterday…when [he] merely took the
early and late morning and the afternoon off."[5]

But this was too easy—and anyway, it didn't lessen the deep and
abiding unhappiness I felt about the situation. I realized I was making the classic error of cherishing something beyond reasonable
expectation. Yet I simply couldn't shake it off. I knew that in a sense
I was simply *making myself unhappy*, refusing to surrender what could
be given up. But it was all dying very hard. In strong moments I convinced myself that philosophy was a subject too important to leave to
academic philosophers, that it was time to move on in some other
fashion. Then I would remember my colleagues' smugness, their
endless store of reasoned disapproval for anything happening outside the academy and—not least—their pointlessly comfortable

lives, untroubled by thoughts of struggling to make ends meet. And I was angry again.

Christianity was born, Nietzsche said, when *ressentiment* became creative. Out of a sense of grievance I found energy to work harder. Yet I found I could not thoroughly enjoy the successes that came— not, anyway, in the sense of accepting where I was and not wishing at the same time to be somewhere else. Happiness, as Aristotle and Spinoza and Russell all agree, is in some large measure about mental hygiene: having the strength of character to think carefully about situations, to accept the implications of your rational decisions, to moderate desire, and to act on the information that comes to you.[6] Happiness is never simply a choice, though it involves many hard decisions. It is, rather, a transformation of one's life through work, luck, and dedication. But it is true that attitude plays a very important role in our being happy. Socrates said the good life and the happy life were indistinguishable. It was *that* philosophical challenge, I realize, and nothing to do with this or that scholarly debate or question, that I was having trouble meeting.

When I was younger, my father, who had a drinking problem and was going to Alcoholics Anonymous meetings, used to post around the house various reproductions of the AA serenity prayer. "God grant me the serenity to accept the things I cannot change," it goes, "the courage to change the things I can, and the wisdom to know the difference." I found this irritating at the time, partly because I was angry with him and the situations his drinking created for me and the rest of the family, but mostly because I considered the prayer banal to the point of self-parody, unappealing in its lack of passion. Lately I have come to think rather differently, and not only because I have drunk too much myself now and then and done some regrettable things as a result. I find it helps to remember the perhaps counterintuitive fact that something's being true does not necessarily make it spectacular.

"The golden mean is an uninteresting doctrine," Russell says at one point in *The Conquest of Happiness,* "and I can remember when I was young rejecting it with scorn and indignation, since in those days it was heroic extremes that I admired. Truth, however, is not always interesting, and many things are believed because they are interesting although, in fact there is little other evidence in their favor." So here's to this unspectacular but important truth about happiness: it lies in some large measure in how we comport ourselves, in how we frame and mold our desires, in how well we can accept the many facts about us and the world that are painful or ugly. Here's to the courage not only to change the things we can but to accept the very human state of affairs that happiness sometimes lies within our grasp, if only we will close our fingers around it. Here's to, finally, the awareness that getting everything you want is not the source of happiness but of unhappiness, for when striving ceases so does life. "[T]o be without some of the things you want," says Russell, "is an indispensable part of happiness."

Earlier I wrote of Boethius's *Consolation of Philosophy,* with its unstable but still powerful conviction that taking the long view, walking the road of acceptance, is the means to reconciling ourselves to our fate. If we can read him without the Christian apologetics—not his intention, to be sure—what Boethius celebrates is not the resignation that masks defeat and drowns ambition but the wisdom that accepts what cannot be changed while actively attacking what can. That kind of acceptance begins with the underrated cognitive and moral faculty—the intellectual virtue—of distinguishing between misfortune and injustice. I see now—but only now, after long years of struggle—that the consolation of philosophy must lie, for me, in accepting that academia is *not* the only place in the world where I, or anyone else, might lead a life worth living. ("Academentia," a friend of mine calls the obsessive mental condition of believing the opposite: a common affliction.) And the happy irony is that I have never been, and could never be, a better or more complete lover of wisdom—a more perfect philosopher—than at the moment I reached that conclusion.

I am still open to any offers of lifetime job security—who isn't? But in the meantime I am, like every athlete interviewed before the big game and every actor called to Broadway, just happy to be here.

In a place where Fred and Ginger always end up together, dancing into the darkness to Gershwin or Berlin or Kern, the angels of my content. I know very well they are not real, merely the nimble tricksters of cinematic sophistication, another vehicle of better living in which love triumphs in white tie and tails. I also know that they are not mine to own, that even my cherished wistful experiences are constantly in danger of being stolen from me and repackaged by the all-consuming machinery of the culture.

Yet I know too, in neither delusion nor wishfulness, but rationally and with all critical cylinders firing, that the message Fred and Ginger bring to me is unspectacularly true. Human happiness, sustained in both virtuous action and rigorous contemplation, is possible on this benighted earth. It is, as Aristotle said, nothing less than the fulfillment of our nature. In those moments, I know that my feelings and judgments of happiness are safely mine as long as I have the strength of mind to make them so. The producers, advertisers, and hawkers are powerless in the face of my individual decision, even in the midst of all these imperatives of better living, to be free. No matter how hard they try, they can't take that away from me.

So I raise my glass to the dancing figures, and salute them.

Acknowledgments

Unlike some books, this one has a fairly precise point of origin, a certain event involving children, playgrounds, and the adult thought that the only kind of pure happiness humans can know is the kind children find in play. I no longer believe that is so—I'm not sure I really did then—but the incident is nonetheless what inspired me to pursue happiness in the form of this discussion. That journey has taken me on a different path than I imagined I would follow and involved some painful reassessments and reconfigurations, but for being there at the delusionally confident moment when I decided to tackle a subject as expansive as happiness, I thank Charlie Foran and Mary Ladky, their daughters Anna and Claire, Ken and Tina Whyte and their daughter Thea. Needless to say, none of them is responsible for anything unpleasant that has happened in the long journey from that moment to this.

Aristotle said the highest expression of virtue, and (it follows) the genuinely happy life, were to be found in the cultivation of true friendship. I have been blessed with a group of friends who bear him out. Their good companionship, wise counsel, and laser-guided wit, sometimes provided in thrice-daily phone conversations, voluminous e-mail exchanges, or long evenings of social dissection, have made this book possible. In many cases, these people shared material about happiness and its problems with me; in a few, they figure in the preceding pages, the essential supporting characters of my story. All of them are present in ways both explicit and implicit. I thank them all but in particular, Anne Bains, Sara Borins, Todd Ducharme, Allan Hepburn, Naomi Klein, Chris Kutz, Dana

Lerman, Barry McCartan, Jessica Riskin, Suzanne Stein, and Janice Zawerbny.

Special thanks are owing to my editor and friend Jackie Kaiser. As always, she superbly managed the rare combination of being supportive but critical, encouraging yet tough. Thanks also to Meg Taylor, who finished the substantive edit when insistent biology forced a change of plan; Catherine Marjoribanks, who copyedited the manuscript and compiled the index; and Cynthia Good, Karen Cossar, and Scott Sellers at Penguin, for their work in making this book as good as it could be. Paula Thiessen secured permissions for quoted materials, where necessary. Nancy Friedland spent a very funny afternoon with me in one of Toronto's temples of commerce, seeking (and finding) the perfect author photo for this book. And my agents, Bruce Westwood and Jennifer Barclay, have shown a degree of enthusiasm and forbearance that is greatly appreciated.

Audiences at the McLuhan Seminar at the University of Toronto, the Art Gallery of Ontario, the School of the Art Institute of Chicago, the Floating Gallery in Winnipeg, the University of Western Ontario, the University of Alberta, the University of Waterloo, the University of Windsor, the University of St. Michael's College, the University of Toronto at Scarborough, Guelph University, Brock University, the Philosophy Course Union at the University of Toronto, York University, and the Canadian Museum Association in Ottawa provided useful feedback on some early drafts of material contained herein. Some small sections of this book appeared in infant versions or as part of larger arguments in the following publications: *Mix, The Philosophical Forum, Muse, Saturday Night, Utne Reader, The Chronicle of Higher Education, The Globe and Mail, Descant,* and *Adbusters.* I thank the editors of all of them for their interest in my work. I am most grateful to my students, especially those in recent courses on philosophy and culture and in a lively version of introductory philosophy taught during the 1997–98 academic year, for forcing me to see new levels of meaning in texts I arrogantly thought I understood.

Thanks also to Alison Bond in New York and to Doug Pepper

and Susan Westendorf at Crown Publishers for their faith in, and help with, the U.S. edition of this book.

Thanks finally and most of all to Gail Donaldson, who has been my constant companion, even when not physically present, during the personal and cultural navigations that inform so much of this book—and my life. You will understand what I mean when I say she is my best friend.

Notes

CHAPTER 1

1. Howard Mumford Jones, *The Pursuit of Happiness* (Cambridge: Harvard University Press, 1953), p. 6, in a chapter on what he calls "The Glittering Generality," borrowing the phrase from Rufus Choate's wry 1856 comment on the natural law provisions of the U.S. Constitution. Copyright © 1957 by the President and Fellows of Harvard College. Reprinted by permission of Harvard University Press. This and all further quotations used by permission.

2. Eric Hoffer, *The Passionate State of Mind and Other Aphorisms* (New York: Harper & Row, 1955). See also Paul Nowell Elbin, *The Paradox of Happiness* (New York: Hawthorn Books, 1975).

3. John Ralston Saul, *The Doubter's Companion: A Dictionary of Aggressive Common Sense* (Toronto: Viking, 1994), pp. 153–54.

4. Quoted in Sanjida O'Connell, "How Your Genes Put a Smile on Your Face," *Toronto Star* (1 September 1996), pp. A1 and A4.

5. Rae Corelli, "Get Happy!" *Maclean's* (16 September 1996). Also Daniel Goleman, "Forget Money: Nothing Can Buy Happiness," *USAir* (November 1996), pp. 70–90 (inter.); and Goleman, "Happiness Is... Genetic, Researchers Say," *New York Times* (15 July 1996), reprinted in *Globe and Mail* (16 July 1996).

6. Rem B. Edwards, *Pleasures and Pains: A Theory of Qualitative Hedonism* (Ithaca: Cornell University Press, 1979), p. 117. For other examples of analytic philosophy's struggles with happiness, see Anthony Kenny, "Happiness," in Joel Feinberg, ed., *Moral Concepts* (Oxford: Oxford University Press, 1969), pp. 43–52; and R. Kraut, "Two Conceptions of Happiness," *Philosophical Review* 88 (1979): 167–97.

7. L. Wayne Sumner, "Welfare, Happiness, and Pleasure," *Utilitas* 4:2 (November 1992), p. 213.

8. Ludwig Wittgenstein, *Tractatus Logico-Philosophicus,* D. F. Pears and B. F. McGuinness, trans. (London: Routledge & Kegan Paul, 1961 [German orig. 1921]), remark 6.43 (p. 72).

9. W. Newton-Smith, "A Conceptual Investigation of Love," in Alan Montefiore, ed., *Philosophy and Personal Relations* (London, 1973), pp. 118–19; quoted in Michael Tanner's witty essay "The Language of Philosophy," in Leonard Michaels and Christopher Ricks, eds., *The State of the Language* (Berkeley: University of California Press, 1980), pp. 458–66.

10. M. Scott Peck is the acknowledged master of this tone. In his book *A World Waiting to Be Born* (New York: Bantam, 1993), he retails with relish stories of slick executives, hostile and critical, who are overcome with emotion at his workshops, often while talking about God or their mothers. Describing the small percentage of people who walk out of his community-building gatherings, Peck says this: "It is as if, for some reason, they cannot bear all the love in the room. We do not know the reason. Occasionally they offer explanations, but these seem spurious." (Maybe they were too polite to say they had to go puke.)

11. Cover, *Psychology Today* (July/August 1996).

12. Siimon Reynolds, *Become Happy in Eight Minutes* (New York: Plume, 1996), p. 55.

13. It turns out that goldfish are popular not only with G-and-T-swilling libertines like myself but also children, who apparently consume the little crackers in record numbers during car trips. The Pepperidge Farm people clearly think children will respond to the smiley faces as cuter than the originals and therefore preferable. By the way, I have been asked by a fellow fan to go on record and say that the cheddar cheese flavor of goldfish are *infinitely better* than the plain ones. I would be distressed to see the nonsmiling ones go the way of all flesh, but the plain-flavored ones could happily die out in my view as long as the cheesy ones remain.

14. James Servin, "Are We Happy Yet? The Era of Angst Is Finally Over," *Bazaar* (September 1997), p. 300.

15. These statistics, and a careful discussion of the ethical issues arising from psychopharmaceutical use, are found in Salem Alaton, "A Pill for All Reasons," *Globe and Mail* (9 November 1996), pp. D1 and D3.

16. See James Langton, "Orange Flavoured Prozac to Be Aimed at Kids," *Sunday Telegraph* (London) (17 August 1997). My thanks to Mike Gordon for this information.

17. Francis Hutcheson, *Inquiry into the Origin of our Ideas of Beauty and Virtue* (Edinburgh: 1725), Treatise II, "Concerning Moral Good and Evil," sec. 3, p. 8.

18. Gabrielle-Emilie de Breteuil, Marquise du Châtelet, *Discours sur le bonheur*, Robert Mauzi, ed. (Paris: Société de l'édition "Les Belles Lettres," 1961). Mme du Châtelet's *discours* is in the tradition that was, arguably, begun by the pseudonymous author Alain, whose *Propos le bonheur* is an early example of this literary-philosophical treatment of the subject. I thank Allan Hepburn for drawing my attention to this text, and for providing this elegant translation.

19. For examples of this line of inquiry, see the essays by philosophers and economists collected in Martha Nussbaum and Amartya Sen, eds., *The Quality of Life* (Oxford: Oxford University Press, 1992).

20. A. John McSweeney and Thomas L. Creer, "Health-Related Quality-of-Life Assessment in Medical Care," *Disease-a-Month* XLI:I (January 1995), pp. 1–72, at p. 7.

21. Albert Camus, *The Myth of Sisyphus and Other Essays*, Justin O'Brien, trans. (New York: Vintage, 1955), pp. 3 and 91.

22. For the best available treatment of this growing self-consciousness in modernity, see Charles Taylor, *Sources of the Self: The Making of the Modern Identity* (Cambridge: Harvard University Press, 1989), esp. Part III, "The Affirmation of Ordinary Life."

23. For the standard reading of the liberal political tradition in these terms, see C. B. Macpherson, *The Political Theory of Possessive Individualism* (Oxford: Oxford University Press, 1982).

24. The classic statement of postmodernity's "incredulity towards meta-narratives" is Jean-François Lyotard, *The Postmodern Condition: A Report on Knowledge* (Minneapolis: University of Minnesota Press, 1984). Transhumanist philosophy lacks a definitive manifesto in book form,

but for an array of Transhumanist and Extropian literature, see www.aleph.se/Trans and its various linked websites.

25. The word *happiness* appears in English sometime around 1530, but was probably not yet in wide usage at that time. In fourteen dictionaries published between 1670 and 1760, only three include definitions of happiness. Thereafter, such definitions are increasingly common, possibly reflecting the influence of the early-modern thinkers on educated discourse. Politically, the notion of an explicit *right* to happiness was a long time coming. Happiness does not appear as a basic element in any of: the English Petition of Rights against Charles I, the British Declaration of Rights in 1688, the statement of basic rights in the Stamp Act Congress of 1765, or even John Adams's declaration of the First Continental Congress of October 1774, which spoke of "life, liberty, and property." Not until George Mason's May 1776 Virginia Declaration of Rights was the pursuit of happiness added to that list, an addition reiterated more famously by Thomas Jefferson in July of that year in the Declaration of Independence. See Jones, *The Pursuit of Happiness,* pp. 8–17.

26. In that sense I am using "machine" in much the same way as the late French philosopher Gilles Deleuze. In Deleuze's view, machines include *all* power apparatuses, from institutions to rule-governed symbol systems like writing. For an accessible discussion of these ideas, see his *Negotiations 1972–1990,* Martin Joughin, trans. (New York: Columbia University Press, 1995). Deleuze took Camus's Sisyphean challenge seriously, by the way, but reached the opposite conclusion: he committed suicide in 1995, leaping to his death from the window of his Paris apartment.

27. Lawrence Solomon, "Editorial," *The Next City* (Spring 1996).

28. People also tend to forget that there are also material *bads,* like the huge collection of bizarre and unmanageable furniture collected by my buddies Ian and Dorceta during their grad-school days. Some people would consider this judgment of mine on their possessions just a matter of taste, but in this instance anyway I incline to the robust metaphysical confidence of Plato. Good things are good and bad things are not, and anybody with eyes can see the difference.

29. Mariella Bertelli, "The Shirt of a Happy Person," *Why* (Summer 1996), p. 59. The story, a retold fable, has a king set off in search of the shirt of a happy person, which he needs to cure his young son of a persistent melancholy. He searches hither and yon until, finally, he finds a man who proclaims himself happy. The king, overjoyed, asks for his shirt. But the man can't oblige—he doesn't own a shirt. "Now," the piece concludes, "is there anybody truly happy out there? Someone who could give a shirt to the Prince?"

30. Immanuel Kant, *Groundwork of the Metaphysics of Morals,* H. J. Paton, trans. (London: Hutchinson, 1948 [German orig. 1785]). "Happiness is the condition of a rational being in the world with whom everything goes according to his wish and will," Kant added in his *Critique of Practical Reason* (Thomas K. Abbott, trans. [Indianapolis: Bobbs-Merrill, 1949; orig. 1788]). "It rests, thus, on the harmony of physical nature with his ends and purposes. But the rational being in the world is not the cause of the world and of physical nature. There is, therefore, not the least ground in the moral law for any necessary connection between morality (i.e., virtue) and proportionate happiness." Kant believed, indeed, that only God could bring virtue and happiness into line: "the *summum bonum,* the union of virtue and happiness, is possible in the world only on the supposition of a Supreme Being having a causality corresponding to moral character."

    The view that Kant was simply *hostile* to happiness is actually a bit crude. For an extended, and nuanced, account of the place of happiness in Kantian moral theory, see Victoria S. Wike, *Kant on Happiness in Ethics* (Albany: SUNY Press, 1994). Nevertheless, Kant did regard happiness as pathological in the strict sense of being a matter of feeling, not reason, and therefore heteronomous—changeable, not self-legislated, hence not to be relied upon—when what we require in a basis of morality is the autonomous authority of duty.

31. Details of Ekman's FACS research are taken from Daniel Zalewski, "Written on the Face," *Lingua Franca* (September 1997), pp. 19–20. Ekman claims that FACS can be used to interpret mammalian behavior across cultural and species boundaries and is a more reliable indicator of emotion than self-reporting—though he does admit that faking is possible. See his *Telling Lies* (New York: Norton, 1985) and his

recent edited anthology *What the Face Reveals* (New York: Oxford University Press, 1997). "Another barrier to progress," Zalewski notes dryly, "is FACS's speed. At present, five minutes of videotape takes around twelve hours to transcribe" (p. 20).

Chapter 2

1. Philip Zimbardo, "What messages are behind today's cults?" *APA Monitor* (May 1997), p. 14.

2. In some cases, names and personal details of the people in this story have been altered in order to protect their privacy.

3. I have drawn some details of this account from Jess Feist, *Theories of Personality,* 3rd ed. (New York: Harcourt Brace, 1985), pp. 591–630.

4. Aristotle, *Metaphysics,* I: 2 (982b23). In the same vein, Hegel believed that only in parts of the earth where material survival was made less pressing—the temperate zones—could peoples become "world-historical": that is, active in the manifestation of freedom. The same may be said of individuals with respect to the basic needs of food and shelter. See Hegel, *Introduction to the Philosophy of History,* Leo Rauch, trans. (Indianapolis: Hackett, 1988), ch. 5.

5. A. H. Maslow, *Motivation and Personality,* 2nd ed. (New York: Harper & Row, 1970), p. 38. All further quotations from Maslow, with the exception of letters, are from this text at, respectively, pp. 163, 164, 45, and 150.

6. Quoted in Feist, *Theories of Personality,* p. 595.

7. Feist, *Theories of Personality,* p. 609.

8. W. B. Frick, *Humanistic Psychology: Interviews with Maslow, Murphy and Rogers* (Columbus, Ohio: Merrill, 1971), p. 36.

9. Horace Fletcher, *Happiness as Found in Forethought Minus Fearthought* (New York, 1913), pp. 1, 7, 19–20. This and other examples of early-century happiness tracts are taken from Jones, *The Pursuit of Happiness,* ch. 5.

10. Lorine Pruette, "Getting an Early Start on Happiness," *Woman's Home Companion* (January 1937), p. 9.

11. Luther Conant Jr., "A 10-Day Plan for Happiness," *Woman's Home Companion* (October 1950).

12. "Everybody Happy?" *Radio Times* (24–30 August 1996), p. 12.

13. "TV/Radio," *The Scotsman* (28 August 1996), p. 18.

14. Charlotte Raven, "I Don't Feel Cheerful When I'm Ordered to Be Happy," *The Guardian* (17 October 1996); reprinted in *The Toronto Star* (19 October 1996); used by permission.

15. S. T. Coleridge, *The Three Graves,* IV, xii.

16. Constance Penley, *NASA/TREK* (New York: Verso, 1997), p. 141.

17. On a less obvious front, *Star Trek* has even spawned a new form of utopian metafiction: a genre of homosexual reworkings of the original series, with Kirk and Spock in prominent roles as lovers, that is known as slash fiction. This second-order utopia, communicated in cheaply produced zines and renegade conventions, revises the original material by making the fans themselves—in this case, oddly enough, mainly straight women—the authors of an ideal vision of sexual equality, love, and technological comfort. See also Penley's *NASA/TREK* for details of this genre, at pp. 120–45.

18. Bill Bryson, *Notes from a Small Island* (London: Minerva, 1996), pp. 72–74; reproduced by permission of Greene & Heaton Limited.

19. In a conditional statement, i.e., one where the logical connector is an if/then relation, the first term is known as the *antecedent* and the second as the *consequent.* Affirming the consequent means taking the second term of a valid conditional proposition as true and "deriving" the antecedent term from it: this is to mistake a sufficient condition for a necessary one. To see why this is fallacious reasoning, consider an example. Let us say it is true to state this: "If it is raining outside, then the pavement is wet." Fine; it is a *sufficient condition* of the pavement's being wet that it be raining outside. Yet from this true statement it does not follow that "If the pavement is wet, then it is raining outside." For it is not a *necessary* condition of the pavement's being wet that it be raining outside. (The pavement might be wet because the street cleaner just went by or because I have just emptied a bucket of water on it.) Affirming the consequent is one of the commonest logical errors and one that is often hard to spot.

20. Or *risen* gaze, if we are already inclined (as Plato was) to think nonappetitive things higher in nature and goodness than mere wants.

21. Bertrand Russell, *The Conquest of Happiness* (New York: Liveright,

1958), p. 73. Copyright © 1930 by Horace Liveright, Inc., renewed © 1958 by Bertrand Russell. Reprinted by permission of Liveright Publishing Corporation. All further quotations from Russell are taken from this text and used by permission. The idea receives its most extensive and vigorous treatment in Spinoza's *Ethics,* where he argues that all feelings of regret or unhappiness disappear when we view the world rationally, which is to say from the standpoint of eternity *(Ethics,* Part II, prop. 44, corollary 2). But in this form the injunction is, according to one contemporary philosopher, "uninterestingly weak." It tells us nothing about how to live.

22. Oliver Goldsmith, "Happiness, In a Great Measure, Dependant on Constitution," in Arthur Friedman, ed., *Collected Works,* Volume I (Oxford: Oxford University Press, 1966), pp. 384–88; used by permission.

23. Sigmund Freud, *Civilization and Its Discontents,* James Strachey, trans. (New York: Norton, 1966 [orig. German edition 1930]), p. 49. Translation copyright © 1961 by James Strachey, renewed 1989 by Alix Strachey. Reprinted by permission of W. W. Norton & Company, Inc. All further quotations from Freud are taken from this text and used by permission.

24. Hanns Sachs, "Psychotherapy and the Pursuit of Happiness," *Imago* Vol. I (1939): 356–64; at p. 360.

25. The Austrian philosopher of science Karl Popper is credited with articulating falsifiability—the ability of a claim to be shown false—as the hallmark of true empirical science. A true (scientific) claim is one that could be proved false, but so far hasn't been; by contrast, a claim that cannot ever be shown false is not really a claim at all—it is ideology, myth, or pseudo-science, a thought that admits no possible refutation. See Popper, *The Logic of Scientific Discovery* (New York: Basic Books, 1959; originally *Logik der Forschung,* Vienna, 1935).

CHAPTER 3

1. Other SSRIs include Zoloft and Welbutrin; because of allegedly less severe side effects and more precise targeting of serotonin than are found in other neurotransmitters (e.g., dopamine and norepinephrine), they have largely replaced earlier generations of antidepressants

such as tricylcins and tetracyclins in the repertoire of most psychiatrists and general practitioners.

2. *The Compendium of Pharmaceuticals and Specialties,* 32nd ed. (Toronto: Canadian Pharmaceutical Association, 1997), p. 1315.

3. Greg Critser, "Oh, How Happy We Will Be: Pills, Paradise, and the Profits of the Drug Companies," *Harper's Magazine* (June 1996), pp. 38–46.

4. Reported in Christian Tyler, "A Philosopher's Tale," *Financial Post* (26 September 1996), p. 25.

5. See Critser, "Oh, How Happy We Will Be," pp. 39–40.

6. Douglas Coupland, *Microserfs* (New York: HarperCollins, 1995), p. 165.

7. Elizabeth Telfer explores the distinction in a fine study called, simply, *Happiness* (New York: St. Martin's Press, 1980). The essence of the division lies in the respective Greek roots of the labels in question: "hedonistic" is from *hédoné,* simple and especially bodily pleasure, while "eudaimonistic" is from *eudaimonia,* an untranslatable word that implies considered approval of a body of (virtuous) actions or traits. Bertrand Russell, in *The Conquest of Happiness,* says, in a similar but not quite identical vein, "The two sorts [of happiness] might be distinguished as plain and fancy, or animal and spiritual, or of the heart and of the head" (p. 143).

8. The opposite was true when I first wrote it and so I originally decided to let it stand in the final text. But I must tell you, in all honesty, that I do now own two Giorgio Armani suits. And they make me very happy indeed.

9. In a provocative essay unfortunately marred by a surfeit of cyber-theory jargon, Alan Shapiro argues that this minor key has been present in the *Star Trek* lexicon since its very inception with the original series's pilot episode (later broadcast in two parts as "The Menagerie"). In the story, the original *Enterprise* commander, Captain Pike (Jeffrey Turner), first refuses and then accepts an alien attempt to house him in a virtual-reality zoo in which his manufactured experiences will be consumed by cerebral humanoids so advanced they can no longer generate feelings themselves. See Shapiro, "Kirk Was Never the Original," in *Digital Delirium,* Arthur and Marilouise Kroker, eds. (New York: St. Martin's Press, 1997), pp. 74–81.

10. For a diverting, and definitive, account of the social and cultural creation of the weekend in modern industrialized societies, see Wytold Ribczynski, *Waiting for the Weekend* (New York: Viking, 1991).

11. Kingsley Amis, *Difficulties with Girls* (New York: Summit, 1988), p. 218.

12. Freud, *Civilization and Its Discontents*, p. 24. For Freud, the reality principle was a combination of deferred expectations, moderated desires, and repressed expectations that helped us cope with the inevitable failure to realize all our wishes in the world. The process of socialization is, in large measure, a matter of converting the quasi-instinctual pleasure principle into something that is, of necessity, more suited to the world we inhabit. In this way, Freud is an advocate of the lowered-gaze theory of happiness: we purchase happiness of a kind at the price of transforming or deadening our desires.

13. James Atlas, "The Fall of Fun," *The New Yorker* (18 November 1996), p. 62.

14. Marshall McLuhan, *Understanding Media: The Extensions of Man* (Cambridge: MIT Press, 1994 [orig. 1964]); quotation is taken from selections in *Essential McLuhan,* Eric McLuhan and Frank Zingrone, eds. (Toronto: Anansi, 1995), p. 168.

15. Kingsley Amis, *The Biographer's Moustache* (London: Flamingo, 1996), p. 199.

16. Evelyn Waugh, *Vile Bodies* (Harmondsworth: Penguin Books, 1938 [orig. 1930]), p. 177.

17. L. J. Davis, "The Encyclopedia of Insanity," *Harper's Magazine* (February 1997), pp. 61–66. I have relied on this sharp-tongued negative review of DSM-IV for a number of the details in this section.

18. Davis, "The Encyclopedia of Insanity," p. 64.

19. Paula Caplan, *They Say You're Crazy: How the World's Most Powerful Psychiatrists Decide Who's Normal* (Reading, Mass.: Addison-Wesley, 1995). This book contains references to Caplan's articles, including her *Canadian Psychology* article proposing Dominant Delusional Personality Disorder.

20. Reprinted under the title "Why the Happy Are Nuts" in *Harper's Magazine* (January 1993), pp. 23–25.

21. Nick Hornby, *High Fidelity* (New York: Riverhead Books, 1995), p. 25. Reprinted by permission of Riverhead Books, a division of the Putnam

Publishing Group, from *High Fidelity* by Nick Hornby. Copyright © 1995 by Nick Hornby. "Maybe we all live life at too high a pitch, those of us who absorb emotional things all day," the narrator says later (p. 169), "and as a consequence we can never feel merely *content:* we have to be unhappy, or ecstatically, head-over-heels happy, and those states are difficult to achieve within a stable, solid relationship. Maybe Al Green is directly responsible for more than I realized."

22. All statistics reported in the article "Placebos—Where the Cure Really Is in the Patient's Mind," *Financial Post* (26 October 1996).

23. From "Have Faith! Is That the Prozac Secret?" *Toronto Star* (1 August 1996).

24. The encounter was even stranger than I have suggested in the main text: it took place in the communal sauna of a run-down nudist colony in upstate New York. David Sedaris, *Naked* (New York: Little, Brown, 1997), pp. 270–71.

25. Aldous Huxley, *Brave New World* (Harmondsworth: Penguin Books, 1974), pp. 178–79.

26. Moira Farr, "Is Everybody Happy? The Pushy Politics of Prozac," *This Magazine* (August 1994), pp. 31 and 32; used by permission. Farr's book-length memoir and analysis of depression is called *After Daniel: A Suicide Survivor's Tale* (Toronto: HarperCollins, 1999).

27. Reported by Michael Kesterton in his "Social Studies" column, *Globe and Mail* (18 January 1997), p. A28.

CHAPTER 4

1. The seventeenth-century English philosopher John Locke was the first to address the problem of personal identity explicitly, arguing (incorrectly) that memory was the sole criterion of personhood; see his *Essay Concerning Human Understanding,* Campbell Fraser, ed. (Oxford: Oxford University Press, 1894), Book 2, ch. 27. In the eighteenth century, David Hume argued (also incorrectly) that persons were simply bundles of perceptions, with no identity beyond that; see *A Treatise on Human Nature,* L. A. Selby-Bigge, ed. (Oxford: Oxford University Press, 1896), Book I, Part 4, sec. 6. The literature on personal identity since then has been dominated by disputes between those who center

it in memory and those who find it in the body, and by ever more elaborate thought-experiments—transposed bodies, disappearing selves, clones—designed to generate various puzzles about identity.

2. Nicholson Baker, *U and I: A True Story* (New York: Random House, 1991), pp. 104–105.

3. James F. Balch and Phyllis A. Balch, *Prescription for Nutritional Healing,* 2nd ed. (Garden City: Avery, 1997), p. 224.

4. Nancy Mitford, *Christmas Pudding* (New York: Carroll & Graf, 1987 [orig. 1975]), p. 130.

5. Robert Penn Warren, *All the King's Men* (New York: Harcourt Brace, 1964), p. 438.

6. I guess I should admit that I stole this pun from Nicholson Baker, that consummate phrase-maker and master of self-conscious precision, who uses it in *U and I.* But the Schwarzenegger gloss is mine—and anyway, Baker knows all about the subtle temptations, and pleasures, of small acts of literary theft. See, for example, his long essay "Lumber" in *The Size of Thoughts* (New York: Random House, 1996), pp. 207–355.

7. Raymond Williams, "Advertising: The Magic System," in Simon During, ed., *The Cultural Studies Reader* (New York: Routledge, 1993), pp. 320–36, at p. 321. The italics are mine.

8. Malcolm Gladwell, "The Science of Shopping," *The New Yorker* (4 November 1996), pp. 66–75; "The Coolhunt," *The New Yorker* (17 March 1997), pp. 78–88; and "Listening to Khakis," *The New Yorker* (28 July 1997), pp. 54–65. All direct quotations are taken from "The Coolhunt."

9. Plato's theory of linked goods is articulated in many places, notably in Book II of *The Republic.* G. E. Moore's views on the good as unanalyzable can be found in his work *Principia Ethica* (Cambridge: Cambridge University Press, 1903), which contains Moore's famous claim, influential with the Bloomsbury Group, concerning the happy (and hence ethical) life: "it is obvious that personal affection and aesthetic enjoyment include by far the greatest goods with which we are acquainted." The theory of emotivism, which argues that ethical judgments are on the order of mere exclamations or expressions of taste, was most influentially discussed by R. M. Hare in his book *The Language of Morals* (Oxford: Oxford University Press, 1952).

10. Our own quotidian philosophers, cultural critics, are attempting to do some of this work. Tom Frank, editor-in-chief of *The Baffler* in Chicago, published a superb essay arguing that the notion of hip was too riddled with commercial viruses to be retained ("Hip Is Dead," *The Nation* [1 April 1996], pp. 16–19), and recently completed a book, *The Conquest of Cool* (Chicago: University of Chicago Press, 1997), which did the same for cool. It was excerpted in *Harper's Magazine* (November 1997), pp. 32–38. "Hip and square are now permanently locked together, like the images of Coke and Pepsi, in a self-perpetuating pageant of workplace deference and advertising outrage," Frank writes, of the cooption of the idea of rebellion by commercial forces. "Impervious to criticism of any kind, and virtually without historical memory, hip has become the public philosophy of the age of flexible accumulation" (p. 38).

11. A hermeneutic circle is a circle of interpretation, whereby the thing interpreted cannot be approached without prejudices or preconceptions (for a total lack of them, even if possible, would make understanding impossible). Those prejudices are then re-formed or confirmed by the thing itself. The process can be continuous, prejudices and thing feeding back one to another in a dynamic relation. In this sense (as Gladwell says of cool), one indeed has to know a thing already before one can know it. But this sort of circle does not, cannot, support the essentialism he falls into, and so one cannot be "trapped" in the way he suggests: interpretation is liberating, and it alters both the interpreter and the thing interpreted.

12. Theodor Adorno and Max Horkheimer, "The Culture Industry: Enlightenment as Mass Deception," in Simon During, ed., *The Cultural Studies Reader*, pp. 29–43.

13. A couple of other happy-face tidbits, reaching beyond the routine annexation of the image for retail merchants like Wal-Mart: I recently saw a T-shirt with an image of the standard yellow face, only the mouth was not bowed in a smile but flat-lined in neutral; underneath were the words "Yeah. Whatever." A study of tipping habits in restaurants (*Journal of Applied Social Psychology*, 1996) reported the interesting result that female waiters who drew a happy face on the bill got higher average tips from customers, while male waiters who did the same got lower

ones. I always make it a point to give lower tips to happy-face-drawing waiters, myself, part of a larger program of reductions for things like kneeling next to the table, commenting on something I said to my companion, or dotting *i*'s with hearts.

14. I mean by this the sorts of things analyzed by Roland Barthes in his series of essays entitled *Mythologies,* Annette Lavers, trans. (London: Paladin, 1973), and the similar collection, written in tribute to Barthes by Gilbert Adair, called *Myths and Memories* (London: Fontana, 1986). These close readings of cultural markers expose the way ideological assumptions—about class, about work, about social difference—are twined through apparently innocuous things like laundry detergent, car design, and the standard bistro meal of steak frites (a precursor to Adair's fish-and-chips example).

15. Dick Hebdige, *Subculture: The Meaning of Style* (London: Routledge, 1979), p. 11; used by permission.

16. Hebdige, *Subculture,* p. 12. The ideological uses of "common sense" can run in the other direction too: that is, when a conservative politician undertakes, as Mike Harris did in the Canadian province of Ontario, a "common sense revolution." Here the *idea* of common sense is brought into the fore as a stamp of approval for a very particular political agenda. For a careful assessment of the descriptive and pejorative senses of ideology, see Raymond Geuss, *The Idea of a Critical Theory* (Cambridge: Cambridge University Press, 1981), ch. 1. And for the uses of "common sense" as a trope in philosophical (and to some extent political) rhetoric, you might look at my modestly titled article, "The Plain Truth About Common Sense: Skepticism, Metaphysics, and Irony," *Journal of Speculative Philosophy* 9:3 (Fall 1995): pp. 169–88.

17. Stuart Hall, "Culture, Media and the 'Ideological Effect,'" in J. Curran et al., eds., *Mass Communication and Society* (London: Arnold, 1977).

18. Louis Althusser, *For Marx* (London: Allen Lane, 1969).

19. I have in mind such things as Lewis Lapham's brilliantly grumpy editorials in *Harper's Magazine,* the witty "Varnish Remover" column in the on-line magazine *Slate* (www.slate.com), some of the angry editorials in the on-line magazine *Suck* (www.suck.com), parts of *Shift* and the *Utne Reader,* Leslie Savan's now-defunct ad column in the *Village Voice,*

Naomi Klein's column in the *Toronto Star,* the Chicago-based journal *The Baffler,* and just about everything in the superb Vancouver-based guerrilla media magazine *Adbusters.*

20. Howard Mumford Jones, *The Pursuit of Happiness,* pp. 132–33.

21. In an early episode of Chris Carter's controversial television series *Millennium,* a group of doomed young men forced to participate in direct telephone marketing—a kind of advertising-age vision of hell, also pilloried effectively in Michael Tolkin's bitter 1993 film *The New Age*—are shown various motivational slogans on a massive screen as they dial and pitch, dial and pitch. "Facilitate envy" was one of them.

22. Robert Nozick, *Anarchy, State, and Utopia* (New York: Basic Books, 1974), pp. 239–40.

23. Robert J. Samuelson, *The Good Life and Its Discontents: The American Dream in the Age of Entitlement 1945–1995* (New York: Vintage, 1995). See also the evidence marshaled by economist Paul Krugman, "The CPI and the Rat Race," *Slate* (21 December 1996). Media critic Neil Postman has made the argument about television's role in fostering unrealistic expectations a staple of his recent interviews and public statements.

24. "One of the causes of unhappiness among intellectuals in the present day," Bertrand Russell said in 1958, "is that so many of them, especially those whose skill is literary, find no opportunity for the independent exercise of their talents, but have to hire themselves out to rich corporations directed by Philistines, who insist upon their producing what they themselves regard as pernicious nonsense" *(The Conquest of Happiness,* pp. 217–18).

25. In this respect envy can be theoretically distinguished, as Nozick notes, from related notions like jealousy, spite, begrudgingness, and competitiveness. In Nozick's schema there are four possibilities with respect to the issue of whether you and someone else possess a thing:

	He	*You*
1.	has it	have it
2.	has it	don't have it
3.	doesn't have it	have it
4.	doesn't have it	don't have it

You are *envious* if you prefer 4 to 2, while also preferring 3 to 4. You are *jealous* if you prefer 1 to 2, but are indifferent between 3 and 4. You are *begrudging* if you prefer 3 to 1, while also preferring 3 to 4. You are *spiteful* if you prefer 4 to 1, while also preferring 3 to 4. You are *competitive* if you prefer 3 to 4, while being indifferent between 1 and 4.

But in practice these conditions are often coextensive. "A competitive person is begrudging," Nozick concludes. "A spiteful person is begrudging. There are envious people who are not jealous... [t]hough...most jealous people are envious. And surely it is a psychological law that spiteful people are envious." Nozick, *Anarchy, State, and Utopia,* p. 239.

26. Krugman, "The CPI and the Rat Race." All further quotations by Krugman are from this article. *Slate* is at www.slate.com.

27. Michael Frayn, *A Landing on the Sun* (New York: Viking, 1991), p. 142.

CHAPTER 5

1. Friedrich Nietzsche, *The Genealogy of Morals,* Essay III, sec. 14, Walter Kaufmann and R. J. Hollingdale, trans. (New York: Vintage, 1967), p. 124.

2. As an amateur in the field of philosophy—his subject was classics—and as a critic of the Scholastic orthodoxy of his time, Hobbes was also given to taking swipes at academic philosophers. Discussing "Absurdity" in *Leviathan,* he notes that no creature but man is subject to it, for it is an error of reason. "And of men, those are of all most subject to it, that professe Philosophy." See Hobbes, *Leviathan,* C. B. Macpherson, ed. (Harmondsworth: Penguin Books, 1968), p. 113. All further Hobbes quotations are from this edition.

3. John Locke, *Second Treatise of Government,* C. B. Macpherson, ed. (Indianapolis: Hackett, 1980 [orig. 1690]), pp. 19 and 47.

4. See Locke, *An Essay Concerning Human Understanding,* Book II, ch. 21, sec. 42.

5. Josiah Quincy Jr., *Observations on the Act of Parliament Commonly Called the Boston Port-Bill* (Boston, 1774), p. 28.

6. *The Writings of Thomas Jefferson,* A. A. Lipscomb and A. E. Bergh, eds. (20 vols., Washington, D.C., 1905), Part XIII, pp. 135–36. Jefferson's letter, dated 22 March 1812, is addressed to F. A. Van der Kemp.

7. John Adams, *Works,* Part IV, p. 193. From *Thoughts on Government.*

8. Benjamin West, *The New-England Almanack; or, Lady's and Gentleman's Diary for the Year of Our Lord Christ, 1766* (Providence, 1765), no pagination.

9. *Writings of George Washington* (Bicentennial edition, Washington), sec. 35, p. 432.

10. *The Writings of Thomas Jefferson,* Part XII, p. 369; from a letter to Kosciusko, dated 26 February 1810.

11. Certainly the redistribution of wealth would solve many a social problem. "I think it quite certain that a real change in the relations of human beings to possessions would be of more help in [altering antisocial behavior] than any ethical commands," Freud writes; "but the recognition of this fact among socialists has been obscured and made useless for practical purposes by a fresh idealistic misconception of human nature" *(Civilization and Its Discontents,* p. 90).

12. *The Spectator,* edited by G. Gregory Smith (8 vols., London, 1887–1898), Vol. i, p. 59.

13. From "Worship" in *The Conduct of Life: The Works of Ralph Waldo Emerson,* James Elliott Cabot, ed. (Standard Library edition; 14 vols.; Boston and New York, 1883–1983), Part VI, p. 215.

14. Henry David Thoreau, *Walden* (New York: Time Inc., 1962 [orig. 1854]), pp. 86–88. Like Hobbes before him, Thoreau took well-judged aim at the academic philosophers who ignored him in his own day, and continue to do so now despite the efforts of able apologists like Stanley Cavell of Harvard University (see, e.g., Cavell, *The Senses of Walden* [San Francisco: North Point Press, 1980]). "There are nowadays professors of philosophy, but not philosophers," Thoreau wrote. "To be a philosopher is not merely to have subtle thoughts, nor even to found a school, but so to love wisdom as to live, according to its dictates, a life of simplicity, independence, magnanimity, and trust. It is to solve some of the problems of life, not only theoretically, but practically" *(Walden,* pp. 12–13).

15. Michael Pollan, *Second Nature: A Gardener's Education* (New York: Dell, 1991), p. 5. Pollan's argument that the garden is where nature and culture meet, illuminating both, is instructive; but I would be inclined to

go further and say that our very idea of nature is constructed out of cultural cloth, and the garden is simply (but powerfully) the door through which we attempt to enter nature—a project that cannot succeed, for we cannot leave our cultural selves behind.

16. See, for these examples, Bill McKibben, "Curbing Nature's Paparazzi," *Harper's Magazine* (November 1997), pp. 19–24; adapted from McKibben's essay "The Problem with Wildlife Photography," *Double-Take* (Fall 1997).

17. Respectively, 10 Wallace 273; 16 Wallace 36; and III US 746.

18. *Herman v. The State*, 8 Indiana 545 (appendix); quoted and discussed in Jones, *The Pursuit of Happiness*, pp. 33–38.

19. Jones, *The Pursuit of Happiness*, pp. 47–48 and following, discusses these cases in detail. I have relied on that discussion here.

20. The story was the opening example in Ackerman's popular seminar on "Justice" at the Yale Law School in the late 1980s and an important part of his book *Social Justice in the Liberal State* (New Haven: Yale University Press, 1980), Sec. 13, "The Pursuit of Happiness," esp. pp. 45–49.

21. Bentham's calculus, often thought to epitomize the nineteenth-century mania for moral algorithm, was quite explicit and detailed, proceeding along seven separate vectors of measurement: (1) intensity, (2) duration, (3) certainty, (4) proximity, (5) fecundity (that is, likelihood of bringing more of the same), (6) purity, and (7) extent (that is, the number of people affected). This array was then put into practice by following a six-step calculation procedure which began with distinguishing between pleasures and pains and ended with counting the number of people "whose interests appear to be concerned" with a given pleasure or pain. See Jeremy Bentham, *An Introduction to the Principles of Morals and Legislation*, J. H. Burns and H. L. A. Hart, eds. (London, 1970).

22. J. S. Mill, *Utilitarianism* (Indianapolis: Bobbs-Merrill, 1959 [orig. 1863]), p. 10. Unless otherwise noted, all further Mill quotations are taken from this text.

23. Bentham, *An Introduction to the Principles of Morals and Legislation*, p. 74.

24. From *Athenaeus* XII 547a (U 512); this passage is supposed to be a citation from Epicurus's treatise *On One's Final End*. See Eugene O'Connor, trans., *The Essential Epicurus* (Buffalo, N.Y.: Prometheus Books, 1993).

25. Epicurus, *Principal Doctrines,* Part V; in Brad Inwood and L. P. Gerson, trans., *The Epicurus Reader* (Indianapolis: Hackett, 1994).

26. L. W. Sumner, "Welfare, Happiness, and Pleasure," p. 199. This vague conception is, to be fair, Sumner's starting point, not his conclusion, in a careful survey of the prospects for hedonistic welfare.

27. The Princeton University mathematician John Nash was awarded the Nobel Prize for his work on the original dilemma. Anatole Rappaport of the University of Toronto wrote a well-known "tit for tat" computer program that maximizes utility in iterated prisoner's dilemmas; it begins by cooperating and then simply repeats the last choice of the opposite number. All of the most successful long-term strategies for the dilemma are "nice" in this sense: they do not defect first.

    Nash, by the way, suffered from schizophrenia following his influential discovery and was given a sinecure at Princeton's Institute for Advanced Study, where he became a familiar figure haunting the hallways. Speculation that there is a connection between rational-choice theory and mental illness is merely malicious.

28. This and subsequent quotations from Heilbroner are from his book *Teachings from the Worldly Philosophy* (New York: Norton, 1996), passim.

29. For an extended critique of this dominance, see Donald P. Green and Ian Shapiro, *Pathologies of Rational Choice Theory* (New Haven: Yale University Press, 1996).

30. Taken from John Cassidy's excellent article "The Decline of Economics," *The New Yorker* (2 December 1996), pp. 50–60, at p. 58.

31. William Paley, *The Principles of Moral and Political Philosophy,* in Alburey Castell et al., eds., *An Introduction to Modern Philosophy* (New York: Macmillan, 1994), p. 297.

32. Jonathan Edwards, *The Works of President Edwards* (4 vols.; New York and London, 1844), Part IV, p. 276. "The idea," adds Howard Mumford Jones *(The Pursuit of Happiness,* p. 2), "is at least as old as Tertullian."

CHAPTER 6

1. Epictetus, *The Enchiridion,* Thomas W. Higginson, trans. (Indianapolis: Bobbs-Merrill, 1948), Article I.

2. Laura Wexler, "Thinking, Not Shrinking," *Utne Reader* (January–

February 1997), pp. 50–51. The idea of directly selling philosophical advice (as opposed to professing the subject in the academic fashion) always reminds me of a story told by one of my professors at Yale, a great man, now dead, named Maurice Natanson. It was meant to illustrate the Socratic wisdom that nobody can do your philosophical reflection for you.

A deeply troubled man is walking down the street. He is worried about his life, its emptiness and lack of direction. He is confused and unhappy. He turns a corner and suddenly comes upon a dirty storefront filled with an assortment of old furniture and appliances and, in the corner, a small sign that says "Philosophy done here." An old bearded man, the very figure of deep wisdom, is pottering about behind a small counter. Salvation at last! A professional philosopher, hanging out a shingle, and there to save him! He rushes into the store—only to be told by the old man that the sign is for sale.

3. Spinoza, *Ethics,* Part IV, prop. 54. The Latin title of this work—*Ethica ordine geometrico demonstrata*—hints at Spinoza's attempt to derive ethical guidelines rationally, using only the deductive methods of geometry, moving from axiom to postulate to proof. The result is one of the most difficult, and strangest, books of the early modern period.

4. Nietzsche, *The Wanderer and His Shadow,* p. 323. A similar view is defended in Emerson's essay "Self-Reliance."

5. Rüdiger Bittner, "Is It Reasonable to Regret Things One Did?" *Journal of Philosophy* 89:5 (May 1992), p. 267. All further quotations from Bittner are taken from this article. Bittner's argument is a combination of fine distinctions and aggressive common sense. "The word 'reasonable' is to be understood here in its everyday sense, roughly equivalent to phrases like 'it's a good idea,' 'it makes sense,' 'it is recommendable.' Thus the question can also be expressed as follows: Should we regret bad things we did?" (p. 262).

6. Bernard Williams, "Moral Luck," in *Moral Luck* (New York: Cambridge University Press, 1981), p. 29. Williams is Bittner's main target in arguing against the connection between regret and moral character. As an Aristotelian, Williams believes we are responsible even for unforeseen and unintended consequences of our actions—hence the notion of

moral luck, and the tragic possibilities of human life. Bittner not only considers that position absurd, he thinks regretting even intended and foreseen consequences is irrational.

7. Julia Annas, *The Morality of Happiness* (New York: Oxford University Press, 1993), p. 10, n. 24; used by permission. Annas's book is the best account I know of ancient ethical theory and the central role played in that theory by robust notions of happiness.

8. They are, respectively, More's *Dialogue of Comfort against Tribulation,* Raleigh's *The History of the World,* Bunyan's *Grace Abounding* and a large part of *The Pilgrim's Progress,* De Sade's *Justine,* Dostoevsky's *House of the Dead,* and Hitler's *Mein Kampf.* See Anthony Storr, *Solitude: A Return to the Self* (New York: Free Press, 1988), ch. 4. Copyright © 1988 by Anthony Storr. Reprinted by permission of The Free Press, a division of Simon & Schuster.

9. Thus theodicy, from the Greek *theos* (god) and *diké* (justice). See V. E. Watts's introduction to his translation of *The Consolation* (Harmondsworth: Penguin Books, 1969), which I have relied on, p. 19.

10. *The Allegory of Love* (Oxford, 1936), p. 46.

11. Voltaire, *Candide: Or Optimism,* Robert M. Adams, trans. (New York: Norton, 1966 [orig. 1759]), p. 77.

12. The standard statement of this theory is Mihaly Ciskszentmihalyi, *Flow: The Psychology of Optimal Experience* (New York: Harper & Row, 1990). Ciskszentmihalyi's position on optimal experience obviously owes a good deal to Maslow, but it has deeper roots in Emerson and Thoreau—not to mention Cicero and Aristotle.

13. "Kitsch causes two tears to flow in quick succession," Kundera writes in *The Unbearable Lightness of Being.* "The first tear says: How nice to see the children running on the grass! The second tear says: How nice to be moved, together with all mankind, by children running on the grass! It is the second tear that makes kitsch kitsch."

14. The thought experiment of the experience-machine is a favorite of Robert Nozick's. See *Anarchy, State, and Utopia,* pp. 42–45; and *The Examined Life: Philosophical Meditations* (New York: Basic Books, 1989), pp. 104–108. See also James Griffin, *Well-Being: Its Meaning, Measurement, and Moral Importance* (Oxford: Oxford University Press, 1986), p. 9, who argues against the view that happiness can be reduced to

mental states. The limitations of this thought experiment are carefully discussed by Sumner, "Welfare, Happiness, and Pleasure," pp. 215–17, including some relevant mention of *Total Recall* and *Star Trek: The Next Generation*.

15. Alasdair MacIntyre, *After Virtue*, 2nd ed. (London: Duckworth, 1981), p. 219.

16. Eric J. Cassell, "The Nature of Suffering and the Goals of Medicine," *New England Journal of Medicine* 306 (1982): 639–45; quoted in Sumner, "Welfare, Happiness, and Pleasure," pp. 210–11.

17. Sumner, "Welfare, Happiness, and Pleasure," p. 212.

18. Reported in the *Globe and Mail* (22 May 1997), p. A26.

CHAPTER 7

1. Trillin is the acknowledged master of this genre of food writing—see his collection of *New Yorker* food pieces, *American Fried* (New York: Doubleday, 1974)—though Jane and Michael Stern have been doing good things in the pages of *Gourmet* magazine for the last few years and recently published a book entitled *Eat Your Way Across the USA: 500 Diners, Lobster Shacks, Buffets, Pie Palaces, and Other All-American Eateries* (New York: Bantam, 1997).

2. See, for example, the sharply written book *Data Smog: Surviving the Information Glut* (New York: HarperCollins, 1997), by journalist David Shenk. Some of Shenk's objections to Informatian Age rah-rah—that the illusion of perfect individual autonomy actually undermines democracy, creating an equality of isolated market niches—are (if I may say so) anticipated in my book *Dreams of Millennium* (Toronto: Viking, 1996), ch. 4, "The Virtual Future."

3. David Denby, "Buried Alive: Our Children and the Avalanche of Crud," *The New Yorker* (15 July 1996), pp. 48–59.

4. Neil Postman, *Amusing Ourselves to Death: Public Discourse in the Age of Show Business* (New York: Viking, 1985), p. 67. See also Marshall McLuhan, *Understanding Media*.

5. Postman, *Amusing Ourselves to Death,* p. 69. B. W. Powe makes a similar argument for the political nullity of an overwhelming data-load in his book *A Canada of Light* (Toronto: Somerville House, 1997 [orig. *A Tremendous Canada of Light* (Toronto: Coach House, 1993)]), albeit in

a more poetic and hopeful vein than Postman's grumpy critique. Powe thinks communications technology can foster "lightness," or the civil openness to the Other that he thinks characteristic of Canadian political culture. Pierre Bourdieu's essay *Sur la télévision* (Paris: Liber, 1997) is an even more polemical condemnation of what Bourdieu calls *les fast-thinkers:* the sort of faux-intellectuals that talk-television tends to create, the people who substitute opinion for discourse; see also Emily Eakin, "Bourdieu Unplugged," *Lingua Franca* (August 1997), pp. 22–23. While agreeing with much of the substance of these critiques, I have argued that it is possible to communicate deep ideas, and to engage in real public discourse, on television. See Kingwell, "The Intellectual Possibilities of Television," *The Chronicle of Higher Education* (12 December 1997), p. b7.

6. Paul Virilio, *Speed and Politics* (New York: Semiotext(e), 1995 [orig. *Vitesse et politique: essai de dromologie* (Paris: Galilée, 1977)]).

7. That is, for example, the argument of Grant McCracken's three-volume on-line book *Plenitude* (available at www.cultureby.com). While I share McCracken's optimism about the possibilities of cultural critique and innovation in an age of invigorating variety, I find I cannot be as sanguine as he seems to be about the dangers saturation poses to individual projects of self-creation. Most people find the cultural volume that is so obvious today paralysing, or simply enervating, not liberating. They are not prepared or (it seems) able to view the growing volume as the Platonic metaphysical plenitude, the full creation of everything that might be, that McCracken celebrates. (In fact the idea of plenitude receives a fuller and more influential treatment in medieval and early modern philosophical theology, where the notion of God's bounty is seen to imply that all things that might be created *have* been created: God's will is a deed, and here possibility is actuality.)

8. Evelyn Waugh, *Decline and Fall* (Harmondsworth: Penguin, 1937 [orig. 1928]), p. 186.

9. Jean-François Lyotard, "Defining the Postmodern," in Simon During, ed., *The Cultural Studies Reader,* pp. 170–73, at p. 173.

10. David Denby, *Great Books: My Adventures with Homer, Rousseau, Austen,*

and Other Indestructible Writers of the Western World (New York: Simon & Schuster, 1996).

11. For the influence of the clock on the velocity of human experience, and its attendant connection to a reduction in some forms of happiness, see Neil Postman, *Technopoly: The Surrender of Culture to Technology* (New York: Knopf, 1992) and James Hillman, *The Soul's Code: In Search of Character and Calling* (New York: Random House, 1996).

12. Storr, *Solitude,* pp. ix, xi, and xii; used by permission. Storr's book is the best discussion I know of the human value of solitary experience; but see also Ester Schaler Buchholz, *The Call of Solitude: Alonetime in a World of Attachment* (New York: Simon & Schuster, 1997). B. W. Powe has argued that for intricate cultural reasons solitude is more possible in Canada than in the United States. See *A Canada of Light* and *The Solitary Outlaw* (Toronto: Lester & Orpen Dennys, 1987). The latter, like the former, was revised and re-released in 1997 by Somerville House, Toronto.

13. These findings about married well-being are well known, although often misquoted to suggest an asymmetry, that women are happier single and men married. See Jessie Bernard, *The Future of Marriage* (New York: World Publishing, 1972; reissued by Yale University Press, 1982), where the original stats are presented and then used, oddly, to argue the asymmetrical conclusion. (Bernard concludes, without any warrant, that women's reports of married happiness are merely responses to social or conventional pressure.) The misinterpretation became canonical in textbooks published through the 1980s and '90s. Some examples: "Bernard's investigation showed that the psychological costs of marriage were great for women" (from *Changing Families* [1994]). "We do know, for instance, that marriage has an adverse effect on women's mental health" (from *Sociology of Marriage and the Family* [1995]). "If marriage is so difficult for wives, why do the majority surveyed judge themselves as happy?...Happiness is interpreted by wives in terms of conformity. Since they are conforming to society's expectations, this must be happiness" (from *Diversity in Families* [1996]).

In a 1997 report called *Closed Hearts, Closed Minds: The Textbook Story of Marriage,* members of the mildly right-of-center Institute for American Values argued, it seems rightly, that the textbook perpetuation of an asymmetry thesis with respect to happiness in marriage was "a national embarrassment." They exposed the books in question for their shoddy research and faulty methodology. Details of the controversy were reported in Margaret Wente, "Marriage by the Book," the *Globe and Mail* (20 September 1997), p. D7.

14. John Lanchester, *The Debt to Pleasure* (London: Picador, 1996), p. 44.

15. Francis Bacon, "Of Gardens," in *The Essays or Counsels, Civil and Moral, of Francis Lord Verulam* (Mount Vernon: Peter Pauper Press, n.d.), p. 178.

16. The most illuminating examination of this process I know, in the context of contemporary media-driven culture, is Stuart Hall's careful (but rather dense) essay "Encoding, Decoding," in Simon During, ed., *The Cultural Studies Reader,* pp. 90–103. "Certain codes may, of course, be so widely distributed in a specific language community or culture, and be learned at so early an age, that they appear not to be constructed—the effect of an articulation between sign and referent—but to be 'naturally' given," Hall writes. "This has the (ideological) effect of concealing the practices of coding which are present. But we must not be fooled by appearances" (p. 95).

17. The cultural anthropologist Michel de Certeau is illuminating on the productive possibilities that, paradoxically, seem to reside in consumption: tactical maneuvers of transformation, alteration, subversion. Using the very systems of representation that stand over against them, resistant consumer-producers can engage in a critique of consumption that "redistributes its space; it creates at least a certain play in that order, a space for maneuvers of unequal forces and for utopian points." See M. de Certeau, *The Practice of Everyday Life,* Steven Rendall, trans. (Berkeley: University of California Press, 1984), p. 18; also Henry Jenkins, *Textual Poachers: Television Fans and Participatory Culture* (New York: Routledge, 1992), ch. 6.

18. There is an extensive technical literature on this topic which I will not attempt to cite here. But for an overview, including references and assessment of its implications for contemporary political theory, see Mark Kingwell, *A Civil Tongue: Justice, Dialogue and the Politics of Pluralism* (University Park: Penn State Press, 1995), especially chs. 1 and 2.

19. Jonathan Lear, "The Disappearing 'We,'" *Proceedings of the Aristotelian Society,* Supplementary Volume, 1984.

CHAPTER 8

1. There is an extensive literature on the narrative hypothesis in the fields of psychology and philosophy, much of it quite technical. As before, I will not attempt to cite it in detail here, but good examples include M. Freeman, *Rewriting the Self: History, Memory and Narrative* (New York: Routledge, 1993); Jerome Bruner, *Acts of Meaning* (Cambridge: Harvard University Press, 1990); T. R. Sarbin, ed., *Narrative Psychology: The Storied Nature of Human Conduct* (New York: Praeger, 1986); and M. White and D. Epston, *Narrative Means to Therapeutic Ends* (New York: Norton, 1990).

2. This example was first used by the philosopher Judith Baker, whose excellent paper on the subject I was asked to comment on some time ago. I have altered the example somewhat and expanded it a great deal. Baker's paper was presented at a meeting of the Ontario Philosophical Association (York University, Toronto, 1995); my comment also addressed another paper, equally illuminating, by William Pullman of the University of Western Ontario.

3. MacIntyre, *After Virtue,* p. 218. MacIntyre's subtle analysis of narrative, self, and virtue is a superior example of nontechnical moral philosophy; see especially ch. 15. I should note that MacIntyre's version of Aristotelian virtue theory is hostile to the idea of happiness, but mainly because he reads happiness as a utilitarian concept. I presume he would not quarrel with the notion of *eudaimonistic* happiness, though he would argue that we cannot recover it as straightforwardly as I am suggesting.

4. Bertrand Russell, *The Conquest of Happiness,* pp. 113–15. Russell's solution for this particular form of unhappiness, which he labels "persecution mania," is summed up in the following tart maxims (p. 119): (1) "remember that your motives are not always as altruistic as they seem to yourself"; (2) "don't overestimate your own merits"; (3) "don't expect others to take as much interest in you as you do yourself"; and (4) "don't imagine that most people give enough thought to you to have any desire to persecute you."

5. EN 1097b3–7. I have relied throughout on Terence Irwin's fine translation of the *Nicomachean Ethics* (Indianapolis: Hackett, 1985). Citations are given in the standard form.

6. In Book I of the *Ethics* Aristotle offers ten separate arguments against Plato's theory of the Form of the Good, familiar to readers of *The Republic* and other dialogues, and adds a few others elsewhere. I won't go into them here, but they mostly concern the judgment that a variety of uses of the adjective *good* does not provide warrant for thinking there must be some linking, overarching notion of the Good.

7. Seneca, *De Vita Beata,* in *Seneca: Moral Essays,* John W. Basore, trans. (3 vols., Loeb Classical Library: London and New York, 1928–35), Part II, p. 107.

8. Dorothy Thompson, "The Right to Happiness," *Ladies' Home Journal* (April 1941), p. 6.

9. Annas, *The Morality of Happiness,* p. 4. Annas is hopeful about this middle course, but urges "the unexciting virtue of intellectual caution" to avoid falling too easily into the view that Aristotle's ideas about virtue can be straightforwardly ours (p. 5).

10. F. H. Bradley, *Ethical Studies* (Oxford: Oxford University Press, 1876), Essay VI, p. 215.

11. For this contrast, see Henry Sidgwick, *The Methods of Ethics* (London, 1907), p. 106.

12. Ogden Nash, "Kind of an Ode to Duty," in *The Face Is Familiar: The Selected Verse of Ogden Nash* (Garden City: Garden City Publishing, 1941), pp. 175–76.

13. Bernard Williams, *Ethics and the Limits of Philosophy* (London: Routledge & Kegan Paul, 1985), p. 9.

14. I make an argument like this in my essay "Defending Political Virtue," *Philosophical Forum* 27:3 (Spring 1996): 244–68. I know that this talk of virtues might appear to be somewhat at odds with the liberalism I defended in some earlier works, including my book *A Civil Tongue;* but even there, when I defended the abstraction of right over good for political purposes, I was trying to find the shared ethical substance that might still remain in Western societies—in particular the political virtue of civility—even after we surrender the idea of a unified ethical life.

15. This important aspect of Aristotle's ethical theory has lately received new attention. See Stephen A. White, *Sovereign Virtue: Aristotle on the Rela-*

tion Between Happiness and Prosperity (Stanford: Stanford University Press, 1992), esp. chs. 1 and 2. Aristotle thought that generosity *(eleutheriotes)* and magnificence *(megaloprepeia)* were virtues, and the large outlay of money in "honorable" ways was part of the complete exercise of virtue— a position, foreign to the Christian worldview, which demands a certain amount of wealth in order to be fully good. "A poor person could not be magnificent since he lacks the means for large and fitting expenditures; and if he attempts it, he is foolish, since he spends more than what is worthy and right for him, when in fact it is correct spending that expresses virtue" (EN 1122b27-29; but for a different interpretation, see White, pp. 210–13). For more on this, see my entry on "Liberality" in *Philosophy of Law: An Encyclopedia* (New York: Garland, 1998).

16. Annas's careful account of Aristotle's ultimate inability to resolve the question is illuminating. See *The Morality of Happiness,* ch. 18.

17. Plato, *Republic,* 353e5–354a2. I have used a modified version of G. M. A. Grube's translation (Indianapolis: Hackett, 1974), p. 27.

18. This is a fairly common occurrence in Plato's dialogues. Earlier in *The Republic* the old man Cephalus retires under a barrage of probing questions from Socrates, and in the dialogue *Euthyphro,* the title character engages Socrates for a while only to dash off when the going gets rough. You cannot wonder that the Athenians put the little troublemaker to death.

POSTSCRIPT

1. David Shields, *Remote* (New York: Knopf, 1996), p. 201. "Someone somewhere says that a darkened movie theater reminds us of being in the womb and that the images we see evoke the worlds we dreamed before we were born. This seems to me to be simply true: by far my favorite moment in a movie theater comes when the final trailer is over, the last house lights dim off, and the otherwise dormant right side of my brain takes over completely."

2. Stanley Cavell, *Pursuits of Happiness: The Hollywood Comedy of Remarriage* (Cambridge: Harvard University Press, 1981), pp. 4–5.

3. Heinrich Heine, *Gedanken und Einfälle,* sec. I. Quoted in Freud, *Civilization and Its Discontents,* p. 57, in a discussion of the unnaturalness of

the Christian injunctions to "love thy neighbor as thyself" and to "love thine enemy."

4. F. M. Cornford, *Microcosmographia Academica: Being a Guide for the Young Academic Politician* (Cambridge: Bowes & Bowes, 1908), p. 11.

5. Kingsley Amis, *Lucky Jim* (Harmondsworth: Penguin Books, 1961), pp. 84 and 92.

6. From Ernest R. Groves and Phyllis Blanchard, *Introduction to Mental Hygiene* (American Social Sciences Series: New York, 1930), p. 454: "Mental hygiene is the application of science in an effort to help men, women, and children make sane adjustments. It recognizes the biological meaning of adaptation to environment... It frankly sees personal and social happiness in the belief that this normally follows wholesome adjustment." This school of psychology has been largely discredited, as have its overblown scientific pretensions; yet the central idea remains surprisingly resilient—not to mention pretty cogent.

Bibliography

Ackerman, Bruce. *Social Justice in the Liberal State*. New Haven: Yale University Press, 1980.

Adair, Gilbert. *Myths and Memories*. London: Fontana, 1986.

Adorno, Theodor, and Max Horkheimer. "The Culture Industry: Enlightenment as Mass Deception." In *The Cultural Studies Reader,* ed. Simon During. New York: Routledge, 1993.

Alaton, Salem. "A Pill for All Reasons." *Globe and Mail* (9 November 1996).

Althusser, Louis. *For Marx*. London: Allen Lane, 1969.

Amis, Kingsley. *The Biographer's Moustache*. London: Flamingo, 1996.

———. *Difficulties with Girls*. New York: Summit, 1988.

———. *Lucky Jim*. Harmondsworth: Penguin Books, 1961.

Annas, Julia. *The Morality of Happiness*. New York: Oxford University Press, 1993.

Anon. "Everybody Happy?" *Radio Times* (24–30 August 1996).

Anon. "Have Faith! Is That the Prozac Secret?" *Toronto Star* (1 August 1996).

Anon. "Placebos—Where the Cure Really Is in the Patient's Mind." *Financial Post* (26 October 1996).

Anon. "TV/Radio." *Scotsman* (28 August 1996).

Argyle, Michael. *The Psychology of Happiness*. New York: Methuen, 1987.

Aristotle. *Metaphysics*. Translated and edited by J. L. Ackrill. In *A New Aristotle Reader*. Princeton: Princeton University Press, 1987.

———. *Nicomachean Ethics*. Translated by Terence Irwin. Indianapolis: Hackett, 1985.

Atlas, James. "The Fall of Fun." *The New Yorker* (18 November 1996).

Bacon, Francis. "Of Gardens." In *The Essays or Counsels, Civil and Moral, of Francis Lord Verulam*. Mount Vernon: Peter Pauper Press, n.d.

Baker, Nicholson. "Lumber." In *The Size of Thoughts*. New York: Random House, 1996.

———. *U and I: A True Story*. New York: Random House, 1991.

Balch, James F., and Phyllis A. Balch. *Prescription for Nutritional Healing*. Second Edition. Garden City, N.J.: Avery, 1997.

Barrow, Robin. *Happiness*. Oxford: M. Robinson, 1980.

Barthes, Roland. *Mythologies*. Translated by Annette Lavers. London: Paladin, 1973.

Benett, W. *Justice and Happiness*. Oxford: Clarendon, 1911.

Bentall, Richard P. "A Proposal to Classify Happiness as a Psychiatric Disorder." *Journal of Medical Ethics* (June 1992). Reprinted as "Why the Happy Are Nuts." *Harper's Magazine* (January 1993).

Bentham, Jeremy. *An Introduction to the Principles of Morals and Legislation*. Edited by J. H. Burns and H. L. A. Hart. Darien, Conn.: Hafner, 1970.

Bernard, Jessie. *The Future of Marriage*. New York: World Publishing, 1972; reissued by Yale University Press, 1982.

Bertelli, Mariella. "The Shirt of a Happy Person." *Why* (Summer 1996).

Bittner, Rüdiger. "Is It Reasonable to Regret Things One Did?" *Journal of Philosophy* 89:5 (May 1992): 262–73.

Bloomfield, Harold H. *Happiness: The TM Program, Psychiatry, and Enlightenment*. New York: Dawn Press, 1976.

Boethius, Anicius. *The Consolation of Philosophy*. Translated by V. E. Watts. Harmondsworth: Penguin Books, 1969.

Bourdieu, Pierre. *Sur la télévision*. Paris: Liber, 1997.

Bradburn, Norman H. *In Pursuit of Happiness*. Chicago: University of Chicago Press, 1963.

Bradley, F. H. *Ethical Studies*. Oxford: Oxford University Press, 1876.

Brochmann, Georg. *Humanity and Happiness*. London: Gollancz, 1951.

Bruner, Jerome. *Acts of Meaning*. Cambridge, Mass: Harvard University Press, 1990.

Bryson, Bill. *Notes from a Small Island*. London: Minerva, 1996.

Buchholz, Ester Schaler. *The Call of Solitude: Alonetime in a World of Attachment*. New York: Simon & Schuster, 1997.

Camus, Albert. *The Myth of Sisyphus and Other Essays*. Translated by Justin O'Brien. New York: Vintage, 1955.

Canadian Pharmaceutical Association. *The Compendium of Pharmaceuticals and Specialties.* Thirty-Second Edition. Toronto: Canadian Pharmaceutical Association, 1997.

Caplan, Paula. *They Say You're Crazy: How the World's Most Powerful Psychiatrists Decide Who's Normal.* Reading, Mass.: Addison-Wesley, 1995.

Cassell, Eric J. "The Nature of Suffering and the Goals of Medicine." *New England Journal of Medicine* 306 (1982): 639–45.

Cassidy, John. "The Decline of Economics." *The New Yorker* (2 December 1996).

Cavell, Stanley. *Pursuits of Happiness: The Hollywood Comedy of Remarriage.* Cambridge: Harvard University Press, 1981.

———. *The Senses of Walden.* San Francisco: North Point Press, 1980.

Cicero, Marcus Tullius. *Tusculan Disputations.* Edited and translated by A. E. Douglas. Warminster, U.K.: Aris & Phillips, 1990.

Ciskszentmihalyi, Mihaly. *Flow: The Psychology of Optimal Experience.* New York: Harper & Row, 1990.

Conant, Luther, Jr. "A 10-Day Plan for Happiness." *Woman's Home Companion* (October 1950).

Corelli, Rae. "Get Happy!" *Maclean's* (16 September 1996).

Cornford, F. M. *Microcosmographia Academica: Being a Guide for the Young Academic Politician.* Cambridge, U.K.: Bowes & Bowes, 1908.

Coupland, Douglas. *Microserfs.* New York: HarperCollins, 1995.

Critser, Greg. "Oh, How Happy We Will Be: Pills, Paradise, and the Profits of the Drug Companies." *Harper's Magazine* (June 1996).

Davis, L. J. "The Encyclopedia of Insanity." *Harper's Magazine* (February 1997).

De Bono, Edward. *The Happiness Purpose.* Harmondsworth: Penguin Books, 1979.

De Breteuil, Gabrielle-Emilie, Marquise du Châtelet. *Discours sur le bonheur.* Edited by Robert Mauzi. Paris: Société de l'édition "Les Belles Lettres," 1961.

De Certeau, M. *The Practice of Everyday Life.* Translated by Steven Rendall. Berkeley: University of California Press, 1984.

Deleuze, Gilles. *Negotiations 1972–1990.* Translated by Martin Joughin. New York: Columbia University Press, 1995.

Denby, David. "Buried Alive: Our Children and the Avalanche of Crud." *The New Yorker* (15 July 1996).

———. *Great Books: My Adventures with Homer, Rousseau, Woolf, and Other Indestructible Writers of the Western World.* New York: Simon & Schuster, 1996.

Dougherty, Jude P., editor. *The Good Life and Its Pursuit.* New York: Paragon House, 1984.

Eakin, Emily. "Bourdieu Unplugged." *Lingua Franca* (August 1997).

Edwards, Jonathan. *The Works of President Edwards.* New York and London, 1844.

Edwards, Rem B. *Pleasures and Pains: A Theory of Qualitative Hedonism.* Ithaca: Cornell University Press, 1979.

Ekman, Paul. *Telling Lies.* New York: Norton, 1985.

———, editor. *What the Face Reveals.* New York: Oxford University Press, 1997.

Elbin, Paul Nowell. *The Paradox of Happiness.* New York: Hawthorn Books, 1975.

Eliot, Charles W. *The Happy Life.* New York: Cromwell, 1905.

Emerson, Ralph Waldo. "Worship." In *The Conduct of Life: The Works of Ralph Waldo Emerson.* Edited by James Elliott Cabot. Boston and New York: 1883–1983.

Epictetus. *The Enchiridion.* Translated by Thomas W. Higginson. Indianapolis: Bobbs-Merrill, 1948.

Epicurus. *Principal Doctrines.* In *The Epicurus Reader.* Translated by Brad Inwood and L. P. Gerson. Indianapolis: Hackett, 1994.

Eysenck, Michael W. *Happiness: Facts and Myths.* Hove: Erlbaum, 1990.

Farr, Moira. "Is Everybody Happy? The Pushy Politics of Prozac." *This Magazine* (August 1994).

Feist, Jess. *Theories of Personality.* Third Edition. New York: Harcourt Brace, 1985.

Fletcher, Horace. *Happiness as Found in Forethought Minus Fearthought.* New York, 1913.

Frank, Thomas. *The Conquest of Cool.* Chicago: University of Chicago Press, 1997.

———. "Hip Is Dead." *The Nation* (1 April 1996).

———. "The Marriage of Hip and Square." *Harper's Magazine* (November 1997).

Frayn, Michael. *A Landing on the Sun*. New York: Viking, 1991.

Freeman, M. *Rewriting the Self: History, Memory and Narrative*. New York: Routledge, 1993.

Freud, Sigmund. *Civilization and Its Discontents*. Translated by James Strachey. New York: Norton, 1966 [orig. 1930].

Frick, W. B. *Humanistic Psychology: Interviews with Maslow, Murphy and Rogers*. Columbus, Ohio: Merrill, 1971.

Geuss, Raymond. *The Idea of a Critical Theory*. Cambridge: Cambridge University Press, 1981.

Gladwell, Malcolm. "The Coolhunt." *The New Yorker* (17 March 1997).

———. "Listening to Khakis." *The New Yorker* (28 July 1997).

———. "The Science of Shopping." *The New Yorker* (4 November 1996).

Goldsmith, Oliver. "Happiness, In a Great Measure, Dependant on Constitution." In *Collected Works*, ed. Arthur Friedman. Volume I. Oxford: Oxford University Press, 1966.

Goleman, Daniel. "Forget Money: Nothing Can Buy Happiness." *USAir* (November 1996).

———. "Happiness Is…Genetic, Researchers Say." *Globe and Mail* (16 July 1996 [reprinted from the *New York Times*, 15 July 1996]).

Green, Donald P., and Ian Shapiro. *Pathologies of Rational Choice Theory*. New Haven: Yale University Press, 1996.

Griffin, James. *Well-Being: Its Meaning, Measurement, and Moral Importance*. Oxford: Oxford University Press, 1986.

Groves, Ernest R., and Phyllis Blanchard. *Introduction to Mental Hygiene*. American Social Sciences Series: New York, 1930.

Gumpert, Martin. *The Anatomy of Happiness*. New York: McGraw-Hill, 1951.

Hall, Stuart. "Culture, Media and the 'Ideological Effect.'" In *Mass Communication and Society*, ed. J. Curran et al. London: Arnold, 1977.

———. "Encoding, Decoding." In *The Cultural Studies Reader*, ed. Simon During. New York: Routledge, 1993.

Hare, R. M. *The Language of Morals*. Oxford: Oxford University Press, 1952.

Hebdige, Dick. *Subculture: The Meaning of Style*. London: Routledge, 1979.

Hegel, G. W. F. *Introduction to the Philosophy of History*. Translated by Leo Rauch. Indianapolis: Hackett, 1988.

Heilbroner, Robert. *Teachings from the Worldly Philosophy*. New York: Norton, 1996.

Hillman, James. *The Soul's Code: In Search of Character and Calling.* New York: Random House, 1996.

Hobbes, Thomas. *Leviathan.* Edited by C. B. Macpherson. Harmondsworth: Penguin Books, 1968 [orig. 1651].

Hoffer, Eric. *The Passionate State of Mind and Other Aphorisms.* New York: Harper & Row, 1955.

Hornby, Nick. *Fever Pitch.* New York: Riverhead Books, 1995.

Hume, David. *A Treatise on Human Nature.* Edited by L. A. Selby-Bigge. Oxford: Oxford University Press, 1896.

Hutcheson, Francis. *Inquiry into the Origin of our Ideas of Beauty and Virtue.* Edinburgh, 1725.

Huxley, Aldous. *Brave New World.* Harmondsworth: Penguin Books, 1974 [orig. 1932].

Jefferson, Thomas. *The Writings of Thomas Jefferson.* Edited by A. A. Lipscomb and A. E. Bergh. Washington, D.C., 1905.

Jenkins, Henry. *Textual Poachers: Television Fans and Participatory Culture.* New York: Routledge, 1992.

Jones, Howard Mumford. *The Pursuit of Happiness.* Cambridge: Harvard University Press, 1953.

Kant, Immanuel. *Critique of Practical Reason.* Translated by Thomas K. Abbott. Indianapolis: Bobbs-Merrill, 1949 [orig. 1788].

———. *Groundwork of the Metaphysics of Morals.* Translated by H. J. Paton. London: Hutchinson, 1948 [orig. 1785].

Kenny, Anthony. "Happiness." In *Moral Concepts,* ed. Joel Feinberg. Oxford: Oxford University Press, 1969.

Kingwell, Mark. *A Civil Tongue: Justice, Dialogue and the Politics of Pluralism.* University Park: Pennsylvania State University Press, 1995.

———. "Defending Political Virtue." *Philosophical Forum* 27:3 (Spring 1996): 244–68.

———. *Dreams of Millennium: Report from a Culture on the Brink.* Toronto: Viking, 1996.

———. "The Intellectual Possibilities of Television." *Chronicle of Higher Education* (12 December 1997).

———. "Liberality." In *Philosophy of Law: An Encyclopedia.* New York: Garland, 2000.

———. "The Plain Truth About Common Sense: Skepticism, Metaphysics, and Irony." *Journal of Speculative Philosophy* 9:3 (Fall 1995): 169–88.

Klein, Richard. *Cigarettes Are Sublime.* Durham: Duke University Press, 1993.

———. *Eat Fat.* New York: Pantheon, 1996.

Kraut, R. "Two Conceptions of Happiness." *Philosophical Review* 88 (1979): 167–97.

Krugman, Paul. "The CPI and the Rat Race." *Slate* [www.slate.com] (21 December 1996).

Lanchester, John. *The Debt to Pleasure.* London: Picador, 1996.

Langton, James. "Orange Flavoured Prozac to Be Aimed at Kids." (London) *Sunday Telegraph* (17 August 1997).

Lasch, Christopher. *The Culture of Narcissism: American Life in an Age of Diminishing Expectations.* New York: Norton, 1978.

Lear, Jonathan. "The Disappearing 'We.'" *Proceedings of the Aristotelian Society,* Supplementary Volume, 1984.

Lewis, C. S. *The Allegory of Love.* Oxford, 1936.

Locke, John. *An Essay Concerning Human Understanding.* Edited by Campbell Fraser. Oxford: Oxford University Press, 1894.

———. *Second Treatise of Government.* Edited by C. B. Macpherson. Indianapolis: Hackett, 1980 [orig. 1690].

Lyotard, Jean-François. "Defining the Postmodern." In *The Cultural Studies Reader,* ed. Simon During. New York: Routledge, 1993.

———. *The Postmodern Condition: A Report on Knowledge.* Minneapolis: University of Minnesota Press, 1984.

MacIntyre, Alasdair. *After Virtue: A Study in Moral Theory.* Second Edition. London: Duckworth, 1981.

Macpherson, C. B. *The Political Theory of Possessive Individualism.* Oxford: Oxford University Press, 1982.

Marx, Karl. *The German Ideology.* In *The Marx-Engels Reader,* ed. Robert C. Tucker. New York: Norton, 1978.

Maslow, Abraham H. *Motivation and Personality.* Second Edition. New York: Harper & Row, 1970.

McCracken, Grant. *Plenitude* (on-line book). www.cultureby.com.

McFall, Lynne. *Happiness.* New York: Peter Lang, 1989.

McKibben, "Curbing Nature's Paparazzi." *Harper's Magazine* (November 1997).

McLuhan, Eric, and Frank Zingrone, editors. *Essential McLuhan*. Toronto: Anansi, 1995.

McLuhan, Marshall. *Understanding Media: The Extensions of Man*. Cambridge: MIT Press, 1994 [orig. 1964].

McSweeney, A. John, and Thomas L. Creer. "Health-Related Quality-of-Life Assessment in Medical Care." *Disease-a-Month* XLI:I (January 1995): 1–72.

Mill, John Stuart. *On Liberty*. New York: Norton, 1975 [orig. 1859].

———. *Utilitarianism*. Indianapolis: Bobbs-Merrill, 1959 [orig. 1863].

Mitford, Nancy. *Christmas Pudding*. New York: Carroll & Graf, 1987 [orig. 1975].

Moore, G. E. *Principia Ethica*. Cambridge: Cambridge University Press, 1903.

Morris, Desmond. *Happiness*. Birmingham: University of Birmingham Press, 1984.

Murray, Charles. *In Pursuit of Happiness and Good Government*. New York: Simon & Schuster, 1988.

Nash, Ogden. "Kind of an Ode to Duty." In *The Face Is Familiar: The Selected Verse of Ogden Nash*. Garden City, N.J.: Garden City Publishing, 1941.

Newton-Smith, W. "A Conceptual Investigation of Love." In *Philosophy and Personal Relations,* ed. Alan Montefiore. London, 1973.

Nietzsche, Friedrich. *On the Genealogy of Morals*. Translated by Walter Kaufmann and R. J. Hollingdale. New York: Vintage, 1967.

Nozick, Robert. *Anarchy, State, and Utopia*. New York: Basic Books, 1974.

———. *The Examined Life: Philosophical Meditations*. New York: Basic Books, 1989.

Nussbaum, Martha, and Amartya Sen, editors. *The Quality of Life*. Oxford: Oxford University Press, 1992.

O'Connell, Sanjida. "How Your Genes Put a Smile on Your Face." *Toronto Star* (1 September 1996).

Paley, William. *The Principles of Moral and Political Philosophy*. In *An Introduction to Modern Philosophy,* ed. Alburey Castell et al. Sixth Edition. New York: Macmillan, 1994 [orig. 1785].

Peck, M. Scott. *A World Waiting to Be Born*. New York: Bantam, 1993.

Penley, Constance. *NASA/TREK*. New York: Verso, 1997.

Penn Warren, Robert. *All the King's Men*. New York: Harcourt, Brace, 1964.

Pieper, Josef. *Happiness and Contemplation*. New York: Pantheon, 1958.

Plato. *Euthyphro*. Translated by Lane Cooper. In *Plato: The Collected Dialogues,* ed. Edith Hamilton and Huntington Cairns. Princeton: Princeton University Press, 1961.

———. *The Republic*. Translated by G. M. A. Grube. Indianapolis: Hackett, 1974.

Pollan, Michael. *Second Nature: A Gardener's Education*. New York: Dell, 1991.

Popper, Karl. *The Logic of Scientific Discovery*. New York: Basic Books, 1959 [orig. 1935].

Postman, Neil. *Amusing Ourselves to Death: Public Discourse in the Age of Show Business*. New York: Viking, 1985.

———. *Technopoly: The Surrender of Culture to Technology*. New York: Knopf, 1992.

Powe, B. W. *A Canada of Light*. Toronto: Somerville House, 1997.

———. *The Solitary Outlaw*. Toronto: Somerville House, 1997.

Powys, John Cowper. *The Art of Happiness*. New York: Simon & Schuster, 1935.

Pruette, Lorine. "Getting an Early Start on Happiness." *Woman's Home Companion* (January 1937).

Quincy, Josiah, Jr. *Observations on the Act of Parliament Commonly Called the Boston Port-Bill*. Boston, 1774.

Raven, Charlotte. "I Don't Feel Cheerful When I'm Ordered to Be Happy." *Guardian* (17 October 1996); reprinted in the *Toronto Star* (19 October 1996).

Reynolds, Siimon. *Become Happy in Eight Minutes*. New York: Plume, 1996.

Rouner, Leroy S., editor. *In Pursuit of Happiness*. Notre Dame: Notre Dame University Press, 1995.

Russell, Bertrand. *The Conquest of Happiness*. New York: Liveright, 1958.

Russell, Countess Dora Winifred Black. *The Right to Be Happy*. New York: Harper, 1927.

Rybczynski, Witold. *Waiting for the Weekend*. New York: Viking, 1991.

Sachs, Hanns. "Psychotherapy and the Pursuit of Happiness." *Imago* Vol. I (1939): 356–64.

Samuelson, Robert J. *The Good Life and Its Discontents: The American Dream in the Age of Entitlement*. New York: Vintage, 1995 [reissued, with a new afterword, 1997].

Sarbin, T. R., editor. *Narrative Psychology: The Storied Nature of Human Conduct*. New York: Praeger, 1986.

Saul, John Ralston. *The Doubter's Companion: A Dictionary of Aggressive Common Sense*. Toronto: Viking, 1994.

Sedaris, David. *Naked*. New York: Little, Brown, 1997.

Seneca. *De Vita Beata*. In *Seneca: Moral Essays*. Translated by John W. Basore. London and New York: Loeb Classical Library, 1928–35.

Servin, James. "Are We Happy Yet? The Era of Angst Is Finally Over." *Bazaar* (September 1997).

Shapiro, Alan. "Kirk Was Never the Original." In *Digital Delirium*, eds. Arthur and Marilouise Kroker. New York: St. Martin's Press, 1997.

Shenk, David. *Data Smog: Surviving the Information Glut*. New York: Harper-Collins, 1997.

Shields, David. *Remote*. New York: Knopf, 1996.

Sidgwick, Henry. *The Methods of Ethics*. London, 1907.

Smith, G. Gregory, editor. *The Spectator*. London: 1887–1898.

Solomon, Lawrence. "Editorial." *The Next City* (Spring 1996).

Spinoza, Benedict. *Ethics*. Translated and edited by G. H. R. Parkinson. London: J. M. Dent, 1989.

Stearns, Peter. *American Cool: Constructing a Twentieth-Century Emotional Style*. New York: New York University Press, 1994.

Stern, Jane and Michael. *Eat Your Way Across the USA: 500 Diners, Lobster Shacks, Buffets, Pie Palaces, and Other All-American Eateries*. New York: Bantam, 1997.

Storr, Anthony. *Solitude: A Return to the Self*. New York: Free Press, 1988.

Sumner, L. Wayne. "Welfare, Happiness, and Pleasure." *Utilitas* 4:2 (November 1992): 199–223.

Tanner, Michael. "The Language of Philosophy." In *The State of the Language*, ed. Leonard Michaels and Christopher Ricks. Berkeley: University of California Press, 1980.

Taylor, Charles. *Sources of the Self: The Making of the Modern Identity*. Cambridge: Harvard University Press, 1989.

Teilhard de Chardin, Pierre. *On Happiness*. London: Collins, 1973.

Telfer, Elizabeth. *Happiness.* New York: St. Martin's Press, 1980.

Thompson, Dorothy. "The Right to Happiness." *Ladies' Home Journal* (April 1941).

Thoreau, Henry David. *Walden.* New York: Time Inc., 1962 [orig. 1854].

Trillin, Calvin. *American Fried.* New York: Doubleday, 1974.

Tyler, Christian. "A Philosopher's Tale." *Financial Post* (26 September 1996).

Virilio, Paul. *Speed and Politics.* New York: Semiotext(e), 1995.

Voltaire. *Candide: Or Optimism.* Translated by Robert M. Adams. New York: Norton, 1966 [orig. 1759].

Waugh, Evelyn. *Decline and Fall.* Harmondsworth: Penguin, 1937 [orig. 1928].

———. *Vile Bodies.* Harmondsworth: Penguin Books, 1938 [orig. 1930].

Wente, Margaret. "Marriage by the Book." *Globe and Mail* (20 September 1997).

West, Benjamin. *The New-England Almanack: Or, Lady's and Gentleman's Diary for the Year of Our Lord Christ, 1766.* Providence: 1765.

Wexler, Laura. "Thinking, Not Shrinking." *Utne Reader* (January–February 1997).

White, M., and D. Epston. *Narrative Means to Therapeutic Ends.* New York: Norton, 1990.

White, Stephen A. *Sovereign Virtue: Aristotle on the Relation Between Happiness and Prosperity.* Stanford: Stanford University Press, 1992.

Wike, Victoria S. *Kant on Happiness in Ethics.* Albany: SUNY Press, 1994.

Williams, Bernard. *Ethics and the Limits of Philosophy.* London: Routledge & Kegan Paul, 1985.

———. "Moral Luck." In *Moral Luck.* New York: Cambridge University Press, 1981.

Williams, Raymond. "Advertising: The Magic System." In *The Cultural Studies Reader,* ed. Simon During. New York: Routledge, 1993.

Wittgenstein, Ludwig. *Tractatus Logico-Philosophicus.* Translated by D. F. Pears and B. F. McGuinness. London: Routledge & Kegan Paul, 1961 [orig. 1921].

Zalewski, Daniel. "Written on the Face." *Lingua Franca* (September 1997).

Zimbardo, Philip. "What Messages Are Behind Today's Cults?" *APA Monitor* (May 1997).

Index

About the Author

Philosopher and social critic Mark Kingwell was born in Toronto in 1963. He is the author of two previous award-winning books, *A Civil Tongue* (1995) and *Dreams of Millennium* (1997), and is a contributing editor to *Saturday Night, Shift,* and *Descant* magazines. His essays and articles have appeared in more than 40 other publications, including *Harper's, Utne Reader, The New York Times Magazine,* and *Adbusters,* where he is a columnist. He holds a Ph.D. from Yale University and is currently associate professor of philosophy at the University of Toronto.